BLOOM'S PERIOD STUDIES

BLOOM'S PERIOD STUDIES

English Romantic Poetry

Edited and with an introduction by
Harold Bloom
Sterling Professor of the Humanities
Yale University

CHELSEA HOUSE
PUBLISHERS
An imprint of Infobase Publishing

Bloom's Period Studies: English Romantic Poetry

Chelsea House
An imprint of Infobase Publishing
132 West 31st Street
New York NY 10001

ISBN-10: 0-7910-7680-6
ISBN-13: 978-0-7910-7680-4

For Library of Congress Cataloging-in-Publication Data, please contact the publisher.

 ISBN: 0-7910-7680-6

Chelsea House books are available at special discounts when purchased in bulk quantities for businesses, associations, institutions, or sales promotions. Please call our Special Sales Department in New York at (212) 967-8800 or (800) 322-8755.

You can find Chelsea House on the World Wide Web at
http://www.chelseahouse.com

Contributing Editor: Pamela Loos
Cover designed by Terry Mallon

Printed in the United States of America

IBT EJB 10 9 8 7 6 5 4 3

This book is printed on acid-free paper.

Contents

Editor's Note

My Introduction is the essay entitled "The Internalization of Quest-Romance," still in print as the opening piece of *Romanticism and Consciousness* (Norton, 1970) and also in *Poetics of Influence: New and Selected Criticism* (Henry Schwab, New Haven) 1988. A shorter version appeared originally in *The Yale Review* (Summer, 1969) and was expanded in *The Ringers In the Tower* (Chicago, 1971).

I reprint the essay here as Introduction because, after a third of a century, I find it best represents my lifetime thought on the Romantic poets. Were I to revise it now, I probably would emphasize the role of Shakespeare, particularly of his *Hamlet*, as an influence on English Romanticism at least as central as that of Milton.

The essays in criticism gathered here begin with the Irish Nobel laureate Seamus Heaney's meditation upon his two grand precursors, William Wordsworth and William Butler Yeats.

The great Wordsworthian critic Geoffrey Hartman links the prophetic sagas of the Hebrew Bible to High Romantic poetics, while Helen Vendler, a superb close reader, provides a fresh and vitalistic interpretation of Keats's well-read "Ode on a Grecian Urn."

John Clubbe and Ernest J. Lovell, Jr. argue that Byron, Shelley, and Keats were far more skeptical than Blake, Wordsworth, and Coleridge, after which Jerome J. McGann sets himself against what he regards as "the Romantic ideology" supposedly imposed upon these poets by certain latter-day critics.

William Keach finds in Shelley's irregular rhymes a visionary resonance that celebrates the mind's power over a universe of death, while the satiric narrator of Byron's *Don Juan* is seen by Frederick L. Beaty as being wholly adequate to his subject. Next, Stuart Curran juxtaposes British and Continental Romantic poetry, while John L. Mahoney contemplates the personally tragic later poetry of Coleridge.

Fiercely learned, Thomas McFarland employs Frederich Schlegel and Coleridge against Paul de Man's ironizing preference for "allegory" over "symbol" in Romantic poetics, after which David Perkins analyzes Coleridge's famous Introductory Note to *Kubla Khan*.

Paul de Man speaks for himself, quite powerfully, on the temporal complexity in Wordsworth, while Stephen Gurney contrasts Byron and Shelley, whose ambivalent friendship is a poem in itself.

My honored teacher, M. H. Abrams, the dean of Romantic studies, usefully sets forth the "material base" of Keats's achievement, after which G.A. Rosso ends this volume by pondering Blake's Rahab symbol in relation to the Harlot of the Revelation of St. John the Divine.

HAROLD BLOOM

Introduction

Freud, in an essay written sixty years ago on the relation of the poet to daydreaming, made the surmise that all aesthetic pleasure is forepleasure, an "incitement premium" or narcissistic fantasy. The deepest satisfactions of literature, in this view, come from a release of tensions in the psyche. That Freud had found, as almost always, either part of the truth or at least a way to it, is clear enough, even if a student of Blake or Wordsworth finds, as probably he must, this Freudian view to be partial, reductive, and a kind of mirror image of the imagination's truth. The deepest satisfactions of reading Blake or Wordsworth come from the realization of new ranges of tensions in the mind, but Blake and Wordsworth both believed, in different ways, that the pleasures of poetry were only forepleasures, in the sense that poems, finally, were scaffoldings for a more imaginative vision, and not ends in themselves. I think that what Blake and Wordsworth do for their readers, or can do, is closely related to what Freud does or can do for his, which is to provide both a map of the mind and a profound faith that the map can be put to a saving use. Not that the uses agree, or that the maps quite agree either, but the enterprise is a humanizing one in all three of these discoverers. The humanisms do not agree either; Blake's is apocalyptic, Freud's is naturalistic, and Wordsworth's is—sometimes sublimely, sometimes uneasily—blended of elements that dominate in the other two.

Freud thought that even romance, with its elements of play, probably commenced in some actual experience whose "strong impression on the writer had stirred up a memory of an earlier experience, generally, belonging to childhood, which then arouses a wish that finds a fulfillment in the work in question, and in which elements of the recent event and the old memory should be discernible." Though this is a brilliant and comprehensive

From *Romanticism and Consciousness*. © 1969 by Harold Bloom.

thought, it seems inadequate to the complexity of romance, particularly in the period during which romance as a genre, however displaced, became again the dominant form, which is to say the age of Romanticism. For English-speaking readers, this age may be defined as extending from the childhood of Blake and Wordsworth to the present moment. Convenience dictates that we distinguish the High Romantic period proper, during which the half-dozen major English poets did their work, from the generations that have come after them, but the distinction is difficult to justify critically.

Freud's embryonic theory of romance contains within it the potential for an adequate account of Romanticism, particularly if we interpret his "memory of an earlier experience" to mean also the recall of an earlier insight, or yearning, that may not have been experiential. The immortal longings of the child, rather variously interpreted by Freud, Blake, and Wordsworth, may not be at the roots of romance, historically speaking, since those roots go back to a psychology very different from ours, but they do seem to be at the sources of the mid-eighteenth-century revival of a romance consciousness, out of which nineteenth-century Romanticism largely came.

J.H. Van den Berg, whose introduction to a historical psychology I find crucial to an understanding of Romanticism, thinks that Rousseau "was the first to view the child as a child, and to stop treating the child as an adult." Van den Berg, as a doctor, does not think this was necessarily an advance: "Ever since Rousseau the child has been keeping its distance. This process of the child and adult growing away from each other began in the eighteenth century. It was then that the period of adolescence came into existence." Granting that Van den Berg is broadly correct (he at least attempts to explain an apparent historical modulation in consciousness that few historians of culture care to confront), then we are presented with another in a series of phenomena, clustering around Rousseau and his age, in which the major change from the Enlightenment to Romanticism manifested itself. Some of these are analyzed in this volume, by Barfield, Van den Berg, and Frye in particular, not so much as changes in consciousness, but as changes in figuration. Changes in consciousness are of course very rare and no major synthesizer has come forth as yet, from any discipline, to demonstrate to us whether Romanticism marks a genuine change in consciousness or not. From the Freudian viewpoint, Romanticism is an "illusory therapy" (I take the phrase from Philip Rieff), or what Freud himself specifically termed an "erotic illusion." The dialectics of Romanticism, to the Freudians, are mistaken or inadequate, because the dialectics are sought in Schiller or Heine or in German Romantic philosophy down to Nietzsche, rather than in Blake or the

English Romantics after him. Blake and Coleridge do not set intellect and passion against one another, any more than they arrive at the Freudian simplicity of the endless conflict between Eros and Thanatos. Possibly because of the clear associations between Jung and German Romanticism, it has been too easy for Freudian intellectuals to confound Romanticism with various modes of irrationalism. Though much contemporary scholarship attempts to study English and continental Romanticism as a unified phenomenon, it can be argued that the English Romantics tend to lose more than they gain by such study.

Behind continental Romanticism there lay very little in the way of a congenial native tradition of major poets writing in an ancestral mode, particularly when compared to the English Romantic heritage of Spenser, Shakespeare, and Milton. What allies Blake and Wordsworth, Shelley and Keats, is their strong mutual conviction that they are reviving the true English tradition of poetry, which they thought had vanished after the death of Milton, and had reappeared in diminished form, mostly after the death of Pope, in admirable but doomed poets like Chatterton, Cowper, and Collins, victims of circumstance and of the false dawn of Sensibility. It is in this highly individual sense that English Romanticism legitimately can be called, as traditionally it has been, a revival of romance. More than a revival, it is an internalization of romance, particularly of the quest variety, an internalization made for more than therapeutic purposes, because made in the name of a humanizing hope that approaches apocalyptic intensity. The poet takes the patterns of quest-romance and transposes them into his own imaginative life, so that the entire rhythm of the quest is heard again in the movement of the poet himself from poem to poem.

M.H. Abrams, in an essay included in this volume, brilliantly traces these patterns of what he calls "the apocalypse of imagination." As he shows, historically they all stem directly from English reactions to the French Revolution, or to the intellectual currents that had flowed into the Revolution. Psychologically, they stem from the child's vision of a more titanic universe that the English Romantics were so reluctant to abandon. If adolescence was a Romantic or Rousseauistic phenomenon of consciousness, its concomitant was the very secular sense of being twice-born that is first discussed in the fourth chapter of *Émile*, and then beautifully developed by Shelley in his visionary account of Rousseau's second birth, in the concluding movement of *The Triumph of Life*. The pains of psychic maturation become, for Shelley, the potentially saving though usually destructive crisis in which the imagination confronts its choice of either sustaining its own integrity, or yielding to the illusive beauty of nature.

The movement of quest-romance, before its internalization by the High Romantics, was from nature to redeemed nature, the sanction of redemption being the gift of some external spiritual authority, sometimes magical. The Romantic movement is from nature to the imagination's freedom (sometimes a reluctant freedom), and the imagination's freedom is frequently purgatorial, redemptive in direction but destructive of the social self. The high cost of Romantic internalization, that is, of finding paradises within a renovated man, shows itself in the arena of self-consciousness. The quest is to widen consciousness as well as to intensify it, but the quest is shadowed by a spirit that tends to narrow consciousness to an acute preoccupation with self. This shadow of imagination is solipsism, what Shelley calls the Spirit of Solitude or *Alastor*, the avenging daimon who is a baffled residue of the self, determined to be compensated for its loss of natural assurance, for having been awakened from the merely given condition that to Shelley, as to Blake, was but the sleep of death-in-life. Blake calls this spirit of solitude a Spectre, or the genuine Satan, the Thanatos or death instinct in every natural man. One of the essays by Geoffrey H. Hartman in this volume concerns the Romantic search for an anti-self-consciousness, a way out of the morass of inwardness. Modernist poetry in English organized itself, to an excessive extent, as a supposed revolt against Romanticism, in the mistaken hope of escaping this inwardness (though it was unconscious that this was its prime motive).

Modernist poets learned better, as their best work, the last phases of W. B. Yeats and Wallace Stevens, abundantly shows, but criticism until recently was tardy in catching up, and lingering misapprehensions about the Romantics still abide. Thus, Irving Howe, in an otherwise acute essay on literary modernism, says of the Romantic poets that "they do not surrender the wish to discover in the universe a network of spiritual meaning which, however precariously, can enclose their selves." This is simply not true of Blake or Wordsworth or Shelley or Keats, nor is the statement of Marius Bewley's that Howe quotes approvingly, that the Romantics' central desire is "to merge oneself with what is greater than oneself." Indeed, both statements are excellent guides to what the major Romantics regarded as human defeat or a living death, as the despairing surrender of the imagination's autonomy. Since neither Howe nor Bewley is writing as an enemy of the Romantics, it is evident that we still need to clear our minds of Eliotic cant on this subject.

Paul de Man terms this phenomenon the post-Romantic dilemma, observing that every fresh attempt of Modernism to go beyond Romanticism ends in the gradual realization of the Romantics' continued priority. Modern poetry, in English, is the invention of Blake and of Wordsworth, and I do not know of a long poem written in English since which is either as legitimately difficult or as rewardingly profound as *Jerusalem* or *The Prelude*. Nor can I find a modern lyric, however happily ignorant its writer, which develops beyond or surmounts its debt to Wordsworth's great trinity of *Tintern Abbey*, *Resolution and Independence*, and the *Intimations of Immortality* ode. The dreadful paradox of Wordsworth's greatness is that his uncanny originality, still the most astonishing break with tradition in the language, has been so influential that we have lost sight of its audacity and its arbitrariness. In this, Wordsworth strongly resembles Freud, who rightly compared his own intellectual revolution to those of Copernicus and Darwin. Van den Berg quietly sees "Freud, in the desperation of the moment, turning away from the present, where the cause of his patients' illnesses was located, to the past; and thus making them suffer from the past and making our existence akin to their suffering. It was not necessary." Is Van den Berg right? The question is as crucial for Wordsworth and Romanticism as it is for Freud and psychoanalysis. The most searching critique of Romanticism that I know is Van den Berg's critique of Freud, particularly the description of "The Subject and his Landscape" included in this anthology:

> Ultimately the enigma of grief is the libido's inclination toward exterior things. What prompts the libido to leave the inner self? In 1914 Freud asked himself this question—the essential question of his psychology, and the essential question of the psychology of the twentieth century. His answer ended the process of interiorization. It is: the libido leaves the inner self when the inner self has become too full. In order to prevent it from being torn, the I has to aim itself on objects outside the self; "... ultimately man must begin to love in order not to get ill." So that is what it is. Objects are of importance only in an extreme urgency. Human beings, too. The grief over their death is the sighing of a too-far distended covering, the groaning of an overfilled inner self.

Wordsworth is a crisis-poet, Freud a crisis-analyst; the saving movement in each is backwards into lost time. But what is the movement of loss, in poet and in analyst? Van den Berg's suggestion is that Freud unnecessarily sacrificed the present moment, because he came at the end of a tradition of intellectual error that began with the extreme Cartesian dualism, and that progressively learned to devalue contact between the self and others, the self and the outer world, the self and the body. Wordsworth's prophecy, and Blake's, was overtly against dualism; they came, each said, to heal the division within man, and between man and the world, if never quite between man and man. But Wordsworth, the more influential because more apparently accessible of the two (I myself would argue that he is the more difficult because the more problematic poet), no more overcame a fundamental dualism than Freud did. Essentially this was Blake's complaint against him; it is certainly no basis for us to complain. Wordsworth made his kind of poetry out of an extreme urgency, and out of an overfilled inner self, a Blakean Prolific that nearly choked in an excess of its own delights. This is the Egotistical Sublime of which Keats complained, but Keats knew his debt to Wordsworth, as most poets since do not.

Wordsworth's Copernican revolution in poetry is marked by the evanescence of any subject but subjectivity, the loss of what a poem is "about." If, like the late Yvor Winters, one rejects a poetry that is not "about" something, one has little use for (or understanding of) Wordsworth. But, like Van den Berg on Freud, one can understand and love Wordsworth, and still ask of his radical subjectivity: was it necessary? Without hoping to find an answer, one can explore the question so as to come again to the central problem of Romantic (and post-Romantic) poetry: what, for men without belief and even without credulity, is the spiritual form of romance? How can a poet's (or any man's) life be one of continuous allegory (as Keats thought Shakespeare's must have been) in a reductive universe of death, a separated realm of atomized meanings, each discrete from the next? Though all men are questers, even the least, what is the relevance of quest in a gray world of continuities and homogenized enterprises? Or, in Wordsworth's own terms, which are valid for every major Romantic, what knowledge might yet be purchased except by the loss of power?

Frye, in his theory of myths, explores the analogue between quest-romance and the dream: "Translated into dream terms, the quest-romance is the search of the libido or desiring self for a fulfillment that will deliver it from the anxieties of reality but will still contain that reality." Internalized romance—and *The Prelude* and *Jerusalem* can be taken as the greatest examples of this kind—traces a Promethean and revolutionary quest, and cannot be translated into dream terms, for in it the libido turns inward into the self. Shelley's *Prometheus Unbound* is the most drastic High Romantic version of internalized quest, but there are more drastic versions still in our own age, though they present themselves as parodistic, as in the series of marvelous interior quests by Stevens, that go from *The Comedian As the Letter C* to the climactic *Notes Toward a Supreme Fiction*. The hero of internalized quest is the poet himself, the antagonists of quest are everything in the self that blocks imaginative work, and the fulfillment is never the poem itself, but the poem beyond that is made possible by the apocalypse of imagination. "A timely utterance gave that thought relief" is the Wordsworthian formula for the momentary redemption of the poet's sanity by the poem already written, and might stand as a motto for the history of the modern lyric from Wordsworth to Hart Crane.

The Romantics tended to take Milton's Satan as the archetype of the heroically defeated Promethean quester, a choice in which modern criticism has not followed them. But they had a genuine insight into the affinity between an element in their selves and an element in Milton that he would externalize only in a demonic form. What is heroic about Milton's Satan is a real Prometheanism and a thoroughly internalized one; he can steal only his own fire in the poem, since God can appear as fire, again in the poem, only when he directs it against Satan. In Romantic quest the Promethean hero stands finally, quite alone, upon a tower that is only himself, and his stance is all the fire there is. This realization leads neither to nihilism nor to solipsism, though Byron plays with the former and all fear the latter.

The dangers of idealizing the libido are of course constant in the life of the individual, and such idealizations are dreadful for whole societies, but the internalization of quest-romance had to accept these dangers. The creative process is the hero of Romantic poetry, and imaginative inhibitions, of every kind, necessarily must be the antagonists of the poetic quest. The special puzzle of Romanticism is the dialectical role that nature had to take in the revival of the mode of romance. Most simply, Romantic nature poetry, despite a long critical history of misrepresentation, was an anti-nature poetry, even in Wordsworth who sought a reciprocity or even a dialogue with nature, but found it only in flashes. Wordsworthian nature, thanks to Arnold and the critical tradition he fostered, has been misunderstood, though the insights of recent critics have begun to develop a better interpretative tradition, founded on A. C. Bradley's opposition to Arnold's view. Bradley stressed the strong side of Wordsworth's imagination, its Miltonic sublimity, which Arnold evidently never noticed, but which accounts for everything that is major in *The Prelude* and in the central crisis lyrics associated with it. Though Wordsworth came as a healer, and Shelley attacked him, in *Mont Blanc*, for attempting to reconcile man with nature, there is no such reconciliation in Wordsworth's poetry, and the healing function is performed only when the poetry shows the power of the mind over outward sense. The strength of renovation in Wordsworth resides only in the spirit's splendor, in what he beautifully calls "possible sublimity" or "something evermore about to be," the potential of an imagination too fierce to be contained by nature. This is the force that Coleridge sensed and feared in Wordsworth, and is remarkably akin to that strength in Milton that Marvell urbanely says he feared, in his introductory verses to *Paradise Lost*. As Milton curbed his own Prometheanism, partly by showing its dangers through Satan's version of the heroic quest, so Wordsworth learned to restrain his, partly through making his own quest-romance, in *The Prelude*, an account of learning both the enormous strength of nature, and nature's wise and benevolent reining-in of its own force. In the covenant between Wordsworth and nature, two powers that are totally separate from each other, and potentially destructive of the other, try to meet in a dialectic of love. "Meet" is too hopeful, and "blend" would express Wordsworth's ideal and not his achievement, but the try itself is definitive of Wordsworth's strangeness and continued relevance as a poet.

If Wordsworth, so frequently and absurdly called a pantheist, was not questing for unity with nature, still less were Blake, Shelley, and Keats, or their darker followers in later generations, from Beddoes, Darley, and Wade down to Yeats and Lawrence in our time. Coleridge and Byron, in their very different ways, were oddly closer both to orthodox Christian myth and to pantheism or some form of nature-worship, but even their major poems hardly approximate nature poetry. Romantic or internalized romance, especially in its purest version of the quest form, the poems of symbolic voyaging that move in a continuous tradition from Shelley's *Alastor* to Yeats's *The Wanderings of Oisin*, tends to see the context of nature as a trap for the mature imagination. This point requires much laboring, as the influence of older views of Romanticism is very hard to slough off. Even Northrop Frye, the leading romance theorist we have had at least since Ruskin, Pater, and Yeats, says that "in Romanticism the main direction of the quest of identity tends increasingly to be downward and inward, toward a hidden basis or ground of identity between man and nature." The directional part of this statement is true, but the stated goal I think is not. Frye still speaks of the Romantics as seeking a final unity between man and his nature, but Blake and Shelley do not accept such a unity as a goal, unless a total transformation of man and nature can precede unity, while Wordsworth's visions of "first and last and midst and without end" preserve the unyielding forms both of nature and of man. Keats's closest approach to an apocalyptic vision comes when he studies Moneta's face, at the climax of *The Fall of Hyperion*, but even that vision is essentially Wordsworthian, seeing as it does a perpetual change that cannot be ended by change, a human countenance made only more solitary in its growing alienation from nature, and a kind of naturalistic entropy that has gone beyond natural contraries, past "the lily and the snow."

Probably only Joyce and Stevens, in later Romantic tradition, can be termed unreconstructed naturalists, or naturalistic humanists. Later Romantics as various as Eliot, Proust, and Shaw all break through uneasy natural contexts, as though sexuality was antithetical to the imagination, while Yeats, the very last of the High Romantics, worked out an elaborate sub-myth of the poet as antithetical quester, very much in the mode of Shelley's poetry. If the goal of Romantic internalization of the quest was a wider consciousness that would be free of the excesses of self-consciousness, a consideration of the rigors of experiential psychology will show, quite rapidly, why nature could not provide an adequate context. The program of Romanticism, and not just in Blake, demands something more than a natural man to carry it through. Enlarged and more numerous senses are necessary, an enormous virtue of Romantic poetry clearly being that it not only demands such expansion but begins to make it possible, or at least attempts to do so.

The internalization of romance brought the concept of nature, and poetic consciousness itself, into a relationship they had never had before the advent of Romanticism in the later eighteenth century. Implicit in all the Romantics, and very explicit in Blake, is a difficult distinction between two modes of energy, organic and creative (Orc and Los in Blake, Prometheus bound and unbound in Shelley, Hyperion and Apollo in Keats, the Child and the Man, though with subtle misgivings, in Wordsworth). For convenience, the first mode can be called Prometheus and the second "the Real Man, the Imagination" (Blake's phrase, in a triumphant letter written when he expected death). Generally, Prometheus is the poet-as-hero in the first stage of his quest, marked by a deep involvement in political, social, and literary revolution, and a direct, even satirical attack on the institutional orthodoxies of European and English society, including historically oriented Christianity, and the neoclassic literary and intellectual tradition, particularly in its Enlightenment phase. The Real Man, the Imagination, emerges after terrible crises in the major stage of the Romantic quest, which is typified by a relative disengagement from revolutionary activism, and a standing aside from polemic and satire, so as to bring the search within the self and its ambiguities. In the Prometheus stage, the quest is allied to the libido's struggle against repressiveness, and nature is an ally, though always a wounded and sometimes a withdrawn one. In the Real Man, the Imagination stage, nature is the immediate though not the ultimate antagonist. The final enemy to be overcome is a recalcitrance in the self, what Blake calls the Spectre of Urthona, Shelley the unwilling dross that checks the spirit's flight, Wordsworth the sad perplexity or fear that kills or, best of all, the hope that is unwilling to be fed, and Keats, most simply and perhaps most powerfully, the Identity. Coleridge calls the antagonist by a bewildering variety of names since, of all these poets, he is the most hag-ridden by anxieties, and the most humanly vulnerable. Byron and Beddoes do not so much name the antagonist as mock it, so as to cast it out by continuous satire and demonic farce. The best single name for the antagonist is Keats's Identity, but the most traditional is the Selfhood, and so I shall use it here.

Only the Selfhood, for the Romantics as for such Christian visionaries as Eckhart before them, burns in Hell. The Selfhood is not the erotic principle, but precisely that part of the erotic that cannot be released in the dialectic of love, whether between man and man, or man and nature. Here the Romantics, all of them I think, even Keats, part company with Freud's dialectics of human nature. Freud's beautiful sentence on marriage is a formula against which the Romantic Eros can be tested: "A man shall leave father and mother—according to the Biblical precept—and cleave to his wife; then are tenderness and sensuality united." By the canons of internalized romance, that translates: a poet shall leave his Great Original (Milton, for the Romantics) and nature—according to the precept of Poetic Genius—and cleave to his Muse or Imagination; then are the generous and solitary halves united. But, so translated, the formula has ceased to be Freudian and has become High Romantic.

In Freud, part of the ego's own self-love is projected onto an outward object, but part always remains in the ego, and even the projected portion can find its way back again. Somewhere Freud has a splendid sentence that anyone unhappy in love can take to heart: "Object-libido was at first ego-libido and can be again transformed into ego-libido," which is to say that a certain degree of narcissistic mobility is rather a good thing. Somewhere else Freud remarks that all romance is really a form of what he calls "family-romance;" one could as justly say, in his terms, that all romance is necessarily a mode of ego-romance. This may be true, and in its humane gloom it echoes a great line of realists who culminate in Freud, but the popular notion that High Romanticism takes a very different view of love is a sounder insight into the Romantics than most scholarly critics ever achieve (or at least state).

All romance, literary and human, is founded upon enchantment; Freud and the Romantics differ principally in their judgment as to what it is in us that resists enchantment, and what the value of that resistance is. For Freud it is the reality principle, working through the great disenchanter, reason, the scientific attitude, and without it no civilized values are possible. For the Romantics, this is again a dialectical matter, as two principles intertwine in the resistance to enchantment—one "organic," an anxiety principle masquerading as a reality principle and identical to the ego's self-love that never ventures out to others, and the other "creative," which resists enchantment in the name of a higher mode than the sympathetic imagination.

This doubling is clearest in Blake's mythology, where there are two egos, the Spectre of Urthona and Los, who suffer the enchantments, real *and* deceptive, of nature and the female, and who resist, when and where they can, on these very different grounds. But, though less schematically, the same doubling of the ego into passive and active components is present in the other poets wherever they attempt their highest flights and so spurn the earth. The most intense effort of the Romantic quest is made when the Promethean stage of quest is renounced, and the purgatorial crisis that follows moves near to resolution. Romantic purgatory, by an extraordinary displacement of earlier mythology, is found just beyond the earthly paradise, rather than just before it, so that the imagination is tried by nature's best aspect. Instances of the interweaving of purgatory and paradise include nearly everything Blake says about the state of being he calls Beulah, and the whole development of Keats, from *Endymion*, with its den or cave of Quietude, on to the structure of *The Fall of Hyperion*, where the poet enjoys the fruit and drink of paradise just before he has his confrontation with Moneta, whose shrine must be reached by mounting purgatorial stairs.

Nothing in Romantic poetry is more difficult to comprehend, for me anyway, than the process that begins after each poet's renunciation of Prometheus; for the incarnation of the Real Man, the Imagination, is not like psychic maturation in poets before the Romantics. The love that transcends the Selfhood has its analogues in the renunciatory love of many traditions, including some within Christianity, but the creative Eros of the Romantics is not renunciatory though it is self-transcendent. It is, to use Shelley's phrasing, a total going-out from our own natures, total because the force moving out is not only the Promethean libido, but rather a fusion between the libido and the active or imaginative element in the ego; or, simply, desire wholly taken up into the imagination. "Shelley's love poetry," as a phrase, is almost a redundancy, Shelley having written little else, but his specifically erotic poems, a series of great lyrics and the dazzling *Epipsychidion*, have been undervalued because they are so very difficult, the difficulty being the Shelleyan and Romantic vision of love.

Blake distinguished between Beulah and Eden as states of being (Frye's essay, "The Keys to the Gates," included in this anthology, is definitive on this distinction), the first being the realm of family-romance and the second of apocalyptic romance, in which the objects of love altogether lose their object dimension. In family-romance or Beulah, loved ones are not confined to their objective aspect (that would make them denizens of Blake's state of Generation or mere Experience), but they retain it nevertheless. The movement to the reality of Eden is one of re-creation, or better, of knowledge not purchased by the loss of power, and so of power and freedom gained *through* a going-out of our nature, in which that last phrase takes on its full range of meanings. Though Romantic love, particularly in Wordsworth and Shelley, has been compared to what Charles Williams calls the Romantic Theology of Dante, the figure of Beatrice is not an accurate analogue to the various Romantic visions of the beloved, for sublimation is not an element in the movement from Prometheus to Man.

There is no useful analogue to Romantic or imaginative love, but there is a useful contrary in the melancholy wisdom of Freud on natural love, and the contrary has the helpful clarity one always finds in Freud. If Romantic love is the sublime, then Freudian love is the pathetic, and truer of course to the phenomenon insofar as it is merely natural. To Freud, love begins as ego-libido, and necessarily is ever after a history of sorrow, a picaresque chronicle in which the ever-vulnerable ego stumbles from delusion to frustration, to expire at last (if lucky) in the compromising arms of the ugliest of Muses, the reality principle. But the saving dialectic of this picaresque is that it is better thus, as there is no satisfaction in satisfaction anyway, since in the Freudian view all erotic partners are somewhat inadequate replacements for the initial sexual objects, parents.

Romantic love, to Freud, is a particularly intense version of the longing for the mother, a love in which the imago is loved, rather than the replacement. And Romantic love, on this account, is anything but a dialectic of transformation, since it is as doomed to overvalue the surrogate as it compulsively overvalues the mother.

Our age begins to abound in late Romantic "completions" of Freud, but the Romantic critiques of him, by Jung and Lawrence in particular, have not touched the strength of his erotic pessimism. There is a subtly defiant attempt to make the imago do the work of the imagination by Stevens, particularly in the very Wordsworthian *The Auroras of Autumn*, and it is beautifully subversive of Freud, but of course it is highly indirect. Yet a direct Romantic counter-critique of Freud's critique of Romantic love emerges from any prolonged, central study of Romantic poetry. For Freud, there is an ironic loss of energy, perhaps even of spirit, with every outward movement of love away from the ego. Only pure self-love has a perfection to it, a stasis without loss, and one remembers again Van den Berg's mordant observation on Freud: "Ultimately the enigma of grief is the libido's inclination toward exterior things." All outward movement, in the Freudian psychodynamics, is a fall that results from "an overfilled inner self," which would sicken within if it did not fall outwards, and downwards, into the world of objects, and of other selves. One longs for Blake to come again and rewrite *The Book of Urizen* as a satire on this cosmogony of love. The poem would not require that much rewriting, for it can now be read as a prophetic satire on Freud, Urizen being a superego certainly overfilled with itself, and sickening into a false creation or creation-fall. If Romantic love can be castigated as "erotic illusion," Freudian love can be judged as "erotic reduction," and the prophets of the reality principle are in danger always of the Urizenic boast:

> I have sought for a joy without pain,
> For a solid without fluctuation
> Why will you die O Eternals?
> Why live in unquenchable burnings?

The answer is the Romantic dialectic of Eros and Imagination, unfair as it is to attribute to the Freudians a censorious repressiveness. But to Blake and the Romantics, all available accounts of right reason, even those which had risen to liberate men, had the disconcerting tendency to turn into censorious moralities. Freud painfully walked a middle way, not unfriendly to the poetic imagination, and moderately friendly to Eros. If his myth of love is so sparse, rather less than a creative Word, it is still open both to analytic modification and to a full acceptance of everything that can come out of the psyche. Yet it is not quite what Philip Rieff claims for it, as it does not erase "the gap between therapeutic rationalism and self-assertive romanticism." That last is only the first stage of the Romantic quest, the one this discussion calls Prometheus. There remains a considerable gap between the subtle perfection to which Freud brought therapeutic rationalism, and the mature Romanticism which is self-transcendent in its major poets.

There is no better way to explore the Real Man, the Imagination, than to study his monuments: *The Four Zoas*, *Milton*, and *Jerusalem*; *The Prelude* and the *Recluse* fragment; *The Ancient Mariner* and *Christabel*; *Prometheus Unbound*, *Adonais*, and *The Triumph of Life*; the two *Hyperions*; *Don Juan*; *Death's Jest-Book*; these are the definitive Romantic achievement, the words that were and will be, day and night. What follows is only an epitome, a rapid sketch of the major phase of this erotic quest. The sketch, like any which attempts to trace the visionary company of love, is likely to end in listening to the wind, hoping to hear an instant of a fleeting voice.

The internalization of quest-romance made of the poet-hero a seeker not after nature but after his own mature powers, and so the Romantic poet turned away, not from society to nature, but from nature to what was more integral than nature, within himself. The widened consciousness of the poet did not give him intimations of a former union with nature or the Divine, but rather of his former selfless self. One thinks of Yeats's Blakean declaration: "I'm looking for the face I had / Before the world was made." Different as the major Romantics were in their attitudes towards religion, they were united (except for Coleridge) in *not* striving for unity with anything but what might be called their Tharmas or id component, Tharmas being the Zoa or Giant Form in Blake's mythology who was the unfallen human potential for realizing instinctual desires, and so was the regent of Innocence. Tharmas is a shepherd-figure, his equivalent in Wordsworth being a number of visions of man against the sky, of actual shepherds Wordsworth had seen in his boyhood. This Romantic pastoral vision (its pictorial aspect can be studied in the woodcuts of Blake's Virgil series, and in the work done by Palmer, Calvert, and Richmond while under Blake's influence) is Biblical pastoralism, but not at all of a traditional kind. Blake's Tharmas is inchoate when fallen, as the id or appetite is inchoate, desperately starved and uneasily allied to the Spectre of Urthona, the passive ego he has projected outward to meet an object-world from which he has been severed so unwillingly. Wordsworth's Tharmas, besides being the shepherd image of human divinity, is present in the poet himself as a desperate desire for continuity in the self, a desperation that at its worst sacrifices the living moment, but at its best produces a saving urgency that protects the imagination from the strong enchantments of nature.

In Freud the ego mediates between id and superego, and Freud had no particular interest in further dividing the ego itself. In Romantic psychic mythology, Prometheus rises from the id, and can best be thought of as the force of libido, doomed to undergo a merely cyclic movement from appetite to repression, and then back again; any quest within nature is thus at last irrelevant to the mediating ego, though the quest goes back and forth through it. It is within the ego itself that the quest must turn, to engage the antagonist proper, and to clarify the imaginative component in the ego by its strife of contraries with its dark brother. Frye, writing on Keats, calls the imaginative ego *identity-with* and the selfhood ego *identity-as*, which clarifies Keats's ambiguous use of "identity" in this context. Hartman, writing on Wordsworth, points to the radical Protestant analogue to the Romantic quest: "The terror of discontinuity or separation enters, in fact, as soon as the imagination truly enters. In its restraint of vision, as well as its peculiar nakedness before the moment, this resembles an extreme Protestantism, and Wordsworth seems to quest for 'evidences' in the form of intimations of continuity."

Wordsworth's greatness was in his feeling the terror of discontinuity as acutely as any poet could, yet overcoming this terror nevertheless, by opening himself to vision. With Shelley, the analogue of the search for evidences drops out, and an Orphic strain takes its place, for no other English poet gives so continuous an impression of relying on almost literal inspiration. Where Keats knew the Selfhood as an attractive strength of distinct identity that had to be set aside, and Wordsworth as a continuity he longed for yet learned to resist, and Blake as a temptation to prophetic wrath and withdrawal that had to be withstood, Shelley frequently gives the impression of encountering no enchantment he does not embrace, since every enchantment is an authentic inspiration. Yet this is a false impression, though Yeats sometimes received it, as in his insistence that Shelley, great poet as he certainly was, lacked a Vision of Evil. The contrary view to Yeats is that of C. S. Lewis, who held that Shelley, more than any other "heathen" poet (the word is from Lewis), drove home the truth of Original Sin.

Both views are mistaken. For Shelley, the Selfhood's strong enchantment, stronger even than it is for the other Rómantics, is one that would keep him from ever concluding the Prometheus phase of the quest. The Selfhood allies itself with Prometheus against the repressive force Shelley calls Jupiter, his version of Blake's Urizen or Freud's superego. This temptation calls the poet to perpetual revolution, and Shelley, though longing desperately to see the tyrannies of his time overturned, renounces it at the opening of *Prometheus Unbound*, in the Imagination's name. Through his renunciation, he moves to overturn the tyranny of time itself.

There are thus two main elements in the major phase of the Romantic quest, the first being the inward overcoming of the Selfhood's temptation, and the second the outward turning of the triumphant Imagination, free of further internalizations—though "outward" and "inward" become cloven fictions or false conceptual distinctions in this triumph, which must complete a dialectic of love by uniting the Imagination with its bride, who is a transformed ongoing creation of the Imagination rather than a redeemed nature. Blake and Wordsworth had long lives, and each completed his version of this dialectic. Coleridge gave up the quest, and became only an occasional poet, while Byron's quest, even had he lived into middle age, would have become increasingly ironic. Keats died at twenty-five, and Shelley at twenty-nine; despite their fecundity, they did not complete their development, but their death-fragments, *The Fall of Hyperion* and *The Triumph of Life*, prophesy the final phase of the quest in them. Each work breaks off with the Selfhood subdued, and there is profound despair in each, particularly in Shelley's; but there are still hints of what the Imagination's triumph would have been in Keats. In Shelley, the final despair may be total; but the man who had believed so fervently that the good time would come had already given a vision of imaginative completion in the closing Act of *Prometheus Unbound*, and we can go back to it and see what is deliberately lacking in *The Triumph of Life*. What follows is a rapid attempt to trace the major phase of quest in the four poets, taking as texts *Jerusalem* and *The Prelude*, and the *Fall* and *Triumph*, these two last with supplementary reference to crucial earlier erotic poems of Keats and Shelley.

Of Blake's long poems the first, *The Four Zoas*, is essentially a poem of Prometheus, devoting itself to the cyclic strife between the Promethean Orc and the moral censor, Urizen, in which the endless cycle between the two is fully exposed. The poem ends in an apocalypse, the explosive and Promethean *Night the Ninth, Being The Last Judgment*, which in itself is one of Blake's greatest works, yet from which he turned when he renounced the entire poem (by declining to engrave it). But this renunciation was completed not before he attempted to move the entire poem from the Prometheus stage to the Imagination, for Blake's own process of creative maturation came to its climax while he worked on *The Four Zoas*. The entrance into the mature stage of the quest is clearly shown by the two different versions of *Night the Seven*, for the later one introduces the doubling of the ego into Spectre of Urthona and Los, Selfhood or *Identity-As*, and Imagination or *Identity-With*. Though skillfully handled, it was not fully clarified by Blake, even to himself, and so he refused to regard the poem as a definitive vision.

Its place in his canon was filled, more or less, by the double-romance *Milton* and *Jerusalem*. The first is more palpably in a displaced romance mode, involving as it does symbolic journeys downwards to our world by Milton and his emanation or bride of creation, Ololon, who descend from an orthodox Eternity in a mutual search for one another, the characteristic irony being that they could never find one another in a traditional heaven. There is very little in the poem of the Prometheus phase, Blake having already devoted to that a series of prophetic poems, from *America* and *Europe* through *The Book of Urizen* and on to the magnificent if unsatisfactory (to him, not to us) *The Four Zoas*. The two major stages of the mature phase of quest dominate the structure of *Milton*. The struggle with the Selfhood moves from the quarrel between Palamabron (Blake) and Satan (Hayley) in the introductory "Bard's Song" on to Milton's heroic wrestling match with Urizen, and climaxes in the direct confrontation between Milton and Satan on the Felpham shore, in which Milton recognizes Satan as his own Selfhood. The recognition compels Satan to a full epiphany, and a subsequent defeat. Milton then confronts Ololon, the poem ending in an epiphany contrary to Satan's, in what Blake specifically terms a preparation for a going forth to the great harvest and vintage of the nations. But even this could not be Blake's final Word; the quest in Milton is primarily Milton's and not Blake's, and the quest's antagonist is still somewhat externalized.

In *Jerusalem*, *The Prelude*'s only rival as the finest long poem of the nineteenth century, Blake gives us the most comprehensive single version of the Romantic quest. Here there is an alternation between vision sweeping outwards into the nightmare world of the reality principle, and a wholly inward vision of conflict in Blake's ego between the Spectre and Los. The poet's antagonist is himself, the poem's first part being the most harrowing and tormented account of genius tempted to the madness of self-righteousness, frustrated anger, and solipsistic withdrawal even in the Romantic period. Blake-Los struggles on against this enchantment of despair, until the poem quietly, almost without warning, begins to move into the light of a Last judgment, of a kind passed by every man upon himself. In the poem's final plates the reconciliation of Los and his emanative portion, Enitharmon, begins, and we approach the completion of quest.

Though Blake, particularly in *Jerusalem*, attempts a continuity based on thematic juxtaposition and simultaneity, rather than on consecutiveness, he is in such sure control of his own procedure that his work is less difficult to summarize than *The Prelude*, a contrast that tends to startle inexperienced readers of Blake and of Wordsworth. *The Prelude* follows a rough naturalistic chronology through Wordsworth's life down to the middle of the journey, where it, like any modern reader, leaves him in a state of preparation for a further greatness that never came. What is there already, besides the invention of the modern lyric, is a long poem so rich and strange it has defied almost all description.

The Prelude is an autobiographical romance that frequently seeks expression in the sublime mode, which is an invitation to aesthetic disaster. *The Excursion* is an aesthetic disaster, as Hazlitt, Byron, and many since happily have noted, yet there Wordsworth works within rational limits. *The Prelude* ought to be an outrageous poem, but its peculiar mixture of displaced genre and inappropriate style *works*, because its internalization of quest is the inevitable story for its age. Wordsworth did not have the Promethean temperament, yet he had absolute insight into it, as *The Borderers* already had shown.

In *The Prelude*, the initial quest phase of the poet-as-Prometheus is diffuse but omnipresent. It determines every movement in the growth of the child's consciousness, always seen as a violation of the established natural order, and it achieves great power in Book VI, when the onset of the French Revolution is associated with the poet's own hidden desires to surmount nature, desires that emerge in the great passages clustered around the Simplon Pass. The Promethean quest fails, in one way in the Alps when chastened by nature, and in another with the series of shocks to the poet's moral being when England wars against the Revolution, and the Revolution betrays itself. The more direct Promethean failure, the poet's actual abandonment of Annette Vallon, is presented only indirectly in the 1805 *Prelude*, and drops out completely from the revised, posthumously published *Prelude* of 1850, the version most readers encounter.

In his crisis, Wordsworth learns the supernatural and superhuman strength of his own imagination, and is able to begin a passage to the mature phase of his quest. But his anxiety for continuity is too strong for him, and he yields to its dark enchantment. The Imagination phase of his quest does not witness the surrender of his Selfhood and the subsequent inauguration of a new dialectic of love, purged of the natural heart, as it is in Blake. Yet he wins a provisional triumph over himself, in Book XII of *The Prelude*, and in the closing stanzas of *Resolution and Independence* and the Great Ode. And the final vision of *The Prelude* is not of a redeemed nature, but of a liberated creativity transforming its creation into the beloved:

> Prophets of Nature, we to them will speak
> A lasting inspiration, sanctified
> By reason, blest by faith: what we have loved
> Others will love, and we will teach them how;
> Instruct them how the mind of man becomes
> A thousand times more beautiful than the earth
> On which he dwells, above this frame of things ...

Coleridge, addressed here as the other Prophet of Nature, renounced his own demonic version of the Romantic quest (clearest in the famous triad of *Kubla Khan*, *Christabel*, and *The Ancient Mariner*), his wavering Prometheanism early defeated not so much by his Selfhood as by his Urizenic fear of his own imaginative energy. It was a high price for the release he had achieved in his brief phase of exploring the romance of the marvelous, but the loss itself produced a few poems of unique value, the *Dejection Ode* in particular. The essay on the Greater Romantic Lyric, included in this book, is M. H. Abrams' pioneering and greatly illuminating explanation of how Coleridge preceded Wordsworth in the invention of a new kind of poetry that shows the mind in a dialogue with itself. The motto of this poetry might well be its descendant, Stevens' "The mind is the terriblest force in the world, father, / Because, in chief, it, only, can defend / Against itself. At its mercy, we depend / Upon it." Coleridge emphasizes the mercy, Wordsworth the saving terror of the force. Keats and Shelley began with a passion closer to the Prometheus phase of Blake than of Wordsworth or Coleridge. The fullest development of the Romantic quest, after Blake's mythology and Wordsworth's exemplary refusal of mythology, is in Keats's *Endymion* and Shelley's *Prometheus Unbound*.

In this second generation of Romantic questers the same first phase of Prometheanism appears, as does the second phase of crisis, renounced quest, overcoming of Selfhood, and final movement towards imaginative love, but the relation of the quest to the world of the reality principle has changed. In Blake, the dream with its ambiguities centers in Beulah, the purgatorial lower paradise of sexuality and benevolent nature. In Wordsworth, the dream is rare, and betokens either a prolepsis of the imagination abolishing nature, or else a state the poet calls "visionary dreariness," in which the immediate power of the mind over outward sense is so great that the ordinary forms of nature seem to have withdrawn. But in Keats and Shelley, a polemical Romanticism matures, and the argument of the dream with reality becomes an equivocal one.

Romanticism guessed at a truth our doctors begin to measure; as infants we dream for half the time we are asleep, and as we age we dream less and less. The doctors have not yet told us that utterly dreamless sleep directly prophesies or equals death, but it is a familiar Romantic conceit, and may prove to be true. We are our imaginations, and die with them.

Dreams, to Shelley and Keats, are not wish fulfillments. It is not Keats but Moneta, the passionate and wrong-headed Muse in *The Fall of Hyperion*, who first confounds poets and dreamers as one tribe, and then insists they are totally distinct and even sheer opposites, antipodes. Freud is again a clear-headed guide; the manifest and latent content of the dream can be distinct, even opposite, but in the poem they come together. The younger Romantics do not seek to render life a dream, but to recover the dream for the health of life. What is called real is too often an exhausted phantasmagoria, and the reality principle can too easily be debased into a principle of surrender, an accommodation with death-in-life. We return to the observation of Van den Berg, cited earlier: Rousseau and the Romantics discovered not only the alienation between child and adult, but the second birth of psychic maturation or adolescence. Eliot thought that the poet of *Adonais* and *The Triumph of Life* had never "progressed" beyond the ideas and ideals of adolescence, or at least of what Eliot had believed in *his* own adolescence. Every reader can be left to his own judgment of the relative maturity of *Ash Wednesday* and *The Witch of Atlas*, or *The Cocktail Party* and *The Cenci*, and is free to formulate his own dialectics of progression.

The Promethean quest, in Shelley and in Keats, is from the start uneasy about its equivocal ally, nature, and places a deeper trust in the dream; for at least the dream itself is not reductive, however we reduce it in our dissections. Perhaps the most remarkable element in the preternatural rapidity of maturation in Keats and Shelley is their early renunciation of the Prometheus phase of the quest, or rather, their dialectical complexity in simultaneously presenting the necessity and the inherent limitation of this phase. In *Alastor*, the poem's entire thrust is at one with the Poet-hero's self-destruction; this is the cause of the poem's radical unity, which C. S. Lewis rightly observed as giving a marvelous sense of the poet's being at one with his subject. Yet the poem is also a daimonic shadow in motion; it shows us nature's revenge upon the imagination, and the excessive price of the quest in the poet's alienation from other selves.

On a cosmic scale, this is part of the burden of *Prometheus Unbound*, where the hero, who massively represents the bound prophetic power of all men, rises from his icy crucifixion by refusing to continue the cycles of revolution and repression that form an ironic continuity between himself and Jupiter. Demogorgon, the dialectic of history, rises from the abyss and stops history, thus completing in the macrocosmic shadow what Prometheus, by his renunciation, inaugurates in the microcosm of the individual imagination, or the liberating dream taken up into the self. Shelley's poetry after this does not maintain the celebratory strain of Act IV of his lyrical drama. The way again is down and out, to a purgatorial encounter with the Selfhood, but the Selfhood's temptations, for Shelley, are subtle and wavering, and mask themselves in the forms of the ideal. So fused do the ideal and these masks become that Shelley, in the last lines he wrote, is in despair of any victory, though it is Shelley's Rousseau and not Shelley himself who actually chants:

> ... thus on the way
> Mask after mask fell from the countenance
> And form of all; and long before the day
>
> Was old, the joy which waked like heaven's glance
> The sleepers in the oblivious valley, died;
> And some grew weary of the ghastly dance,
>
> And fell, as I have fallen, by the wayside—

For Shelley, Rousseau was not a failed poet, but rather the poet whose influence had resulted in an imaginative revolution, and nearly ended time's bondage. So Rousseau speaks here not for himself alone, but for his tradition, and necessarily for Coleridge, Wordsworth, and the Promethean Shelley as well, indeed for poetry itself. Yet rightly or wrongly, the image Shelley leaves with us at his end is not this falling-away from the quest, but the image of the poet forever wakeful amidst the cone of night, illuminating it as the star Lucifer does, fading as the star, becoming more intense as it narrows into the light.

The mazes of romance in *Endymion* are so winding that they suggest the contrary to vision, a labyrinthine nature in which all quest must be forlorn. In this realm, nothing narrows to an intensity, and every passionate impulse widens out to a diffuseness, the fate of Endymion's own search for his goddess. In reaction, Keats chastens his own Prometheanism, and attempts the objective epic in *Hyperion*. Hyperion's self-identity is strong but waning fast, and the fragment of the poem's Book III introduces an Apollo whose self-identity is in the act of being born. The temptation to go on with the poem must have been very great after its magnificent beginnings, but Keats's letters are firm in renouncing it. Keats turns from the enchantments of identity to the romance-fragment, *The Fall of Hyperion*, and engages instead the demon of subjectivity, his own poetic ambitions, as Wordsworth had done before him. Confronted by Moneta, he meets the danger of her challenge not by asserting his own identity, but by finding his true form in the merged identity of the poethood, in the high function and responsibilities of a Wordsworthian humanism. Though the poem breaks off before it attempts the dialectic of love, it has achieved the quest, for the Muse herself has been transformed by the poet's persistence and integrity. We wish for more, necessarily, but only now begin to understand how much we have received, even in this broken monument.

I have scanted the dialectic of love in all of these poets. Romantic love, past its own Promethean adolescence, is not the possessive love of the natural heart, which is the quest of the Freudian Eros, moving always in a tragic rhythm out from and back to the isolated ego. That is the love Blake explicitly rejected:

> Let us agree to give up Love
> And root up the Infernal Grove
> Then shall we return and see
> The worlds of happy Eternity
>
> Throughout all Eternity
> I forgive you you forgive me ...

The Infernal Grove grows thick with virtues, but these are the selfish virtues of the natural heart. Desire for what one lacks becomes a habit of possession, and the Selfhood's jealousy murders the Real Man, the imagination. All such love is an entropy, and as such Freud understood and accepted it. We become aware of others only as we learn our separation from them, and our ecstasy is a reduction. Is this the human condition, and love only its mitigation?

> To cast off the idiot Questioner who is always questioning,
> But never capable of answering ...

Whatever else the love that the full Romantic quest aims at may be, it cannot be a therapy. It must make all things new, and then marry what it has made. Less urgently, it seeks to define itself through the analogue of each man's creative potential. But it learns, through its poets, that it cannot define what it is, but only what it will be. The man prophesied by the Romantics is a central man who is always in the process of becoming his own begetter, and though his major poems perhaps have been written, he has not as yet fleshed out his prophecy, nor proved the final form of his love.

SEAMUS HEANEY

The Makings of a Music: Reflections on Wordsworth and Yeats

What interests me is the relationship between the almost physiological operations of a poet composing and the music of the finished poem. I want to explore the way that certain postures and motions within the poet's incubating mind affect the posture of the voice and the motion of rhythms in the language of the poem itself. I want to see how far we can go in seeking the origins of a poet's characteristic 'music'.

I chose the word 'makings' for the title because it gestures towards the testings and hesitations of the workshop, the approaches towards utterance, the discovery of lines and then the intuitive extension of the vital element in those lines over a whole passage. If you like, I am interested in the way Valery's two kinds of poetic lines, *les vers donnés* and *les vers calculés*, are combined. The given line, the phrase or cadence which haunts the ear and the eager parts of the mind, this is the tuning fork to which the whole music of the poem is orchestrated, that out of which the overall melodies are worked for or calculated. It is my impression that this haunting or *donné* occurs to all poets in much the same way, arbitrarily, with a sense of promise, as an alertness, a hankering, a readiness. It is also my impression that the quality of the music in the finished poem has to do with the way the poet proceeds to respond to his *donné*. If he surrenders to it, allows himself to be carried by its initial rhythmic suggestiveness, to become somnambulist after its invitations, then we will have a music not

From *Preoccupations: Selected Prose, 1968–1978.* © 1980 by Seamus Heaney.

unlike Wordsworth's, hypnotic, swimming with the current of its form rather than against it. If, on the other hand, instead of surrendering to the drift of the original generating rhythm, the poet seeks to discipline it, to harness its energies in order to drive other parts of his mind into motion, then we will have a music not unlike Yeats's, affirmative, seeking to master rather than to mesmerize the ear, swimming strongly against the current of its form.

Of course, in any poetic music, there will always be two contributory elements. There is that part of the poetry which takes its structure and beat, its play of metre and rhythms, its diction and allusiveness, from the literary tradition. The poetry that Wordsworth and Yeats had read as adolescents and as young men obviously laid down certain structures in their ear, structures that gave them certain kinds of aural expectations for their own writings. And we are all used to the study of this kind of influence: indeed, as T.S. Eliot has attested, we have not developed our taste in poetry until we can recognize with pleasure the way an individual talent has foraged in the tradition. But there is a second element in a poet's music, derived not from the literate parts of his mind but from its illiterate parts, dependent not upon what Jacques Maritain called his 'intellectual baggage' but upon what I might call his instinctual ballast. What kinds of noise assuage him, what kinds of music pleasure or repel him, what messages the receiving stations of his senses are happy to pick up from the world around him and what ones they automatically block out—all this unconscious activity, at the pre-verbal level is entirely relevant to the intonations and appeasements offered by a poet's music.

We have developed methods for tracing and expressing the relevance and significance of the first kind of influence, the literary influence, and much of the illuminating work on Wordsworth has been in this area. I remember with particular gratitude the late W. J. Harvey's inaugural lecture at Queen's University, in which he analysed the opening lines of *The Prelude* to show how those lines were influenced by the closing lines of *Paradise Lost*. Once it has been pointed out to us that Wordsworth's joy in open country and his sense of release from the bondage of the city are consciously set in the penumbra of Adam and Eve's expulsion from Eden, and that the language of Wordsworth's lines invites us to read his freedom in the context of that expulsion, then the whole lift of the passage is increased, and the wave of Wordsworth's feeling is rendered seismic by one discreet literary allusion.

But I seek my text a little further on in that passage, where the poet tells us that his poetry came to him on this occasion spontaneously and that he poured it out, told it to the open fields. Then come these four lines, precise, honest, revealing:

> My own voice cheered me, and, far more, the mind's
> Internal echo of the imperfect sound;
> To both I listened, drawing from them both
> A cheerful confidence in things to come.

Although Wordsworth is here describing the activity of composing aloud, of walking and talking, what the poetry reaches into is the activity of listening. 'My own voice cheered me'—in the words of the old joke, he is entranced by the exuberance of his own verbosity. The act of composition is a cheering one. But even though he is listening to the sound of his own voice, he realizes that this spoken music is just a shadow of the unheard melody, 'the mind's internal echo'. He is drawn into himself even as he speaks himself out, and it is this mesmerized attention to the echoes and invitations within that constitutes his poetic confidence. We need only recall for contrast the way W.H. Auden addressed himself to the discussion of the act of writing, always tackling it in terms of metre, stanza forms, philology, always keeping in front of us the idea of the poem as 'a verbal contraption', to see how intimately and exactly Wordsworth is touching into the makings of his music in those lines.

What we are presented with is a version of composition as listening, as a wise passiveness, a surrender to energies that spring within the centre of the mind, not composition as an active pursuit by the mind's circumference of something already at the centre. The more attentively Wordsworth listens in, the more cheerfully and abundantly he speaks out.

We have ample evidence of Wordsworth's practice of composing aloud. In *The Prelude* he tells us how he paced the woods with his dog running a bit ahead of him, so that the dog's barking would warn him of strangers and he could then quieten his iambic drone and not be taken for an idiot. We have also the evidence gathered by the Reverend Canon Rawnsley among the peasantry of Westmorland that he was not always successful in passing undetected:

> But thear was anudder thing as kep' fwoaks off, he hed a terr'ble girt deep voice ... I've knoan folks, village lads and lasses, coming ower by t'auld road aboon what runs fra Grasmer to Rydal, flayt a'most to death there by t' Wishing Gate to hear t' girt voice a groanin' and mutterin' and

thunderin' of a still evening. And he had a way of standin' quite
still by t' rock there in t' path under Rydal, and fwoaks could
hear sounds like a wild beast coming frat' rocks, and childer
were scared fit to be dead a'most.

And elsewhere Rawnsley's informant told of Mrs. Wordsworth's
difficulties also:

Mrs. Wudsworth would say, 'Ring the bell,' but he wouldn't
stir, bless ye. 'Goa and see what he's doing,' she'd say, and we
wad goa up to study door and hear him a mumbling and
bumming through hit. 'Dinner's ready, sir,' I'd ca' out, but he'd
goa mumbling on like a deaf man, ya see. And sometimes Mrs.
Wordsworth'ud say, 'Goa and brek a bottle, or let a dish fall
just outside door in passage.' Eh dear, that maistly wad bring
him out, wad that.

But the most instructive account of the poet's habits is surely the one given
by Hazlitt, who visited the Wordsworths at Alfoxden in June 1798. Hazlitt
heard the poetry read first by Coleridge and then by Wordsworth.
Admittedly, he does not actually witness Wordsworth in the process of
composition, but he does tell us about the quality and sway of the poet's
speaking voice in his essay 'My First Acquaintance with the Poets':

We went over to Alfoxden again the day following, and
Wordsworth read us the story of *Peter Bell* in the open air; and
the comment made upon it by his face and voice was very
different from that of some later critics! Whatever might be
thought of the poem, 'his face was a book where men might
read strange matters,' and he announced the fate of his hero in
prophetic tones. There is a *chaunt* in the recitation of both
Coleridge and Wordsworth, which acts as a spell upon the
hearer, and disarms the judgement. Perhaps they have deceived
themselves by making habitual use of this ambiguous
accompaniment. Coleridge's manner is more full, animated and
varied; Wordsworth's more equable, sustained and internal.
The one might be termed more *dramatic*, the other more
lyrical. Coleridge has told me that he himself liked to compose
in walking over uneven ground, or breaking through the
straggling branches of a copse wood; whereas Wordsworth

always wrote (if he could) walking up and down a straight gravel walk, or in some spot where the continuity of his verse met with no collateral interruption.

Wordsworth's chaunt acted as a spell upon the hearer, whether that hearer were Hazlitt or Wordsworth himself. It *en*chaunted. It was 'equable, sustained, internal', three adjectives which we might apply to the motion of Wordsworth's blank verse also. The continuity of the thing was what was important, the onward inward pouring out, up and down the gravel path, the crunch and scuffle of the gravel working like a metre or a metronome under the rhythms of the ongoing chaunt, those 'trances of thought and mountings of the mind' somehow aided by the automatic, monotonous turns and returns of the walk, the length of the path acting like the length of the line. And I imagine that the swing of the poet's body contributed as well to the sway of the voice, for Hazlitt tells us that 'there was something of a roll, a lounge in his gait, not unlike his own Peter Bell.' The poet as ploughman, if you like, and the suggestive etymology of the word 'verse' itself is pertinent in this context. 'Verse' comes from the Latin *versus* which could mean a line of poetry but could also mean the turn that a ploughman made at the head of the field as he finished one furrow and faced back into another. Wordsworth on the gravel path, to-ing and fro-ing like a ploughman up and down a field, his voice rising and falling between the measure of his pentameters, unites the old walking meaning of *versus* with the newer, talking sense of verse. Furthermore, Wordsworth's *poetic* voice, the first voice of his poetry, that voice in which we overhear him talking to himself, the motions of this voice remind me powerfully of the motions of ploughhorses as described by the poet Edwin Muir:

> Their hooves like pistons in an ancient mill
> Move up and down, yet seem as standing still.

The high moments of Wordsworth's poetry occur when the verse has carried us forward and onward to a point where line by line we do not proceed but hang in a kind of suspended motion, sustained by the beat of the verse as a hanging bird is sustained by the beat of its wing, but, like the bird, holding actively to one point of vantage, experiencing a prolonged moment of equilibrium during which we feel ourselves to be conductors of the palpable energies of earth and sky:

> Oh, when I have hung
> Above the raven's nest, by knots of grass
> Or half-inch fissures in the slippery rock
> But ill sustained, and almost, as it seemed
> Suspended by the blast which blew amain,
> Shouldering the naked crag, oh, at that time,
> While on the perilous ridge I hung alone,
> With what strange utterance did the loud dry wind
> Blow through my ears; the sky seemed not a sky
> Of earth, and with what motion moved the clouds.

This is perhaps an obvious moment, when the wind of heaven and the 'corresponding mild creative breeze' of inspiration sustain the voice and suspend the consciousness in its hovering. But it does not always require such extreme sensation to generate the trance. For example, at the end of that 'equable, sustained internal' narrative 'The Ruined Cottage', what Wordsworth calls 'the calm oblivious tendencies / Of nature' pervade the music, a music of coming to rest, of understanding:

> She sleeps in the calm earth, and peace is here.
> I well remember that those very plumes,
> Those weeds, and the high spear grass on that wall,
> By mist and silent raindrops silvered o'er,
> As once I passed, did to my mind convey
> So still an image of tranquillity,
> So calm and still, and looked so beautiful
> Amid the uneasy thoughts which filled my mind,
> That what we feel of sorrow and despair
> From ruin and from change, and all the grief
> The passing shows of being leave behind,
> Appeared an idle dream that could not live
> Where meditation was. I turned away
> And walked along my road in happiness.

We know that the phrase 'the still, sad music of humanity' will apply to this, but it is too abstract, not kinetic enough. There is a cumulative movement in the Pedlar's lines that does not so much move the narrative forward as intensify the lingering meditation, just as the up and down walking does not forward a journey but habituates the body to a kind of dreamy rhythm. And in this entranced state, the casual concerns of the mind, the proper sorrow for the wounded life of Margaret imaged in the overgrown cottage garden, such things are allayed by apprehensions of a longer, deeper tranquillity. To put it another way, 'the one life of Joy' imbues the music, is intoned by it, and can be apprehended from it. And nowhere do we experience this more potently than in the eight lines of 'A slumber did my spirit seal':

> A slumber did my spirit seal;
>   I had no human fears:
> She seemed a thing that could not feel
>   The touch of earthly years.
>
> No motion has she now, no force;
>   She neither hears nor sees;
> Rolled round in earth's diurnal course
>   With rocks, and stones, and trees.

The music begins with 'slumber' and ends with 'diurnal', and the eight lines turn on the poles of those sturdy vowels as surely, slowly, totally as the earth turning. Unless we can hear the power and dream in the line 'Rolled round in earth's diurnal course', I do not think we can ever properly hear Wordsworth's music. The quintessential sound of it is in 'diurnal', a word that comes up again at the end of the skating passage in *The Prelude*:

> Not seldom from the uproar I retired
> Into a silent bay, or sportively
> Glanced sideway, leaving the tumultuous throng,
> To cut across the reflex of a star
> That fled, and, flying still before me, gleamed
> Upon the glassy plain; and oftentimes,
> When we had given our bodies to the wind,
> And all the shadowy banks on either side
> Came sweeping through the darkness, spinning still
> The rapid line of motion, then at once
> Have I, reclining back upon my heels,
> Stopped short; yet still the solitary cliffs
> Wheeled by me—even as if the earth had rolled
> With visible motion her diurnal round!
> Behind me did they stretch in solemn train,

Feebler and feebler, and I stood and watched
Till all was tranquil as a dreamless sleep.

The exhilaration of the skating, the vitality of the verbs, 'gleaming', 'sweeping', 'spinning', 'wheeling', the narrative push, the *cheerfulness*, to use one of the poet's favourite positive words—all these things have their part to play in the overall effect of this writing. But what distinguishes it as Wordsworthian is the gradual allaying of the sensation which is not, however, a diminution of awareness. It is as if a lens of apprehension opens wide and holds open. It is achieved by pacing, a slow, gathering but not climactic movement, repetitive but not monotonous, a walking movement. We might say, in fact, that Wordsworth at his best, no less than at his worst, is a pedestrian poet. As his poetic feet repeat his footfalls, the earth seems to be a treadmill that he turns; the big diurnal roll is sensed through the poetic beat and the world moves like a waterwheel under the fall of his voice.

I introduce the water metaphor because any account of Wordsworth's music must sooner or later come to the river, but before we do so, I want to linger in the wood above Dove Cottage where the poet occasionally composed. At the moment all is quiet there, but it is an active quiet, the late morning of 29 April 1802:

We then went to John's Grove, sate a while at first. Afterwards William lay, and I lay in the trench under the fence—he with his eyes shut and listening to the waterfalls and the birds. There was no one waterfall above another—it was a sound of waters in the air—the voice of the air. William heard me breathing and rustling now and then but we both lay still and unseen by one another. He thought it would be as sweet thus to lie in the grave, and hear the *peaceful* sounds, of the earth and just to know that our dear friends were near.

Dorothy and her brother are as intimate with process here as the babes in the wood, and if there is something erotic about the rustling of those leaves, there is something cthonic about the energies fundamental to the whole experience. Phrases like 'diurnal course' and 'diurnal roll' are underwritten by sensation and take their lifeline from moments like this. The couple listen, they surrender, the noise of water and the voice of the air minister to them. The quick of this moment is like the quick of the poem 'A slumber did my spirit seal': it dramatizes the idea of 'wise passiveness' and makes the listening ear as capable of gathering might into itself as Yeats's 'gazing heart'. All the typical Wordsworthian verbs have been guaranteed: powers sink in, mould, impress, frame, minister, enter unawares.

Wordsworth had to grope along the grains of the language to find the makings of a music that would render not so much what Hopkins called the inscape as the instress of things, known physically and intuitively at such times. His great strength and originality as a writer came first of all from his trusting the validity of his experience, from his courageous and visionary determination to *ériger en lois ses impressions personnels*. But the paraphrasable content of Wordsworth's philosophy of nature would remain inert had he not discovered the sounds proper to his sense. Nature forms the heart that watches and receives but until the voice of the poet has been correspondingly attuned, we cannot believe what we hear. And so we come to the beautiful conception of the River Derwent as tutor of his poetic ear. The tongue of the river, he implies, licked him into poetic shape; the essential capacity was, from the beginning, the capacity to listen

> Was it for this
> That one, the fairest of all rivers, loved
> To blend his murmurs with my nurse's song,
> And from his alder shades and rocky falls,
> And from his fords and shallows, sent a voice
> That flowed along my dreams? For this didst thou,
> O Derwent, travelling over the green plains
> Near my 'sweet birth place', didst thou, beauteous stream,
> Make ceaseless music through the night and day
> Which with its steady cadence tempering
> Our human waywardness, composed my thoughts
> To more than infant softness, giving me
> Among the fretful dwellings of mankind
> A knowledge, a dim earnest, of the calm
> Which Nature breathes among the fields and groves?
> Beloved Derwent, fairest of all streams,
> Was it for this that I, a four years child,
> A naked boy, among thy silent pools
> Made one long bathing of a summer's day,
> Basked in the sun, or plunged into thy streams,
> Alternate, all a summer's day, or coursed

Over the sandy fields, and dashed with flowers
Of yellow grunsel; or, when crag and hill,
The woods, and distant Skiddaw's lofty height,
Were bronzed with a deep radiance, stood alone
A naked savage in the thunder shower?

As in the other passages already quoted, the movement of this one also enacts the insights it presents. The river flows into dreams and composes. The passage flows, shifts through times and scenes, mixes, drifts and comes to rest with the child composed into a stilled consciousness, a living tuning fork planted between wood and hill, bronzed in the sunset.

Moreover, in that original cluster of sound and image which Wordsworth divines at the roots of his poetic voice—a river streaming hypnotically in the background, a stilled listener hovering between waking and dreaming—in this cluster of sound and image we find prefigured other moments which were definitive in his life as a poet and which found definition in his distinctive music. I am thinking of the soldier whom he encounters at dawn in Book IV of *The Prelude*, and of the Leech Gatherer; and, in particular, of the way his listening to their speech becomes a listening in and sounding forth of a something else, that something which deeply interfuses silence with sound, stillness with movement, talk with trance, and which is radical to the sound and sense he makes as a poet:

The old Man still stood talking by my side;
But now his voice to me was like a stream
Scarce heard; nor word from word could I divide;
And the whole body of the Man did seem
Like one whom I had met with in a dream;
Or like a man from some far region sent,
To give me human strength, by apt admonishment.

I hope I am not indulging in special pleading when I draw attention to the rhyming of 'stream' and 'dream', and notice that shortly after this 'feet' is rhymed with 'repeat', and then 'me', 'silently' and 'continually' are harmonized. I am convinced that these words are conducting us towards something essential to the poetry.

I have been talking about the 'first voice' of Wordsworth's poetry, as that term was defined by Gottfried Benn and approved by T. S. Eliot, that is 'the voice of the poet talking to himself—or to nobody', the voice that is found to express 'a dark embryo', 'a something germinating in him for which he must find words.' Admittedly there is another voice in Wordsworth, which he was conscious of himself and which comes about, when, as he says in his Preface to *Lyrical Ballads*, the poet

> bring[s] his feelings near to those of the persons whose feelings he describes, nay, for short periods of time perhaps ... let[s] himself slip into an entire delusion, and even confound[s] and identifies his feelings with theirs.

'Peter Bell', 'The Idiot Boy' and 'The Thorn' come to mind, yet in these poems I suspect that there was nothing fundamentally dramatic about Wordsworth's surrender to the speech of the character. It was not a question of the poet's voice performing a part but of the poet's voice being possessed; it was not a question of technical cool, of finding a dramatic pitch, rather a matter of sympathetic warmth, of sinking into a mood of evocation. And in this the Wordsworthian process differs radically from the Yeatsian, just as the satisfaction and scope of their musics differ.

Both Yeats and Wordsworth liked to speak their lines, both intoned, yet both had difficulty in the actual writing of the poem. I have stressed the primary generating surrender that Wordsworth seems to have made to his *donnés* because it seems to me that that was definitive of his music. Yet it is also true that Dorothy's *Journals* are full of evidence that the composition of long poems like 'Michael' affected him nervously and physically; he became sick and exhausted by the strain of the writing, and Mary Moorman even speculates that he may have felt his career as a poet menaced by these symptoms. Nevertheless, the strain does not show in the verse and Wordsworth continued to think of the poetic act as essentially an act of complaisance with natural impulses and tendencies.

It is otherwise with Yeats. With him, the act is not one of complaisance but of control. In fact, one of the earliest references to Yeats's habit of composing aloud is in a letter written by his father in 1884, and there the father speaks of his son's procedure as 'manipulation'. 'His bad metres arise', J. B. Yeats wrote, 'from his composing in a loud voice manipulating of course the quantities to his taste.' Where we can think of Wordsworth going into a trance, mesmerized by the sound of his own voice, we have to think of Yeats testing and trying out different voices and deciding on which will come most resonantly from the mask. Consider, for example, his performance in the following passage, written near the end of his career:

> Every now and then, when something has stirred my
> imagination, I begin talking to myself. I speak in my own
> person and dramatize myself, very much as I have seen a mad
> old woman do upon the Dublin quays, and sometimes detect
> myself speaking and moving as if I were still young, or walking
> perhaps like an old man with fumbling steps. Occasionally I
> write out what I have said in verse, and generally for no better
> reason than because I remember that I have written no verse
> for a long time.

The self-consciousness of this little scene is very different from the
unselfconscious Wordsworth making his turns on the gravel path. There
is something roguish in the passage, a studied, throwaway effect—the
impetus behind the writing, for example, being put down casually to the
fact that the poet happens to remember that another lyric is due about
now. Nevertheless, we feel that Yeats's account of himself acting out the
poem's origin, turning the *donné* into display, is proper to the Yeatsian
posture. Yeats does not listen in but acts out. The origin of the poetry is
not a matter of sinking in but of coming up against, the mature music is
not a lulling but an alerting strain. Padraic Colum once spoke of Yeats's
poems having to be handled as carefully as a blade, and the image reminds
us of Yeats's own ambitions for the work, poems 'the poet sings them with
such airs / That one believes he has a sword upstairs'; poems 'cold and
passionate as the dawn'; plays where he hopes 'the passion of the verse
comes from the fact that the speakers are holding down violence or
madness—down, *hysterica passio*. All depends on the completeness of the
holding down, on the stirring of the beast underneath.' It is just such a
note we hear in the major poems, as in 'The Tower':

> Now shall I make my soul,
> Compelling it to study
> In a learned school
> Till the wreck of body,
> Slow decay of blood,
> Testy delirium
> Or dull decrepitude,
> Or what worst evil come—
> The death of friends, or death
> Of every brilliant eye
> That made a catch in the breath—

Seem but the clouds of the sky
When the horizon fades,
Or a bird's sleepy cry
Among the deepening shades.

This is theatrical in its triumph, and many of the high moments in the
Collected Poems share its rhetorical cast. At its worst that rhetoric is
bragging; at its level best it has, to use Denis Donoghue's finely tuned
adjective, an equestrian authority, which arises from Yeats's certainty that
'all the old writers, the masculine writers of the world, wrote to be spoken
or to be sung, and in a later age to be read aloud for hearers who had to
understand swiftly or not at all.' This Yeats who declared himself
impatient with 'poetical literature, that is effeminate in its continual
insistence upon certain moments of strained lyricism', sought a music that
came ringing back off the ear as barely and resonantly as a shout caught
back off a pillar in an empty church. It is indeed the music of energy
reined down, of the mastered beast stirring:

A sudden blow: the great wings beating still
Above the staggering girl, her thighs caressed
By the dark webs, her nape caught in his bill,
He holds her helpless breast upon his breast ...

Turning and turning in the widening gyre
The falcon cannot hear the falconer;
Things fall apart; the centre cannot hold;
Mere anarchy is loosed upon the world,
The blood-dimmed tide is loosed, and everywhere
The ceremony of innocence is drowned ...

Grant me an old man's frenzy,
Myself must I remake
Till I am Timon and Lear
Or that William Blake
Who beat upon the wall
Till Truth obeyed his call ...

In Yeats, the voice muscles its way over the obstacle course of the form and
flexes like an animated vine on the trellis of its metric and rhyme scheme.
We are aware of the finished poem as an impressive thing in itself but

somehow more impressive because of a threshold of difficulties now overcome. Those difficulties, of course, he exulted in: 'The Fascination of What's Difficult' complains of more things than the toil of artistic creation, but its rebounding utterance is won out of that central struggle:

> The fascination of what's difficult
> Has dried the sap out of my veins, and rent
> Spontaneous joy and natural content
> Out of my heart. There's something ails our colt
> That must, as if it had not holy blood
> Nor on Olympus leaped from cloud to cloud,
> Shiver under the lash, strain, sweat and jolt
> As though it dragged road-metal. My curse on plays
> That have to be set up in fifty ways,
> On the day's war with every knave and dolt,
> Theatre business, management of men.
> I swear before the dawn comes round again
> I'll find the stable and pull out the bolt.

The words fly off there like stones in a riot; this is not a region to wander in but a combat zone where rhymes collide and assertions strike hard music off one another like quarter-staffs striking. 'My curse on plays / That have to be set up in fifty ways'—yet it is one of Yeats's remarks, in *Explorations*, about the revision of his plays which throws light upon an important element in the makings of his music:

> I have written a good many plays in verse and prose and almost all those plays I have rewritten after performance, sometimes again and again, and every rewriting that has succeeded upon the stage has been an addition to the masculine element, an increase in the bony structure.

We can see how the bony structure has grown in this instance when we compare the sonnet with the first jottings in Yeats's notebook

> *Subject* To complain of the fascination of what's difficult. It spoils spontaneity and pleasure, and wastes time. Repeat line ending difficult and rhyme on bolt, exalt, colt, jolt. One could use the thought that the winged and broken colt must drag a cart of stones out of pride because it is difficult and end by

denouncing drama, accounts, public contests, all that is merely difficult.

For Yeats, composition was no recollection in tranquillity, not a delivery of the dark embryo, but a mastery, a handling, a struggle towards maximum articulation. Paradoxically, one can employ George Bernard Shaw's dictum on style—'Effectiveness of assertion is the alpha and omega of style'—to suggest the direction and endeavour of Yeats's writing. Paradoxically, because Shaw's arguing voice was anathema to the young poet who was to write later in *Autobiographies* that Shaw discovered it was possible 'to write with great effect without music, without style either good or bad, to eliminate from the mind all emotional implication and prefer plain water to every vintage'. Yet it is this virtue of 'effectiveness of assertion' that is common to both.

There is a relation between the process of composition and the feel of the completed poem all through Yeats's work. From the beginning things had to be well made, the soul had to be compelled to study, the images had to be masterful:

> A line will take us hours maybe;
> Yet if it does not seem a moment's thought,
> Our stitching and unstitching has been naught.
> Better go down upon your marrow bones
> And scrub a kitchen pavement, or break stones
> Like an old pauper, in all kinds of weather;
> For to articulate sweet sounds together
> Is to work harder than all these ...

Scrubbing pavements, breaking stones—these things are contrasted with the craft of verse only to partake of its nature in the context of the poem itself. The abrasive and unyielding are necessarily present in the creative encounter, the mill of the mind has its work to do, for, as the lady affirms a little later in 'Adam's Curse', 'we must labour to be beautiful'. Thoughts do not ooze out and into one another, they are hammered into unity. 'All reality', Yeats notes in a 'Diary Written in 1930', 'comes to us as the reward of labour.' And at the end of his life, in 'A General Introduction to my Work', the theme of labour and deliberate effort comes up again: 'I compel myself to use those traditional metres that have developed with the language.' Yet even traditional metres had to be subdued to the Yeatsian element:

> It was a long time before I had made a language to my liking; I
> began to make it when I discovered some twenty years ago that
> I must seek, not as Wordsworth thought, words in common
> use, but a more powerful and passionate syntax, a complete
> coincidence between period and stanza.

The concern is for syntax the controller, the compelling element that
binds the constituent elements of sense into active unity.

But it is not only in Yeats's writings about composition that this urge
to mastery can be discovered. It becomes most obvious in his manuscripts,
in the evidence there of relentless concentration and self-criticism, in the
evolution of driving verse from metrical monotony and, in many cases,
plain ugly sentences. It is clear that the unwavering ceremonious
procedures of his verse depend upon the way he wrought strongly for
finish in the act of composition itself. One is reminded of a phrase by that
other 'masculine' talent, Gerard Manley Hopkins, who spoke of 'a strain
of address'; and Hopkins also spoke of 'that feeling of physical constraint
that I want'.

All this is relevant to the success of a poem like 'Death'. 'Death' does
not depend upon the way words woo themselves; the consonantal music
and the short line work against any collusion between the vowels, the
consonants and line-breaks acting as forcing agents, ramrodding the
climax rhyme by rhyme

> Nor dread nor hope attend
> A dying animal;
> A man awaits his end
> Dreading and hoping all;
> Many times he died,
> Many times rose again.
> A great man in his pride
> Confronting murderous men
> Casts derision upon
> Supersession of breath;
> He knows death to the bone—
> Man has created death.

Again, it is that accumulating pressure in the movement, the sense of
passion held down, that we are responding to. The poem's arch is built on
repetitions that strain away from one another by reason of the sense they

are making, but press in upon one another by reason of the repeated vocable. Dread, hope, man, many times, death—the weight of the utterance forces these words against themselves and the rhymes on died/pride and breath/death form the unshakeable arch of the structure. Affirmation arises out of oppositions.

'Long-legged Fly' is a poem that is absolute in its poetic integrity, that commands us both by the stony clarity of its sounds and the deep probes of its images, though 'images' is too weak a word, is somehow inaccurate: it is more that every element in the poem is at once literal and symbolic. It is a transcendent realization of the things I was trying to get at: what is the relationship between the creative moment in the life of an individual and the effect of that moment's conception throughout history?

That civilization may not sink,
Its great battle lost,
Quiet the dog, tether the pony
To a distant post;
Our master Caesar is in the tent
Where the maps are spread,
His eyes fixed upon nothing,
A hand under his head.
Like a long-legged fly upon the stream
His mind moves upon silence.

That the topless towers be burnt
And men recall that face,
Move most gently if move you must
In this lonely place.
She thinks, part woman, three parts a child
That nobody looks; her feet
Practise a tinker shuffle
Picked up on a street.
Like a long-legged fly upon the stream
Her mind moves upon silence.

That girls at puberty may find
The first Adam in their thought,
Shut the door of the Pope's chapel,
Keep those children out.
There on that scaffolding reclines

Michael Angelo.
With no more sound than the mice make
His hand moves to and fro.
Like a long-legged fly upon the stream
His mind moves upon silence.

The creative mind is astraddle silence. In my reading, the long-legged fly
has a masculine gender and while there is a sense of incubation permeating
the whole poem, there is also a sense of intent siring. The image recalls
the first chapter of the Book of Genesis, where God the Father's mind
moves upon chaos, and the image functions within the poem like the nerve
of a thinking brain, a brain that concedes the clangour and objectivity of
historical events, the remorselessness of action, the unstoppable flow of
time. It concedes all this but simultaneously affirms the absoluteness of
the moment of silence, the power of the mind's motion along and against
the current of history. The poem dramatizes concentration brought to the
point of consummation. The act of the mind, in Michael Angelo's case,
exerts an almost glandular pressure on history and what conducts that
pressure is the image in the beholder's eye. In a similar way, as I have tried
to show, poetry depends for its continuing efficacy upon the play of sound
not only in the ear of the reader but also in the ear of the writer.

GEOFFREY HARTMAN

The Poetics of Prophecy

In our honorific or sophomoric moods, we like to think that poets are
prophets. At least that certain great poets have something of the audacity
and intensity—the strong speech—of Old Testament prophets who claimed
that the word of God came to them. "The words of Jeremiah, the son of
Hilkiah ... To whom the word of the Lord came in the days of Josiah ..." It
is hard to understand even this introductory passage, for the word for
"words," *divre* in Hebrew, indicates something closer to "acts" or "word
events," while what the King James version translates as "to whom the
word of the Lord came," which hypostatizes the Word, as if it had a being
of its own, or were consubstantial with what we know of God, is in the
original simply *hajah devar-adonai elav*, "the God-word was to him." We
don't know, in short, what is going on; yet through a long tradition of
translation and interpretation we feel we know. Similarly, when
Wordsworth tells us that around his twenty-third year he "received"
certain "convictions," which included the thought that despite his
humbler subject matter he could stand beside the "men of old," we seek
gropingly to make sense of that conviction. "Poets, even as Prophets,"
Wordsworth writes,

> each with each
> Connected in a mighty scheme of truth,

From *High Romantic Argument: Essays for M. H. Abrams*, edited by Lawrence Lipking. © 1981
by Cornell University.

Have each his own peculiar faculty,
Heaven's gift, a sense that fits him to perceive
Objects unseen before ...
An insight that in some sort he possesses,
A privilege whereby a work of his,
Proceeding from a source of untaught things
Creative and enduring, may become
A power like one of Nature's.

[1850 *Prelude* xiii.301–12]

In the earlier (1805) version of *The Prelude* "insight" is "influx," which relates more closely to a belief in inspiration, or a flow (of words) the poet participates in yet does not control: "An influx, that in some sort I possess'd."

I will somewhat neglect in what follows one difference, rather obvious, between poet and prophet. A prophet is to us, and perhaps to himself, mainly a *voice*—as God himself seems to him primarily a voice. Even when he does God in many voices, they are not felt to stand in an equivocal relation to each other: each voice is absolute, and vacillation produces vibrancy rather than ambiguity. In this sense there is no "poetics of prophecy"; there is simply a voice breaking forth, a quasivolcanic eruption, and sometimes its opposite, the "still, small voice" heard after the thunder of Sinai. I will try to come to grips with that difference between poet and prophet later on; here I should only note that, being of the era of Wordsworth rather than of Jeremiah, I must look back from the poet's rather than from the prophet's perspective, while acknowledging that the very concept of poetry may be used by Wordsworth to reflect on—and often to defer—the claim that he has a prophetic gift.

There is another passage in *The Prelude* that explores the relation between poet and prophet. Wordsworth had been to France during the Revolution, had followed that cataclysmic movement in hope, had seen it degenerate into internecine politics and aggressive war. Yet despite the discrediting of revolutionary ideals, something of his faith survived, and not only faith but, as he strangely put it, "daring sympathies with power." In brief, he saw those terrible events in France as necessary and even divinely sanctioned. To explain his mood Wordsworth writes a confessional passage that also gives his most exact understanding of prophecy:

But as the ancient Prophets, borne aloft
In vision, yet constrained by natural laws

With them to take a troubled human heart,
Wanted not consolations, nor a creed
Of reconcilement, then when they denounced,
On towns and cities, wallowing in the abyss
Of their offences, punishment to come;
Or saw, like other men, with bodily eyes,
Before them, in some desolated place,
The wrath consummate and the threat fulfilled;
So, with devout humility be it said,
So, did a portion of that spirit fall
On me uplifted from the vantage-ground
Of pity and sorrow to a state of being
That through the time's exceeding fierceness saw
Glimpses of retribution, terrible,
And in the order of sublime behests:
But, even if that were not, amid the awe
Of unintelligible chastisement,
Not only acquiescences of faith
Survived, but daring sympathies with power,
Motions not treacherous or profane, else why
Within the folds of no ungentle breast
Their dread vibration to this hour prolonged?
Wild blasts of music thus could find their way
Into the midst of turbulent events;
So that worst tempests might be listened to.
                                        [1850 *Prelude* x.437–63]

This eloquent statement has many complexities; but it is clear that
though Wordsworth felt himself "uplifted from the vantage-ground / Of
pity and sorrow," he did not leave them behind in this moment of sublime
vision and terrible purification. It is certainly a remarkable feature of a
prophet like Jeremiah that "borne aloft / In vision" he yet takes with him
"a troubled human heart." Like Jonah, he tries to evade the commission,
though not, like Jonah, by running away but rather by claiming he is not
of age when it comes to speech ("Then said I, Ah, Lord GOD! behold, I
cannot speak: for I am a child"). Jeremiah even accuses God, in bitterness
of heart, of the very thing of which God accused Israel: of seducing the
prophet, or of being unfaithful (Jeremiah 20:7ff).
      Wordsworth expresses most strongly a further, related aspect of
prophetical psychology: the ambivalent sympathy shown by the prophet

for the powerful and terrible thing he envisions. This sympathy operates even when he tries to avert what must be, or to find a "creed of reconcilement." The poet's problem vis-à-vis the Revolution was not, principally, that he had to come to terms with crimes committed in the name of the Revolution or of liberty. For at the end of the passage from which I have quoted he indicates that there had been a rebound of faith, a persuasion that grew in him that the Revolution itself was not to blame, but rather "a terrific reservoir of guilt / And ignorance filled up from age to age" had "burst and spread in deluge through the land." The real problem was his entanglement in a certain order of sensations which endured to the very time of writing: he owns to "daring sympathies with power," "motions," whose "dread vibration" is "to this hour prolonged," and whose harmonizing effect in the midst of the turbulence he characterized by the oxymoron "Wild blasts of music."

We understand perfectly well that what is involved in Wordsworth's sympathy with power is not, or not simply, a sublime kind of *Schadenfreude*, And that no amount of talk about the pleasure given by tragedy, through "cathartic" identification, would do more than uncover the same problem in a related area. The seduction power exerts, when seen as an act of God or Nature, lies within common experience. It does not of itself distinguish poets or prophets. What is out of the ordinary here is the "dread vibration": a term close to music, as well as one that conveys the lasting resonance of earlier feelings. How did Wordsworth's experience of sympathy with power accrue a metaphor made overt in "wild blasts of music"?

The tradition that depicts inspired poetry as a wild sort of natural music ("Homer the great Thunderer, [and] the voice that roars along the bed of Jewish Song") circumscribes rather than explains these metaphors. When we take them to be more than commonplaces of high poetry we notice that they sometimes evoke the force of wind and water as blended sound (cf. "The stationary blasts of waterfalls," 1850 *Prelude* vi.626), a sound with power to draw the psyche in, as if the psyche also were an instrument or element, and had to mingle responsively with some overwhelming, massive unity. Despite the poet's imagery of violence, the ideal of harmony, at least on the level of sound, is not given up. The soul as a gigantic if reluctant aeolian harp is implicitly evoked.

How strangely this impulse to harmony is linked with violent feelings can be shown by one of Wordsworth's similes. Similes are, of course, a formal way of bringing together, or harmonizing, different areas of experience. From Coleridge to the New Critics the discussion of formal poetics has often focused on the valorized distinction between fancy and imagination, or on the way difference is reconciled. Shortly before his reflection on the ancient prophets, and when he is still describing the indiscriminate carnage unleashed by Robespierre, Wordsworth has recourse to a strange pseudo-Homeric simile comparing the tempo of killings to a child activating a toy windmill:

> though the air
> Do of itself blow fresh, and make the vanes
> Spin in his eyesight, that contents him not,
> But, with the plaything at arm's length, he sets
> His front against the blast, and runs amain,
> That it may whirl the faster.
> [1850 *Prelude* x.369–74]

An aeolian toy is used, explicitly now, to image a sublime and terrible order of events. The instrument is given to the wind, so that it may go faster; yet this childish sport is set in an ominous context. The innocent wish to have something go fast reflects on the child whose mimicry (as in the Intimations Ode) suggests his haste to enter the very world where that haste has just shown itself in heinous form. Though there is something incongruous in the simile, there is also something fitting: or at least a drive toward fitting together incongruous passions of childhood and adulthood; and may this drive not express the dark "workmanship that reconciles / Discordant elements" by a mysterious, quasi-musical "harmony" (1850 *Prelude* i.340ff.)? Here the reconciling music, by which the mind is built up, is already something of a "wild blast"; and when we think of the passage on prophecy to follow, on Wordsworth's "daring sympathies with power," we realize that what is involved in these various instances—lust for carnage, vertigo-sport, the child's impatience to grow up, the poet's fit of words, and the prophet's sympathy with the foreseen event, however terrible—is an anticipatory relation to time, a hastening of futurity.

The music metaphor, associated with wind and water sound, occurs in yet another context close to apocalyptic feelings. (By "apocalyptic" I always mean quite specifically an anticipatory, proleptic relation to time, intensified to the point where there is at once desire for and dread of the end being hastened. There is a potential inner turning against time, and against nature insofar as it participates in the temporal order.) Wordsworth's dream in *Prelude* V of the Arab saving stone and shell from the encroaching flood, also identified as the two principal branches of humane learning, mathematics and literature, is given an explicitly apocalyptic frame. The poet is meditating on books "that aspire to an unconquerable life," human creations that must perish nevertheless. Quoting from a Shakespeare sonnet on the theme of time, he reflects that we "weep to have" what we may lose: the weeping represents both the vain effort and the proleptic regret, so that the very joy of possessing lies close to tears, or thoughts deeper than tears. Only one detail of the ensuing dream need concern us. It comes when the Arab asks the dreamer to hold the shell (poetry) to his ear. "I did so," says the dreamer,

> And heard that instant in an unknown tongue,
> Which yet I understood, articulate sounds,
> A loud prophetic blast of harmony;
> An Ode, in passion uttered, which foretold
> Destruction to the children of the earth
> By deluge, now at hand.
>
> [1850 *Prelude* v.93–98]

A "blast of harmony" is not only a more paradoxical, more acute version of the metaphor in "blast of music," but we recognize it as an appropriate figure for the shouting poetry also called prophecy. In the lines that follow, Wordsworth stresses the dual function of such poetry: it has power to exhilarate and to soothe the human heart. But this is a gloss that conventionalizes the paradox in "blast of harmony" and does not touch the reality of the figure.

Our task is to understand the reality of figures, or more precisely, the reality of "blast of harmony," when applied to prophecy, or prophetic poetry. I will suggest, on the basis of this figure, that there is a poetics of prophecy; and I will study it by reading closely two episodes in *The Prelude* entirely within the secular sphere: the "spot of time" alluding to the death of the poet's father, and the ascent of Snowdon. After that a transition to the prophetic books, and to Jeremiah in particular, may lie open.

2

The death of Wordsworth's father is not attended by unusual circumstances. As Claudius says in a play we shall refer to again: a "common theme / Is death of fathers." Yet it is precisely the commonplace that releases in this case the "dread vibration." The thirteen-year-old schoolboy is impatient to return home for the Christmas holidays, and climbs a crag overlooking two highways to see whether he can spot the horses that should be coming. From that bare, wind-blown crag he watches intensely, and shortly after he returns home his father dies. That is all: a moment of intense, impatient watching, and then, ten days later, the death. Two things without connection except contiguity in time come together in the boy, who feels an emotion that perpetuates "down to this very time" the sights and sounds he experienced waiting for the horses. Here is Wordsworth's account in full:

> There rose a crag,
> That, from the meeting-point of two highways
> Ascending, overlooked them both, far stretched;
> Thither, uncertain on which road to fix
> My expectation, thither I repaired,
> Scout-like, and gained the summit; 'twas a day
> Tempestuous, dark, and wild, and on the grass
> I sate half-sheltered by a naked wall;
> Upon my right hand couched a single sheep,
> Upon my left a blasted hawthorn stood;
> With those companions at my side, I watched,
> Straining my eyes intensely, as the mist
> Gave intermitting prospect of the copse
> And plain beneath. Ere we to school returned,—
> That dreary time,—ere we had been ten days
> Sojourners in my father's house, he died,
> And I and my three brothers, orphans then,
> Followed his body to the grave. The event,
> With all the sorrow that it brought, appeared
> A chastisement; and when I called to mind
> That day so lately past, when from the crag
> I looked in such anxiety of hope;
> With trite reflections of morality,
> Yet in the deepest passion, I bowed low
> To God, Who thus corrected my desires;
> And, afterwards, the wind and sleety rain,
> And all the business of the elements,
> The single sheep, and the one blasted tree,
> And the bleak music from that old stone wall,
> The noise of wood and water, and the mist
> That on the line of each of those two roads

Advanced in such indisputable shapes;
All these were kindred spectacles and sounds
To which I oft repaired, and thence would drink,
As at a fountain; and on winter nights,
Down to this very time, when storm and rain
Beat on my roof, or, haply, at noon-day,
While in a grove I walk, whose lofty trees,
Laden with summer's thickest foliage, rock
In a strong wind, some working of the spirit,
Some inward agitations thence are brought,
Whate'er their office.
                          [1850 *Prelude* xii.292–333]

The secular and naturalistic frame of what is recorded remains intact. Yet the experience is comparable in more than its aura to what motivates prophecy. Though there is no intervention of vision or voice, there is something like a special, burdened relation to time. Wordsworth called the episode a "spot of time," to indicate that it stood out, spotlike, in his consciousness of time, that it merged sensation of place and sensation of time (so that time was *placed*), even that it allowed him to physically perceive or "spot" time.

The boy on the summit, overlooking the meeting point of two highways, and stationed between something immobile on his right hand and his left, is, as it were, at the center of a stark clock. Yet the question, How long? if it rises within him, remains mute. It certainly does not surface with the ghostly, prophetic dimension that invests it later. At this point there is simply a boy's impatient hope, "anxiety of hope," as the poet calls it (l.313), a straining of eye and mind that corresponds to the "far-stretched" perspective of the roads. But the father's death, which supervenes as an "event" (l.309), converts that moment of hope into an ominous, even murderous anticipation.

In retrospect, then, a perfectly ordinary mood is seen to involve a sin against time. The boy's "anxiety of hope," his wish for time to pass (both the "dreary time" of school and now of watching and waiting) seems to find retributive fulfillment when the father's life is cut short ten days later. The aftermath points to something unconscious in the first instance but manifest and punishing now. The child feels that his "desires" have been "corrected" by God. What desires could they be except fits of extreme—apocalyptic—impatience, brought on by the very patience or dreary sufferance of nature, of sheep and blasted tree? That the boy bowed low to God, who corrected his desires, evokes a human and orthodox version of nature's own passion.

A similar correction may be the subject of "A slumber did my spirit seal," where a milder sin against time, the delusion that the loved one is a "thing" exempt from the touch of years, is revealed when she dies and becomes a "thing" in fact. The fulfillment of the hope corrects it, as in certain fairy tales. In Wordsworth, hope or delusion always involves the hypnotic elision of time by an imagination drawn toward the "bleak music" of nature—of a powerfully inarticulate nature.

Yet in both representations, that of the death of the father and that of the death of the beloved, there is no hint of anything that would compel the mind to link the two terms, hope against time and its peculiar fulfillment. The link remains inarticulate, like nature itself. A first memory is interpreted by a second: the "event" clarifies an ordinary emotion by suggesting its apocalyptic vigor. But the apocalyptic mode, as Martin Buber remarked, is not the prophetic. Wordsworth's spots of time are said to renew time rather than to hasten its end. A wish for the end to come, for time to pass absolutely, cannot explain what brought the two happenings together, causally, superstitiously, or by a *vaticinum ex eventu*.

Perhaps the apocalyptic wish so compressed the element of time that something like a "gravitation" effect was produced, whereby unrelated incidents fell toward each other. It is, in any case, this process of conjuncture or binding that is mysterious. Not only for the reader but for Wordsworth himself. A more explicit revelation of the binding power had occurred after the death of the poet's mother. Wordsworth's "For now a trouble came into my mind / From unknown causes" (1850 *Prelude* ii.276–77) refers to an expectation that when his mother died the world would collapse. Instead it remains intact and attractive.

> I was left alone
> Seeking the visible world, nor knowing why.
> The props of my affection were removed,
> And yet the building stood, as if sustained
> By its own spirit!
> [1850 *Prelude* ii.277–81]

What he had previously named, describing the relationship between mother and infant, "the gravitation and the filial bond," continues to operate without the mother. This event contrary to expectation is the "trouble"; and the "unknown causes" allude to the gravitation, or glue or binding, that mysteriously sustains nature, and draws the child to it in the mother's absence. Even loss binds; and a paradox emerges which focuses on the fixative rather than fixating power of catastrophe, on the nourishing and reparative quality of the. "trouble." Wordsworth, too benevolent perhaps, suggests that time itself is being repaired: that the pressure of eternity on thought (the parent's death) creates an "eternity of thought" (1850 *Prelude* i.402). The survivor knows that the burden of the mystery can be borne, that there is time for thought.

Whether or not, then, we understand Wordsworth's experience fully, the "spots of time" describe a trauma, a lesion in the fabric of time, or more precisely, the trouble this lesion produces and which shows itself as an extreme consciousness of time. Not only is there an untimely death in the case of the father, but it follows too fast on the boy's return home. As in *Hamlet*, "The time is out of joint. O cursed spite / That ever I was born to set it right!" The righting of the injury somehow falls to the poet. "Future restoration" (1850 *Prelude* xii.286), perhaps in the double sense of a restoration of the future as well as of a restoration still to come, is the task he sets himself.[1]

Prophecy, then, would seem to be anti-apocalyptic in seeking a "future restoration," or time for thought. But time, in Wordsworth, is also language, or what the Intimations Ode calls "timely utterance." That phrase contains both threat and promise. It suggests the urgent pressure that gives rise to speech; it also suggests that an animate response, and a harmonious one, is possible, as in Milton's "answerable style," or the pastoral cliche of woods and waters mourning, rejoicing or echoing in timely fashion the poet's mode. Ruskin referred to it as the pathetic fallacy but Abraham Heschel will make pathos, in that large sense, the very characteristic of prophetic language.

More radically still "timely utterance" means an utterance, such as prophecy, or prophetic poetry, which founds or repairs time. The prophet utters time in its ambiguity: as the undesired mediation, which prevents fusion, but also destruction. It prevents fusion by intruding the voice of the poet, his troubled heart, his fear of or flight from "power"; it prevents destruction by delaying God's decree or personally mediating it. Wordsworth speaks scrupulous words despite his sympathy with power and his attraction to the muteness or closure foreseen. By intertextual bonding, by words within words or words against words, he reminds us one more time of time.

We cannot evade the fact that the anxious waiting and the father's death are joined by what can only be called a "blast of harmony." The two moments are harmonized, but the copula is poetic as well as prophetic. For the conjunction of these contiguous yet disparate happenings into a "kindred" form is due to a "working of the spirit" that must be equated with poetry itself. While in the boy of thirteen the process of joining may have been instinctual, the poet recollects the past event as still working itself out; the incident demonstrated so forceful a visiting of imaginative power that later thought is never free of it. What is remarkable in this type-incident—and so remarkable that it keeps "working" on the mind "to this very time"—is not only the "coadunation," as Coleridge would have said, or "In-Eins-Bildung" (his false etymology for the German *Embildungskraft*, or imagination), but also that it is a "blast," that the workmanship reconciling the discordant elements anticipates a final, awesome unification. Hope is always "anxious" in that it foresees not just unity but also the power needed to achieve unity, to blast things into that state. The fear, then, that mingles with apocalyptic hope also stills it, or brings it close to "that peace / Which passeth understanding" (1850 *Prelude* xiv.126–27), because of the uncertain, terrible nature of this final bonding, which evokes in the episode on the crag a bleak and bleating music and images of stunned, warped, blasted, inarticulate being.

3

I turn to the climatic episode of *The Prelude*, the ascent of Snowdon in Book xiv. Disregarding all but its barest structure, we see that it again presents a sequence of two moments curiously harmonized. The theme of time enters as *elided* when the moon breaks through the mist and into the absorbed mind of the climber. "Nor was time given to ask or learn the cause, / For instantly a light upon the turf / Fell like a flash ..." (xiv.37–39). This moment of prevenient light is followed as suddenly by a wild blast of music: the roar of waters through a rift in the mist. The second act or "event" is here an actual sound, separated off from sight and almost hypostatized as a sound. It is quite literally a "blast of harmony": "The roar of waters ... roaring with one voice."

The appearance of the moon out of the mist is not, however, as unmotivated as might appear. It realizes an unuttered wish, "Let there be light," as the poet climbs through the darkness to "see the sun rise." Spotting the moon fulfills his hope in an unexpected way, which also foreshortens time. The mind of the poet is disoriented; but then time is lengthened as the sight of the moonstruck scene takes over in a kind of silent harmonization. If my hypothesis is correct, there is something truly magical here. The effect ("And there was light") utters the cause—that is, utters the scriptural text ("Let there be light") lodging as desire in the poet. Silence emits a "sound of harmony" (xiv.98–99) analogous to the music of the spheres. Not the poet but heaven itself declares the glory, the "And there was light" as "night unto night showeth knowledge." Wordsworth seems to behold visibly the "timely utterance" with which Genesis begins—the very harmony between cause and effect, between fiat and actualizing response—and this spectacle seems to be so ghostly a projection of nature itself (rather than of his own excited mind) that he claims it was "given to spirits of the night" and only by chance to the three human spectators (xiv.63–65).

Yet if the first act of the vision proper proves deceptive, because its motivation, which is a scriptural text, or the authority of that text, or the poet's desire to recapture that fiat power, remains silent and inward, the second act, which is the rising of the voice of the waters, also proves deceptive, even as it falsifies the first. The sound of the waters (though apparently unheard) must have been there all along, so that what is shown up by the vision's second act is a premature harmonizing of the landscape by the majestic moon: by that time-subduing object all sublime. Time also becomes a function of the desire for harmony as imagination now foreshortens and now enthrones the passing moment, or, to quote one of many variants, "so moulds, exalts, indues, combines, / Impregnates, separates, adds, takes away / And makes one object sway another so ..." In the poet's commentary there is a further attempt at harmonizing, when moon and roaring waters are typified as correlative acts, the possessions of a mind

> That feeds upon infinity, that broods
> Over the dark abyss, intent to hear
> Its voices issuing forth to silent light
> In one continuous stream
>
> [xiv.71–74]

An image of communion and continuity is projected which the syntax partially subverts, for "its" remains ambiguous, and we cannot say for sure whether the voices belong to the dark abyss or the heavenly mind. What remains of this rich confusion are partial and contradictory structures of unification, which meet us "at every turn" in the "narrow rent" of the text, and add up less to a "chorus of infinity" than again to a "blast of harmony."

4

For prophet as for poet the ideal is "timely utterance," yet what we actually receive is a "blast of harmony." In Jeremiah a double pressure is exerted, of time on the prophet and of the prophet on time. The urgency of "timely utterance" cuts both ways. Moreover, while the prophet's words must harmonize with events, before or after the event, the word itself is viewed as an event that must harmonize with itself, or with its imputed source in God and the prophets. A passage such as Jeremiah 23:9–11 describes the impact of the God-word in terms that not only are conventionally ecstatic but also suggest the difficulty of reading the signs of authority properly, and distinguishing true from false prophet. "Adultery" seems to have moved into the word-event itself.

> Concerning the prophets:
> My heart is broken within me,
> all my bones shake;
> I am like a drunken man,
> like man overcome by wine,
> because of the LORD
> and because of his holy words.
> For the land is full of adulterers;
> because of the curse the land mourns....

The time frame becomes very complex, then. On an obvious level the God-word as threat or promise is interpreted and reinterpreted in the light of history, so that Jeremiah's pronouncements are immediately set in their time. "The words of Jeremiah, the son of Hilkiah ... to whom the word of the Lord came in the days of Josiah ..." The ending *jah*, meaning "God," reveals from within these destined names the pressure for riming events with God. Jeremiah's prophecies are political suasions having to do with Israel's precarious position between Babylon on one border and Egypt on the other in the years before the destruction of Jerusalem by Nebuchadnezzar. The very survival of Israel is in question; and the prophet is perforce a political analyst as well as a divine spokesman. He speaks at risk not only in the hearing of God but also in that of Pashur, who beat him and put him in the stocks (20:1–4), in that of so-called friends who whisper "Denounce him to Pashur," and in that of King Zedekiah, the son of Josiah, king of Judah, who sends Pashur (the same or another) to Jeremiah, saying, "Inquire of the Lord for us" about Nebuchadnezzar, king of Babylon (21:1–3).

On another level, however, since the book of Jeremiah knows that the outcome is "the captivity of Jerusalem" (1:3), a question arises as to the later force of such prophecy. Near the onset of Jeremiah's career a manuscript of what may have been a version of Deuteronomy was found, and a dedication ceremony took place which pledged Judah once more to the covenant. The issue of the covenant—whether it is broken, or can ever be broken—and the part played in this issue by the survival of a book such as Jeremiah's own is another aspect of the prophet's utterance. Can one praise God yet curse oneself as the bearer of his word (20:13–14)? Or can Judah follow God into the wilderness once more, showing the same devotion as when it was a bride (2:2)? "I utter what was only in view of what will be.... What is realized in my history is not the past definite of what was, since it is no more, or even the present perfect of what has been in what I am, but the future anterior of what I shall have been for what I am in the process of becoming." That is Jacques Lacan on the function of language.

Indeed, the contradictions that beset "timely utterance" are so great that a reversal occurs which discloses one of the founding metaphors of literature. When Jacques Lacan writes that "symbols ... envelop the life of man in a network so total that they join together, before he comes into the world, those who are going to engender him 'by flesh and blood'; so total that they bring to his birth, along with the gifts of the stars, if not with the gifts of the fairies, the shape of his destiny; so total that they give the words that will make him faithful or renegade, the law of the acts that will follow him right to the very place where he is not yet and even beyond his death; and so total that through them his end finds its meaning in the last judgement, where the Word absolves his being or condemns it," he is still elaborating Jeremiah 1:4. "Now the word of the LORD came to me saying, 'Before I formed you in the womb I knew you, and before you were born I consecrated you; I appointed you a prophet to the nations.'" This predestination by the word and unto the word—the "imperative of the Word," as Lacan also calls it, in a shorthand that alludes to the later tradition of the Logos—is then reinforced by Jeremiah 1:11–12. "And the word of the LORD came to me saying, 'Jeremiah, what do you see?' And I said, 'I see a rod of almond.' Then the LORD said to me, 'You have seen well, for I am watching over my word to perform it.'"

Here the pun of "rod of almond" (*makel shaqued*) and "[I am] watching" (*shoqued*) is more, surely, than a mnemonic or overdetermined linguistic device: it is a rebus that suggests the actualizing or performative relationship between words and things implied by the admonition: "I am watching over my word to perform it." The admonition is addressed to the prophet, in whose care the word is, and through him to the nation; while the very image of the rod of almond projects not only a reconciliation of contraries, of punishment (rod) and pastoral peace (almond), but the entire problem of timely utterance, since the almond tree blossoms unseasonably early and is as exposed to blasting as is the prophet, who seeks to avoid premature speech: "Ah, Lord God! Behold, I do not know how to speak, for I am only a child."

The forcible harmonizing of *shaqued* and *shoqued*, the pressure of that pun, or the emblematic abuse of a pastoral image, alerts us to the difficult pathos of prophetic speech. What does "watching over the word" involve? The prophets are politically and psychically in such a pressure-cooker situation ("I see a boiling pot," Jeremiah 1:13) that a powerful contamination occurs. Their words cannot always be distinguished from those of God in terms of who is speaking. The prophet identifies now with God and now with his people; moreover, his only way of arguing with the Lord is through words and figures given by the latter. Lacan would say that there is an inevitable inmixing of the Discourse of the Other. Jeremiah argues with God in God's language; and such scripture formulas as "according to thy word" recall this confused, and indeterminate situation.

When, in famous lyric verses, Jeremiah admits that he cannot speak without shouting, and what he shouts is "violence and destruction" (20:8), it is as if the God-word itself had suffered a crisis of reference. For this typical warning is now directed not against Israel but against God: it refers to the condition of the prophet who feels betrayed as well as endangered. Jeremiah's hymn begins: "O Lord, you seduced me, and I was seduced," where "seduce," *pittiytani*, can mean both sexual enticement and spiritual deception—as by false prophets. No wonder that at the end of this hymn, the most formal and personal in the entire book, there is a surprising and unmotivated turn from blessing ("Sing to the LORD; praise the LORD") to cursing ("Cursed be the day on which I was born!" 20:13–18). However conventional such a curse may be, and we find a famous instance in Job, it cannot but be read in conjunction with "Before I formed you in the womb I knew you." Jeremiah's "Cursed be the day" is a Caliban moment; God has taught the prophet to speak, and so to curse; or it is a Hamlet moment, the prophet being "cursed" by his election to set the time right. But more important, the curse is the word itself, the violence done by it to the prophet. He feels it in his heart and bones as a burning fire (20:9). The word that knew him before he was conceived has displaced father and mother as begetter: when he curses his birth his word really curses the word. Jeremiah is not given time to develop; he is hurled untimely into the word. The words of the prophet and the words of God can be one only through that "blast of harmony" of which Wordsworth's dream still gives an inkling.

5

When even an intelligent contemporary discussion of "The Prophets as Poets" talks of a "symphony of the effective word" and "the gradual union of person and word," and sees prophecy advancing historically from "word as pointer to word as the thing itself," it adopts metaphors as solutions. The animating fiat spoken by God in the book of Genesis, which founds the harmonious correspondence of creative principle (word) and created product (thing), is literalized by a leap of faith on the part of the intelligent contemporary reader.

Yet with some exceptions—Wolfgang Binder and Peter Szondi on the language of Hölderlin, Erich Auerbach on Dante and figural typology, Northrop Frye on Blake, M. H. Abrams and E. S. Shaffer on the Romantics, Stanley Cavell on Thoreau—it is not the literary critics but the biblical scholars who have raised the issue of secularization (or, what affinity is there between secular and sacred word?) to a level where it is more than a problem in commuting: how to get from there to here, or vice versa. Since Ambrose and Augustine, and again since the Romantic era, biblical criticism has developed together with literary criticism; and still we are only beginning to appreciate their mutual concerns.

It is no accident that the career of Northrop Frye has promised to culminate in an Anatomy of the Bible, or in a summa of structural principles that could harmonize the two bodies of the logos: scripture and literature. By labeling an essay "The Poetics of Prophecy," I may seem to be going in the same direction, and I certainly wish to; yet I think that the relationship between *poetics* and *prophetics* cannot be so easily accommodated. The work of detail, or close reading, ever remains, and quite possibly as a task without an ending. Even when we seek to climb to a prospect where secular and sacred hermeneutics meet on some windy crag, we continue to face a number of unresolved questions that at once plague and animate the thinking critic.

One question is the status of figures. They seem to persist in language as indefeasible sedimentations or as recurrent necessity, long after the megaphone of prophetic style. Moreover, because of the priority and survival of "primitive" or "oriental" figuration, such distinctions as Coleridge's between fancy and imagination tend to become the problem they were meant to resolve. Strong figurative expression does not reconcile particular and universal, or show the translucence of the universal in the concrete: there is such stress and strain that even when theorists value one mode of imaginative embodiment over another—as symbol over allegory or metaphysical wit—they admit the persistence and sometimes explosive concurrence of the archaic or depreciated form.

Another important question is the status of written texts in the life of society or the life of the mind. Almost every tradition influenced by Christianity has aspired to a spiritualization of the word, its transformation and even disappearance as it passes from "word as pointer to word as thing itself." A logocentric or incarnationist thesis of this kind haunts the fringes of most studies of literature, and explains the welcome accorded at present to semiotic counterperspectives. Textual reality, obviously, is more complex, undecidable, and lasting than any such dogma; and the dogma itself is merely inferred from historically ramified texts.

A last question concerns intertextuality. From the perspective of scripture intertextuality is related to canon formation, or the process of authority by which the bibles (*biblia*) we call the Bible were unified. The impact of scripture on literature includes the concept of (1) peremptory or preemptive texts and (2) interpreters who find the unifying principle that could join books into a canon of classics. From a secular perspective these books, whether classified as literature or as scripture, have force but no authority; and to bring them together into some sort of canon is the coup of the critic, who harmonizes them by the force of his own text. His work reveals not their canonicity but rather their intertextuality; and the most suggestive theory along these lines has been that of Harold Bloom.

The impact, according to him, of a preemptive poem on a later one is always "revisionary": the one lives the other's death, deviating its meaning, diverting its strength, creating an inescapable orbit. "Revisionary" suggests, therefore, a relationship of force: again, a blast of harmony rather than a natural or authoritative unification.

For a reason not entirely clear to me, Bloom wishes to establish English poetry after Milton as a Milton satellite. Milton becomes a scripture substitute with the impressive and oppressive influence of scripture itself. Later poets must harmonize with Milton, willingly or unwillingly: even their deviations are explained by attempts to escape the Milton orbit. Yet I have shown that Wordsworth may imitate a scripture text ("Let there be light") with a power of deviousness that is totally un-Miltonic.

Milton and Nature, Wordsworth saw, were not the same. His return to scripture is not to its precise verbal content, though it is an implicit content (Genesis, light, voice) that infuses the texture of the vision on Snowdon. The form of the fiat, however, predominates over its content; and what we are given to see is not scripture reenacted or imaginatively revised—new testamented—but the unuttered fiat in its silent yet all-subduing aspect. What Wordsworth names and represents as Nature is the fiat power working tacitly and harmoniously, reconciling discordant elements, building up the mind and perhaps the cosmos itself.

Snowdon's Miltonic echoes, therefore, which recapitulate a portion of the story of creation as retold in the seventh book of *Paradise Lost*, are allusions whose status is as hard to gauge as those to *Hamlet* in the "spot of time" referring to the father's death. The converging highways, moreover, in that spot of time could lead the contemporary reader (perhaps via Freud) to Oedipus, so that a question arises on the relation of revisionary to hermeneutic perspectives, making the intertextual map more tricky still. Yet Wordsworth's vision, natural rather than textual in its apparent motivation, can still be called revisionary because a prior and seminal text may be hypothetically reconstituted.

The act of reconstitution, however, now includes the reader in a specific and definable way. The *poet* as reader is shown to have discovered from within himself, and so recreated, a scripture text. The *interpreter* as reader has shown the capacity of a "secular" text to yield a "sacred" intuition by a literary act of understanding that cannot be divided into those categories. On the level of interpretation, therefore, we move toward what Schleiermacher called *Verstehen*, on the basis of which a hermeneutic is projected that seeks to transcend the dichotomizing of religious and nonreligious modes of understanding and of earlier (prophetic) and later (poetic-visionary) texts.

6

Returning a last time to Wordsworth: much remains to be said concerning the "gravitation and the filial bond" that links earlier visionary texts to his own. The reader, in any case, also moves in a certain gravitational field; and I have kept myself from being pulled toward a Freudian explanation of the nexus between the boy's "anxiety of hope" and the guilty, affective inscription on his mind of a natural scene. My only finding is that should a God-word precede in Wordsworth, it is rarely foregrounded, but tends to be part of the poem's ground as an inarticulate, homeless or ghostly, sound. It becomes, to use one of his own expressions, an "inland murmur."

In the second act of Snowdon this sound comes out of the deep and is suddenly the very subject, the "Imagination of the whole" (1805 *Prelude* xiii.65). Though the text behind that sound cannot be specified, it is most probably the word within the word, the Word that was in the Beginning (John 1:1), and which uttered as from chaos, "Let there be light." In Milton the first words of the "Omnific Word" are "Silence, ye troubl'd Waves, and thou Deep, peace" (*Paradise Lost* vii.216), a proto-fiat Wordsworth may have absorbed into his vision of silence followed by his more radical vision of the power in sound.

When the poet writes, "The sounding cataract haunted me like a passion" ("Tintern Abbey"), there is again no sense of a proof text of any kind. We recognize a congruity of theme between this waterfall and the "roar of waters" heard on Snowdon, and perhaps associate both with Psalm 42: "Deep calls unto deep at the thunder of thy cataracts." Such allusions may exist, but they are "tidings" born on the wave of natural experience. Yet a prophetic text does enter once more in the way we have learned to understand. The word "passion," by being deprived of specific reference, turns back on itself, as if it contained a muted or mutilated meaning. By a path more devious than I can trace, the reader recovers for "passion" its etymological sense of "passio"—and the word begins to embrace the pathos of prophetic speech, or a suffering idiom that is strongly inarticulate or musical, like the "earnest expectation of the creature ... subjected ... in hope" of which Paul writes in Romans (8:19–20), like sheep, blasted tree, and the boy who waits with them, and the barely speaking figures that inhabit the poet's imagination. The event, in Wordsworth, is the word of connection itself, a word event (the poem) that would repair the bond between human hopes and a mutely remonstrant nature, "subjected in hope."

"Do you know the language of the old belief?" asks Robert Duncan. "The wild boar too / turns a human face." Today the hope in such a turning includes the very possibility of using such language. A mighty scheme not of truth but of troth—of trusting the old language, its pathos, its animism, its fallacious figures—is what connects poet and prophet. When Wordsworth apostrophizes nature at the end of the Intimations Ode, he still writes in the old language, yet how precariously, as he turns toward what is turning away:

And O, ye Fountains, Meadows, Hills and Groves,
Forebode not any severing of our loves!

Note

1. Ordinary language, like ordinary incident, does indeed become very condensed and tricky here. "Thither I repaired," writes Wordsworth of the crag (l.286), and again, toward the end, "to which I oft repaired" (l.325), referring to the voluntary, sometimes involuntary, return of memory to the haunting scene. This "repaired" means simply "to go," the "re-" functioning as an intensifying particle. But in the second use of the word, the "re-" inclines the word toward its original sense of "return," or more specifically, "return to one's native country," *repatriare*. So that the first "repaired" may already contain proleptically the sense of returning to the father's house: climbing the crag is the first step in a conscious yet unconscious desire to overgo time and repatriate oneself, return home, to the father. The relation of "repair" to its etymological source is as tacit as unconscious process; so it may simply be a sport of language that when Wordsworth introduces the notion of "spots of time" a hundred or so lines before this, he also uses the word, though in its other root meaning of "restore," from *reparare*:

> There are in our existence spots of time,
> That with distinct pre-eminence retain
> A renovating virtue, whence, depressed
> By false opinion and contentious thought,
> Or aught of heavier or more deadly weight,
> In trivial occupations, and the round
> Of ordinary intercourse, our minds
> Are nourished and invisibly repaired;
>   [1850 *Prelude* xii.208–15]

Though the young Wordsworth repairs to that which should nourish and repair (his father's house), he finds on the crag houseless or homeless phenomena, which hint at a stationary and endless patience. Whether "repair" may also have echoed in Wordsworth's mind as the repairing of man and nature (ll.298–302, which call hawthorn and sheep his "companions," as well as "kindred" [l.324], suggest his integration into a nonhuman family at the very point that the human one seems to fall away) must be left as moot as the foregoing speculations. The latter may suggest, however, not only the overdetermination of Wordsworth's deceptively translucent diction, but the consistency of his wish to join together what has been parted.

Bibliographical Note

The locus classicus of Coleridgean poetics is found in Chapters 13 and 14 of the *Biographia Literaria* (1818), "On the Imagination, or Esemplastic Power," etc. *Aids to Reflection* (1824) and a mass of miscellaneous lectures and readings contain many subtle and varying attempts to distinguish between symbolical and allegorical, analogous and metaphorical language, and so forth. Coleridge's reflections on the subject of style and unity are much more intricate than my general comment suggests; see, for one example, "On Style," reprinted in *Coleridge's Miscellaneous*

Criticism, ed. T.M. Raysor (Cambridge, Mass., 1936), pages 214–17. Yet even there German-type speculation is mixed with practical and preacherly admonition. The major German influence in regard to art, revelation, and the question of unity (or "identity philosophy") was, of course, Schelling. Martin Buber's distinction between apocalyptic and prophetic is made in "Prophecy, Apocalyptic, and the Historical Hour," in *On the Bible* (New York, 1968). For Abraham Heschel on pathos, see *The Prophets* (New York, 1962). The intelligent contemporary discussion on prophets as poets is in David Robertson's chapter of that title in *The Old Testament and the Literary Critic* (Philadelphia, 1977). Robertson acknowledges his debt to Gerhard von Rad's *Old Testament Theology*, volume 2. To the literary scholars mentioned in my essay, I should add Paul de Man's and Angus Fletcher's work on the theory of allegory; Walter Benjamin's seminal reconsideration of baroque allegory in *The Origin of German Tragic Drama* (originally published in 1928); and articles by Robert W. Funk on the parable in the New Testament and in Kafka. Frank Kermode is also working on the parable and has begun publishing on the idea of canon formation. Elinor Shaffer's *Kubla Khan and the Fall of Jerusalem* (Cambridge, England, 1976) links up more specifically than Basil Willey movements in Bible criticism and considerations of literary form. Her chapter entitled "The Visionary Character" is especially valuable in summarizing the movement of thought whereby poets, critics, and theologians came to consider Holy Writ as composed of different poetic and narrative genres, and faced the question of how to value nonapostolic (generally "apocalyptic" rather than "prophetic") visionariness. My quotations from Jacques Lacan can be found in *Ecrits: A Selection* (New York, 1977), pages 68 and 86. The issue of secularization in literary history is central to M. H. Abrams' *Natural Supernaturalism* (1971) and has elicited, in the Anglo-American domain, many partial theories from Matthew Arnold to Daniel Bell. Stanley Cavell's *The Senses of Walden* (1971) reveals a Wordsworthian type of underwriting in Thoreau, and one so consistent in its allusions to earlier epics and scriptures that *Walden* begins to emerge as a sacred book.

HELEN VENDLER

Truth the Best Music:
The *Ode on a Grecian Urn*

We must presume, since Keats went on after writing the *Ode to a Nightingale* to write the *Ode on a Grecian Urn* (as near a twin to the earlier ode as one poem can be to another),[2] that his experiments in analyzing, distinguishing, and objectifying his thoughts and feelings about creation, expression, audience, sensation, thought, beauty, truth, and the fine arts were still in some way unsatisfactory to him. And yet he was not ready to examine "art" in some general way: abandoning nonrepresentational "natural" music as his metaphor, he took as metaphor another special case, the one (because of the Elgin marbles) most in the public-eye, the case of sculpture.[3] He has, we realize, given in and joined his phantoms of *Indolence* on their urn; but in this new speculative enterprise he has somewhat changed the cast of characters, retaining Love and Poesy (as maiden and pipe player) but discarding Ambition, and adding new figures to which we shall come.

The *Ode on a Grecian Urn* squarely confronts the truth that art is not "natural," like leaves on a tree, but artificial. The sculptor must chisel the stone, a medium external to himself and recalcitrant. In restricting itself to one sense, the *Urn* resembles *Nightingale*, but in the *Urn* the sense is sight, not hearing. The *Urn* suppresses hearing, as the *Ode to a Nightingale* had suppressed sight (and as both suppress the "lower senses" of touch and taste). If *Nightingale* is an experiment in thinking about art in terms of pure, "natural," nonrepresentational music prolonged in time, the *Urn* is an experiment in thinking about art in terms of pure, "artificial," representational visuality extended in space (a space whose extension, in Keats's special case, rounds on itself—the urn is a self-limiting frieze). As we have seen, precisely because the nightingale's song is nonrepresentational it can ignore that world "where men sit and hear each other groan"; because it is nonconceptual or nonphilosophical it can avoid those sorrows and leaden-eyed despairs inseparable from thought. The *Ode to a Nightingale* can therefore bypass (until the questions which break its trance end the poem) the question of truth, and expatiate in its consideration of sensation and beauty, suggesting, by its darkness, that the more indistinct and dim and remote that beauty, the better. Beauty, in the form of the bird's song without words, stimulates the reverie of the musing Fancy, which endlessly projects itself on a perfect void—the essentially vacant, if transfixing, song of the nightingale.

All of this changes with the *Ode on a Grecian Urn*. Keats now proposes, with respect to art as he understands it and wishes to practice it, that art is a constructive and conscious shaping of a medium, and that what is created is representational, bearing some relation to "Truth." He proposes to examine this premise through a deliberately invented vehicle for understanding, a carved marble Hellenic urn.[4] Recognizable represented forms—male, female, and animal—appear on the urn (crowding to the borders of composition the leaves and grass so dear to decoratively breeding Fancy; the leaves are the nostalgic tribute to the earlier naive view of the artist as one who puts forth leaves as naturally as trees). The attitudes conferred by Keats on his represented forms are also clearly recognizable and unambiguous: they are attitudes of sexual pursuit and flight, of music-making and courtship, and of communal religious performance. Instinctive and civilized actions alike are represented: human beings—and perhaps even the gods themselves (though they are here indistinguishable from human beings)[5]—are the natural inhabitants of this medium. The forms, and the attitudes in which they are displayed, are beautiful—in the largest sense of that word (a sense Keats had imbibed from the Elgin marbles), a sense which includes the striking, the conflictual, and the memorable as well as the graceful and decorous. The urn seems in fact remarkably like life, framing as it does vivid moments of action or feeling.

This advance in Keats's conceiving of what art is like—an advance over the less complex (because instinctually expressive and nonrepresentational) postulate of the nightingale ode—requires a different response to the artifact. The actions represented on the urn excite in the beholder an empathy like that solicited in the listener by the *melos* of the nightingale, but they, unlike the birdsong, are allowed to provoke him to early questions. The constitutive trope of the *Urn* is interrogation, that trope of the perplexed mind.[6]

Three times the poet "enters" a scene on the urn; but, as I see the progress of the poem, he enters each successive scene with a different view, as spectator, of what the urn is and what it does. Each entrance can be represented conceptually as a different Keatsian hypothesis about what is offered us by aesthetic experience, each provoking a different conclusion on our part about propriety of response. Keats once again plays the part of "audience," as he had in *Nightingale*; but he has turned from listener to spectator (or so we at first believe—the terms were always problematic to him, since his own art of written poetry entails in its audience both a seeing and a listening). Keats has, by eliminating alive self-expressive artist (like the bird), turned his attention more profoundly to what an artifact in and of itself, without first-person expressive or biographical context, may be said to convey. And by making his symbol not ambiguously "natural" (as was the "music" of the Dryad-bird) but unarguably man-made in a highly intellectual and conventionalized form, he can examine the question of the capacities and limits of an aesthetic medium far more exactly than he could in *Nightingale*.

Keats's first hypothesis about aesthetic experience, evoked by the orgiastic first scene on the urn, is that art tells us a story, a history, about some people who are not ourselves. The proper response to the urn in this instance is then to question it, to ask of it, "Who are these people, and what are they doing?"—the question of a believer in naive mimetic art, in art as illustration. It is the question Keats himself had asked in *Psyche* when he saw the embracing couple: "Who wast thou, O happy, happy dove?" It was the question that had irritated him when he could not at first solve the identities of the urn-figures in *Indolence*, since he had been acquainted with Phidian statues rather than with vases; the figures "were strange to me, as may betide / With vases, to one deep in Phidian lore." To ask "What men or gods are these?" is to suppose that there is a simple and satisfiable relation between beholder and art object, that the beholder can eventually know the "truth" of the leaf-fringed legend that haunts about the shape of the urn, determining its figurative decoration. In *Indolence*, Keats had eventually recognized that the figures which had been haunting some urn, and had departed from it to come and haunt him, were called (allegorically) Love, Ambition, and Poesy. They might have been called (mythologically) Venus, Cupid, and Psyche, or (historically) Achilles, Hector, and Helen; in any case, they had names. He had not at that time envisaged an art of visible but unspecifiable forms, forms deriving their interest neither from the emotions (allegorized), nor from mythology, nor from historical fact. All of Keats's early questions in the ode ("What men or gods are these? What maidens loth? / What mad pursuit? What struggle to escape?") could be given their "true" answers, he thinks, if only he knew the lost legend that the dead sculptor presumably had in mind, and here illustrated.

Keats's second hypothesis about aesthetic response is evoked by the second scene, which shows a piper accompanying a youth courting a maiden. This second hypothesis (prompted by his own use of allegorical frieze in *Indolence* and *Nightingale*) proposes that the urn represents not mythologically or historically identifiable figures acting out some known (if lost) legend, but rather what would nowadays be called a universal or archetypal "Truth"—in this instance" truth of the unity of Love, Beauty, and Art, symbolized by the classic icon of a lover courting a maiden to music. The archetype is idealized—that is to say, it represents a human fantasy: that the lover will forever love, and the beloved be forever fair, and their courtship give rise to, and be accompanied by, an eternally refreshed art, "songs forever new." In this hypothesis, the urn is not representing other people, mythological or historical but is allegorically representing ourselves and our feelings—except that it shows us ourselves and our actions "in a finer tone."[7] Our proper response to the urn is, under this hypothesis, to give up useless questions of what historical or mythological story it illustrates, rejoice in its extreme beauty, regret the discrepancy that exists between the fantasized and the real, and yet recognize the truth of our aspirations (here, toward a "happy" art accompanying constancy in love and perpetuity of beauty) represented in the actualized fantasy Keats is now attempting to reverse his declaration in *Nightingale* that "Beauty cannot keep her lustrous eyes, / Or new Love pine at them beyond tomorrow." If not in life, at least in the truthful allegorical representation of our idealism, "For ever wilt thou love, and she be fair!"

The response stimulated by the second hypothesis—a response of sympathy with an idealized human state—is incompatible with the response solicited by the first hypothesis, that query about historical or legendary names and places. In the second response, the speaker is not exercised to discover originating legend or narrative, but naively once again enters wholly into the pictured scene, temporarily "forgetting" that he is contemplating a vase, and taking in the sculptured spectacle purely as life: "More happy love! more happy, happy love! ... / For ever panting, and for ever young."

Keats, I believe, saw both of these naive responses (in which he shows his spectator of the vase fully participating) as in themselves alone not adequate to art. Art does not exist to offer historical truth alone, whether social or divine or sylvan; neither is it created primarily to offer the moral truth of accessible archetypal ideals. Consequently, in exhibiting each of these two responses, Keats does not permit the excitement generated by them to survive. The mind cannot rest in either hypothesis. In the first instance, the questions rise to a frenzy—"What pipes and timbrels? What wild ecstasy?"—but the frenzy toward specification is instantly quieted by a change of orchestration, as Keats allows the excited mind which posed the questions to abandon historical inquiry and try to begin, rationally, to consider the, import of art. Keats turns to generalization and to philosophical diction, introducing a new movement, one of thought rather than empathy, as he meditates on the relative capacities of music, poetry, and the visual arts.

This new movement rejects the "heard melodies" so praised in the ode Keats had just completed on the nightingale (those melodies addressing the sensual ear) in favor of spatial and visual melodies which address the spirit. However, the criterion of aesthetic praiseworthiness here is still "sweetness" or *melos*. The bitterly truthful or the dissonant seem as yet to have no place in Keats's conception of this sculptural art, which is said to have "sweeter" melodies than music, and to express a "flowery" tale (like that embowered one of Cupid and Psyche, perhaps) "more sweetly" than Keats's own art of poetry could do.

This philosophical meditation on the superiority of spiritual to sensual melody interrupts the speaker's naive participation in the initial orgiastic scene; in the same way, a reflection on earthly passion and its putative inferiority to sculptured passion interrupts his second naive entry, this time an entry into the love on the urn. Once again, Keats draws a hierarchical comparison—not, now, one favoring visual art over sensual music or "our" rhyme, but rather one favoring the love on the urn over our "breathing human passion" far below it. To recapitulate: neither the naive factual questioning nor the naive thoughtless empathy is allowed to continue undisturbed: one is checked by a debate on the relative sweetness of music, rhyme, and sculpture, the other by a bitter intellectual recollection of the realities of human passion.[8] In each case, the poet's self—first the self as artist in a putatively deficient medium (since rhyme, like music, is addressed to the sensual ear), and second the self as embittered lover—rises to pit itself in some "philosophic" way against its own spontaneous, immediate, and "naive" response to the urn.

Undaunted, the speaker attempts a third time to "enter" the urn, and Keats proposes, in his fourth stanza, a new and more adequate hypothesis about the aesthetic experience offered by an artifact, and our aesthetic response: The urn, he suggests, is not just the illustration of a legend or tale about other people; nor is it just a representation, in archetypal and idealized form, of our human aspirations. Rather, it is most truly described as a self-contained anonymous world, complete in itself, which asks from us an empathic identification supremely free both of factual inquiry and of self-interest. Naive museum-goers demand either a known story, or the representation of a state visibly analogous to one of their own. It is easy to be merely narratively curious: "What men or gods are these?" It is even easier, by analogy with ourselves, to love a lover: "More happy love! more happy, happy love!" To the first of these naive responders, art is like a newspaper photograph, in need of an explanatory caption; to the second, art is like a mirror, in which he narcissistically luxuriates. But Keats, contemplating his third scene—a ritual sacrificial procession—foreign, ancient, remote from anything he has himself known—asks not about an antecedent legend but investigates instead the boundaries of representation: What group has the artist now selected? To what altar is the heifer being led? From what town does the procession issue?[9]

Keats confronts in this way the necessary limits of representational art. All mimetic art represents some fragment of life, and implies a preceding dramatic disposition of its figures and a narrative chain of consequences for them, an antecedent and subsequent existence of these momentarily visible forms. The artist selects some element of life and focuses his attention on it, composing it so memorably that even if it is foreign to our life or experience—as a Greek ritual procession is not familiar in the way that the lust or love of the first two scenes might be— still we are so taken by this representation that we ask not the myth or history that will conveniently classify its characters and actions but rather the questions "Who?" "Whence?" and "Whither?"—not with detached anthropological or literary curiosity but with entire intimacy and yearning. If we could answer these last questions—and by hypothesis we cannot, since the urn is both visually limited and tacit we would know origins and ends. Who are we; whither are we led by that mysterious priest; whence have we come to this place where we stand? The self-complete world of the work of art exerts a force drawing us to a pathos, not our own, not visibly reflecting our own immediate experience. In imagining the little town where the procession began and the green altar where it will end, Keats allows for the continuing naiveté of belief never entirely lost even in the most self-forgetful aesthetic response. In this last hypothesis, the sense of solid reality created by the urn draws us into a cooperative venture in which, by extrapolating outward to altar and town, we "see" (as in certain optical illusions) much more information than is actually provided. Given a created procession, we ourselves cooperatively create its destination and its origin—its religious whither and whence.

While this third hypothesis—in which the audience, prompted by the visible artifact, engages by its interrogation in an act of cooperative mutual creation with the artist—is more satisfying than the purely mimetic, historical hypothesis of the artifact-as-illustration given in the first stanza, or the purely expressive and allegorical one of the artifact-as-mirror proposed in the second and third stanzas, it is also, because the most sophisticated hypothesis, the most alienating. We might be grateful to the urn while it was instructing us in historical or legendary truths about divine or human action; we might warm to it while it represented, through a universal archetype, truths of emotion at once eternal and personal. But once we recognize that it is primarily neither culturally instructional (a "sylvan historian") nor flatteringly truthful to our narcissistic wishes—that it is neither about someone else nor about us, but rather about its own inventions into which we are enticed and on which we exercise our own pathos in return—we see it as necessarily artificial, a work in a given medium by a given hand. The return out of trance into consciousness, exhibited once in *Nightingale*, is here deliberately made to occur three times, with each exit from a scene into which one has entered. While we are "within" the urn, we are not outside it; while we are outside reflecting on it, we are not "within" it. Like the figures on the urn, we cannot at once be in the town where we live and on the urn.

I have been speaking, on the whole, as though Keats, looking at an urn, were pressed, by the intensity of his feelings, to three successively more complex and intelligent responses. In point of fact, of course, Keats invents his three urn-scenes—of orgiastic pursuit to music, of courtship to music, and of religious observance—to which his three hypotheses of response will be attached. The first turbulent scene is invented as one likely to stimulate archaeological questions which could be satisfied by the "truths" of a museum notice: "This scene represents a ceremonial orgy in honor of the god such-and-such; participants attempted ecstatic sexual experience by the use of intoxicants, and ritual music was played on the kind of pipe represented here," and so on. The second idyllic scene is invented as one which has the tendency to evoke psychological "truth" of an easy reductiveness: "In every civilization we find the eternal pair, youth and maiden; we recognize here the idealized posture of youthful first love and pastoral song." But the third religious scene is invented as one presenting the real test of aesthetic response. Once we pass (as museum visitors) beyond a wish for the explanatory factual truths of historical or cultural captions, and beyond the narcissistic stage of being interested only in "lyric" art which we can see as a reflection of something in ourselves, we can confront art as art is in itself, in its ultimate formal anonymity and otherness. It is not "they"—men or gods. It is not "I" or "we." Or it is not primarily these. It is itself. And, by its nature, it draws us to itself, we do not impose our concerns upon it.

Keats's triple hypothesis engenders the compositional rhythm of the poem, its large structural form. Whereas *Nightingale* traces first a withdrawal from the world, then an engagement with the music of the bird, and later an involuntary disengagement at the admission of thought (a single parabolic trajectory), the *Urn*, as I have said, repeats a comparable form three times, once for each scene. I recapitulate here in formal terms what I have already described thematically. The opening address to the urn—grateful but equilibrated and archaeological—gives way to a mounting voyeuristic excitement, as the beholder surrenders to the orgiastic scene. This excitement is not allowed a gradual subsidence. Instead, at the very moment of its interrogatory climax, it is admonished by a reproof of the sensual, as the wild ecstasy is replaced, in a striking whitening of voice, by soft pipes which play "not to the sensual ear" but rather "to the spirit ditties of no tone." Yet a second time, while seeing the young lovers on the urn, the speakers excitement is heightened; he feels, this time, not the excitement of a voyeur, but that of a passionate sympathizer. This fever of identification, defensively over-prolonged through an extra stanza, is suddenly cooled, in the midst of its exclamatory *accelerando* (just as the earlier factual questions had been broken into in mid-career), by the memory of human passion, with its paradoxical simultaneous cloying and persisting thirst. In both of these cases, the irruption of the reflective mind is sudden, unforeseen, and apparently unpreventable: mind bursts in—whether in questions or in reflection—on receptive sensation as a force no longer able to be repressed. Keats's easy sense of being able to outwit the "dull brain"—with its perplexing questions[10] and its retarding of trance—has vanished forever. The brain breaks in; and what is more, Keats welcomes it, and entertains it; he is genuinely interested in meditating on the relation between heard and unheard melodies, on art addressed to the ear vis-à-vis art addressed to the spirit. And in fact the brain is never really banished; even to the orgiastic figures it had addressed its intellectual questions; even in describing the lovers it incorporates its knowledge of earthly change in the elegiac and contrastive language through which the sympathy for them is addressed.

When, the third time, the speaker bends to the urn, he has lost his voyeuristic and narcissistic motives. The speaker is—really for the first time—the truly aesthetic spectator, viewing the scene with a speculative curiosity which is no longer idle nor hectic. He no longer makes a self-absorbed, contrastive referral to his own human case, but rather extends himself in a generous loss of self in the other. He enters into the life of the religious scene, prolonging it forward and backward with tenderness and feeling, investing the procession with the weight of life's mysteries of whence and whither without altering its otherness, both cultural and historic. The priest remains mysterious, a figure for Fate leading life on (derived as he is from the priest in *Psyche*, he is yet the devotee of no one deity); the little town remains unknowable, a figure for the invisibility of origins; the green altar remains unseen, and undescribed (unlike Psyche's fane), a figure for a veiled end.

When this last intensity of engagement with the urn fails (as, like the preceding ones, it must), it fails because Keats has seen too far into the core of an eternal destruction. This destruction is not melodramatic and fierce, like the mutual ravening of all created beings which Keats had flinched at in his epistle to Reynolds. That earlier destruction was something outside aesthetic experience, which nonetheless blighted that experience—"It forces us in summer skies to mourn: / It spoils the singing of the nightingale" (*Dear Reynolds*, 84–85). Here, in the *Urn*, no such sensational interference from the outside is envisaged: the destruction of aesthetic reverie arises rather from the necessary obliteration inherent in process itself. All processions, by the very fact of their existence as processions, leave their origins behind; all travel is sacrificial of its origins. There is no agent for this destruction: the townsfolk are not banished by an enemy; if their little town has a citadel, Keats tells us deliberately that it is a peaceful one. The mysterious priest has something of the folk-tale force of a pied piper: we are all led willingly on, by many pieties, into life and then out of it. Life's sadness does not lie in the bitterness of sexual rhythms with their ultimate exhaustion, those rhythms underlying the *Nightingale* ode; it does not even lie, as Keats had thought, in the perplexing intellect which interrupts or retards sensual reverie; rather, it lies in the very existence of origins, processions, and ends, in the fact of process.

These precocious insights left Keats with a poem four-fifths complete, with its great fourth stanza—expressing his furthest reach— already written. The poem had begun, we recall, with a comparison of the urn with rhyme—to the disadvantage of rhyme. The urn's whole and simultaneous visual art, where everything can be present (and presented) at once, seemed to Keats, fresh from his disillusion with the nightingale, sweeter than a temporally experienced art like music or poetry. The reason for this preference is exposed in the second and third stanzas: what is seen whole and simultaneously need never come to an end, whereas the defect of a temporal art, like the song of the nightingale or the rhyme of the poet, is that it bids adieu, and fades. Visual art is not fugitive—or so it would at first appear.

But as Keats explores his successive responses to visual art through his invented scenes on the urn, he discovers that there is a rhythm of engagement and disengagement by which the mind imposes its own temporality on the stasis of visual art. To the first scene, the beholder attributes a rhythm of pursuit and escape, a more excited version of the rhythm of the later procession. The inflamed men or gods come from somewhere; the maidens loth are struggling to escape to some haven. This invention of origins (Tempe? Arcady?) and ends (escape) accounts in part for the rhythms of engagement and disengagement. But a far more powerful force toward disengagement resides in every spectator's intermittent awareness, in contemplating any work of art, that the scene before his eyes is not a real but a represented one. Keats's first involuntary disengagement is caused by this knowledge; having seen the pipes and timbrels represented, he knows that they are not real, that they pipe unheard except to the spirit. This art is a dumb-show, and the pipes are in fact silent; but Keats, in an effort to mitigate the strict knowledge of disengagement, avoids the uncompromising word "silent" and calls the pipes, instead, "soft." We of course know that they are so soft as to be "unheard"; they play ditties "of no tone." The word "silent," though here repressed, waits in the wings and appears, insistently, in the last two stanzas. Keats's response to the urn therefore becomes a classic case of the dilemma which the psychologists of perception (using the classic figure of the duck-rabbit) call the dilemma of figure and ground. If the spectator focuses on one aspect, the other recedes into the background, and vice versa. In this case, the dilemma is that of subject matter and medium, of "men" and "marble." While Keats pressingly interrogates the urn's figures, he cannot think of them as other than real: "What men or gods are these? ... For ever wilt thou love ... O mysterious priest ..." On the other hand, as soon as he allows his consciousness of the marble medium to arise, he loses his sense of the figural representations as "real," and a disjunction in tone marks the breaking of the spell.[11] There are, as I have said, three such disjunctions in the poem (I italicize the mo-ment of the tonal reversal):

> What pipes and timbrels? What wild ecstasy?
> *Heard melodies are sweet ...*

> For ever panting and for ever young;
> *All breathing human passion far above ...*

> What little town ...
> Is emptied of this folk, this pious morn?
> *And, little town, thy streets for evermore*
> *Will silent be.*

In concluding his poem Keats wished, it seems to me, to give equal credence to each side of these junctures, to recognize fully both his participation in the represented "reality" and his awareness of the constituting medium removing those representations from actual life. Since, in Keats's view, one cannot experience sensory participation in the represented scene and intellectual awareness of the medium at one and the same time,[12] and since attention can change focus so rapidly from what is being represented to the medium of representation and back again, Keats has to affirm two wholly incompatible responses, never simultaneous, one always canceling the other, but both of them authentic, both of them provided by the artifact, both of them "aesthetic."

It was in his second stanza that Keats had most wonderfully allowed the two responses, to matter and to medium, free play. He permits there a rapidly alternating perception first of one and then of the other, and he uses identical language for the two experiences in order to show that they compete on identical terrain. Commentary often refers to the impossibility of deciding which are "bad" and which "good" of the many "can's" and "cannot's" in this stanza. To the piper and the youth, Keats says in turn, "Thou canst not leave thy song," which is meant to be good but has overtones of coercion; "Never, never canst thou kiss," which is surely bad; and "She cannot fade,"[13] which is surely good. In this stanza, the poet still sees medium and subject matter in (to quote Wordsworth) "a constant interchange of growth and blight." The marble medium confers certain benefits ("She cannot fade") and certain limitations ("Thou hast not thy bliss"). The lines focus alternately on life matter—the beauty of the maiden, the ardor of the lover—and on the coercions of the marble medium—"Never, never canst thou kiss." The quick shuttling back and forth in the speaker's mind between immersion in the fervent matter and recognition of the immobile medium represents a tension as yet unconceptualized in the poem (that is, one not yet "philosophically" or "reflectively" analyzed).

In the following stanza, the third, Keats defensively attempts to suppress interrogation by suppressing one half of his response, his awareness of the limits of the medium. Thus he hopes to enter wholly into the static happiness of the represented matter, which attempts a return to Psyche's timeless bower: "Ah, happy, happy boughs! ... And happy melodist ... More happy love! More happy, happy love! / For ever warm ..." The difference between this bower and that of Psyche is that into this bower has intruded the vocabulary of time, in the thoughts of shed leaves and springs that have been bidden adieu. And the undistinguished nature of the language of this stanza demonstrates the necessary failure of invention when the momentum of the poem is deliberately halted, stalled in its most recent perception. The needle of receptive sensation sticks, we might say, in its last phrase. The strain of maintaining timelessness in the vocabulary of time climaxes in the return of the repressed, as the sexual consummation prohibited by the atemporal visual medium of the urn takes place violently in Keats's recollection, leaving "a burning forehead, and a parching tongue."

Keats returns to the problem of subject matter and medium at the end of his poem. Shocked by the "deceiving" ability of representational art to persuade his belief not only in the represented procession but equally in the green altar and the fantasized town, he recoils intellectually from participation in subject matter into pure awareness of medium, becoming the apparently detached, but in reality the cheated, spectator. He no longer anthropomorphizes the urn into bride, child, or historian—all names which had been prompted by a wish to assimilate the artifact itself to its representational function—but rather addresses it as pure medium, as an Attic shape, a fair attitude, embroidered by the chisel of its carver with marble men and maidens.[14] But, as in the earlier attempt to suppress the intellect in the third stanza, one half of the response-field cannot be maintained alone. Marble men and maidens suddenly "swell into reality"[15] and walk on real earth "with forest branches and the trodden weed." It is hopeless to try to maintain a detached attitude: the scene is cold marble and it is trodden weeds, both and each, one moment the carved, the next the real.

The dilemma the urn presents is one insoluble to description. We can, if we like, see the whole ode as Keats's extreme test of his negative capability, in a moment when "Things cannot to the will / Be settled, but they tease us out of thought." He had written those words to Reynolds after composing his first sketch for the fourth stanza of the *Urn*, a sketch in which an easy "pictorial" simultaneity is preserved by a refusal to inquire into the expressive limits of painting, or into origins and ends. There, Keats had invented a present-tense "natural" scene which looks neither before nor after:

> The sacrifice goes on; the pontif knife
> Gleams in the sun, the milk-white heifer lows,
> The pipes go shrilly, the libation flows:
> A white sail skews above the green-head cliff,
> Moves round the point, and throws her anchor stiff.
> The mariners join hymn with those on land.
>   (*Dear Reynolds*, 20–25)

The ode will not permit itself such easy solutions as this eternally present one.

Aesthetic experiences, as well as intellectual ones, ask us to exist in "uncertainties, Mysteries, doubts, without any irritable reaching after fact & reason" (*Letters*, I, 193). Certain concepts, too, provoke this uncertainty; one of these, in Keats's view, is the concept of eternity. Is eternity an infinite sequence of temporal successions or rather an unchanged permanency? Keats has fluctuated between the two senses of "eternity" earlier in the ode, in his repeated use of "ever," "never," "for ever," and "for evermore." The first notion of eternity—as an infinite sequence of active, continuing, successive motions—is expressed in phrases like "For ever wilt thou love" and "For ever piping songs for ever new" (phrases that remind us of the gardener Fancy, who breeding flowers will ever breed new ones); while the second notion of eternity—as unmoving, fixed, and deathlike—arises in the lines about boughs that cannot shed their leaves and streets that "for evermore / Will silent be." One sort of "forever" (the *Psyche* "forever") belongs, as I have said, to the "swelling reality" represented by the subject matter, love "for ever panting"; the other sort of "forever" belongs to the static limitations of the nontemporal medium. One sort of "forever" is expressive and warm—"for ever piping" and "for ever warm"; the other sort of "forever" is silent and cold, like the streets forevermore silent and the cold Pastoral. As "artificial" artifact rises into the ascendant over "natural" action in the mind of the perceiver, the "silent" streets give birth to the generalizing phrase "silent form," and the "marble" men give birth to the phrase "Cold Pastoral!" (When we last saw the word "pastoral" it was natural and vegetative in the "pastoral eglantine" of *Nightingale*; now it is no longer associated with nature, but with art, and with genre.)

Perhaps there is no formulation adequate to the alternating awareness of subject matter and medium, of "nature" and "artifact" in aesthetic response. But it seems to me that the ending of the *Urn* has been unfairly criticized because neither Keats's intention nor his accomplishment has been entirely understood. (Though Keats's leaving his intent obscure may represent a flaw in execution, it does not excuse us from attempting to penetrate that intent.) The fiction of the ode is that of a poet coming, in woe, to a work of art, interrogating it, and being solaced by it. We know that Keats had himself remarked on how differently we contemplate things when we see them not equally but in distress of mind. "Difficulties," he said, "make our Prime Objects a Refuge as well as a Passion" (*Letters*, I, 141). He was speaking here of our aims rather than of our objects of contemplation, but we may say that in the ode he sees the urn as a refuge as well as a passion, as a friend to man in woe. Instead of repudiating, as he had done in the *Nightingale* ode, the tranced Fancy which makes illusion swell into reality, he now thinks of conscious representational artifice as a refuge, enabling man to "enter into the existence" of other modes of being, as he entered into the existence of the sparrow picking about the gravel (*Letters*, I, 186). (It is significant that the word "Fancy" is not used here, nor in subsequent odes; that word does not denote the truth-value that Keats is now attributing to art.)

There are lesser and better ways of entering into the existence of other beings. Keats had already explored one mode, which precluded all memory of the world left behind, in his meditation in *Nightingale* on lyric as pure, spontaneous, nonrepresentational melodiousness evocative of rich sensations. Now, by adding the truth of representation, and the truth of "unnatural" artifice consciously shaping a form, to the beauty of sensation, Keats can explore more complicated modes of aesthetic response—those which I have here named, too crudely, as voyeuristic, narcissistic, and disinterestedly aesthetic. All of them, however, cause that journey outward from habitual self into some other thing which seems, such is the force of creation, to swell into reality. On the other hand, the philosophic mind knows that in truth—at least in the truth of "consequitive reasoning" as Keats called it—the art object (here the urn) exists in a given medium (here the carved marble). "A complex mind," says Keats, is "one that is imaginative and at the same time careful of its fruits—who would exist partly on sensation partly on thought—to whom it is necessary that years should bring the philosophic Mind" (*Letters*, I, 186). Sensation and Thought are respectively aligned, in this famous letter to Bailey, to Beauty and Truth. Truth is, for Keats, the property of the conscious or waking mind, that mind which both sees aspects of life and meditates on them conceptually, Adam's mind which woke to the truth of Eve. (I use Keats's own vocabulary, however imprecise, as the one least falsifying to his thought: "The Imagination may be compared to Adam's dream—he woke and found it truth," as he explained to Bailey.)[16] Keats had decided to omit the question of truth from his poem of sensation, *Nightingale*, but he found he could not continue to write without admitting to the precincts of verse the perplexities of the brain as well as the delights of sensation. The urn's original charming names of bride, child, and sylvan historian, fictively naturalizing metaphors, are all projects of sensation rather than of thought; thought must treat the urn as artifact. When Keats allows philosophical thought to accompany his sensations of visual response, that thought sees the emotions and acts of the beautiful represented forms, but also recognizes the gap in psychological continuity between perception of matter and perception of medium. Allowing thought as well as sensation full play, Keats recognizes that his own voluntary submission to the art object entails not only empathy but also the detached recognition of its specific medium—causing that successive rhythm of entrance and exit which he had found so painful when he believed it to be caused exclusively by the deceptive cheating of a temporally dissolving Fancy. Now, seeing the dialectic between empathy and reflection as an ineluctable process of consciousness, he can regain an equilibrium of feeling before the urn, and give it a self-elucidating speech which will be true to its paradoxical union of stimuli to sensation and thought alike.

The urn, as we last see it, is not a historian but rather an epigrammatist. It is, astonishingly, no longer silent, as it had been during Keats's prolonged interrogation. It finally speaks because the speaker has ceased to ask it those historical and extrapolatory questions which it is not equipped to answer. The urn is only a "silent form" when the wrong kinds of truth are asked of it. As soon as Keats sees it as a friend of man (rather than as a historian or an archaeologist) it speaks, and becomes an oracular form, saying (as oracles often do) two things equally true. It says "Beauty is Truth" when we are looking at it with the eyes of sensation, seeing its beautiful forms as actual people, alive and active. It says "Truth is Beauty" when we are looking at it with the eyes of thought, seeing it, as the mind must see it, as a marble inscribed by intentionality, the true made beautiful by form. The two messages do not coincide; they alternate. Like a lighthouse, the urn beams one message, then the other, as we respond alternately to its human verisimilitude (which solicits our empathy) or to its triumphant use of its resistant medium (which solicits our admiration). The urn can speak of nothing but itself, and its self-referentiality is nowhere clearer than in the interior completeness of its circular epigram, which encounters our ironic sense of its limitation. When the urn says, commenting on its own motto, that that is all men know on earth and all they need to know, we realize that it makes that announcement from the special perspective of its own being, the tuneless being of the artwork in the Platonic realm where Truth and Beauty are indistinguishable. It speaks to us from its own eternity at once so liberating and so limited. Keats's choice of a circular frieze, rather than a linear one, confirms the urn's self-enclosing and self-completing form.

Nonetheless, the urn, unlike the uncaring, "natural" *Nightingale*, speaks to man.[17] It is, in the phrase Keats used as well for Milton, "a friend to man," and it exemplifies the "great end" attributed, in *Sleep and Poetry*, to poetry, "that it should be a friend / To sooth the cares, and lift the thoughts of man" (246–247). The art of the urn-sculptor is, like the art of the poet in *Psyche*, mimetic, but it is mimetic in a philosophical way, not a photographic one; it does not copy some lost historical model, but rather it chooses evocative human postures. It is beautiful, like the song of the nightingale, but it is, in a way the bird's song cannot be, representationally true. Although it is expressive, it is not solely self-expressive, like the bird's song; although it has been made by an artist, it does not exhibit his motives (as Keats's earlier urn, in *Indolence*, had borne his motives Love, Ambition, and Poesy). Rather, it expresses a variety of cultural motives, not a homogeneous or personal set, and is therefore a broadly socially expressive form. And it is deliberate, a reworking of nature with tools, even a violation (by its chiseling) of nature, not a spontaneous ecstatic outpouring or budding.

The poet himself utters the closing words in which the urn's motto and commentary are encapsulated as a quotation:

> When old age shall this generation waste,
>   Thou shalt remain, in midst of other woe
>   Than ours, a friend to man, to whom thou say'st,
> "Beauty is truth, truth beauty,"—that is all
>   Ye know on earth, and all ye need to know.

The last two lines are spoken by the urn,[18] which places special emphasis on the mottolike epigram before going on to comment on its unique worth. But the whole last sentence of the poem is the sentence of the speaker who, in his prophecy, recounts what the urn will say to succeeding generations. The speaker has reached, by the end of the poem, a prophetic amplitude of statement, looking before and after. With his philosophic mind, he foresees the time when his own generation will be wasted by old age, as previous generations have been in their turn; in that time to come, another young generation will be feeling woe as he has felt it, and will come to the urn; as he has to me, for refuge and solace. In its generosity this picture of parallel relations between generations represents an advance over the cruel representation, in *Nightingale*, of hungry filial generations each treading the past parental generation down. In his closing stanza, Keats is now above and beyond his own past immediate encounters with the urn-scenes; his detachment is now comparable to the detachment of the urn itself. But his mind is more capacious, in this last stanza, than the being of the urn is. Keats's mind here encompasses past, present, and future; youth, woe, age, the wasting of time, and the coming of another generation—all those horrors from which he had so strenuously averted his gaze in *Nightingale*. Keats's mind judges and places the single experience of seeing the urn in the total human experience of the life and death of generations. The sublimity—and ecstasy—of art is therefore granted as one moment along the span of life, a moment in which, by the intensity of art, all disagreeables are made to evaporate "from their being in close relationship with Beauty & Truth" (*Letters*, I, 192). The disagreeables—age, death, woe—have reasserted themselves in the mind of the speaker both during the poem (in his reflective moments) and at the end of the poem. But he gives the last, solacing word to the urn, because it utters that word afresh to each new generation—yet he encapsulates that last word in his own last overarching sentence of praise for art.

The divinity physically worshiped in this ode is the art object, the urn. The divinities conceptually celebrated are the twin divinities of

Beauty *and* Truth, Sensation *and* Thought. The divinity imaginatively celebrated is that greeting of the spirit that takes place between the audience and the art object. The object provides the beautiful carved forms of the three scenes; the spirit moves to enter into and share the life of each scene, and even, in the third instance, helps to extend that life into imagined new creation. Together the object and the spirit create the aesthetic reverie, real and unreal at once. If it is true that, as we read Keats's fourth stanza, our sense of a beautiful train of anonymous figures led by a mysterious priest from obscure origins to an ultimate sacrificial rite in an unknown place is all we know of beauty and truth on earth and all we need to know, then Keats's urn has kept its promise to our generation as to his.

If we now turn to a more exact inquiry into the language of the *Urn*, we must raise, first of all, the central question it provokes. The ode has become notorious for one of its stratagems of language—the resort to the Platonic absolutes, Beauty and Truth. It omits only Goodness, sometimes (as in Spenser's *Hymns*) called Love. Keats's resort to the Platonic dyad governs the whole poem: it means that he had set his mind resolutely on an assault on philosophical language, as he then conceived it. His earlier approach in *Nightingale* to the philosophical problem of the relation of "life" to "art" tried to treat the problem metaphorically, opposing day to night, waking to dreaming, silence to song, suffering to ecstasy, and so on. In the *Urn*, Keats determines not to resort to descriptive metaphor alone, but also to confront intellectually; not only to find images, but to enunciate propositions; not "to console," but "plainly to propound" (Stevens). The pictorial and descriptive language which had governed *Nightingale* had, even there, been adequate only to the central rapt trance; the "real" world of "life" had called up in Keats his antiquated personifications of spectre-thin Youth, palsied Age, lustrous-eyed Beauty, and pining Love; while the pain of his own mortal lot, once he readmitted the perplexing mind, had called up a propositional utterance of a defensive explicitness, "Thou wast not born for death, immortal Bird!" These elements in *Nightingale* give birth to several elements of the diction of the *Urn*. The *Urn*'s implicitly contrastive judgments (boughs that, unlike real boughs, cannot shed their leaves; love, unlike human love, forever panting; and so on) spring directly from *Nightingale*'s contrastive emphasis on the immortality of the bird; and the urn's constant Lover and unfading Maiden are clearly, as I have said above, derivations-by-contrast from the prospectively fading Beauty and faithless Lover of *Nightingale*. But the *Urn*-language ("She cannot fade, though thou hast not thy bliss, / For ever wilt thou love, and she be fair!") is deliberately stripped of *visibilia*. Beauty is robbed of her lustrous eyes and the Lover has not even so expressive a verb as "pine"; he simply "loves," she is simply "fair." Evidently the reader who comes to the *Urn* expecting throughout the ode the rich intensification of language that he found in *Nightingale* will be disappointed: where are his Keatsian luxuries? Of course they are not entirely absent; but Keats is placing stern and deliberate shackles on himself in the central part of his poem, deciding to mistrust his proliferating adjectival fancy and to write instead in the plainest outline. By "the plainest outline" I mean first of all his choosing the simplest possible emblems of desire (a lover loving, a maiden being fair, a piper piping, trees in leaf), and second his choosing the plain language of pure, unqualified proposition (rhyme's tales are sweet, but sculpture's tales are sweeter; heard melodies are sweet, but unheard ones are sweeter; songs to the sensual ear are dear, but those to the spirit are more endeared; human love saddens, cloys, and parches, but that on the urn is far superior).[19] Thus, for the first three stanzas (with some exceptions which I will mention later), the wish to write with a sober and unmistakable truth both of figural presentation and of intellectual assertion led Keats to a certain baldness of unequivocal judgment ("more sweetly," "sweeter," "more endear'd," "far above"), wholly unlike the native tentativeness which sprang, in him, from his exploratory and negatively capable sensibility. The wish to be truthful and to speak in propositions rather than in descriptions also led him to state the obvious in the barest of skeletal statements, aligning a series of blunt verbs:

thou	canst not leave thy song
nor ever	can those trees be bare
never	canst thou kiss
she	cannot fade
thou	hast not thy bliss
for ever	wilt thou love, and she be fair
ye	cannot shed your leaves
nor ever	bid the spring adieu

These sentences employ forms of extreme propositional simplicity; they are verbal "yes" and "no", markers:

leave song?	No
be bare?	No

kiss?	No
fade?	No
have bliss?	No
love for ever?	Yes
be fair?	Yes
shed leaves?	No
bid spring adieu?	No

In being addressed to figures (the melodist, the lover, and the boughs) who presumably would know whatever the poet is telling them about their state, the sentences might also seem to display a false ingenuousness or whimsicality. And yet we know the power of these stanzas; and we all agree that the fiction they adopt, as the speaker describes to the urn-figures the mixed blessing of their state, is a way for Keats to displace first-person utterance. (He does not, incidentally, address the maiden as he does the male lover and the male piper; the two males are fantasy-figures for himself as bold lover and unwearied melodist, and his empathy joins them, not her.)

In the absence of adjectival sensuality, Keats attempts by two means to give his "propositional" language some richness. He repeats central words (as in "ye soft *pipes* play on, / Not to the sensual *ear*, but more endear'd, / *Pipe* to the spirit ... / *For ever piping* songs *for ever* new"). But even more than to the repetition of words, Keats resorts to the repetition of syntactic patterns, to a rigid, hypnotic pattern of apostrophe followed by either assertion or negation in a chain of "ever" and "never," "not" or "no." The pattern is just varied enough so as not to be absolutely predictable: a "canst not" is followed by a "can" and by a "never canst" and "cannot"; in the midst of the declarative "can's" and "cannot's" comes the sudden, touching "Yet, do not grieve"—the first sketch for the poet's later consolation of Autumn, "Think not of them." The semantic and syntactic repetitiveness rises in the third stanza of the ode to a form of babble, in which what is being said is palpably subordinated to the effect of incoherent envy—"Ah happy, happy boughs! ... and happy melodist ... more happy love! more happy, happy love! For ever warm ... for ever panting." It has usually been assumed that Keats lost control of his poem in this stanza; Bate (p. 513) speaks of the "strain" here comparable to that felt in "Already with thee!" in *Nightingale*. It is perhaps misguided, though, to think of Keats as a helpless spirit to whom poems happened; it is more probable that instinctive aesthetic aims led him compositionally down certain paths—in this case, the path of propositions—which exacted a certain price. The trouble with propositions, for someone of Keats's earlier aesthetic inclinations, was that they seemed not to embody feeling. A statement of what is or is not true is, of itself, emotionally neutral; and Keats's first set of propositions about the figures on the urn, following his initial questions, attempt the form of that declarative neutrality: "Thou canst not leave / Thy song"; "[Never] can those trees be bare"; "She cannot fade"; "For ever wilt thou love." Dissatisfied with blank propositional statement, Keats suppresses questions and rewrites the propositions, turning the original declarative mode to an exclamatory form: "Ah happy, happy boughs! *that cannot shed your leaves*; and happy melodist *for ever piping*; more happy love! *for ever panting*." Keats's revolt against the propositional form is already evident in his interpolations of feeling in the apostrophes "*fair* youth" and "*bold* lover" as well as in his pained "do not grieve" and his sympathetic "though thou hast not thy bliss." He is even false to the strictly propositional form (itself expressively appropriate to the eternal present tense of the atemporal urn) when he moves into the future tense of prophecy: instead of the more proper "Forever dost thou love; she is forever fair," he offers what he regards as a consolatory vista of future years to his bold but unsatisfied lover: "For ever wilt thou love, and she be fair!"

One cannot, however, write every passage twice, first saying what is or is not, and then rephrasing it with an "applied" emotional coloring by affixing to every declarative statement an exclamatory addendum. These two stanzas, then—stanzas two and three—urge us, by their very inefficiency as stratagem, backward to the language of the beginning of the ode and forward to the language of the last two stanzas.

I have already spoken of Keats's wish to incorporate representational "truth" in this ode. This thematic wish necessarily provoked a second—a desire to incorporate propositional "truth" in the language of the poem. Keats's resolve to incorporate "truth" in this ode led him to the poem's first naive view of truth as a set of simple answers to simple questions, names and stories to answer who and why. Keats then passed on to a second hypothesis: if truth is not identificatory names and stories (the truth of fact or of history), perhaps it is true declarative propositions (the truth of philosophy)—but to be true to emotion as well as to fact, the "philosophical" propositions must be invested with rhetorical coloration, and therefore he is led to attach his exclamation (the truth of feeling). Finally, some of his propositions must state not only what is, but in what order relative things are to be placed, in what way some are better than others (the truth of value); consequently, we see Keats resorting to judgmental or hierarchical propositions of the sort "X is sweeter than (or more endeared than, or far above) Y."

But Keats cannot all command the strings, and his language wishes to escape his new puritanical effort to say what is true—factually, philosophically, emotionally, and judgmentally—rather than to narrate or complain or describe or wish, as he had chiefly done in the earlier odes. The language escapes its propositional aridity in the opening five lines of the ode, and it also escapes in the fourth stanza—those two passages where the poem becomes most beautiful, and most itself. The first stanza of the *Urn* offers us a far more complex mind, holding far more intellectual possibilities in view, than any single stanza of the earlier odes. It contains some reminiscence of earlier work, including the sense of past mythology borrowed from *Psyche* (as "What men or gods are these?" recalls "Who wast thou?"), and Keats's self-presentation as poet present in all previous odes. But the urn's initial appellations, in their intellectual complexity, are unlike any epithets in *Indolence* or *Psyche* or *Nightingale*. "Thou still unravish'd bride of quietness" and "Thou foster-child of silence and slow time" offer us a different depth from the descriptive "Thou light-winged Dryad of the trees," though they are cut to the same syntactic pattern. A Dryad has fairy wings and belongs in trees; but a bride and unravishment and quietness are not necessarily related to an urn, nor is a foster child necessarily linked to silence or time. The epithets in *Indolence* ("a fair maid, and Love her name"; "Ambition, pale of cheek"; "my demon Poesy") and in *Psyche* ("O latest born and loveliest vision"; "O brightest"; "the gardener Fancy"; "the warm Love") are like the epithets in *Nightingale* ("immortal Bird"; "warm South"; "deceiving elf") in being simple and conventional in their expression and in their categories of reference. But the complex mind writing the *Urn* connects stillness and quietness to ravishment and a bride (as John Jones says, p. 220, surely the bridal Urn is Eve, Adams dream as he awoke and found it Truth); this complex mind also interrelates silence, the lapsing of ages, death, and fosterage; it connects history to the woods, and stories to flowers, and it judges sculpture against poetry; it puts legends with leaves, interweaving both with the haunting presence of the invisible in culture— all in relation to a carved form and its auxiliary ornament; it alternates men with gods, the natural with the pastoral, Tempe with Arcady; it joins music to activity, and ecstasy to struggle. The mind generating this first stanza is surely a more interesting and fruitfully confused mind than the one which generated the opening of *Indolence* or *Psyche* or *Nightingale*. It is a mind striving against its tendency to exclude. (In *Indolence* the mind had wished to exclude its own compulsion toward action, temporality, and form; in *Psyche* it had wished to exclude both time and the embodiment of reverie in a physical medium; in *Nightingale* it had wished to exclude its consciousness of suffering.) Now nothing is to be excluded—neither the past nor the present, neither the peaceful nor the ecstatic nor the violent, neither men nor gods, neither truth nor legend, neither sexuality nor chastity, neither figuration nor location, neither origins nor ends, neither activity nor stillness, neither life nor art, neither music nor silence.

We find our satisfactions variously in art; but one of the greatest satisfactions is our sense that the artist is being faithful to all he knows of experience, and is determined, within the limits of his medium, to exclude nothing. The *Urn* (unlike *Indolence*, *Psyche*, and *Nightingale*) originates in a decision to embrace representationally all that is; and to tell, in some way, the truth about it. But after the inexpressibly fruitful first stanza, for two stanzas Keats writes a more lax verse, first condemning himself, in the service of philosophical truth, to the enunciating of propositions, and then, in the service of the truth of feeling, turning the same propositions into exclamations. Finally he utters the proposition which I believe voices the generating motive of the poem—the necessary self-exhaustion and self-perpetuation of sexual appetite.

It may be true that one needs only that paradoxical human sense of cloying and thirsting to engender, by contrast, the unfading love and beauty of the couple on the urn. But we must recall here the two forms of sexuality on the urn—the mad pursuit of the maidens loth and their consequent struggle to escape, and the contrasting entirely idyllic portrait of the loving lover and the fair beloved (each scene accompanied by its appropriate music). It seems to me that the rather theatrical evoking of cloying and parching speaks rather to the Byronic sexuality of pursuit and struggle rather than to Keats's new, scarcely as yet believed in, hope for a permanent tie to Fanny Brawne. In his words of July, just after writing the odes, "For myself I know not how to express my devotion to so fair a form: I want a brighter word than bright, a fairer word than fair ... In case of the worst that can happen, I shall still love you" (*Letters*, II, 123). The second-scene figures on the urn, then, represent in themselves not only things, unattainable (eternity, immobility) but also things Keats believed in—love, constancy, fidelity, beauty, and truth. To these constants, the cloying and parching did not apply; the only power which can touch the verities, Keats believed, was death. The true opponent to the urn-experience of love is not satiation but extinction. It is not the transience of erotic feeling but the transience of life itself which is the obstacle the ode must confront; and it does so in its greatest invention, its fourth stanza.

The great imaginative discoveries of this stanza—its invisible altar-goal and its invisible town-origin—are not inventions of sensation but of thought. The green altar and the little town correspond, in being "what-is-not-on-the-urn," to the fading youth and palsied age and groaning men of *Nightingale*—those things not present in the Nightingale's world. It is evident now how completely Keats has abandoned his *Nightingale* idea of a suffering world and a pain-free art. Art, on the urn—by including struggle, resistance, and sacrificial procession as well as love and youth—has begun its effort to be all-inclusive, to let in "the disagreeables." What is excluded on the urn, then, is only what we cannot ever know—whence we came, whither we are going, those mysteries of eternity. Keats reverses the coloration we might expect for the point of origin and the point of sacrificial conclusion; while we might have expected the sacrificial to be the empty and the desolate, and the point of origin to be leafy, populated, and pristine, Keats displaces his fear of death onto the abandoned town, which itself takes on the qualities of the life we shall have vacated when we die. In exhibiting, in this third scene, our social role rather than our private role—in placing us all as members of a linked cultural procession of pious folk—Keats sacrifices the pride of solitary position that had made him, in *Indolence*, the self-sufficient dreamer refusing the social solicitations of Love or Ambition or Poesy. A similar solitariness had led him to cast himself in a starring (if "tuneless") role as Psyche's priest-poet (and, displaced as Cupid, as Psyche's lover). The social sympathy stirring in *Nightingale* (for the condemned youth and the palsied old) led Keats only to an anguished flight away from such sympathies. In the *Urn*, social sympathy leads Keats to a self-abnegating place in the anonymous (almost, we wish to say, choral) procession. In refining human music to the sacrifice, Keats takes an even more ascetic position. The orgy had its pipes and timbrels; the calmer tableau of love had its happy melodist; but the only sound in the scene of sacrifice is the premonitory lowing of the heifer (a transmutation, of course, of the ecstatic song of the nightingale). Both pipes and hymns had been included in Keats's first imagining of the sacrificial scene in the epistle to Reynolds ("The pipes go shrilly, the libation flows: ... / The mariners join hymn with those on land"). The new absence of art-music at the close of the ode is a striking omission, given Keats's insistence in the *Urn* on melodies heard and unheard, and given the careful insertion of art-melody into the first two scenes of lust and love. The effect produced is of a falling-silent of accompaniment, and of the incapacity of music to express either the final animal utterance of the victim or the final silence of the little town. Even unheard melodies do not encompass that pathos. The easy, natural music of *Indolence* ("the throstle's lay"), the internal music of *Psyche* ("tuneless numbers," a "delicious moan / Upon the midnight hours") and the full-throated spontaneous music ("full-throated ease," "such an ecstasy!") of *Nightingale* will never again rise spontaneously in Keats. *Lamia's* delusive music vanishes with the palace it supports; and there is no music in *The Fall of Hyperion*. The great recovery of music in *To Autumn* comes in the final acoustic "noise" of bleats, whistles, and twitters.

As I have said, these felicities of the fourth stanza of the *Urn*—the invoked but invisible origin and end, the absence of art-music—are inventions of thought, not of sensation. And yet the language of this greatest stanza of the ode (especially in light of its contrast with the other stanzas and other odes) demands comment. The stanza returns, as we recall, to the third-person questioning of the first stanza, in asking (though with a different, nonfactual, tonality), "Who are these coming to the sacrifice?" It then begins to recapitulate the second stanza by replicating its second-person addresses ("Ye soft pipes ... Fair youth ... Bold lover") in its second-person address to the priest ("O mysterious priest"). The heifer with its "drest" garlanded flanks has replaced *Psyche's* rosy sanctuary "dress[ed]" with the wreathed garlands on the trellis, as adornment for the sacrificial morn replaces adornment for the love-night. The *Ode to a Nightingale* is, like *Psyche* (and, in its prolongation of drowsiness into the morning, *Indolence*), a night-poem; the *Urn*, by coming into the light of day and rousing itself on "this pious morn" to sacrificial activity, exhibits a stoic bravery, to be continued in the later odes. After the one-line overture "Who are these coming to the sacrifice?" the three equal movements of three lines each give the fourth stanza an equanimity and spaciousness not found in the other stanzas of the ode. The last question of the poem, though it follows the direct question to the priest, returns to the third-person formulation of the opening questions ("What men or gods?")—"What little town ... is emptied" today? The town's three competing imagined locations (by river, or by sea shore, or mountain-built) make the town literally unknowable. The greater becomes our surprise, then, when the tender second-person address, hitherto reserved to things or persons visible on the urn (pipes, boughs, lover, melodist, priest), is extended, with an effect of indescribable pathos, to the invisible and unknowable little town:

> And, little town, thy streets for evermore
> Will silent be; and not a soul to tell
> Why thou art desolate, can e'er return.

The *Urn*'s earlier "can's" and "cannot's" are echoed in the line "not a soul ... can e'er return," just as the future tense of the bold prophecy "For ever wilt thou love" is echoed in "Thy streets for evermore / Will silent be." The "for evermore" and "e'er" echo their happier counterparts earlier as well.

When an urn is shifted round, *Indolence* had told us, "the first seen shades *return*"; and Keats had imagined that he could command the *Indolence* phantoms to fade, and "be once more / In masque-like figures on the dreamy urn." But now, refusing the cyclical recurrence of his first view of the urn-figures, and his illusion that they can leave and return to their places on the urn at will, Keats puts a final interdict on all his shades: not a soul "can e'er *return*." It is the frequent internal echoes from ode to ode such as this one (of which we cannot suppose Keats to have been unconscious) which create much of the depth of the odes when they are read together.

In admitting the perpetual silence of the streets of his little town, Keats ceased to struggle, with volleys of questions, against the foster-child of silence. Not a soul will come back from that undiscovered country. In resolving to remain in the presence of the urn without any further questions, Keats exemplifies his own Negative Capability; "not a soul to tell why" is a complete capitulation to mystery, comparable to the acquiescence in ignorance voiced in the epithet "mysterious" applied to the priest. The absence of music in the fourth stanza stands for speechlessness, and for inexpressibility.

After the tranquil and sovereign language of the scenes, visible and invisible, of the fourth stanza, we are shocked—all readers are shocked, to a different degree and in different ways—by the language of the close of the ode. In defending Keats's intent and decisions here, I mean only to defend the necessity of this stage in his noble exploratory progress toward "philosophizing" and toward a language suitable for "philosophizing" in. If, at this point, Keats decided that the language for thinking, even in poetry, must be the abstract and propositional language of philosophy (as he knew it), that was a mistake he was encouraged in by the example of Wordsworth and Coleridge. The language of the close of *Urn* cannot be entirely assimilated to the language used earlier in the ode, and this is a flaw; but we can begin to consider Keats's aims in closing his poem by looking at the epithets by which he characterizes the urn. They are different from his epithets-from-a-devotee in earlier odes, and even from the epithets in earlier lines of this ode. In other odes, and at the beginning of this ode, Keats is often a passive subject, content to be worked upon by his imaginings, ineffectually refusing their solicitations (*Indolence*) or aspiring to participation in a better realm (*Nightingale*) or, at most, proposing to copy a past devotion (*Psyche*). His function as dreamer (*Indolence*), liturgist-priest-lover (*Psyche*), or audience of sensation (*Nightingale*) precludes a critical intellectuality. But the interrogatory mode of *Urn*, which permits the brain full activity, interrupting sensory trance to make judgments and extended reflections, allows as well for consciously intellectual epithets, which attempt a mastery over the object to which they are attached. As I said earlier, "bride of quietness" is a far more complex formulation than "Dryad of the trees" or "amorous glow-worm of the sky"; and yet "bride of quietness," "foster-child of silence," and "sylvan historian" are still epithets of wonder and empathy and pathos, rather than epithets engendered by a critical mind. Attempting to allow the perplexed brain full freedom in his ode, Keats becomes in his last stanza the nineteenth-century intellectual man who is acquainted with archaeological terms and literary genres. "Attic shape" and "Pastoral" are epithets not of rapt subjection but of active intellectual mastery. "I will name you," says Keats, "not in terms you engender upon me ('bride,' 'child') but in terms by which I classify you according to scholarly, intellectual, or critical convention. I have called your youth 'fair' and your maiden 'fair'; those were the words of one entering into your pastoral fiction; now I will call you, yourself, by the standards of aesthetic judgment, a 'fair *attitude*.' I have called you, in awe, the 'foster-child of silence'; now I will call you, in sober truth, a 'silent *form*.' I have called you, imaginatively, a bride and a child, which you in fact are not; but now I will give you a relational name to which you can, in waking certainty, lay functional claim; you are 'a *friend* to man.'"

There are of course fluctuations in feeling, from frigidity to affection, in these epithets of mastery, as commentators have pointed out. I wish simply to make clear that they are all epithets by which Keats attempts to assert his own intellectual rights over the urn, saying that his mind must judge and interpret, as well as respond to, the urn's offering of itself. A flowery tale may be expressed by the urn more "sweetly," perhaps, than it could be by rhyme; but Keats's rhyme wishes to be philosophical, as the urn, being nondiscursive, seemingly cannot be. And yet he will make the urn philosophical. In his final act of intellectual mastery (and generosity), he will give the urn language. He will give it words, ascribe to it a philosophical utterance—his supreme gift to the urn which, until now, could speak only by its pictures.

In writing words for the urn to say, Keats has disturbed his readers. The urn's delphic utterance has the granite solidity possessed only by the most immovable propositions, those which approach tautology: "I am who am," or (another Keatsian one from the *Letters*, I, 279, also cited by Sperry, p. 279), "Sorrow is Wisdom." The attribution of truth to representational art, and the coupling, common in aesthetics, of the terms Truth and Beauty, as the desiderata of art, did not, for Keats, render the terms unproblematic. On the contrary, his own repeated raising of the terms in the *Letters* points to his worrying the problem. His exclusion of "the disagreeables" from previous odes, and their partial inclusion in *Urn*, points up the direction of his concern. He still excludes human death from the urn (except insofar as it is represented by the emptied and invisible town); but by addressing the town in the second person Keats has rendered the deserted town not absent and invisible, but present and engaged with, thereby allowing the pathos of the disagreeable to coexist with truth.

The wish to include the "disagreeable" thought that all art is fictive, medium-bound, and artificial rather than warm, human, and alive accounts for the chilly tone of some parts of the closing stanza. In using the words "shape," "form," "attitude," "marble," "brede," and "Pastoral," Keats is declaring that he will speak in aesthetic, worldly, factual, and critical terms about the urn as an artifact, as an object situated in medium and genre. But the urn has another existence—its virtual existence inside our experience of it. In that existence it exerts its immediate force, scene by scene. Keats must find a concluding language for that warm empathetic experience as well as for the cooler experience of evaluation and taxonomy. He says, thinking once again of the epistle to Reynolds (where he had declared "to philosophize / I dare not yet!"), that the urn "tease[s] us out of thought / As doth eternity." In the epistle, he says that this state—in which one is led beyond the capacities of thought—is one of purgatorial blindness (Keats's purgatory is a realm occupying the vertical space between earth and heaven):

> Things cannot to the will
> Be settled, but they tease us out of thought.
> Or is it that imagination brought
> Beyond its proper bound, yet still confined,—
> Lost in a sort of purgatory blind,
> Cannot refer to any standard law
> Of either earth or heaven? —It is a flaw
> In happiness to see beyond our bourn—
> It forces us in summer skies to mourn:
> It spoils the singing of the nightingale.

This great passage (*Dear Reynolds*, 76–85), written a year before the odes, wishes to place happiness above insight; and it gives rise directly to *Nightingale*'s attempt to keep the bird's singing unspoiled by human mourning. However, this passage already foreshadows the purgatorial emphasis of the letter, a year later, on soul-making. In the *Urn* Keats has (temporarily) left purgatory behind (he will return to it in *The Fall of Hyperion*); he also has decided to change his emphasis, when he talks of art, from the "immortal" (a word implying a being which cannot die, though like the nightingale it may have been born, and can live in time) to the "eternal" (a word which removes all considerations of birth, death, and existence in time). The urn exists (as we enter its "reality") in eternity, and from its vantage point there, where Truth and Beauty are one and the same, it befriends man in woe by making him free of its realm. Its utterance ("That is all / Ye know") is to be linked to other consolatory utterances in Keats, notably the two I have mentioned earlier, "Yet, do not grieve," and "Think not of them." These reassurances are almost maternal: we must think of the urn as saying what it can to us in our perplexity. The urn speaks of knowledge itself; of the sum of our knowledge; and of what we need to know. Since "knowledge" is for Keats a word of "philosophical" weight, the urn's double use of "know" ("all / Ye know ... and all ye need to know") in its address to him (and us) is intended to allay his doubts about the propriety and relevance of a philosophical ambition to his work as man and poet. What word but "know" could end this ode where Keats's project was to admit Thought and Truth to art? What but a propositional sentence, and a repetition by a pun on the two meanings, partitive and summary, of "all," could end this ode which chooses statement over description, and inclusiveness over exclusion? The "mysterious doors / Leading to universal knowledge" (*Endymion*, I, 288–289) could not remain forever shut. The eternal Urn must speak differently from the immortal Bird.

In inventing a language for eternity, Keats resorted to two distinct forms. One is eternally or Platonically true; one is accommodated to human ears. Since we fear that our knowledge is incomplete and insufficient for our state, the urn inclines to us to tell us that what we know (however limited) is sufficient for us, thereby releasing us from the torment of insufficiency. To that degree, the urn speaks our language. But in its oracular condensation of our knowledge into a riddling motto, the urn speaks the only language that Keats can invent which he believes adequate to an eternal being—a language in which he represents in an accommodated propositional form and its converse (X is Y—Y is X) a reality which can only be conceived of as the simultaneous and identical existence (in another realm) of X and Y.

The urn's creed exemplifies, in its bare propositional form and in its use of the diction of Platonic abstraction, Keats's pledge to make truth his best music (*Endymion*, IV, 773). In speaking to men of the extent and sufficiency of their *knowledge* (rather than of their dreams or visions), the urn ratifies the participation of the perplexing brain in aesthetic experience. We recognize in the intellectuality of this last stanza the complex mind (under a different aspect) which we came to know in the opening stanza of the ode. It still perceives finely and concretely (the forest branches, the trodden weed); it still wishes to see the whole (as it saw the totalizing anthropomorphic "shape" of the sylvan historian, it now sees the art-historical Attic "shape" of the vase) as well as the parts; it still aims to incorporate the philosophical diction which speaks of time and eternity, truth and legend, pastoral and thought, with the diction of sensation, which gives visual impressions of men, maidens, and even a heifer (the latter a presence quite unthinkable in *Indolence*, *Psyche*, or *Nightingale*). But in removing itself from the rapt visual and emotional awe of the first stanza, in recalling its own state of sexual woe, in foreseeing its own end in the wasting of its generation, in deciding on its final austere, intellectual epithets for the urn and in putting words into the urn's mouth, the mind of the last stanza represents itself as finally the master of its aesthetic experience, which it can recall at will, speculate on, and find a language (however imperfect) for. Sensation, this mind declares, must coexist with Thought, Beauty with Truth; and the language of Beauty must find a coexistence with the language of Truth.

For the rest of his life Keats was engaged in an investigation of what the language of Truth might be, and whether or not it differed from the language of Sensation, and, if so, how it differed. It is clear from the *Urn* that he believed, at the time he wrote this ode, that the language of Thought was one which expressed itself in propositions purporting to encode truths, of which the perfect form was "X is Y" (the "fallen" form of the Platonic "X is identical to Y"); that it used the abstractions proper to philosophical discourse (of which the chief specimens were words like "Beauty" and "Truth"); that it made intellectual judgments, often expressing a hierarchy of value; and that it was a language of perplexity which interrogated sensation before arriving at propositional formulation. By contrast, the language of Sensation, or of Beauty, seemed to be descriptive and exclamatory, to follow serially upon the registerings of the senses, to be concrete and intense, and to render the synaesthetic convergences, as well as the discreteness, of sensual experience. It was a language not of eternity but of time and space; of things past and passing; of luxuries and of visions. It wished to set aside the "dull brain" which, by thoughts of mortality, perplexed the self's relish in sensation and retarded its flight into trance. The concept of such a language of Sensation represents, I need not say, my abstraction into pure form of Keats's early tendency to luxury. In fact, Keats's perplexing brain is never entirely absent, even in the earliest verse; and "curious conscience ... burrowing like the mole," was, from the beginning, seeking in Keats's poetry a language of its own.[20]

The language of Sensation did not seem adequate to Keats as a vehicle either for tragedy or for heroism. His powerful association of the language of Sensation with the language of lyric led him to think that maturity of mind would have to entail a forsaking of lyric for the epic or dramatic (following the ardors rather than the pleasures of verse, after the manner of Milton); the language of Thought (or even the language of Deed) might then supersede the language of Sensation. We now see *The Fall of Hyperion* as Keats's chief self-conscious effort to write the poetry of Thought, and *Otho the Great* as his attempt to write the poetry of Action. In neither did he succeed as he had hoped. The poetry of Action and the poetry of Thought were both, as we now see, better realized in the ode *To Autumn*.

But before arriving at the conflation of sensation, action, and thought, Keats had to absorb into his ode-world yet another realm, the realm of the "lower" senses. In *Psyche*, as we recall, he had puritanically suppressed all the senses in favor of a dialogue with his own soul, full of historical reminiscence and interior Fancy, defining art as an imitative imaginative activity which preexists (and does not perhaps need) any embodiment in a sense-medium. In *Nightingale*, by focusing on the activity of a single sense (that of hearing) he had been able to include artist, audience, and artifact in his trio of bird, self, and song, but at the price of exalting Beauty and Sensation alone and eliminating representational Truth (including Greek myth) and its poetry of Thought. In the *Urn* the artist is long dead, and only the artifact and its audience remain, but in this art corresponding to the sense of sight, Truth as well as Beauty has become constitutive of creative expression, and the mind is permitted its allegorizing, interrogatory, and propositional functions. Keats's successive scrutinies of natural, creative, but resultless reverie (*Indolence*), of tuneless, imitative numbers (*Psyche*), of wordless, spontaneous, beautiful *melos* (*Nightingale*), and of silent, truthful, objectified representation in a resistant visual medium (*Urn*) are all experiments exhibiting a certain defensiveness in one whose medium, after all, was words, whose art was conscious poetry, whose talent was deeply mythological, and who knew of other senses besides those two "high" ones, sense and hearing. Haunting these odes, up to this point, is the absence of any real exploration of the "lower" senses of taste and touch; and each of these odes is itself incomplete as a metaphor for Keats's total experience of art as he knew it in poetry—its dependence on the senses, its inception in reverie, its fertile, constructive activity in the mind, its powerful embodiment within a resistant medium, its reception by the greeting spirit, its representational validity, its allegorizing tendency, its luxurious beauty, its philosophical truth, its momentary glimpse of divinity, its sense of active intellectual and critical power and mastery. The simple movement of entrance and exit, even in its triple repetition in the *Urn*, is simply not structurally complex enough to be adequate, as a representational form, to what we know of aesthetic experience—or indeed to human experience generally. In the *Ode on Melancholy* Keats will at last admit the "lower" senses to his world of eternal forms, will take on the heroic mastery of action instead of passive subjection or conceptual mastery alone, and will argue the proper relation between psychological experience and aesthetic form. He will also attempt in *Melancholy* to use all his "languages" at once—the language of Greek mythology, the language of allegorical frieze, the language of descriptive sensation, the language of heroic quest, the language of gothic medievalizing, the language of the courtly-love (or "Provençal") tradition, the temporal language of fugitive experience, and the propositional language of eternal verities. If this rich amalgam is, as it proves to be, aesthetically grotesque, it exhibits nonetheless a mind unwilling to abandon any of the linguistic or symbolic resources it has so far discovered.

NOTES

2. I think all commentators are now agreed with Bate that the *Urn* shows "the concentration of a second attempt" (John Keats, p. 510), even though we cannot date these two odes precisely. Sperry rightly insists (p. 268) on "the decisiveness of a context for reading the odes as a progression," and he and I are in agreement on the order *Psyche, Nightingale, Urn, Melancholy, Autumn*. We differ on *Indolence*, which I put first (from its date of conception), and he, by date of appearance, puts after Melancholy.

3. I believe that Keats also raises, in these two odes, the question of the origins of art. In pursuit of this question, some theorists turn to "natural music"

(birdsong) as the origin of human music, which is said to "imitate nature." Other theorists turn to the origins of art in Western history—for example, to the ancient world (which for Keats was the Greek world). More recently, theorists have turned to "primitive" art. In *Nightingale* and *Urn*, Keats seeks instruction from two conventional "wellsprings" of art, nature and the ancient Greek model. See the connection drawn between the sculptural and the mythic (and the opposition of both to "consciousness") in Nancy Goslee's article "Phidian Lore: Sculpture and Personification in Keats's Odes" (*Studies in Romanticism* 21 [1982], 73–86).

4. The urn represents, of course, only one visual possibility among several. The epistle to Reynolds had used a painting to similar effect. Besides Keats's wish to return to the origins of art, he simplifies his case by choosing a monochromatic object, thus restricting his observations to shape undistracted by "Titian colors touch'd into real life." He chooses sculpture over painting as closer (being "in the round") to representational "truth"—and chooses bas-relief over statuary as affording more narrative material. He chooses an urn over a frieze because it has no beginning nor end in outline, and can therefore, by its circular form, represent both eternity and the female better than a rectangular form. (All the addressed objects of veneration of the odes are female.)

5. The figures on the urn do not possess any of the identifying attributes (winged heels, a sheaf of wheat) which would enable us to identify them as gods; nor are they engaged in activities (fighting the Minotaur, for example) which would identify them historically or mythologically.

6. Wallace Stevens' reflection on Keats's wish to repose in the mere enjoyment of Beauty and Sensation, frustrated by his inevitable progression to Thought, Truth, and questions, is contained in *The Ultimate Poem Is Abstract*:

> One goes on asking questions. That, then, is one
> Of the categories. So said, this placid space
>
> Is changed. It is not so blue as we thought. To be blue,
> There must be no questions ...
>   It would be enough
> If we were ever, just once, at the middle, fixed
> In This Beautiful World Of Ours and not as now,
>
> Helplessly at the edge, enough to be
> Complete, because at the middle, if only in sense,
> And in that enormous sense, merely enjoy.

7. Keats seems to have derived the idea of the "finer tone" from *Paradise Lost* (v, 374–376):

> ... *though what if Earth*
> *Be but the shadow of Heaven*, and things therein
> Each to the other like, more than on Earth is thought?
> (Italics indicate Keats's underlining in his copy of *Paradise Lost* now in
> the Keats Museum, Hampstead.)

8. Though the ode is often said to be speaking here about the transiency of

passion, Keats insists (through the *burning* forehead and the *parching* tongue) that sensual fever persists even in sorrow and cloying; his bafflement is more evident than is any sense of the evanescence of passion.

9. Every reader has felt that the factual question "What men or gods are these?" is vastly different in tone from "Who are these coming to the sacrifice?" The second is a question of a procession in motion—"What is the nature of this group coming next?"—rather than a wish for an identifying historical reality.

10. Cf. *Paradise Lost*, VIII, 183–184: "Nor with perplexing thoughts / To interrupt *the sweet of life*" (Keats's underlining).

11. It might at first seem that the tonal "break" is a break between apostrophe (immediacy) and propositional reflection (mediated thought). If such were the case, "art" would remain purely sensational, and reflection would exclude the apostrophic surge of feeling. That this is not so is clear from the procession stanza, where apostrophe is present not only in the querying remark to the priest (part of the "sensational" content), but also in the reflective remark to the town ("thy streets ... will silent be"). In this way the reflective portion of aesthetic response is shown to be as "immediate" and full of feeling as the sensory response itself is.

12. It is a matter of dispute whether one can maintain consciousness of matter and medium at once—can weep for the heroine, so to speak, while admiring the zoom shot. I side with Keats, but there is distinguished opinion on the other side. Even in repeated rereadings, one must choose; empathy of the sort an author would wish to evoke cannot be maintained unbroken while one is considering, say, Dickens' use of evolutionary vocabulary, or Stevens' use of the definite article. As soon as intellectual consideration of medium comes into play, the fiction of the construct lapses.

13. Keats here repeats the *Nightingale*-word "fade" (used of sound becoming faint) and the *Indolence*-word "fade" (used of phantoms vanishing) in yet a third sense, that of Beauty losing her lustrous eyes.

14. I see no evidence for puns here (brede/breed or overwrought maidens). However, I think it likely that the "embroider'd" of *Indolence* and the "breeding ... breed" of *Psyche*, both used of Fancy, engendered the "brede" of the *Urn*.

15. *Letters*, I, 192; Keats is criticizing the aesthetic lifelessness of West's art, and uses the phrase by contrast.

16. For a discussion of the philosophical vocabulary of sensation, see Sperry, ch. I, *passim*.

17. It is touching that the word Keats uses for the expressivity of the urn in his close is "say'st" rather than "showest." Propositional truth can only be expressed in language, Keats's own medium. Representational truth (sensation in the eye) yields (as thought in the mind) propositional truth.

18. This crux now seems settled. See Jack Stillinger, *Twentieth Century Interpretations of Keats's Odes* (Englewood Cliffs, N.J.: Prentice-Hall, 1968), pp. 113–114, where the *consensus gentium* seems to be that the last two lines are spoken by the urn to men.

19. The whole thought structure of the *Urn* is a binary one, as though the governing polarity of Beauty and Truth insensibly worked on Keats's mind so as to make everything present itself (at least in the first instance) in binary form. Bride summons up child; the sylvan historian is better than rhyme; are the shapes deities or mortals; are we in Tempe or Arcady; are these men or gods; who are the males, who are the females; what pursuit, what struggle; what instruments, what ecstasy? "Heard" summons "unheard," the sensual ear is opposed to the spirit; the youth cannot leave his song nor can the trees be bare; the lover cannot kiss yet should not grieve; she cannot fade, he has not his bliss; he will love, she be fair. Some of the pairings are contrastive (pursuit and struggle, males and females) but others are coordinate (instruments and ecstasy, leaving the song and the trees being bare). The binary pattern is visible throughout the poem, though it becomes more graceful as it plays the folk against the priest, the heifer's lowing against her adornments. It is so surprising when the binary pattern is resisted (as in the three imagined situations for the little town) that we almost force the lines back into binary shape—in this case conflating "river" and "sea shore" as though there were an "and" between them instead of an "or," and pairing that one line with its two alternatives against the next line containing a single mountain-location. Of course the equivalency, line for line, helps us to read the phrase in a two-part way,

> What little town by river or sea shore
> Or mountain-built with peaceful citadel,

instead of hearing it as a three-part phrase,

> What little town by river
> or sea shore,
> or mountain-built with peaceful citadel.

If Keats says "Attic shape!" he seems compelled to echo it with "Fair attitude!"; if he says "men" he must say "maidens," if he says "forest branches" he must say "trodden weed." By the time he says "Beauty is Truth" we feel he *must* say "Truth Beauty" or he would be breaking an almost inflexible pattern; similarly, "all ye know on earth" would feel incomplete in this ode without its matching half, "all ye need to know." This binary pattern, so strictly maintained, is not natural to Keats in so compulsive a form. The odes are all stately, and show many parallelisms of diction and syntax; but the norm is exceeded by far in the *Urn*, and suggests a deliberate constraint on reverie.

20. Even in Keats's first poem, a Spenserian description of an enchanted isle, Keats finds himself introducing into his idyll, without any compulsion from the genre, Dido's grief and "aged Lear['s] ... bitter teen"; the early poem to the robin (*Stay, ruby breasted warbler, stay*) envisages bleak storm and a leafless grove, "the gloom of grief and tears."

JOHN CLUBBE AND ERNEST J. LOVELL, JR.

English Romanticism: The Grounds of Belief

In the realm of belief, the second generation of Romantic poets moved beyond their distinguished predecessors toward scepticism. Although Wordsworth and Coleridge returned to the Anglican Church of their birth, neither Byron, Shelley, nor Keats was of any church in his maturity. All three had rejected organized Christianity. Shelley stated he had once been an enthusiastic deist but never a Christian.[1] For Keats the Christian was merely one of many 'Schemes of Redemption',[2] and Byron, characteristically, in the last years of his life was still conducting within himself an interior dialogue between the deistic and the Christian points of view. He requested Murray to send him a copy of Charles Leslie's *Short and Easie Method with the Deists*, but he also told James Kennedy, the Methodist minister who was attempting to bring him to accept orthodox Christianity, that he was 'not perfectly satisfied' with the author's 'mode of reasoning'.[3]

Unlike the earlier poets, no one of this later generation accepted Christ the Redeemer, though each spoke with the highest respect of Him. Keats, we remember, linked Christ and Socrates, even as Shelley had done in line 134 of *The Triumph of Life*. For Shelley, Christ is an 'extraordinary person' whose doctrines were 'quickly distorted' by the Church.[4] Byron as early as 13 September 1811 objected to the '*injustice*' of a diverse 'tyrant'[5] even as Keats objected to 'a certain arbitrary interposition of God ... What a little circumscribe[d] straightened notion!' (KL, II, 101–2).

As had the first generation of English Romantic poets, the second generation also expressed the greatest reverence for the Bible and for Paradise Lost. Byron indicated in his preface to Cain that he had read Milton 'so frequently' before he was twenty that that poet had had a lasting influence upon him. He could not have written his *Vision of Judgment*, despite Southey, if *Paradise Lost* had not been written earlier, and even *Don Juan*, in which, according to Paul Elmer More,[6] Byron adopted the only epic manner left for a poet of the nineteenth century, owes at least a negative debt (and probably much more) to Milton's poem. For Shelley, Milton is in the preface to *Prometheus Unbound* 'the sacred Milton', and Shelley's great 'Lyrical Drama' is in fact more epic than dramatic. Finally, Keats did indeed achieve a Milton-like 'tenour and deep organ tone' in *Hyperion* (I, l. 48).

Like their predecessors, each of the younger poets accepted as a fact the fallen or basically imperfect state of man. Byron wrote his *Cain* in the impassioned terms and tones of a very nearly internal debate between Reason (Lucifer–Cain) and Faith (Adam–Abel). Shelley in *Prometheus Unbound* has man himself responsible for the evil Jupiter, whom he empowers and thus in effect creates. *The Triumph of Life* depicts a defeated and fallen race, without an effective Saviour, and the 'curse imposed on Adam' lives on in *A Defence of Poetry*, where we also learn that there is 'an inexplicable defect of harmony in the constitution of human nature' (SP, 293, 292). Keats's Vale of Soul-Making letter describes a 'System of Salvation' for 'a World of Pains and troubles' obviously in need of it. 'Man is originally "a poor forked creature" subject to the same mischances as the beasts of the forest' (KL, II, 103, 102, 101). Nature likewise is fallen for Keats on 21 April 1819, although not merely in the eye of the beholder: the fish can no more 'philosophise the ice away from the Rivers in winter time' than man can 'exterminate' the 'Poles ..... the sands of Africa, Whirlpools and volcanoes' (I, 101). Similarly cognizant of the destructive forces of nature external to man was Byron. We may recall his 'Darkness', the role of Ocean in *Childe Harold* IV, and the shipwreck canto of *Don Juan*. Shelley was likewise aware, in a note to *Queen Mab*, of the 'wide-wasting earthquake, the storm'.[7] At one time he believed that 'the depravity of the physical and moral nature of man' could be traced back to 'unnatural diet' (such as that of Adam and Eve), which in turn originated in 'some great change in the climates of the earth' (SP, 81, 82).

All the Romantic poets agree then upon the flawed nature of man: it is essentially the sin of pride, Blake's selfhood, the absence of love for others. Evil in man is viewed in terms of separation or separateness, or of solitaries. Thus Wordsworth in *The Excursion* creates the Solitary, disillusioned, disappointed, and somewhat cynical, to be 'educated' by the other main characters, and in *The Recluse* the Wordsworthian persona finds 'a true Community' (I, l. 615), even as the Mariner at the end of Coleridge's poem comes to acknowledge his community with others. The proud and solitary Byronic hero normally achieves no lasting spiritual salvation. Manfred is guilt-laden and tormented, seeking above all else an escape from his remorse. Of the three younger poets, Byron is the most concerned with the suffering inherent in the human condition. For Shelley, 'the principle of self ... is ... the Mammon of the world', worshipped by all but the few in a time when there is 'an excess of the selfish and calculating principle' (SP, 293); as long as Prometheus is ruled by hatred, he is separated from Asia, the love-principle. Keats expresses his views on the question of self in an aesthetic context. Unlike the Wordsworthian poet of the egotistical sublime, the Keatsian poet has 'no self'. This chameleon dramatic poet of greatest empathy is 'an[ni]hilated' by the identity of others and enters fully into their existence (KL, I, 387), even as the spirit of Milton entered into Blake and eventually is redeemed. (As a result, the fictive Blake is also transformed.) But Keats believed, with Shelley, that 'complete disinterestedness of Mind' had been achieved perhaps only by Socrates and Christ (II, 79–80).

For all six poets, then, the solution to the problem of selfhood is the empathetic involvement that Keats suggested. No less than the older generation, the younger sought to escape from the self. This escape may be achieved by a union, communion, or marriage with that which is outside self; essentially an expansionistic urge away from the single centre of consciousness. The Keatsian poet 'is continually in for—and filling some other Body' (KL, I, 387). If a sparrow comes and picks away at the gravel before Keats's window, he picks away too. The spirit of the bird that cuts its airy way through the heavens is *not* closed to Keats's senses five. A key passage here, unlocking much of Keats's art, is that already examined toward the end of Book I of *Endymion* (l. 777ff). If the final goal is 'fellowship with essence', a union of the human and the divine spirits, the means to such salvation is 'self-destroying' love, with which 'we blend, / Mingle, and so become a part of it'; our souls 'interknit' and 'combine' with it. As Douglas Bush has pointed out, the 'clear religion of heaven' is 'Keats's version of Wordsworth's view of nature'[8]—the great difference being of course a difference in emphasis upon nature. The similarity resides in the metaphor of sexual union, with the resulting sensation of 'a sort of oneness' with man and, loosely, with the universe. Keats's 'Platonic' ascent begins with a sensuous apprehension of natural beauty, moves on to art (music and poetry), friendship, and love both mortal and divine, with the greatest number of lines in the passage being given to the love between man and woman. Upon all this one might speculate endlessly and compare with it such pronouncements of Blake's in *The Marriage* as his 'where man is not nature is barren' and 'if the doors of perception were cleansed every [natural] thing would appear to man as it is, infinite';[9] or his complex concept of contraries and their 'marriage', specifically his notions about the sexual union of man and woman, surprisingly like Coleridge's and, less surprisingly, like Shelley's.[10] One thinks also of Coleridge's pious hope of man's 'Reconciliation from this Enmity with Nature' and his persuasion that 'a *Poet's Heart & Intellect* should be ... *intimately* combined & *unified*, with the great appearances in Nature'.[11]

Similarly, Shelley understood that 'the great secret of morals is love, or a going out of our own nature' (SP, 282) so as to achieve an imaginative identification with the non-self. Comparable to Keats's 'enthralments' in *Endymion*, love is, for Shelley, 'the bond and the sanction which connects not only man with man but with every thing which exists' (170). After Prometheus is unbound, the poem ends, as does *Endymion*, with union and marriage. Byron's 'Prometheus', written in July 1816, does not take the story that far and leaves the hero still bound: 'Thy Godlike crime was to be kind' (l. 35).

For a while during the summer of 1816, Byron viewed love as the great principle of the universe, and the narrator of *Childe Harold* III learns temporarily to live not in himself but to become 'portion' of that around him. With that he can 'mingle' and therefore he is 'absorbed' (stanzas 72, 73), even as Shelley's child or poet in reverie feels as if he 'were dissolved into the surrounding universe, or as if the surrounding universe were absorbed into [his] being' (SP, 174). He is 'conscious of no distinction' between the two experiences. Such visionary union assumes a monistic universe, the essence of which is love, Endymion's quest; or as Shelley has the old man in 'The Coliseum' say, love is the 'Power ... which interpenetratest all things, and without which this glorious world were a blind and formless chaos' (227).

We enter into such a world and become one with it in an experience that is clearly imaginative, transcending the limited world of outward sense but beginning in it. The impact of the great basilica of St. Peter at Rome Byron experiences in stanzas 153–9 of *Childe Harold* IV. There his mind 'dilate[s]' and grows 'colossal', even as, earlier, it had expanded in the Alps, which throne 'Eternity in icy halls / Of cold Sublimity' (III, st. 62).

Similarly, Coleridge, standing imaginatively in the Vale of Chamouni (where he had never actually been) and gazing up at Mont Blanc, *hears* the 'dread and silent Mount' 'blending with [his] Thought',

> Till the dilating Soul, enrapt, transfused,
> Into the mighty vision passing—there
> As in her natural form, swelled vast to Heaven.[12]

The persona then calls upon the 'thousand voices' of Earth to praise God, which in the poem's last line they do.

Although the aesthetic, the ethical, and the spiritual (or worshipful or devout) are distinct, they may be closely associated and often are. The imagination of Keats's poet of empathy, 'continuously in for—and filling' such symbolic bodies as sun, moon, or sea but also the divine or holy bodies of men and women, may function on the aesthetic, ethical, or spiritual levels. Perhaps Shelley stated the concept most clearly: we go out of ourselves and identify ourselves 'with the beautiful which exists in thought, action, or person, not our own. A man, to be greatly good, must imagine intensely and comprehensively' (SP, 283). For Blake, the only life was the life lived imaginatively, the existence that annihilated and transcended self. In Book XIV of *The Prelude* Wordsworth finds that 'spiritual Love acts not nor can exist / Without Imagination' (ll. 188–9), a text well illustrated and adorned by Coleridge's Mariner.

The charity of Byron's imagination began at home, it would seem, with himself or with his own mind, or so, maybe, he would have it seem. It permitted that mind to escape from itself in the imaginative contemplation of nature or art in the act of poetic composition. Both Lady Blessington and Shelley saw a 'chameleon' in Byron of some similarities with Keats's chameleon poet of no self or identity. Indeed, Shelley, we may recall, not only discovered a chameleonic quality in all true poets but also concluded that Canto V of *Don Juan* set Byron 'far above all the poets of the day'.[13] Byron's volume including *Cain*, he believed, 'contains finer poetry than has appeared in England since the publication of Paradise Regained.—Cain is apocalyptic—it is a revelation not before communicated to man.'[14] Of himself Byron wrote, 'like all imaginative men, I, of course, embody myself with the character while I *draw* it'.[15] At the very least, for himself the Byronic imagination transformed the world; and the tremendous influence of his poetry makes it clear that it could do the same thing for his readers. Nor did Byron will such imaginative poetry into existence. It is not the product of the calculating reason but 'the feeling of a Former world and Future',[16] thus dependent in important part on experience or memory. It is also, significantly, prophetic, as Shelley said of *Cain*.

The poet who celebrated and exalted the poetry of Pope emphasized even more than Wordsworth the emotional origins of poetry. 'It is the lava of the imagination whose eruption prevents an earthquake', he told his future wife.[17] 'Are not the *passions* the food and fuel of poesy?' he asked,[18] and obviously expected the answer to be affirmative. Here Byron approaches Keats, who claimed that 'all our Passions ... are ... creative of essential Beauty' (KL, I, 184). Elsewhere, Byron wrote that 'poetry is the expression of *excited passion*' and that 'poetry is itself passion, and does not systematize ... does not argue'.[19] On another occasion he seems to express an impersonal theory of poetry: 'a man's poetry is a distinct faculty, or soul, and has no more to do with the everyday individual than the Inspiration with the Pythoness when removed from her tripod'.[20] At times Byron will even speak of poetry as if he were describing a Wordsworthian recollection in tranquillity: 'As for poesy—mine is the *dream* of my sleeping Passions—when they are awake—I cannot speak their language— only in their Somnambulism.'[21] More colourfully, he expresses to Trelawny his more usual position, 'I can only write when the *estro* is upon me.'[22] The term derives from the Greek meaning *gadfly*, hence *stinging frenzy*, and today refers to the period of sexual heat in female animals. In Byron's opinion, then, the imaginative or poetry-producing faculty conceives in a very female and earthy or natural fashion. All these comments suggest that he believed in an organic conception of poetic origin. It is not surprising, then, to find that Byron wished 'to let [his] Genius take its natural direction'.[23]

The other Romantics also endorsed the idea that poetry must come spontaneously. For Keats, 'the Genius of Poetry must work out its own salvation in a man: It cannot be matured by law & precept' (KL, I, 374). In short, it is essentially self-creative, although as Keats well knew it must be nurtured by knowledge and discipline. Blake expressed the autonomous quality of poetic composition in somewhat less organic terms. Referring, it seems, to his *Milton*, he said: 'I may praise it, since I dare not pretend to be any other than the Secretary; the Authors are in Eternity.'[24]

If we view poetry in its origins and end as a process of natural growth or change, so we may also view life. The villain, the tempter, the accuser thus becomes any force that attempts to bind, limit, confine, or inhibit. The second generation of poets shared with the first a strong dislike for bonds or limits upon the individual's natural growth and so also produced a poetry celebrating process, growth and change: for example, Byron's *Don Juan*, Shelley's *Prometheus Unbound*, and Keats's two *Hyperion* poems. The tension between creativity and restriction expresses itself in the conflict between Coleridgean organic and mechanical form, the latter resulting when the poet imposes a system of predetermined rules upon his material. One thinks of Urizen's ten restrictive rules, the thou-shalt-nots.[25] Byron's *Don Juan* may be and has been read as a poem whose central rhythm and controlling concept are determined by his 'sense of life as endless movement and change'. The poem repeatedly satirizes attempts 'to restrain life, to bind and force it into some narrow, permanent form'.[26] Precisely at this point, by sharing their most important assumption, does Byron most easily and inevitably take his place again in the company of the Romantic poets: with Blake breaking the bonds imposed by Urizen, with Wordsworth escaping from the depressing limitations of Godwinian rationalistic theory, with Coleridge celebrating repeatedly the life principle itself.

We recall that Inez ridiculously limited Juan's education, Lambro sold him into slavery, Gulbeyaz forced him to disguise himself as a slave girl in a Turkish harem, and that every one of the heroines, in fact, attempted to capture and bind him. Not in all its cantos does the poem offer a single successful marriage. Indeed, during his entire life Byron resisted artificial restraints upon man's full development as compulsively as did Blake. One thinks of his recurrent interest in the figure of Promethean defiance[27] and of his near obsession with the notion of a vengeful deity who unjustly predetermines the fate of men and thus inhibits their freedom to grow. His own Romantic heroes are usually fated and sometimes very frustrated characters. Byron is, then, the poet and advocate of growth largely because of his insight into the elements that inhibit it. The education of Juan is clear nonetheless: he moves from innocence to experience, even if we are not allowed to look often or deeply into his mind.

Keats's Mansion of Life letter also moves, in its different way, from innocence to experience and beyond. Central to *Hyperion* is the theme of evolution or growth: ''tis the eternal law / That first in beauty should be first in might' (II, ll. 228–9). In that poem the deification of Apollo (which is also the birth of a poet) takes place *because* 'Knowledge enormous' becomes his (III, l. 113). Here and in other Romantic poems the growth is a growth in knowledge of human agony and strife. 'Sorrow is Knowledge', said Manfred (Act I, scene i, l. 10), and over the course of the poem he learns the full extent of that sad truth. As much might be said of

The Prelude, which Coleridge in a letter to Wordsworth called 'the Poem on the growth of your own mind'[28] and which came about as a result of the agonies of Wordsworth's experiences in France and their aftermath. Like Coleridge's 'old Navigator', Wordsworth underwent growth through and as a result of suffering.

At best, following such a growth experience or enlargement of vision, the poet or his poetic character may finally perceive what Keats called 'the ballance of good and evil' (KL, I, 281). Byron observed in 1821 that 'good and evil are pretty equally balanced in this existence',[29] a conclusion he may well have reached shortly after completing *Cain*. Shelley's *Prometheus Unbound* restores the balance of good and evil or imperfection, rejecting any Godwinian theory of man's perfectibility. At the end of the climactic passage closing Act III, after Jupiter has fallen, 'man remains', his lot immeasurably improved, but still man, subject as always to his human passions, to 'chance and death and mutability'. Keats also rejected the doctrine of the perfectibility of man: 'the nature of the world will not admit of it' (KL, II, 101). And Byron never considered such a doctrine: the facts were all against it.

To achieve an insight into the balance of good and evil is to achieve a variety of Coleridgean reconciliation of opposite or discordant qualities, coexisting together and even interpenetrating each other. Such an insight is not wholly distinct from Blake's contraries, 'necessary to Human existence', like his Reason and Energy, the former being in one guise the fallen, satanic Urizen but in another guise the essential 'bound or outward circumference of Energy'.[30] 'In the very temple of Delight', Keats discovered, 'Veiled Melancholy has her sovran shrine.' The inhuman Lamia, possessed of a 'sciential brain' able 'to unperplex bliss from its neighbour pain' (Part 1, ll. 191–2), is kin to Urizen, who, unaware of the law of contraries, 'sought for a joy without pain'.[31] Byron also understood the mixed character of human nature: 'at the very height of ... human pleasure ... there mingle[s] a certain sense of doubt and sorrow'.[32] He concludes that Hope cannot exist without Fear. Keats, in an early sonnet 'To Lord Byron', found Byron's melody 'sweetly sad', his tale one of 'pleasing woe'. Shelley observed, 'tragedy delights by affording a shadow of the pleasure which exists in pain. This is the source also of the melancholy which is inseparable from the sweetest melody' (SP, 292). The idea finds its way into 'To a Skylark': 'Our sweetest songs are those that tell of saddest thought.' Blake had said it all more vividly and violently, Coleridge more philosophically when he found that 'one great principle is common to all' life and all the arts, the 'ever-varying balance, or balancing, of images, notions, or feelings ... conceived as in opposition to each other; in short, the perception of identity and contrariety'.[33]

At times the Romantic poets adopted a formal, ornate, or Miltonic style. But no one of them permitted himself to be bound or limited by a single style. The rich variety of their insights demanded an equally rich variety of styles or modes. A poetry of process, recognizing the mixed nature of human experience and expressing the theme of growth or natural change, will most often express itself in a 'natural' diction, one nourished, however indirectly, by the living spoken language, and in generally informal styles, which, avoiding the elaborate, ornate, and rigidly structured, will nevertheless allow for simplicity and naturalness. Blake professed to be proud that his 'Visions ... have been Elucidated by Children'[34] and some poems in *Songs of Innocence* do appear to be addressed to an audience of children. But aside from these, Blake's diction, once we subtract the proper names of places and persons, seems to be even simpler in numerous passages of the prophecies, which may be without all but the most obvious symbolism or irony. 'No man', Blake asserted, 'can think write or speak from his heart, but he must intend truth.'[35] The ballad style of the *Ancient Mariner* is recognizably akin to that of most of Wordsworth's contributions to *Lyrical Ballads* but easily distinguishable from it. Similarly, the style of Coleridge's conversation poems can never be confused with the conversational style of *Don Juan* or that of Shelley's *Julian and Maddalo*, subtitled *A Conversation*.

Obviously the notion of a conversational style implies tremendous variety, the variety of life itself. Every individual is capable of a number of styles: the Shelleyan voice of Julian is different from that of the *Letter to Maria Gisborne*, and the difference is determined in important part by the differences between Maddalo and Maria. Shelley wrote in the preface to *The Cenci*: 'I entirely agree with those modern critics who assert that in order to move men to true sympathy we must use the familiar language of men.... But it must be the real language of men in general,' he continues in a more Coleridgean strain, 'and not that of any particular class'. Shelley further stresses the element of the artificial when he recommends that his own contemporaries study 'our great ancestors the ancient English poets' (SP, 324). This advice Shelley himself followed, for as much as anything else the style of *The Cenci* is pseudo-Shakespearean. Saying this by no means damns the play, one of the best of the century, for its blank verse can be effectively spoken and the play has had successful productions. The style is 'natural', using 'the familiar language of men' to the extent that it permits a willing suspension of disbelief on the part of an actual theatrical audience. To conclude with the last and first of these poets, Keats called for a return to 'the old Poets' (KL, I, 225). He came to regard the style of *Paradise Lost* as 'a curruption [*sic*] of our Language' and left *Hyperion* incomplete, for he now believed that Miltonic verse could only be written in an 'artful or rather artist's humour'.[36]

The Romantic period was an expansive age, and all its major poets sought to express their free spirits in large, long poems of heroic proportions or implications. Coleridge, the seeming exception, teemed with thoughts in the 1790s for an epic poem, 'The Fall of Jerusalem', but never got it written.[37] In attempting an ambitious poem, the poet might himself become a hero and live heroically. We may note at this point the veneration in which all the Romantic poets held the great seminal writers of Western civilization. Blake, we have seen, valued Moses, Solomon, Homer and Plato. Among the poets of the second generation, one thinks of Byron's love of the Old Testament, Shelley's magnificent translations from Plato, the sense of high adventure that Keats found in Homer. In short, the Romantic poets were not eccentrics (as most of their contemporaries thought) but at the centre of Western literary tradition.

The second generation of Romantic poets had read their Wordsworth and Coleridge, comprehended their questions and answers, and felt a clear need to move on into pastures new. They more or less deliberately built new structures upon a number of typically Wordsworthian and Coleridgean bases. Or at times they refused to build. Quantitatively, they theorized less than their elders. They had little or nothing new to say, for example, about the nature of the symbol, about the relationships among the reason, imagination and fancy, about the reconciliation of man and nature. Byron wrote only two significant critical essays (one of which was not published during his lifetime); Shelley's major critical contributions are his Prefaces and his *Defence of Poetry*, the latter first published in 1840; and Keats left us his letters. This relative paucity of theoretical writing suggests that the second generation distrusted intellectual systems to a greater extent than did the first or had less need of them. Even Blake felt the need to construct an admittedly highly elastic system of his own or be enslaved, he thought, by another man's. Wordsworth was no philosopher but he created a 'philosophy' that is recognizably Wordsworthian, however inconsistent or vague it seems at times. Coleridge's mature philosophy and literary criticism we find magnificently consistent. But Byron clearly distrusted intellectual systems, as did Keats, and Shelley denied in his preface to *Prometheus Unbound*, completed near the end of 1819, that his 'poetical compositions' contained 'a reasoned system on the theory of human life. Didactic poetry is my abhorrence'.[38] Since the second generation of poets shared an unwillingness to submit to intellectual systems, a reductive force inevitably exerts itself in this brief recapitulation of the grounds of belief shared by all six major poets.

We have seen that Byron, Shelley and Keats, hardly less than their three predecessors, pored over the Bible and reverenced *Paradise Lost*. But even though the broad foundations of their Romanticism are both Christian and humanistic, they could not attain the security of belief that their predecessors had attained. They were basically less inclined to arrive at final conclusions. And yet the younger poets agreed with Blake, Wordsworth and Coleridge that man's nature was significantly imperfect and thus in need of redemption. Despite Byron's persisting interest in deistic thought, he is the most orthodox of his contemporaries on the subject of man's inherent imperfections and the need for redemption. Shelley's greatest document of redemption is *Prometheus Unbound*, whereas Keats's is his Vale of Soul-Making letter.

The three younger poets were nearly as interested in the nature of perception as their predecessors, although they were less clearly persuaded that an improved perception would produce a redeemed nature. However, as we have seen, Byron analyzed with great acuity the perceptual experience of Childe Harold in St. Peter's Basilica, where his mind, 'expanded by the Genius of the spot, / Has grown colossal'. For Shelley, nothing exists except as it is perceived, and Keats's old sophist Apollonius in *Lamia* is clearly a counterpart of Blake's Angel in *The Marriage*, whose metaphysics produced the monstrous Leviathan, indeed all that 'we saw'.[39] 'Do not all charms fly', Apollonius asks, 'At the mere touch of cold philosophy?' (Part II, ll. 229–30). We may take his relentless gaze to be a metaphor for his metaphysics, which causes Lamia to disappear and Lycius to die. All this suggests that the younger poets, as well as the older, understood that the mind does not merely mirror a reality external to itself but engages in genuine creative acts of perception. These acts alter the nature of human existence and also transform nature by humanizing it, by rendering the external internal, bringing it indoors, as it were, and thus again reconciling the great polar opposites.

As much as had the earlier, the later generation of Romantic poets viewed the poetic imagination as an ethical or religious imagination. The expansive empathetic power persists as the only power capable of subduing the old enemy, Blakean selfhood, and annihilating the self in man's continuing quest for community. The Romantic poets were repeatedly going away from themselves and from each other, walking away or running away, sometimes in silence and sometimes in despair; but they hungered after community and recognized that the important thing was to know where home was and to try to come back again.[40] The larger structure in several of Blake's poems—*The Book of Urizen*, *Ahania*, and *America*, among others—is circular, ending in a coming together, a coming home, a return to unity and harmony. The conversation poems of Coleridge—who thought the best poems were circular in structure— illustrate his awareness of the need for a return to community. Byron expresses his sense of community most clearly in terms of his guilt-laden, suffering, solitary heroes, who never find a home. (He succeeded in going home again—to Norman Abbey—only through his persona in Canto XIII of *Don Juan*.) Poetically, the sense of community, the felt desire or ability to identify sympathetically and deeply with others, takes the metaphoric form of a chameleon, which is virtually identical with the Byronic concept of *mobilité*.

It would be unwise to close with an image of Romanticism as some massive, transparent triangle constructed of such bloodless concepts as organicism, dynamicism and diversitarianism, or a similarly massive and transparent four-sided figure built of dynamic organicism, imagination, symbolism and the unconscious mind.[41] Rather, it is salutory to remember the ages at death of Byron, Shelley and Keats: thirty-six, twenty-nine and twenty-five respectively. They were, chronologically, young men, unlike Blake in 1824 (the year of Byron's death), aged sixty-seven; Wordsworth, aged fifty-four; and Coleridge, aged fifty-two. We are concerned, in short, not merely with two generations but with an older generation that outlived by many years the younger and lived through experiences that the younger could not duplicate. For whatever reasons, the writers of the first generation achieved a poetically expressed sense of security that we do not find in the later poetry of the second generation. Blake saw the New Jerusalem and described it more than once in his poetry—in 'Night the Ninth' of *The Four Zoas*, for example, and at the end of *Jerusalem*; Wordsworth solved his deepest problems and succeeded in finding 'Home at Grasmere'; the old Mariner had preceded him by several years in going home, where he found a new purpose in life, as Coleridge himself was to do in the Christian church. But Byron, as first-person narrator viewing events at Norman Abbey, returned to his boyish antics as 'the Abbot' of Newstead Abbey, and at the end Juan discovers, concealed beneath the robes of the ghostly Black Friar, only the too solid flesh of 'her frolic Grace—Fitz-Fulke'; Shelley's Prometheus withdraws to his cave with Asia, not to reappear, and we are left with the magnificently inhuman ballet of earth and moon; and Keats's poet-persona can communicate only with the goddess Moneta (the admonisher) and overhear the sadly weakened voices of the fallen Titans.

NOTES

1. SL, I, p. 89. Shelley–Janetta Phillips [? May 1811].

2. KL, II, p. 103.

3. BLJ, VIII, p. 238 (Byron–Murray, 9 October 1821); James Kennedy, *Conversations on Religion with Lord Byron* (London: John Murray, 1830) p. 231.

4. SP, p. 288.

5. BLJ, II, p. 97. See also pp. 88–9.

6. In *The Complete Poetical Works of Byron*, ed. Paul Elmer More (1905; Boston: Houghton Mifflin, 1933) p. 744.

7. SP, p. 112.

8. *John Keats: Selected Poems and Letters* (Boston: Houghton Mifflin, 1959) p. 319.

9. BPP, pp. 37, 39.

10. On Coleridge, see Jonas Spatz, 'The Mystery of Eros: Sexual Initiation in Coleridge's "Christabel"', *PMLA*, 90 (January 1975) pp. 107–16.

11. CCL, IV, p. 575; II, p. 864.

12. 'Hymn before Sun-rise, in the Vale of Chamouni,' ll. 13, 19, 21–3. The poem is all the more impressive since it took its origin not in personal experience but, as is well-known, in Frederike Brun's quite dreadful 'Chamouny beym Sonnenaufgange', itself inspired by Klopstock.

13. SL, II, p. 323. Shelley–Mary Shelley [8–10 August 1821].

14. Ibid., II, p. 388. Shelley–John Gisborne, 26 January 1822.

15. BLJ, IX, pp. 118–19. Byron–Thomas Moore, 4 March 1822.

16. Ibid., VII, p. 37.

17. Ibid., III, p. 179. Byron–Annabella Milbanke, 29 November 1813.

18. Ibid., VII, p. 132. Byron–John Murray, 17 July 1820.

19. Ibid., VIII, p. 146, and LJ, V, p. 582.

20. BLJ, IX, p. 64. Byron–Moore, 16 November 1821.

21. Ibid., V, p. 157. Byron–Murray, 2 January 1817. Equally suggestive of recollection in tranquillity is this passage: 'my first impressions are always strong and confused—& my Memory *selects* & reduces them to order—like distance in the landscape—& blends them better—although they may be less distinct' (ibid., V, p. 221; Byron–Murray, 9 May 1817). Compare an earlier statement: 'While you are under the influence of passions, you only feel, but cannot describe them' (ibid., III, p. 245; journal entry, 20 February 1814).

22. *Records of Shelley, Byron, and the Author*, 2 vols (London: Basil Montagu Pickering, 1878) I, p. 33. The word, a favourite, appears in BLJ, V, pp. 131, 157, 165; VI, p. 49; VIII, p. 166.

23. BLJ, VIII, p. 221. Byron–Murray, 24 September 1821. Although in his satirical poetry he makes a great show of reason and assumes towards its satiric object the superior position of the analyzer and evaluator, Byron, like Shelley and Keats, sensed a fundamental opposition between the faculties of reason and imagination: for example, 'it is only by the excess of imagination they [poets] can arrive at being poets, and this excess debars reason' (*Lady Blessington's 'Conversations of Lord Byron'*, ed. Lovell, p. 115).

24. BL, p. 69. Blake–Butts, 6 July 1803.

25. In *America*, plate 8, BPP, p. 53. See also pp. 26 ('The Garden of Love') and 43 ('A Song of Liberty').

26. Alvin B. Kernan, *The Plot of Satire* (New Haven and London: Yale University Press, 1965) pp. 176, 205.

27. Explored in Clubbe, '"The New Prometheus of New Men": Byron's 1816 Poems and *Manfred*', in *Nineteenth-Century Literary Perspectives* (1974), ed. Clyde de L. Ryals, John Clubbe and B. F. Fisher IV.

28. 30 May 1815, in CCL, IV, p. 573.

29. BLJ, IX, p. 45. 'Detached Thought', no. 95.

30. BPP, p. 34.

31. BPP, p. 70.

32. BLJ, VIII, p. 37. Journal entry, 28 January 1821.

33. *Shakespearean Criticism*, I, p. 181.

34. BL, p. 30. Blake–Trusler, 23 August 1799.

35. BPP, p. 2. On the eighteenth-century roots of Blake's language, see Josephine Miles, *Eras and Modes in English Poetry* (1957), chapter 5, 'The Sublimity of William Blake'.

36. KL, II, pp. 212, 167. Brian Wilkie nicely observes that Keats's self-correction is helpful (*Romantic Poets and Epic Tradition* [Madison: University of Wisconsin Press, 1965] p. 154).

37. E. S. Shaffer, *'Kubla Khan' and The Fall of Jerusalem: The Mythological School in Biblical Criticism and Secular Literature, 1770–1880* (1975), ch. 1.

38. SP, p. 328. Cf. his statement to Keats: 'In poetry I have sought to avoid system & mannerism' (SL, 14 p. 221: 27 July 1820).

39. BPP, p. 40.

40. Hermione de Almeida explores this point in relation to Byron and Joyce. Following C. R. Beye, she writes of the early Greeks: 'The immense emphasis they placed upon the polis was derived from their fast-held notions of man's inseparable connections with place, of his need for a source or center to which he could always return' (*Byron and Joyce through Homer: 'Don Juan' and 'Ulysses'* [New York: Columbia University Press, 1981] p. 184). Maynard Solomon in *Beethoven* (1977)

sensitively discusses the significance of Beethoven's desire to return, late in life, to his birthplace, Bonn.

41. For the former, see Arthur O. Lovejoy, 'The Meaning of Romanticism for the Historian of Ideas', *Journal of the History of Ideas*, 2 (June 1941), especially pp. 272–8; for the latter, René Wellek, 'The Concept of Romanticism in Literary History', *Comparative Literature*, 1 (1949), and Peckham, 'Toward a Theory of Romanticism', *PMLA*, 66 (1951), reprinted in his *Triumph of Romanticism* (1970). See, particularly, section II of Peckham's essay.

Phases of English Romanticism

The despair which characterizes works of this sort should not be read as a mark of artistic weakness. Of course, "Constancy to an Ideal Object" is a "secondary" work in Coleridge's corpus, in two senses: first, its tactics and purposes are defined in terms of precedent and therefore "primary" works like "Kubla Khan"; second, its self-critical relations within the Coleridge canon do not permit it an avenue for making or even anticipating new ideological affirmations. The significance of a book like *Lyrical Ballads* lies in its ability to look before and after. The critique developed in that volume is directed toward precedent ideological structures, but is a critique whose function is to open up new ways of thinking and feeling about the human world. It too is a "secondary" work, then, as are all human works, but its secondariness is not in the field of its own purposes. Self-criticism in *Lyrical Ballads* is subordinated to the adventure of exploring the limits of a new ideological program.

Differences of these kinds remind us that the Romantic Period is marked throughout by various sorts of important differentials, and that current academic interest in the uniformities of Romanticism have tended to obscure both the fact as well as the significance of such differentials. For instance, not all of the writers of this period are Romantic writers, nor are all of the most important writers or works "Romantic" in style or ideological focus. Critics do not mark out such differentials often enough,

---

From *The Romantic Ideology: A Critical Investigation.* © 1983 by The University of Chicago.

and the failure to do so produces serious scholarly distortions of various kinds. Indeed, the differences between the first and the second generation of English Romantics is too often glanced over, and the result has been a somewhat distorted critical view of the Romantic Movement largely considered. This distortion is in fact a function of present ideological commitments, so that any scholarly effort to rectify the distortion must have as much critical impact upon the present as it does upon the past. At this point, then, I should like to introduce some comments upon the different "phases" of the English Romantic Movement. I hope it will be apparent, from the commentary itself, that these remarks involve a critical analysis of Romantic Ideology both in its early nineteenth century formations as well as in its later (literary critical) transformations as we can observe them in our own period and institutions.

Perhaps the best examples of "primary" Romantic works, in the sense I have put forward above, are to be found in the early Blake: in the *Songs*, for example, or *The Marriage of Heaven and Hell*. Works like these possess an unusual confidence in the mutually constructive powers of imagination and criticism when both operate dialectically. *The Marriage of Heaven and Hell*, for example, institutes a broad critique of inherited religion, philosophy, artistic production, and society. Its breadth appears most clearly in the poem's attack upon Swedenborgianism and the New Jerusalem Church, under whose tutelage Blake learned his own powers of criticism and first gained his imaginative freedom. Yet the critique acquires its authority not because it brings every aspect of Blake's social world within its purview, but because it is carried out in a spirit of exuberance and sympathetic imaginative understanding. The unregenerate angel, the starry kings of this world, the crippled gods of the Jewish and Christian dispensations are all brought, like errant children, within the embrace of Blake's benevolent Satanism. Blake chooses to tell poetic tales out of the history of human forms of worship, and generosity comes to replace prohibition as the medium and ground of criticism.

Works of this kind—they are rare in the period—I would call "primary" because they do not bring their own dialectical stance into question. They possess the special historical privilege which attaches to English Romantic poems written before the Reign of Terror, the Directory, and Napoleon's accession to power, as well as the political events in England which took place in response to continental circumstances. Unlike *The Marriage of Heaven and Hell*, the poems in *Lyrical Ballads* are already self-troubled by their own critical structures, and hence already anticipate (or even manifest) the "secondary" forms which will appear in "Peele Castle" or "Constancy to an Ideal Object." Byron first defines the second generation of English Romanticism, in *Childe Harold's Pilgrimage* (1812), with a work which takes its initial stance in a "secondary" posture of Romantic despair and cynicism. Harold Bloom's theory of poetic belatedness seems to me an historical myth designed to explain this fact about most of the important Romantic works: that they are typically reactionary-revisionist, "secondary," and self-critical.

In studying English Romanticism, then, we must be prepared to distinguish three different phases, as it were, of "primary" (visionary) and "secondary" (or revisionist) relationships. In Blake, *The Marriage of Heaven and Hell* is "primary" in relation to works like *Milton* and *Jerusalem*, which are "secondary" and revisionist in this structure of relations. The period covered here stretches from 1789 to approximately 1807–8, or the years between the beginning of the French Revolution to the start of the Peninsular War. In Wordsworth and Coleridge, on the other hand, we can observe a second phase of Romantic relationships. Here the initial works date from the Reign of Terror and they first appear in *Lyrical Ballads*. These works differ from Blake's in that they are already laden with self-critical and revisonist elements. Wordsworth's purely "secondary" phase is brief to the point of nonexistence, for his greatest works—which are rightly judged the touchstone of first generation English Romantic poetry—incorporate vision and its critique from the start. The general historical limits to his important work—approximately 1797 to 1807—help to elucidate the differences which separate Wordsworth from Blake. Within his own corpus, "Peele Castle" is about as close as we come to a genuinely "secondary" work by Wordsworth, though even here the term is not neatly applicable since "Peele Castle" and "Tintern Abbey" are only separated from each other, ideologically and stylistically, by a difference in emphasis. The fact seems to be, as Bloom has observed, that Wordsworth's greatest poems are all marked by a sense of belatedness.

This characteristic of Wordsworth's poetry renders Coleridge's career, from the point of view of literary criticism, all the more significant. The notorious waning of Wordsworth's poetic powers after 1807 signals what for him amounts to a "secondary" poetic phase. In Coleridge, however, the utter despair that might have been Wordsworth's late or "secondary" subject emerges clearly and forcibly in poems like "Limbo," "Constancy to an Ideal Object," "Nature," and "Love's Apparition and Evanishment." These are among the works which stand in a secondary or critical relation to works like "Kubla Khan" and "The Rime of the Ancient Mariner." The despair of such later poetry is the sign of its ideological truthfulness. Since Coleridge's great early poetry is clearly "secondary" and self-critical in its focus, however, we have to approach his later poems in terms of the ideological climate which we associate with the generation of the so-called "Younger Romantics," who occupy a third phase of the English Romantic Movement.

This third phase of Romantic relationships appears most typically in the period stretching from approximately 1808 to 1824—the literary years of a Romanticism in England which is initiated, dominated, and closed by Byron. In its primary phase Byron's work is already so deeply self-critical and revisionist that its ideology—in contrast to Blake, Wordsworth, and the early Coleridge—has to be defined in negative terms: nihilism, cynicism, anarchism. Byron woke to find himself made famous by his despair, even as England's struggle with the purposeless force of Napoleonism was to culminate in the pyrrhic victory of Waterloo, which established the ground for the Holy Alliance and the ghostly return of pre-revolutionary political structures throughout Europe. It is no mere coincidence that Byron, Shelley, and Keats all die out of England, or that Byron's and Shelley's poetry ultimately rests in an expatriate stance. The work of all three is produced in a remarkable span of English history marked, on the one hand, by domestic and foreign events of the greatest moment and, on the other, by the manifest absence of a moral or spiritual focus. Human events seemed dominated by what Shelley called the selfish and calculating principle: at home, the Regency; in the international sphere, Metternich, Castlereagh, and the Quadruple Alliance. Byron's departure from England in 1816 is normally thought of in relation to his marriage separation, but that domestic event merely culminated his desperate Years of Fame, which at the time he characterized in the following epigram.

> 'Tis said Indifference marks the present time,
> Then hear the reason—though 'tis told in rhyme—
> A king who *can't*, a Prince of Wales who *don't*,
> Patriots who *shan't*, and Ministers who *won't*,
> What matters who are in or out of place,
> The *Mad*, the *Bad*, the *Useless*, or the *Base*?

The mordant wit of these lines would resonate, in later years, through international events of an even more dispiriting kind. Byron entered into the Carbonari movement and the Greek struggle with a will, it is true, but with few illusions.

> When a man hath no freedom to fight for at home,
>   Let him combat for that of his neighbours;
> Let him think of the glories of Greece and of Rome,
>   And get knock'd on the head for his labours.
> To do good to mankind is the chivalrous plan,
>   And is always as nobly requited;
> Then battle for freedom wherever you can,
>   And, if not shot or hang'd, you'll get knighted.[12]

The greatest poetry of the later English Romantics, that is to say, was written in a period of intense (and largely successful) Reaction. What made the period especially debilitating to their moral sensibilities was the fact that no one who lived through it was able to say—as Wordsworth once and truly said—that they had known a dawn in whose light it had been bliss to be alive. The French Revolution was no more than a betrayed memory for the later Romantics, the spirit of whose age was very different from the one in which Blake, Wordsworth, and Coleridge produced their most significant work. One of the most profoundly optimistic spirits who ever wrote English poetry, Shelley himself only preserved his human commitments by casting his work into a future tense: a prophetic poetry born, like Isaiah's, in exile and captivity, and not, like Virgil's, in the comforts of Imperial favor. These are the circumstances which give an edge of bleakness even to Shelley's most splendid revolutionary work, and which justify Richard Holmes's summary of *Prometheus Unbound*.

> Prometheus represents suffering, hope, creative skill and the eternal struggle for a potential freedom. He is the symbol of those who struggle for the future; he is the symbol of those who wait the revolution, the new golden age; but he cannot be the symbol of Victory itself.[13]

Unlike Byron, Shelley never believed that it might be possible to make a moral or poetic virtue out of his despair (although this is precisely what Shelley finally did). Nevertheless, we will not feel the meaning or appreciate the significance of his famous ideology of hope if we do not see how deeply it is allied to his sense of hopelessness. The sonnet "England in 1819" expresses this relation with great economy.

An old, mad, blind, despised, and dying king;
Princes, the dregs of their dull race, who flow
Through public scorn,—mud from a muddy spring;
Rulers who neither see, nor feel, nor know,
But leechlike to their fainting country cling,
Till they drop, blind in blood, without a blow.
A people starved and stabbed in the untilled field;
An army, whom liberticide and prey
Makes as a two-edged sword to all who wield;
Golden and sanguine laws which tempt and slay;
Religion Christless, Godless—a book sealed;
A Senate, Time's worst statute, unrepealed,
Are graves from which a glorious Phantom may
Burst, to illumine our tempestuous day.[14]

Nothing could be more exquisitely Shelleyan than that sly, sad pun on the word "sanguine." At the same time, nothing could be more telling than the subjunctive note on which the poem concludes. The sonnet is constructed out of a dreadful list of present-tense realities. What it hopes for, however, is not even a future in which these shall be no more. The poem is more modest and far sadder than that. It hopes for just a future promise, a glimpse of some far goal in time. Here Shelley looks to the possibility that the evils of his day will be at least revealed, that an age dominated by "golden and sanguine laws" will be unmasked and seen for what it is. Such knowledge "may" come, and if it were to come a new day might then be a possibility.

This is the consciousness out of which Shelley's greatest works were created. He was moved by the revolution in Spain, by the Carbonari, and especially by the Greek struggle for independence. But his enthusiasm was guarded with fear and suspicion, not least of all toward himself.

And public attention is now centred on the wonderful revolution in Greece. I dare not, after the events of last winter, hope that slaves can become freemen so cheaply; yet I know one Greek of the highest qualities, both of courage and conduct, the Prince Mavrocordato.[15]

This was written in September 1821. Two weeks before his death his tone had changed, but only for the worse. He returned to his favorite images of blood and gold to characterize the times.

The destiny of man can scarcely be so degraded that he was born only to die: and if such should be the case, delusions, especially the gross and preposterous ones of the existing religion, can scarcely be supposed to exalt it; if every man said what he thought, it could not subsist a day. But all, more or less, subdue themselves to the element that surrounds them, and contribute to the evils they lament by the hypocrisy that springs from them.—England appears to be in a desperate condition, Ireland still worse, and no class of those who subsist on the public labour will be persuaded that *their* claims on it must be diminished. But the government must content itself with less in taxes, the landholder must submit to receive less rent, and the fundholder a diminished interest,—or they will all get nothing, or something worse [than] nothing.—I am glad that my good genius said *refrain*. I see little public virtue, and I foresee that the contest will be one of blood and gold two elements, which however much to my taste in my pockets and my veins, I have an objection to out of them.[16]

The special quality of Shelley's skepticism is a function of certain public and private circumstances, on the one hand, and certain ideological commitments on the other. His belief that poets were the unacknowledged legislators of the world—the emphasis must be placed on "unacknowledged" to specify the Romanticism of the idea—was one shared by all the Romantics, late and early alike. The poet's privilege was insight and vision, the power to apprehend fundamental truths which custom and habit kept hidden from the ordinary person's consciousness. In the early Romantics, the circumstantial threats raised against this conviction not only produced their greatest poetry, it forced them to the most profound defenses and explications of their ideas (the Preface to *Lyrical Ballads*, the "Vision of the Last Judgement," the *Biographia Literaria*). In each case the ideology of poetic vision took its stand in acts of poetic displacement which were able to produce an immediate poetic contact (an aesthesis) with the Idea and "the life of things." We have already observed this effect in a poem like "Kubla Khan"; Blake and Wordsworth exhibit or define its contours at least as clearly, and far more often.

> Imagination—here the Power so called
> Through sad incompetence of human speech,
> That awful Power rose from the mind's abyss

Like an unfathered vapour that enwraps,
At once, some lonely traveller. I was lost;
Halted without an effort to break through;
But to my conscious soul I now can say—
'I recognise thy glory:' in such strength
Of usurpation, when the light of sense
Goes out, but with a flash that has revealed
The invisible world, doth greatness make abode.
                    (*Prelude* VI, 592–602)

And I know that This World is a World of Imagination &
Vision. I see Every thing I paint In This World, but Every body
does not see alike. To the Eyes of a Miser a Guinea is far more
beautiful than the Sun, & a bag worn with the use of Money
has more beautiful proportions than a Vine filled with Grapes.
The tree which moves some to tears of joy is in the Eyes of
others only a Green thing which stands in the way. Some see
Nature all Ridicule & Deformity, & by these I shall not
regulate my proportions; & some scarce see Nature at all. But
to the Eyes of the Man of Imagination, Nature is Imagination
itself. As a man is, so he sees. As the Eye is formed, such are its
Powers. You certainly Mistake, when you say that the Visions
of Fancy are not to be found in This World. To Me This World
is all One continued Vision of Fancy or Imagination. (Letter to
Trusler, 23 Aug. 1799)[17]

When we turn to the later Romantics the differences appear in
character rather than in kind, though they are none the less clear for that.
All the positions taken up by the early Romantics assume more extreme
forms in the later Romantics. The power of imagination to effect an
unmediated (that is, an aesthetic) contact with noumenal levels of reality—
the ideology of such a conviction—shifts toward a naked and powerful
sensationalism in the later Romantics—an aesthetic of arresting surface
effects, a physique of poetry. Shelley's overwhelming verse effects—one
recalls especially Act II scene 5 of *Prometheus Unbound*, or the concluding
stanzas of *Adonais*, or various passages in "Epipsychidion"—illustrate his
version of this new poetic mode very well.

We shall become the same, we shall be one
Spirit within two frames, oh! wherefore two?

One passion in twin-hearts, which grows and grew,
Till like two meteors of expanding flame,
Those spheres instinct with it become the same,
Touch, mingle, are transfigured; ever still
Burning, yet ever inconsumable:
In one another's substance finding food,
Like flames too pure and light and unimbued
To nourish their bright lives with baser prey,
Which point to Heaven and cannot pass away:
One hope within two wills, one will beneath
Two overshadowing minds, one life, one death,
One Heaven, one Hell, one immortality
And one annihilation.

       ("Epipsychidion" 573–87)

One could cite analogous examples out of Byron's kaleidoscope or Keats's voluptuousness, but two of their brief prose remarks are perhaps even more telling:

> the great object of life is Sensation—to feel that we exist—even though in pain. (Letter to Annabelle Milbanke, 6 Sept. 1813)

> O for a Life of Sensations rather than of Thoughts! (Letter to Bailey, 22 Nov. 1817)[18]

From the earliest commentators, like Hazlitt and Hallam, to the most recent, readers have always remarked on this difference between Byron, Shelley, and Keats on the one hand, and Wordsworth and Coleridge on the other, and many have used the difference to set (or insinuate) comparative valuations, usually to the detriment of the later Romantics. Such differences have to do with poetic style and ideology, however, not with the relative success in the poetic craft. Indeed, I do not see how the later Romantics could have written poetry at all without finding an appropriate stylistic means for revealing the special human truths of their worlds—a poetry capable of reciprocating the forms of life and behavior peculiar to the period which extends from the opening of the Peninsular War to Byron's death just prior to the close of the Greek struggle for independence.

These special circumstances affected the earlier Romantics as well. Blake fell silent, Wordsworth fell asleep, and Coleridge fell into his late

Christian *contemptus*. The second generation Romantics, however, fashioned from these evil times a new set of poetic opportunities. Three sorts of poetry may be particularly noted, and although each is most closely associated with one of the three late Romantics, the three modes appear in one form or another, at one time or another, in all of these poets, and even occasionally in the early Romantics. The descriptive terms I am using here to set forth these distinctions are appropriated from the language of critics who have been largely hostile toward the work of the later Romantics.

The tradition which has attacked Byron for his sensationalism and his high-energy rhetoric is well established and has some important subsidiary strains (Byron's anti-intellectualism, his lack of thought, and so forth). Shelley, on the other hand, has always suffered from critics who deplore, or pity, his social commitments and hopes. Shelley is a cureless idealist—a meliorist, a futurist, an escapist with a vaporous style to match his airy thoughts and dreams. Keats, finally, develops his own special forms of escapism which have commonly been ranged under the general heading of his aestheticism. Let me reemphasize here what I have already suggested several times. Although these characterizations bear negative judgments with which I do not agree, they also manipulate what seem to me quite shrewd and accurate critical responses. Shelley's idealism, Byron's sensationalism, and Keats's aesthetic poetry are all displaced yet fundamental vehicles of cultural analysis and critique: a poetry of extremity and escapism which is the reflex of the circumstances in which their work, their lives, and their culture were all forced to develop.

Before looking briefly at each of these poets in turn, let me recall for a moment the eroticism which is a marked feature of all their work. Of the earlier Romantics only Blake took up erotic subjects with a comparable directness, and his work differs from that of the later Romantics in being analytic and critical where they are voluptuous and sensational. This erotic strain in the verse of Byron, Shelley, and Keats has been variously deplored, condescended to, and set aside by a great many critics, particularly on the grounds that such work lacks the highest sort of artistic seriousness. But Shelley's comments on the erotic poetry of the Hellenistic and late Roman periods offers a much finer basis for a critical assessment:

> It is not what the erotic writers have, but what they have not, in which their imperfection consists. It is not inasmuch as they were Poets, but inasmuch as they were not Poets, that they can be considered with any plausibility as connected with the

corruption of their age. Had that corruption availed so as to extinguish in them the sensibility to pleasure, passion, and natural scenery, which is imputed to them as an imperfection, the last triumph of evil would have been achieved. For the end of social corruption is to destroy all sensibility to pleasure; and, therefore, it is corruption. It begins at the imagination—and the intellect as at the core, and distributes itself thence as a paralysing venom, through the affections into the very appetites, until all become a torpid mass in which sense hardly survives. At the approach of such a period, Poetry ever addresses itself to those faculties which are the last to be destroyed, and its voice is heard, like the footsteps of Astraea, departing from the world.[19]

What Shelley observes here is peculiarly apposite to certain aspects of his own period, as he was well aware. His remarks serve to highlight the critical function of such poetry, especially as it operates in decadent and morally imperialist cultures, or as it is judged by sensibilities which maintain and defend the ideologies of those cultures. Eroticism, Shelley argues, is the imagination's last line of human resistance against what he elsewhere called "Anarchy": political despotism and moral righteousness on the one hand, and on the other selfishness, calculation, and social indifference.

NOTES

12. From *The Poems of Byron*, ed. P. E. More (Cambridge, Mass., 1905), 236.

13. Richard Holmes, *Shelley: The Pursuit* (London, 1974), 506.

14. The text here is from the edition of Donald H. Reiman and Sharon B. Powers, *Shelley's Poetry and Prose* (N.Y., 1977). Unless otherwise noted, all poetry will be quoted from this text.

15. *The Letters of Percy Bysshe Shelley*, ed. Frederick L. Jones (Oxford, 1964) II, 350.

16. *Ibid.*, 442.

17. Letter to Trusler, 23 Aug. 1799, in *The Poetry and Prose of William Blake*, ed. David V. Erdman (N.Y., 1965), 676–7.

18. *Byron's Letters and Journals*, ed. Leslie A. Marchand (Cambridge, Mass., 1974) III, 109; *The Letters of John Keats*, ed. H. E. Rollins (Cambridge, Mass., 1958) I, 185.

19. *Shelley's Prose*, 286.

WILLIAM KEACH

Rhyme and the Arbitrariness
of Language

One of the ways in which the language of *The Triumph of Life* 'disfigures' itself, says Paul de Man, is through rhyme:

> If ... compelling rhyme schemes such as 'billow,' 'willow,' 'pillow' or transformations such as 'thread' to 'tread' or 'seed' to 'deed' occur at crucial moments in the text, then the question arises whether these particularly meaningful movements or events are not being generated by random and superficial properties of the signifier rather than by the constraints of meaning.[1]

De Man goes on to say that this 'arbitrary element in the alignment between meaning and linguistic articulation' is not in itself responsible for the instability of meaning in Shelley's text, but is instead part of a larger, more pervasive process by which the poem enacts what he calls 'the figurality of all signification'.[2] One may believe that the poem's 'movements or events' resist being dissolved in de Man's 'all'—inclusive formulation and yet find the more restricted question about rhyme worth pausing over and exploring in greater detail. De Man rightly suggests that *The Triumph of Life* raises the question of rhyme in an urgent way. But more needs to be said about how the poem does this and about how the

From *Shelley's Style*. © 1984 by William Keach.

129

arbitrariness of rhyme bears upon Shelley's declared conception of language as an artistic medium, and upon other poems that challenge the tendency to ignore rhyme or to take it for granted.

By proclaiming that 'language is arbitrarily produced by the Imagination and has relation to thoughts alone,' Shelley embraces more openly and emphatically than any other Romantic poet the Lockean principle that words are arbitrarily related to the thoughts they signify. Rhyme would appear to be a mysterious consequence of linguistic arbitrariness as Shelley conceives it.[3] For in rhyme the arbitrariness of language turns back on itself to produce—or to make it possible for the poet-as-arbiter to produce—phonetic or graphemic as well as semantic links among arbitrary linguistic signs. In the *Defence* Shelley speaks of an interdependent phonetic and semantic order:

> Sounds as well as thoughts have relation both between each other and towards that which they represent, and a perception of the order of those relations has always been found connected with a perception of the order of the relations of thoughts.
>
> (*PP*, 484)

Rhyme is the most conspicuous manifestation of the double order of sounds and thoughts Shelley imagines here. And that rhyme can be surprising, suggestive and compelling is due in part to the happy coincidences an arbitrarily established system makes available. To take one of de Man's examples, 'billow' and 'pillow' are arbitrarily related to the thoughts they respectively signify. Both may be felt to carry some strong onomatopoeic force, but that too is subject to arbitrary conventions specific to the English language (the corresponding Spanish words *oleada* and *almohada*, for instance, might be thought even more mimetically suggestive than 'billow' and 'pillow', although they sound nothing like their English counterparts). But that 'billow' and 'pillow' should rhyme— that these two arbitrarily established signs should echo one another phonetically in a way that formalizes their shared reference to softly rounded, swelling shapes in Shelley's passage about an ethereal, dream-like movement over the surface of water—comes as a mysterious gift from the arbitrary resources of language.

To say, as de Man does, that such verbal events are 'generated by random and superficial properties of the signifier rather than by the constraints of meaning' is to obscure the process by which valuable constraints of meaning may be generated by, or discovered within, random

verbal resources. Charles Tomlinson puts it this way in the poem that gave
Donald Wesling the title for his recent study of rhyme:

> The chances of rhyme are like the chances of meeting—
>   In the fording fortuitous, but once found, binding:
> They say, they signify and they succeed, where to succeed
>   Means not success, but a way forward ...[4]

(1–4)

If a poet must fashion 'A subtler language within language', as Cythna
does on the unstable sands of her island prison in *The Revolt of Islam*
(vii.3112), then the poet who takes his chances with rhyme is taking
advantage of a fortunate fortuitousness within the larger arbitrariness of
language itself. Even the most imaginative production of rhyme is a matter
of finding rather than of creating *ex nihilo*. Rhyming poets must arbitrate
among the arbitrary relations of thoughts and sounds a language offers,
knowing that what they find can become (in Dr Johnson's terms)
capriciously or despotically instead of productively binding, a constraint
on rather than a constraint of meaning.

I want to begin to see what Shelley makes of the chances of rhyme
by looking at two poems—one from the very end, the other from the
beginning of his career—in which rhyme operates under contrasting
formal circumstances, and in which the various implications of his
conviction that 'language is arbitrarily produced by the imagination' are
tested in confrontations with modes of power that are themselves
ultimately arbitrary. The chariot in *The Triumph of Life* moves relentlessly
on in 'a cold glare, intenser than the noon / But icy cold' (77–8), 'on the
silent storm / Of its own rushing splendour' (86–7); the great mountain in
Mont Blanc gleams coldly and silently in the distance, with its precipices
which

> Frost and Sun in scorn of mortal power
> Have piled: dome, pyramid, and pinnacle,
> A city of death, distinct with many a tower
> And wall impregnable of beaming ice.
> Yet not a city, but a flood of ruin
> Is there, that from the boundaries of the sky
> Rolls its perpetual stream ...

(103–9)

In both these poems, but in radically different ways, the arbitrary links available through rhyme are crucial to Shelley's articulation of the mind's encounter with a power which acts 'in scorn of mortal power'. If the terza rima of *The Triumph of Life* threatens to impose a despotic or tyrannical arbitrariness of its own with its sequential chain of terminal commitments and obligations (Shelley could not have shared Dante's belief that the number three was the very opposite of arbitrary), then the 'wildly irregular'[5] and unresolved rhyming of *Mont Blanc poses* the opposite threat of impetuous whimsy and mere randomness. In each case, I want to argue, these are calculated stylistic risks, aspects of Shelley's attempt to appropriate and shape the arbitrariness of language into a medium both reflective of and resistant to a power that defies the mind's desire for meaning.

I

First—and not just arbitrarily—*The Triumph of Life*: we began with Paul de Man's question about the status of rhyme in that poem, and end-rhyme functions there according to a more immediately recognizable and conventional pattern than it does in *Mont Blanc*. Reiman has already given scrupulous attention to Shelley's rhymes in *The Triumph of Life*; I want to re-examine and extend his comments with an emphasis on rhyme's relation to the question of the arbitrary.

The Triumph opens with a rhyme sequence that moves with anticipatory suggestiveness:

> Swift as a spirit hastening to his task
>   Of glory and of good, the Sun sprang forth
> Rejoicing in his splendour, and the mask
>
>   Of darkness fell from the awakened Earth.
> The smokeless altars of the mountain snows
>   Flamed above crimson clouds, and at the birth
>
>   Of light, the Ocean's orison arose ...
>
>   (1–7)

The perfect coincidence of 'task' and 'mask' reinforces the promise of the opening simile and accentuates, through a contextually established contrast, the sun's luminous unmasking of the darkened earth. But the imperfect coincidence of 'forth'/'Earth'/'birth' suggests a dissonant counterplot that foreshadows the sun's disturbingly ambiguous status later in the narrator's 'waking dream' (42). This opening sequence establishes a norm for the play of rhyme in the rest of the poem that is alternately tight and loose, exact and approximate. It also confirms John Hollander's point about how important rhyme can be 'in modulating the effects of terminal cuts' at the end of enjambed lines.[6] Five of the poem's first six lines are enjambed, a proportion only slightly greater than that maintained in the rest of the fragment. In this kind of terza rima, rhyme defines a regular structural pattern which is continually threatened with effacement as lines and tercets are denied grammatical closure. The fact that 'mask' answers to 'task' and 'birth' to 'Earth' offsets the unanswered expectations of closure at the end of the first two tercets. The only line which is grammatically closed disrupts, by virtue of that closure, the integrity of the second tercet; it also ends with the first rhyme word in the poem ('Earth') that fails to answer clearly to its predecessor ('forth'). Rhyming such as this suggests a compositional intelligence fully in touch with the arbitrariness of its expressive medium yet capable of shaping that arbitrariness into, as well as according to, precisely provisional 'constraints of meaning'.

The 'compelling rhyme schemes' instanced by de Man all come from the inset discourse of the distorted figure who 'was once Rousseau' (204). This figure comments on the 'mighty phantoms of an elder day' chained to Life's 'triumphal chair' (252–3): Plato, Socrates, Alexander the Great and Aristotle, who

> 'outlived both woes and wars,
> Throned in new thoughts of men, and still had kept
> The jealous keys of truth's eternal doors
>
> 'If Bacon's spirit [   ] had not leapt
> Like lightning out of darkness; he compelled
> The Proteus shape of Nature's as it slept
>
> 'To wake and to unbar the caves that held
> The treasure of the secrets of its reign—
> See the great bards of old who inly quelled
>
> 'The passions which they sung, as by their strain
> May well be known: their living melody
> Tempers its own contagion to the vein

'Of those who are infected with it—I
Have suffered what I wrote, or viler pain!—

'And so my words were seeds of misery—
Even as the deeds of others.'

(266–81)

For Reiman, Shelley's handling of rhyme towards the end of this passage
is uncharacteristically weak: 'The reduplication of the rhyme in lines
273–82 ("reign/strain/vein/pain" and "melody/I/misery/company") marks
the only obvious place where Shelley was unable to compel the unwilling
dross to the likeness of the beauty he imagined.'[7] Perhaps—but if the
dross of language is so unwilling, why would Shelley have made his task of
shaping it unnecessarily difficult by extending rhyme sequences beyond
the normal requirements of terza rima twice in succession? Although the
incomplete revision of these stanzas means that our judgements about
style must be as provisional as the text itself, there is some evidence, at
least in the first of these reduplicative rhyme sequences, that Shelley was
working towards a moment of extreme intensity in Rousseau's account.
The progression from Nature's 'reign' through 'strain' and 'vein' to 'pain'
marks Rousseau's uncertain relationship to the great figures he comments
on. 'Strain' and 'vein' may both be read as puns whose secondary meanings
connect as well as contrast Rousseau's 'pain' with that experienced by 'the
great bards of old'. Unlike Rousseau they 'quelled / The passions which
they sung', but not without a 'strain' akin to his own suffering; the 'vein'
to which their passions were tempered, like his own, pulses physically as
well as figuratively under the pressure of 'contagion' and 'infected'. The
distinction between words and acts denied by Rousseau's powerful internal
rhyme of 'seeds' and 'deeds'[8] has already been partly undermined in the
distended end-rhyme sequence in the preceding tercets.

One is encouraged to see an incipient coherence in the rhyming
relationships of this obviously unfinished passage by the carefully
managed rhyme in the three preceding tercets. Six of the nine rhyme-
words in those tercets are verbs, and they organize themselves into four
verbs of restraint or withholding ('kept'/'slept'/'held'/'quelled') and two
verbs of urgent action ('leapt'/'compelled'). Bacon's liberating effect on
the domination of Aristotelian thought is enacted in the play of 'leapt'
against 'kept' and 'slept', and of 'compelled' against 'held', rhymes so
semantically alert that they may be said to meet (admittedly in an un-
Popeian spirit) Wimsatt's criterion: 'The words of a rhyme, with their

curious harmony of sound and distinction of sense, are an amalgam of the sensory and the logical, or an arrest and precipitation of the logical in sensory form.'[9] Some of these rhyme-words again exert subtle force on their enjambed line-endings:

> 'If Bacon's spirit [   ] had not leapt
>   Like lightning out of darkness ...'

The rhyme-word 'leapt' sparks across the line-break to fuse with its adverbial complement in a bond accentuated by alliteration and rhythmic stress. 'Slept', on the other hand, modulates the effect of its line- and tercet-ending by setting up a conceptually pointed *contre-rejet* in 'To wake and to unbar'.

The other rhyme sequences which, in de Man's view, betray the subjugation of meaning to 'random and superficial properties of the signifier' occur in Rousseau's controversial encounter with the 'shape all light'

> 'And as I looked the bright omnipresence
>   Of morning through the orient cavern flowed,
> And the Sun's image radiantly, intense
>
> 'Burned on the waters of the well that glowed
> Like gold, and threaded all the forest maze
>   With winding paths of emerald fire—there stood
>
> 'Amid the sun, as he amid the blaze
>   Of his own glory, on the vibrating
> Floor of the fountain, paved with flashing rays,
>
> 'A shape all light, which with one hand did fling
> Dew on the earth, as if she were the Dawn
>   Whose invisible rain forever seemed to sing
>
> 'A silver music on the mossy lawn,
>   And still before her on the dusky grass
> Iris her many coloured scarf had drawn.—
>
> 'In her bright hand she bore a chrystal glass
>   Mantling with bright Nepenthe:—the fierce splendour
>   Fell from her as she moved under the mass

'Of the deep cavern, and with palms so tender
   Their tread broke not the mirror of its billow,
Glided along the river, and did bend her

'Head under the dark boughs, till like a willow
Her fair hair swept the bosom of the stream
   That whispered with delight to be their pillow.—'

                                                              (343–66)

This passage provides a revealing opportunity to watch the compositional will at work as it selects and arranges the arbitrary possibilities of rhyme. Notice the accretion of feminine rhyme, which is far more frequent here than in the poem as a whole. Shelley gradually builds towards the two feminine sequences in lines 359–66 by rhyming on unstressed final syllables at line 343 ('omnipresence') and at line 350 ('vibrating'). The accumulated feminine rhymes, together with the repeated enjambment, help initiate and evoke the gliding, sweeping movement of the 'shape all light'. With the possible exception of 'omnipresence', each of these rhymes is semantically pointed and delicately accommodated to the advances of syntax and figuration. This is true of the masculine rhymes as well, although there is one instance where the demands of terza rima might be thought to assert a momentary despotic control. Would the dew flung upon the earth by the 'shape all light' ever have been transformed into 'silver music' without the pressure exerted on Shelley's figurative imagination by the rhyme-word 'sing'? The answer is yes—this extravagant synaesthetic idea is neither a mere product of the exigencies of rhyme nor a capricious freak, but one aspect of 'that double accompaniment of prismatic color [Iris's scarf] and natural music which repeatedly marks the presence of ideal figures in Shelley's poetry'.[10] Dew and the rain to which it is here compared have in fact sung previously in Shelley's poetry, in a line from Act IV of *Prometheus Unbound* where singing is conspicuously not generated by the demands of rhyme. Ione sees the moon riding in a chariot whose wheels of 'solid clouds, azure and gold' (214),

                               as they roll
Over the grass and flowers and waves, wake sounds
Sweet as a singing rain of silver dew ...

                                                              (233–5)

The manuscript of *The Triumph of Life* shows that Shelley did try a rhyme-word other than 'sing' in line 354—but it was 'ring',[11] confirmation that the desire to transmute light and moisture into musical sound was what dominated his arrangement of arbitrary linguistic possibilities into the dazzling progression from 'vibrating' to 'fling' to 'sing'.

'In the fording fortuitous, but once found, binding.' Much of the rhyming in *The Triumph of Life* displays Shelley's ability to find the fortunate within the fortuitous, to build inventively upon what he finds, and thus to bind line to line and tercet to tercet through his own arbitrations of the arbitrary. Some of the poem's rhymes turn out to be binding outside the passage where Shelley, and then the reader, first find them. On nine occasions rhyme groups are repeated and establish bonds between as well as within individual passages. Twice Shelley repeats the same three rhyme words in the same sequence, and as Reiman says about both instances, 'the apparent coincidence, when examined closely, proves to be ... especially fortunate.'[12] Reiman shows in fine detail how 'beneath'/'death'/'breath' in lines 56–61 and 385–90 and 'form'/'storm'/'deform' in lines 83–8 and 463–8 reinforce complexly infolded parallels between the narrator's initial vision of Life's chariot and Rousseau's recollected experience, and thus contribute to the reader's sense that these two phases of the poem are partial re-enactments of each other. The formal and conceptual relationships among the individual members of these two repeated sequences are precisely judged. Phonetically and syllabically, 'beneath' distinguishes itself from and therefore throws into relief that most ironic of rhyming coincidences, 'death'/'breath'. (Shelley uses this set of rhymes three times in Adonais—stanzas II, XII and XX—but never in this sequence. 'Form'/'storm'/'deform', on the other hand, contains an unusual amount of internal phonetic duplication: it begins and ends with what the French call *rime riche*, the repetition of an entire phonetic, syllable including the initial consonant. One problem with such rhymes, at least in English poetry, is that they often lack the coincidental or arbitrary dimension of most rhyme and depend instead on very obvious lexical transformations; they fall flat unless there is some strong conceptual point to justify the predictable phonetic duplication. The progression of 'form' through 'storm' to 'deform' introduces the element of the arbitrary by separating 'form' and 'deform' with a word which only coincidentally echoes them. And both instances of Shelley's sequence make a strong conceptual point, for it is the storm of Life's triumph that is responsible for deforming the natural and imaginative forms of perception—actually in the case of the distorted (183) and crippled (544) Rousseau, potentially in the case of the narrator.

Forgetting, obliteration and erasure are powerful forces in *The Triumph of Life*.[13] But the articulation of these forces depends upon the counterforces of remembering, literation and repetition. We can see how important rhyme is to Shelley's marshalling of these counterforces by looking at two passages from Rousseau's inset narrative which are about forgetting, obliteration, erasure. The first passage is transitional from Rousseau's sleep of forgetfulness to the appearance of the 'shape all light':

> 'I arose and for a space
> The scene of woods and waters seemed to keep.
>
> 'Though it was now broad day, a gentle trace
>   Of light diviner than the common Sun
> Sheds on the common Earth, but all the place
>
>   'Was filled with many sounds woven into one
> Oblivious melody, confusing sense
>   Amid the gliding waves and shadows dun;
>
> 'And as I looked the bright omnipresence
>   Of morning through the orient cavern flowed,
> And the Sun's image radiantly intense
>
>   'Burned on the waters of the well that glowed
> Like gold, and threaded all the forest maze
>   With winding paths of emerald fire ...'
>
>   (335–48)

When some sixty lines later Rousseau remembers drinking from the shape's cup of Nepenthe, rhymed sounds from the earlier passage return to mark the drink's 'oblivious' effect. He

> 'Touched with faint lips the cup she raised,
> And suddenly my brain became as sand
>
>   'Where the first wave had more than half erased
> The track of deer on desert Labrador,
>   Whilst the fierce wolf from which they fled amazed

'Leaves his stamp visibly upon the shore
  Until the second bursts ...'

(404–10)

The image of 'tracks' or traces being 'half erased' suggests what happens here to 'space'/'trace'/'place' as they are half recalled in 'raised'/'erased'/ 'amazed'. 'Amazed' erases nothing of the forest 'maze' but recalls it entirely—and appropriately, since like Ariadne's thread the sun's reflected image had mnemonically 'threaded all the forest maze / With winding paths of emerald fire'. Such repeated and transformed rhymes are part of Shelley's way of tracing the movements of thought out of one maze and into another, through successive waves of forgetting and remembering.

Many recent accounts of *The Triumph of Life* have emphasized how deeply skeptical it is of human achievement, of imaginative vision, of its own artistic status. De Man extends this skepticism to language itself, to the very principle of verbal signification. But in doing so, he recognizes that Shelley's fragment affirms an irreducible power in the arbitrariness of language, without which language would not be able to question its own mode of meaning: 'The positing power of language is both entirely arbitrary in having a strength that cannot be reduced to necessity, and entirely inexorable in that there is no alternative to it.'[14] One of the ways this 'positing power of language' expresses itself in *The Triumph of Life* is through the positioning of rhyme—through a structuring process in which the arbitrating compositional imagination imposes its will on arbitrary but self-structuring possibilities of language.

II

'Before the chariot had begun to climb
  The opposing steep of that mysterious dell,
Behold a wonder worthy of the rhyme

'Of him who from the lowest depths of Hell
Through every Paradise and through all glory
  Love led serene ...'

(469–74)

It is no accident that Shelley should rhyme on the word 'rhyme' in an allusion to Dante, nor was the decision to compose *The Triumph of Life* in terza rima an arbitrary one. But his decision some six years earlier that

Mont Blanc was a wonder worthy of rhyme presents a much more challenging formal situation. Shelley's own note says that *Mont Blanc* 'rests its claim to approbation on an attempt to imitate the untameable wildness and inaccessible solemnity from which [his] feelings sprang'.[15] 'Untameable wildness' and 'inaccessible solemnity', without and within, both suggest that blank verse might have been the appropriate form for this subject. Wordsworth (in *The Prelude*), Coleridge (in the 'Hymn Before Sunrise, in the Vale of Chamouni')—and John Hollander too (in a wonderful parody of Shelley's poem called 'Mount Blank')[16]—all write about Mont Blanc in blank verse. But Shelley's poem, while creating the impression of blank verse with its massive periods and very frequent enjambment, uses rhyme in its 'attempt to imitate' an experience of the untameable and the inaccessible. Why?

The facts about rhyme in *Mont Blanc* are in themselves striking, particularly when measured against what must have been one of Shelley's formal models, Milton's *Lycidas*.[17] Of the 144 lines in *Mont Blanc*, only three end in words which have no rhyme elsewhere in the poem.[18] Three of the 193 lines in *Lycidas* are also unrhymed. There are only fifteen couplets in Shelley's poem, contrasted with thirty-four in Milton's (ten of these contain lines of different length), and six of the fifteen are relatively faint or imperfect. Curiously, however, two of these six imperfect couplets are repeated: 'for ever'/'river' in lines 9–10 are reversed as 'River'/'for ever' in lines 123–4; 'down'/'throne' in lines 16–17 are repeated phonetically though not semantically in 'down'/'over-thrown' in lines 111–12. Even more curiously, there are eleven instances in *Mont Blanc* of words rhyming with themselves (usually over long stretches of verse), and in three of these eleven instances the same word appears in rhyming position not twice but three times.

One of the remarkable features of this extensive rhyming is the degree to which it is disguised or muted by enjambment. In the text Shelley published in 1817, seventy-three of the poem's 144 lines (one more than half) have no punctuation at the end. In *Lycidas*, by contrast, thirty-three of Milton's 193 lines are without terminal punctuation. In the *Defence* Shelley says of the language of Bacon's prose that 'it is a strain which distends, and then bursts the circumference of the hearer's mind, and pours itself forth ... into the universal element with which it has perpetual sympathy' (*PP*, 485). The images Shelley uses about Bacon in this passage all have their parallels in the imagery of *Mont Blanc* (*burst* actually appears twice in the poem, at lines 11 and 18). There is much in the syntax and versification of *Mont Blanc* that invites us to apply these

images—the recurrent Shelleyan pun on 'strain'; the activities of
distending, bursting and pouring—to Shelley's own style. But noticing the
rhymes in *Mont Blanc* makes us think differently about the straining swell
and flow of Shelley's lines. To treat the poem as if it were written in blank
verse is to close our eyes, ears and minds to one of its greatest sources of
poetic power.

There is no precedent for Shelley's crossing of extended blank-verse
enjambment with irregular rhyme in a poem which raises such
fundamental questions about the mind's powers and limitations. That he
should rhyme with pervasive and provocative irregularity while going so
far to create the feeling of blank verse is in keeping with a poem in which
questions simultaneously propose and interrogate, in which the
experience of blankness itself is both acknowledged and challenged.
Considered from this inclusive perspective, rhyme in *Mont Blanc* is one
important way in which Shelley's verbal imagination structures and
shapes, without giving a closed or determinate pattern to, an experience
which defies structuring and shaping. In a more specific sense, the
cognitive play between or among rhyme words shows Shelley taking
advantage of the way in which the very arbitrariness of linguistic signs he
speaks of in the *Defence* can produce an expressive coincidence and thus a
resource for a mind contending, ultimately, with its own and nature's
blankness. There is no prior reason, for example, why 'waves' (2) and
'raves' (11) should rhyme. But they do, and the fact affords Shelley a
distant yet powerful phonetic link that spans and condenses the relation in
this opening verse paragraph between the mad rush of the 'vast river' and
the 'everlasting universe of things' to which it metaphorically
corresponds. As a dimension of poetic form wrought from the mysterious
arbitrariness of language, Shelley's rhyme becomes both a stay against and
a means of marking the chaos and blankness which are *Mont Blanc*'s special
concerns.

In thinking about the purposes rhyme serves in *Mont Blanc*, we need
to look at the way it functions both in terms of its own inherent
possibilities and in relation to the syntax and rhythm of Shelley's periods.
We must be careful not to isolate rhyme as the vehicle of the structuring,
organizing intellect in easy contrast to the sweeping, impetuous emotional
energy of the long, overflowing sentences: both are aspects of Shelley's
'attempt to imitate' an experience in which philosophical skepticism and
impassioned intuition are held in suspension. Take the second couplet in
the opening verse paragraph:

> Where waterfalls around it leap for ever,
> Where woods and winds contend, and a vast river
> Over its rocks ceaselessly bursts and raves.
>
> $\qquad\qquad\qquad\qquad\qquad\qquad\qquad$ (9–11)

'For ever' and 'river' here seem at once to confirm the proposition with which the poem opens—'The everlasting universe of things / Flows through the mind' (1–2)—and yet to convey a certain probing openness, both because the rhyme is partial, imperfect (the imperfection stands out against the initial repetition of 'Where'/'Where'), and because the absence of any pause after 'river' leaves that line open to flow into the next. This couplet is again left open in part IV, where its reversal shifts the emphasis from 'river' to 'for ever' ('all seems eternal now' the speaker has said in line 75, after first taking in the summit of Mont Blanc). The couplet is followed by 'raves' in line 11, by 'waves' in line 125:

> $\qquad\qquad\qquad\qquad$ and one majestic River,
> The breath and blood of distant lands, for ever
> Rolls its loud waters to the ocean waves,
> Breathes its swift vapours to the circling air.
>
> $\qquad\qquad\qquad\qquad\qquad\qquad\qquad$ (123–6)

The last word in this passage, 'air', is part of what is perhaps the most striking group of postponed or suspended rhyme-words in *Mont Blanc*. Part II ends with the word 'there', with no immediate companion or echo: 'till the breast / From which they fled recalls them, thou art there! (47–8). That this line appears to be unrhymed is appropriate in a passage about the momentary, precarious apprehension of 'some faint image' (47) of the awesome, personified Ravine of Arve. But 'there' does eventually get its complement in the insubstantial 'air' at the end of part IV. Once this very distant rhyme has been completed, it is immediately confirmed at the end of the first line of part V: 'Mont Blanc yet gleams on high:—the power is there' (127). This is the only point in the poem where a couplet spans two verse paragraphs (although 'raves' and 'Ravine' between parts I and II, both of which contain anagrams of the name 'Arve', and 'feel' and 'streams' between parts III and IV, may seem to foreshadow such a spanning). Yet to link two separate sections together by rhyme in this way is also to pull the couplet apart: every resolution in *Mont Blanc* has at least an undertow of dissolution. The 'there'/'air'/'there' sequence is extended a few lines later in part V, but this time the sense of the passage cuts across even the tentativeness of those previous assertions that some presence is 'there': 'in the lone glare of day, the snows descend / Upon that Mountain; none beholds them there' (131–2). The internal rhyme in these lines ('glare'/ 'there') illuminates the discrepancy between the mind's power of perception and its limitations in gaining access to reality's ultimate source. The same daylight which renders things visible in the speaker's immediate realm of experience 'glares' upon the snows of Mont Blanc—but 'there', remote and apart from any beholder, daylight itself seems to lose all connection with human intellection.

The 'there' (48) / 'there' (127) / 'there' (132) pattern is Shelley's finest exploitation in *Mont Blanc* of identical rhyme, of a word rhyming (and re-rhyming) with itself. Homonymic rhyme (punning rhyme, *rime très riche*), in which entire rhyme-words are phonetically identical but semantically different, is a related but distinct phenomenon. Hollander assents to the prejudice against such rhyme when he argues that because of 'the crucial relation between the effect of word stress and the quality of rhyme in English ... *rime très riche* is always in a sense, *rime pauvre*.'[19] But the two instances of it in Mont Blanc indicate how alert Shelley could be to the ways in which even flamboyantly fortuitous rhyme could help him mark the mind's response to the wild and the inaccessible. 'Throne' (17) / 'overthrown' (112) is not a pure example (it is analogous phonetically, though not semantically, to 'form'/'deform' in *The Triumph of Life*), but given Shelley's politics it might appear to be a suggestive one. The suggestiveness is not, however, exactly predictable. Although earthly thrones, so often the embodiments for Shelley of 'Large codes of fraud and woe' (81), are implicitly included in what will be 'overthrown' by the 'Power' in part IV as it flows down from its remote abode, that 'Power' has itself been imaged as occupying a 'secret throne'. So 'throne' stands distantly and indirectly in relation to 'overthrown' as subject, not object, a relation in keeping with Shelley's skeptical ambivalence towards the 'Power'. The fact that both 'throne' and 'overthrown' form imperfect couplets with 'down' (16, 111) further complicates the suggestiveness of this rhyme group.

The other homonymic rhyme in *Mont Blanc* affords a purer example of this phenomenon and more telling evidence of Shelley's resourcefulness in handling what would appear to be deliberately restricted verbal possibilities. At the beginning of part II, when he first names the Ravine of Arve as the immediate location of his experience, he addresses the ravine as 'Thou many-coloured, many-voiced vale' (13). Twelve lines later, when the first of these compound adjectives is expanded and particularized, the 'vale' becomes, or is seen to contain, a 'veil':[20]

> Thine earthly rainbows stretched across the sweep
> Of the ethereal waterfall, whose veil
> Robes some unsculptured image ...
>
> (25–7)

'Poetry', Shelley says in the *Defence*, '... arrests the vanishing apparitions which haunt the interlunations of life, and veiling them, or in language or in form, sends them forth among mankind' (*PP*, 505). One is again tempted to follow this line of thought and figuration and apply the images in *Mont Blanc* to the poem itself, to see the 'ethereal waterfall' as a metaphor for the poem's own verbal veiling of what may be accessible only to momentary, vanishing intuition. The 'veil' in these lines, as so often in Shelley, has a double valence—it simultaneously conceals and reveals— and the movement from 'vale' to 'veil' is by no means entirely negative (compare the function of Iris and 'her many coloured scarf' in *The Triumph of Life*, 357). There is a sense in which this aspect of the 'vale' hides the 'unsculptured image' behind it; there is also a sense, partly enforced by the verb 'Robes', that the 'veil' is what makes this unspecified ('some'), uncreated image exist for the mind at all. Shelley's homonymic rhyme signals the precarious balance and interaction between skepticism and visionary imagination so important in this section and throughout the poem.

Rhyme in *Mont Blanc* is not, then, as 'wildly irregular' as it has been thought to be. It is sufficiently irregular to help evoke the 'untameable wildness' Shelley spoke of: some of the most interesting rhymes in the poem are so distant and so muted by distended syntax that the reader may find them as 'remote' and 'inaccessible' as Mont Blanc itself. With the three unrhymed lines Shelley's rhyme remains open, partly unresolved. Yet rhyme is there as one of the resources with which the poet verbally counters as well as encounters an experience of threatening power and sublimity. A glance at Shelley's final question, together with the sentence that precedes it, may help to confirm our sense of why he did not ask about Mont Blanc in blank verse:

> The secret strength of things
> Which governs thought, and to the infinite dome
> Of heaven is as a law, inhabits thee!
> And what were thou, and earth, and stars, and sea,
> If to the human mind's imaginings
> Silence and solitude were vacancy?
>
> (139–44)

At the beginning of the poem, 'things' (1) became Shelley's first rhyme-word by fording its phonetic complement in 'secret springs' (4), a phrase which appears prominently and characteristically in the opening section of Hume's *Enquiry Concerning Human Understanding* as a metaphor for the unknowable first principle 'by which the human mind is actuated in its operations'.[21] Here at the end of *Mont Blanc*, 'things' fords a rhyme with a different, apparently less skeptical resonance in 'imaginings', although the difference diminishes when one takes in the immediate context of those words: the 'secret strength of things' in line 139; the if-clause and interrogative syntax surrounding 'the human mind's imaginings'. 'Thee' in line 140 forms a couplet with 'sea' and thus supports the initial 'And' through which the final question is joined logically to what precedes it. And does 'vacancy' belong in this rhyming sequence with 'thee' and 'sea'? It both does and does not: the '–cy' suffix rhymes with 'thee' and 'sea', but imperfectly, because it is rhythmically unstressed and because it is attached to the root *vacan(s)*. Shelley simultaneously draws that critical last word into and separates it from the central rhyme of the entire passage—'vacancy' seems both to yield to and to resist the rhyming power of the compositional will—and in the process he makes us conscious of the ambiguous categorizations on which rhyme depends in the first place.

The rhymes of *Mont Blanc* are part of Shelley's response to a landscape and to a philosophical tradition—'to the Arve's commotion, / A loud, lone sound no other sound can tame' (31–2), and to Hume's argument that the 'ultimate springs and principles' of phenomenal reality 'are totally shut up from human curiosity and enquiry', that the mind's attempts to make sense of them as necessity are nothing more than arbitrary impositions:

> every effect is a distinct event from its cause. It could not, therefore, be discovered in the cause, and the first invention or conception of it, *a priori*, must be entirely arbitrary. And even after it is suggested, the conjunction of it with the cause must appear equally arbitrary.[22]
>
> (*An Enquiry Concerning Human Understanding*, IV.1)

Shelley's irregular rhymes do not tame the wildness of a 'sound no other sound can tame', nor can they break the inaccessible silence at the summit of Mont Blanc. But they impose on his and our experience of both an order of language that accepts the arbitrary and submits it to the deliberations of art. They are part of the evidence the poem offers that the arbitrary connections of thought and language need not leave the 'human mind's imaginings' in vacancy.

NOTES

1. 'Shelley disfigured', *Deconstruction and Criticism*, New York, Seabury Press, 1979, 60.

2. ibid., 62.

3. See Harold Whitehall, 'From linguistics to poetry', *Sound and Poetry*, ed. Northrop Frye, New York, Columbia University Press, 1957, 139: 'Rhyme is in a sense the most mysterious of all sound patterns.'

4. Quoted from 'The Chances of Rhyme' in *Selected Poems, 1951–1974*, Oxford, Oxford University Press, 1978. Cf. Cynthia Chase's brief comment on 'les hasards de la rime' in Baudelaire's 'Le Soleil', 'Reading Hegel with Baudelaire', *SIR*, 22, 1983, 260–1.

5. The phrase is Earl Wasserman's, *Shelley: A Critical Reading*, Baltimore, The Johns Hopkins University Press, 1971, 234.

6. *Vision and Resonance: Two Senses of Poetic Form*, New York, Oxford University Press, 1975, 108–10.

7. *Shelley's 'The Triumph of Life': A Critical Study*, Urbana, University of Illinois Press, 1965, 96.

8. See de Man, 'Shelley disfigured', 47–9.

9. 'One relation of rhyme to reason', *The Verbal Icon*, Lexington, University of Kentucky Press, 1954, 165. Cf. Hugh Kenner, 'Pope's reasonable rhymes', *ELH*, 41, 1974, 74–88, especially Kenner's opening remarks on 'a suspicion that the poet of rhyme is playing with fire, flirting with triviality and unworthy coincidence', and his suggestion that the 'problem with such effects [of rhyme] seems to inhere in their look of randomness' (74).

10. Glenn O'Malley, *Shelley and Synesthesia*, Evanston, Northwestern University Press, 1964, 82.

11. Reiman, *Shelley's 'The Triumph of Life'*, 185.

12. ibid., 95.

13. See de Man, 'Shelley disfigured', 50–1 and passim.

14. ibid., 62–3.

15. Shelley's note appears at the end of the Preface to *History of a Six Weeks' Tour through a Part of France, Switzerland, Germany, and Holland*, London, T. Hookham Jr, C. and J. Ollier, 1817.

16. The poem is in *Tales Told of the Fathers*, New York, Atheneum, 1975.

17. See Judith Chernaik, *The Lyrics of Shelley*, Cleveland, Case Western Reserve University Press, 1972, 288 n.4. She points out that the rhymes in the Bodleian MS. of *Mont Blanc* are more regularly interwoven than those of the 1817 printed text and suggests that 'Shelley may have been consciously striving in 1817

for the more irregular rhyme effects of *Lycidas*.' I refer here to the text of *Lycidas* in the *Complete Poems and Major Prose*, ed. Merritt Y. Hughes, New York, Odyssey, 1957. For excellent accounts of Milton's rhyming in *Lycidas*, see Ants Oras, 'Milton's early rhyme schemes and the structure of *Lycidas*', *MP*, 52, 1954–5, 12–22, and Joseph A. Wittreich Jr, 'Milton's "Destin'd urn": the art of *Lycidas*', *PMLA*, 84, 1968, 60–70. Wittreich's analysis is particularly relevant to Shelley's rhyming in *Mont Blanc*, since he argues that Milton's 'encompassing scheme' is not confined to patterns within individual verse paragraphs but 'envelops the poem and its various parts in a massive unity' (61). *Lycidas* is listed among the poems read by Shelley and Mary Shelley in 1815, the year before *Mont Blanc* was written (*Mary Shelley's Journal*, 48).

18. The unrhymed words in *Mont Blanc* are 'forms' (62), 'spread' (65) and 'sun' (133). Neville Rogers, *The Complete Poetical Works of Percy Bysshe Shelley*, Oxford, Clarendon Press, 1975, II, 355, says that Locock also counted 'sky' (108) and 'world' (113) as rhymeless. But if we look at the poem as a whole, 'sky' (108) repeats 'sky' at the end of line 60 and rhymes with 'lie' (19, 54), 'by' (45) and 'high' (52, 70); 'world' (113) repeats 'world' at the end of line 49 and rhymes with 'unfurled' (53). *Lycidas* had traditionally been analyzed paragraph by paragraph, in which case there appear to be ten unrhymed lines. But looking at the total rhyme pattern of the poem as Wittreich does yields only three; see 'Art of *Lycidas*', 63, 69–70.

19. *Vision and Resonance*, 118. See Derek Attridge on the different functions of rhyme in English and French verse in 'Dryden's dilemma, or, Racine refashioned: the problem of the English dramatic couplet', *YES*, 9, 1979, 62–5.

20. Cf. David Simpson, *Irony and Authority in Romantic Poetry*, Totowa, N.J., Rowan & Littlefield, 1979, 233, n.15.

21. Ed L.A. Selby-Bigge, rev. P.H. Nidditch, Oxford, Clarendon Press, 1975, 14. See also 30, 33, 42, 66. 'Secret springs' receives additional emphasis by forming the poem's first couplet with 'brings' in line 5. If this phrase is a Humean allusion, it developed late in Shelley's revisions; he wrote 'secret caves' both in the Bodleian draft and in the recently discovered fair copy. See Chernaik, *The Lyrics of Shelley*, 288, and Judith Chernaik and Timothy Burnett, 'The Byron and Shelley notebooks in the Scrope Davies find', *RES*, n.s. 29, 1978, 45–9.

22. Ed. Selby-Bigge, 30.

FREDERICK L. BEATY

The Narrator as Satiric Device
in *Don Juan*

Early readers of *Don Juan* were at considerable disadvantage in having neither the Dedication nor the prose Preface to Cantos I and II, for in those two introductions the poet initially develops his satiric persona in the tradition of the *vir bonus* who sees the truth and is not afraid to express it. The Preface, cast in the form of a critical parody of Wordsworth's introduction to "The Thorn," is more than just a diatribe against Wordsworth and Southey. It is also an invocation of what Byron considered Dr. Johnson's common-sense approach to the illusions of literary fiction. Johnson, who in the Preface to his edition of Shakespeare (1765) defended the dramatist's neglect of temporal and locational unities, had argued that anyone who mistakes dramatic illusion for reality "may imagine more" and indeed must be considered "above the reach of reason or of truth."[1] In a parallel argument Byron maintains that anyone who can suppose Wordsworth's tale of an unnatural mother and her natural child to have been recounted by a retired sea captain "is requested to suppose by a like exertion of Imagination that the following epic Narrative is told by a Spanish Gentleman in a village in the Sierra Morena."

Certainly McGann is correct in asserting that this Preface initiates an "attack upon the Romantic exaltation of imagination as a divine poetic faculty," for as Byron conceived it, poetic imagining is not a reliable way of creating "truth" but rather a means of analyzing the world that

From *Byron the Satirist*. © 1985 by Northern Illinois University Press.

literature ought to represent.[2] Hence the Preface mocks the creative imagination as essentially deceptive and, moreover, ridicules those so gullible as to believe, through willing suspension of their rational powers, that the ravings and absurdities in "The Thorn" can be attributed to Wordsworth's prosaic narrator. Such people, Byron implies, want to be hoodwinked into believing that an imaginative fiction is preferable to reality. Byron therefore invites them to indulge their imaginations even further—to make fanciful conjectures not only about his narrator's identity but also about a hypothetical English editor who, because he has good reason to detest the laureate, has interpolated the attacks on that "Pantisocratic apostle of Apostasy."

Having recently read the *Biographia Literaria*, Byron was aware of Coleridge's opinion that "The Thorn" had failed as a ventriloquistic experiment because the "dull and garrulous discourser" could not avoid producing a stultifying effect (Chapter XVII). To avoid that pitfall Byron was presumably determined to create a stimulating narrator with whom his intellectually responsible readers might identify—a level-headed, practical man of the world who would render criticism with the incisiveness and conviction of Dr. Johnson. In conjunction with the Preface, the Dedication was designed to establish Byron's persona as a rational, humorous, just, and humane sophisticate in the Augustan poetic tradition. He is the honest realist who loathes the drivel of Wordsworth, the obfuscating metaphysics of Coleridge, the sterile inanity of Southey, the political tergiversation of all the Lakers, the tyranny of Castlereagh, and the inherent pettiness of all who lack truly commendable poetical and political principles. Nor is it difficult to deduce the persona's positive values from what he vehemently deplores.

Partly by means of style, as George M. Ridenour and McGann have shown, Byron relates his Dedication to the classical theory of rhetorical styles.[3] Byron's knowledge of classical critics may not have been comprehensive enough to make him a staunch adherent of what Longinus, Quintilian, and Cicero had postulated about the high, middle, and plain styles. Even so, Byron was well versed in classical literature and was such a devoted student of Pope that he assimilated much of his mentor's stylistic practice. In the Dedication to *Don Juan* the narrator's assertion that he is "wandering with pedestrian Muses" (st. 8) certainly invokes the tradition of Horatian satire; the allusion to Horace's *saturis Musaque pedestri* ("in the satires of my pedestrian muse"—II.6.17) conjures up the image of good-humored raillery, unpretentious realism, and gentlemanly causerie that the more urbane neoclassicists tried to emulate. The offhand manner and colloquial language that Byron's narrator affects are usually in the rhetorical plain style of Horatian satire, recalling Horace's assertions that his verses were, except for meter, more like conversational prose than generally accepted poetry (Satire I.4.38–65). Yet that self-effacing humility does not prohibit Byron from rising to the tone of solemn Old Testament prophecy or the epic grandeur of Juvenalian satire as occasion demands. Hence, for example, Byron employs the appropriate high style when holding up Milton as a desirable model, in contradistinction to the Lakers. In Milton he finds a magnanimous, Promethean man who, because of his political and poetical integrity, was able to create sublime poetry. By contrast to Milton, the provincial Lakers are made to look doubly ridiculous, for their pretensions to soaring "on the winged steed" entail an imaginative flight that is nothing more than a fraudulent escape from reality. And when opposed to Milton's liberalism, Castlereagh's oppressiveness (seen as the perverted cerebral lust of a eunuch) is doubly reprehensible and deserves a style reminiscent of Juvenalian fulmination. After these bitter denunciations in the Dedication, the narrator's assertion that his effusions are "in honest simple verse" contributes an irony surpassing even that which Horace's ingratiating persona casts over his subtle jibes.

Yet the diversity of the narrator's styles deserves to be seen as more than Byron's amalgamated inheritance from the Roman satiric tradition. As A.B. England has observed, the two varieties of verbal structure employed in *Don Juan* can also be traced to two varieties of English satire that flourished in the late seventeenth and early eighteenth centuries. Those passages in which Byron has subjected his material to a formality of language and rhetorical thought—that is, those approximating the lofty Augustan manner of Pope—imply a world order that the poem as a whole does not reflect. The more frequent verbal structure in *Don Juan*, as England has shown, is characterized by a burlesque, almost Hudibrastic, style—one marked by "a high degree of tolerance for disorder, impurity, and discontinuity of rhetoric and diction."[4]

It needs to be pointed out, moreover, that this vacillation, to which many critics have demurred, is an appropriate reflection of the narrator's perspective. And the ottava rima, which allows the poet to build up tensions and then destroy them, is ideally suited to convey this pattern. Man, Byron implies, superimposes a temporary order on his chaotic world, only to find in time that the order has been shattered and that he must set about fashioning a new one. Thus the process from chaos to order to chaos is endless, as each newly imposed order is subject to critical analysis that, by exposing its flaws, effects its collapse. As part of this ineluctable paradigm of nature, man is obliged to resign himself to the comic absurdity of recurrent shambles until he can devise a new construct.

The mask Byron employs for his narrator is in keeping with the tradition of satirists who want their speakers to be part of the scene and yet sufficiently independent of it to be objective. Attempts to detach *Don Juan*'s narrator from its poet have not proved utterly successful because the former is neither a purely fictitious character nor a wholly separable mask but rather a calculated embodiment of selective Byronic features that the poet wished to project. Though as *Don Juan* proceeds the distinction between mask and poet tends increasingly to disappear, Byron tries early in the poem to distance himself from the persona just as he had previously detached himself from the title character in *Childe Harold I*. The narrator's claim that he is "a plain man, and in a single station" (I.22.6) is biographically as inaccurate as his assertion that he "never married" (I.53.7). In the traditional pose of the satirist, he calls himself a "moderate-minded bard" who is quite content with just "a little love"; and unlike voluptuaries, he is satisfied with tried and true pleasures (I.118). Thus he advertises himself as a generally conservative, honest man with middle-of-the-road views. To make the narrator appear to be part of the cast of characters, Byron at the beginning places him amidst the scene of action in Seville, thereby adding conviction to his on-the-spot reporting. Though he boasts not only of having unusual insight into character but also of knowing Don Jose well (I.51.3–4), he seems somewhat obtuse in failing to understand why his well-intentioned interference should be unappreciated. Indeed his meddling in the affairs of Jose and Inez is rewarded, when Juan inadvertently empties "housemaid's water" on the busybody's head (I.24), with ironic justice.

In other instances, however, the narrator is clearly meant to be an alter ego of Byron himself. When, for example, the narrator claims to be a superannuated, thirty-year-old man whose life is over (except, of course, for vicarious enjoyment), he expresses an idea often uttered, though rarely adhered to, by Byron. In fact, the narrator's aging from thirty to thirty-five is perfectly synchronized with the poet's (I.213; XII.2). Certainly the narrator represents his creator when he admits to having been "bred a moderate Presbyterian" (XV.91.8) and to being "half a Scot by birth" (X.17.7). When he concedes that he might have chosen Piccadilly as the site of London scandal but has reasons for leaving "that pure sanctuary alone" (XIII.27), there can be no question that the poet *in propria persona* is referring to his own marital residence. Even more compelling is the unequivocal identification of the narrator with Byron when the former describes himself as "the grand Napoleon of the realms of rhyme" and specifically names some of his works (XI.55–56).

Yet one must realize that the narrator is not Byron's only mask in the poem. From time to time other characters such as Don Juan, Don Jose, and John Johnson express their creator's partial views on reality, and the author's voice encompasses all of them. The dynamic thrust of the poem results primarily from an unresolvable dialectic in which the romantic Juan, who expresses Byron's sentiments more through actions than reflective thoughts, is ironically played off against the worldly narrator. Anne K. Mellor, in her analysis of the opposition between the naïve Juan and the skeptical, cynical narrator, has noted that as the poem proceeds their antithetical views temper one another. As Juan grows older and more worldly through experience, he assumes more of the narrator's perspective despite his perennially "virgin face" (XVII.13.8). As the narrator, reliving his own life through Juan and recollections of past experience, is forced to reevaluate the world, he becomes increasingly aware of the self-imposed limitations of his own blase detachment. The "constant alternation between these widely divergent characters or modes of consciousness," Mellor states, "is itself an analogue for the process of human growth, or self-creation and self-transcendence."[5]

Not only do the narrator's opinions change with the passage of time; at a given moment his views may stand in ironic opposition to one another. The effect of such apparent contradiction upon the reader is twofold. First, he realizes that he cannot wholeheartedly believe whatever the narrator says; and on a more sophisticated level, he also becomes aware that life's problems, as seen from different stances, are incapable of clear-cut, facile solutions. The narrator's cynical comments on the love of Juan and Haidée, for example, may offend the reader who would prefer to empathize with the idyllic lovers. Yet it is the narrator who also conveys the highly romantic depiction of the lovers. Hence the reader must ultimately concede that each of the antithetical viewpoints, far from negating the other, contains partial elements of "truth" and that neither presents the whole picture. Unresolved ironies are the narrator's prime rhetorical means of compelling the reader to see reality from different perspectives and to acknowledge that conflicting ideas are tenable within a larger framework.

What especially endears Byron's jaunty narrator to his readers is that, like Horace, he is willing in his self-analysis to point out his own foibles, thereby strengthening his ties to fallible humanity. As Hazlitt described this propensity in *Don Juan*, "You laugh and are surprised that any one should turn round and *travestie* himself."[6] Only a poet with supreme self-assurance would dare assert that his second canto might suffer the fate of bad poetry in being used to line portmanteaus (II.16.6–8). And in acknowledging that the reader has recently been patient with him, he admits to having been as verbose as an auctioneer (XIII.74.1–4). In its simplest, most direct form such satire assumes the guise of winning self-deprecation ordinarily associated with Socratic irony. The narrator becomes mockingly melodramatic when lamenting that at thirty, with gray hair and squandered heart, he is not what he was in youth; hence his need to take up with "a good old-gentlemanly vice" such as avarice (I.212–16). Furthermore, the foppish outlook he sometimes assumes virtually requires him to poke fun at his own snobbish, self-indulgent tastes, thereby becoming the butt of his own disdain. Yet one senses that he does not completely undermine his posturing but rather reveals its shortcomings. Closely related to such self-parody is his artistic diffidence, manifested through self-conscious commentary on his methodology. When he remarks on the difficulties of selecting a hero or a rhyme, his self-consciousness undermines the superiority to which an artist ordinarily pretends in his final redaction. Admittedly, there may be partial truth in his assertion that "this last simile is trite and stupid" (I.55.8); yet if the narrator (or Byron) had fully believed that, the simile would have been canceled. The poem often conveys the sense of developing casually as it progresses, thus giving rise to Hazlitt's assertion that *Don Juan* is "a poem written about itself."[7] The poet, by allowing his semi-conscious thoughts to rise to the surface, often gives us insight into his own mental processes as he creates, revises, or de-creates.

One of the favorite forms of self-satire in *Don Juan* is that which undermines through contradiction, showing the discrepancy between good intention and actual behavior. This inconsistency indicates not a "seeming myriad of speakers," as Marshall suggested,[8] but a human tendency to vacillate—the *mobilité* to which we are all subject. Though the narrator claims to loathe "that low vice curiosity" (I.23.5), his interest in salacious gossip makes it clear that he is always ready to pry into others' affairs. Similarly, his praise of constancy as a virtue is overthrown at a masquerade by his own wandering fancies, which he ultimately justifies as the pattern of natural change (II.209–14). In a very human way he resolves every spring to reform, but unfortunately his "vestal vow takes wing," leaving him once more to be "reclaim'd" (I.119). Even while affirming that description is his forte, he declares he will not describe and then proceeds to do so (V.52.1); and later he insists: "I won't describe ... I won't reflect, ... I *won't* philosophize, and *will* be read" (X.28). His earlier assertion that "The regularity of [his] design / Forbids all wandering as the worst of sinning" (I.7.3–4) forms the ironic background for his constant digressions, on which he also comments disparagingly (III.96; XIII.12.1; XV.4.5). Yet these digressions, like learning through experience in the external world, are clearly a way of exploring the inner being through suppositions or the free play of associations; they therefore become a means to greater perception. Ultimately he defends even contradictions on the relativistic grounds that there is no absolute truth upon which all humanity can agree but only different perspectives on it (XV.87–90). As a philosophical skeptic, he must conclude that, like everyone else of intellectual integrity, he knows nothing of which he can be certain (XIV.3.1–4). Honest doubt he addresses as "sole Prism / Of the Truth's rays" (XI.2.6–7). Consequently he builds up a succession of ironies based on the tension of apparent contradictions. In time his dialectic crumbles, only to reestablish itself in a new paradox that follows the same progression. To facilitate expression of such fluctuating views, Byron uses the ottava rima with even more versatility than in *Beppo*. Nowhere is its adaptability better suited than as the medium for such a variety of thoughts constantly being recombined and reshaped in new and unexpected ways.

The flexible poetic form also allows the poet to adroitly modulate the persona's involvement in the narrative in accord with artistic need. Especially in the later cantos there are moments when the narrator assumes a casual, self-assured detachment, boasting a Mephistophelean pose, declaring, "I am but a mere spectator" (XIII.7.6), and absolving himself of any responsibility. He claims to "perch upon an humbler promontory" than that of the great philosophers, casting his eye upon whatever suits his story, never straining at versification, but merely rattling on loquaciously like an improviser (XV.19–22). Occasionally, like most satirists, he fancies himself more sinned against than sinning. Although by his own proclamation he is the mildest, meekest, most forgiving man, he is attacked by those who unjustifiably hate him (IX.21). Yet despite his evident annoyance, he aspires to calm self-sufficiency:

> I say, in my slight way I may proceed
>   To play upon the surface of Humanity.
> I write the world, nor care if the world read,

> At least for this I cannot spare its vanity.
> My Muse hath bred, and still perhaps may breed
>   More foes by this same scroll: when I began it,
> I Thought that it might turn out so—*now I know* it,
> But still I am, or was, a pretty poet. (XV.60)

This judicious distancing contributes to the vaunted control exerted by the poet over his narrator, and also by the narrator over his material. Throughout the poem it is the narrator's voice, however changeable, that serves as the chief organizational principle. Repeatedly the narrator utters something such as: "Here I must leave him, for I grow pathetic" (IV.52.1) to show how he completely manipulates his characters, withdrawing from them when their suffering or delight moves him excessively. He even admits to being a puppet master who controls Juan to suit his chaste publisher's whims (IV.97). Thus the poet, positioning himself at the best vantage point for whatever he wishes to communicate, makes his presence felt behind as well as within his story.

Much of the satire is handled with such a light touch that it is almost indistinguishable from comedy, and even when the subject matter is serious, it is often treated in a superficially flippant manner. Yet I cannot agree with Marshall's view that the poem is not satire at all because it provides "no suggestion of the ideal" or that "Don Juan should be regarded as a vast literary joke."[9] The narrator, even while conceding that the world will think him immoral, repeatedly insists that his object is morality (XII.39.2–3; XII.55.4; XII.86.3). In the opening canto he defiantly challenges anyone to assert "that this is not a moral tale, though gay" (I.207), and his protestations become more resolute as the poem continues. He certainly declares a sanative purpose—to do as much through poetry as Newton did to restore fallen man through knowledge (X.1–3). But he believes in achieving that goal by first showing what is wrong, introducing varied topics

>   as subservient to a moral use;
>   Because my business is to *dress* society,
>   And stuff with sage that very verdant goose. (XV.93)

His method is "to show things really as the are, / Not as they ought to be" (XII.40.1–3). In an implied statement of the satirist's positive goal, he asserts that since "gentle readers" have a propensity to close their eyes to what they do not wish to see, it is his moral obligation to open their eyes to reality

(VI.88.1–5). And this passage, significantly, occurs in the canto with which Byron, after having been persuaded to abandon Don Juan, resumed the poem with self-confident vigor. No doubt he exaggerates when he advertises that his fifth canto has "a moral to each error tacked" and when, with one eye upon the Horatian dictum, he asserts it is "formed rather for instructing than delighting" (V.2.4–6). But being deadly solemn, as pious critics would have him be, is not his characteristic approach to the world's evil.

When Madame de Staël accused Byron of abetting immorality, he replied, according to Lady Blessington's account, that he had "sometimes represented vice under alluring forms, but so it was generally in the world, therefore it was necessary to paint it so."[10] Moreover, in his own defense Byron told de Staël that, unlike her, he had never depicted virtue in the guise of dullness or shown vice to be productive of happiness. The narrator in *Don Juan* defends his candor by claiming that his muse is "the most sincere that ever dealt in fiction"; she "treats all things, and ne'er retreats / From any thing" (XVI.2–3). Yet, he insists, she never hurts anyone; her "worst reproof's a smile" (XI.63). To the charge of belittling the value of human life, he answers that his views are no more nihilistic than the pronouncements of many famous moralists (VII.3–6). If he laughs at life, he does so only to check his emotional involvement in the world's sorrows (IV.4.1–2).

Throughout the poem Byron's narrator declares that his determination to effect social reform is not only responsible but heroic since his role as satiric gadfly inevitably provokes antagonism. To bolster his righteous honesty against all detractors, he assumes, in the tradition of the Earl of Shaftesbury, that ridicule is the test of truth; in his opinion, the underlying objection lodged against the first two cantos was that they contained "too much truth" (IV.97.3–4). Unlike his "epic brethren gone before" (I.202), the poet refuses to deal in fabulation. The obligation "of a true poet," he insists, is "to escape from fiction" and present the unvarnished realities of our world (VIII.86,89). The narrator holds up *Don Quixote* as the prototype of the "real Epic" (XIII.8–11), even while lamenting nostalgically that, "Of all tales ... the saddest," it shattered the romantic illusions of chivalry. Accordingly, the descriptions in *Don Juan* are advertised as not only "accurate" but "Epic, if plain truth should prove no bar" (VIII.138.4–5). The narrator claims inspiration not from the mendacious patroness of romance but from the "true Muse" (VIII.1.5). In a similar vein Byron told Lady Blessington, "I always write best when truth inspires me, and my satires, which are founded on truth, have more spirit than all my other productions, for they were written *con amore*."[11]

Since the desired truth, as the narrator interprets it, is tested not by those nebulous assumptions according to which most people live but by concrete reality, he usually identifies it with "fact" (VII.81.2). After completing the first five cantos, Byron wrote Murray: "Almost all Don Juan is *real* life—either my own—or from people I knew" (*BLJ*, VIII, 186). Yet to substantiate claims to veracity, the narrator capriciously refers those who remain incredulous "To history, tradition, and to facts, / To newspapers, whose truth all know and feel, / To plays in five, and operas in three acts" (I.203.1–4). Because those sources are notoriously unreliable, he thereby undermines his own credibility, in effect admitting that his art strives for only an approximation to empirical data. Although he calls himself a "philosopher" (VI.22.1) and a man "fond of true philosophy" (I.220), he means something quite different from what those terms ordinarily imply. His demeaning of Platonism, Stoicism, and Berkeleyan idealism constitutes a conspicuous thrust against systematized philosophy. And when he himself becomes too speculative, relapsing into the insoluble labyrinth of metaphysics, he tries to regain a solid physical basis or even dismisses the subject (I.133–34; VI.22). What he endeavors to be is a friendly sage, like Horace, offering practical, experiential wisdom that will improve human behavior by encouraging man to confront his own nature without illusion. He feels obliged to deal in applicable realities in order to strip the sham from theoretical philosophy, fanciful criticism, and pretenses about motivation.

Yet even the narrator, impelled as he is by the desire to please, sometimes cloaks his true feelings with avowals of good intentions. When the progress of Julia's love leads to adultery, he protests: "And then—God knows what next—I can't go on; / I'm almost sorry that I e'er begun" (I.115.7–8). To make the lubricious tolerable in polite society, he repeatedly proclaims an unwillingness to offend the refined reader. In so doing he reveals that the raw, animalistic impulses of humanity that civilization pretends to have subdued lurk just beneath the surface, waiting to be called forth. The moment he piously announces, after having already divulged highly derogatory information about his characters, that scandal is his aversion and that he detests "all evil speaking, even in jest" (I.51.7–8), the reader is alerted to the blatant discrepancy between assertion and actuality. And since the assumption underlying the narrator's belated self-righteous declarations is that in cultivated society one needs only to affirm his rectitude in order to be exonerated, Byron pokes fun at both the culture that encourages such hypocrisy and the individual who undermines his own integrity to gain social acceptance.

At other times the narrator resorts to clever subterfuge, detours, and double-entendres to circumvent the social barriers to plain speaking. If a suppressed feral nature obtrudes on his civility, he strives, in feline fashion, to cover up the ground as rapidly as he has manured it. After slyly hinting at the intimacy of Inez and Alfonso, he feebly tries to discredit such "lies" by attributing their origin to malicious fabrication (I.66). Sometimes he uses a seemingly innocent word that means something quite different to the worldly wise (e.g., *Phrygian* in the double sense in which Virgil used it), or he coins words like *Cazzani* and *Philo-genitiveness* to cloak his obscenity in esoteric drapery. Nor does the narrator have qualms about affecting a coy refinement, as when he relates that Julia, seeking revenge, denied her husband "several little things he wanted" (I.180.4). At other times his genteel vulgarity dissipates his love of specific detail into vague generality, as when he declares that the harem wondered why Gulbeyaz would buy an odalisque who might then share "her throne and power and every thing beside" (VI.36.8). No matter how risqué the underlying idea may be, he feels compelled in the fashion of a Regency Mr. Spectator to temper wit with veneered morality.

One of the narrator's shrewdest ploys is his asserted withholding of information that might have been brought forth, for when he pretends to gloss over the unspeakable, the reader inevitably assumes the worst. Exactly where or how Juan was concealed in Julia's bed or what happened to Juan and the Ghost at Norman Abbey the narrator positively declines to tell, and his refusal confirms our worst suspicions. As an amiable gossip the narrator is unrivaled in literature because his ruse of staunchly refusing to speculate without verifiable evidence makes his rhetoric overwhelming. Nothing is more convincing than his claim to be withholding information in the interest of fairness: "For my part I say nothing—nothing—but / *This* I will say—my reasons are my own" (I.52.1–2). A man whose conscience virtually forces him to continue, against the superficial rules of etiquette, must, one assumes, be driven by the desire to see justice prevail. From his vast stockpile of possible information the usually omniscient narrator can single out those details which point in the direction of his innuendoes and lead his readers down the path his selectivity has predicated. Through this system of eating his cake and having it too, the narrator unmistakably conveys the reality without ever having expressed it. Sometimes to avoid unsettling his gentler readers he prefers not to complete statements such as his recollections of college life: "For there one learns—'tis not for me to boast, / Though I acquired—but I pass over *that*" (I.53.1–2). Or he tantalizes us by catching himself short: "I say no more—I've said too much" (XVI.77.2). Yet he knows that no perspicacious reader will take such disclaimers seriously. They are all part of the narrator's psychological technique, especially at a crucial moment, for heightening suspense and titillating the reader into demanding more.

It is when the narrator becomes most Olympian that his satire is most devastating, and this lofty condescension, which Hazlitt attributed to Byron's alleged spite and pride, has periodically offended some readers. There are times, to be sure, when the narrator, through the use of substandard language ("And now, my Epic Renegade! what are ye at?"— Dedication 1.5) or a sweeping condemnation of Wordsworth's style as his "aversion," appears to dismiss people and matters as though they were undeserving of consideration. And the obliteration of lawyer Brougham's identity through the assimilation of his name into a pun ("A legal broom's a moral chimney-sweeper"—X.15.1) is accompanied by an equally patronizing tone. Partisan critics ("Praetorian bands") who attempt to set up their candidates for poetical emperor receive the most contemptuous dismissal, for regarding them the narrator contends: "It is hardly worth my while / With such small gear to give myself concern" (XI.62.1–63.3). James R. Sutherland, who regarded Byron's "off-hand, contemptuous manner" as "the new note in English satire," observed: "We can put up with denunciation, for then we are at least being taken seriously; but to be dismissed as a sort of dull joke is highly insulting."[12] Inevitably this technique of brushing aside contemporaries as though they counted for nought proved stinging, even among those who should have recognized that anything truly beneath contempt deserved no comment.

Some of the narrator's oblique declarations of truth are achieved, paradoxically, through outright lying. Certainly no one who had actually bribed the editor of a contemporary review (not even his grandmother's) would advertise his malfeasance (I.209–10). His declaration that he has already bought "public approbation" could have come only from someone completely confident that his indirect attack on William Roberts of the *British Review* and the toadying habits of some writers would be seen as a complete hoax. Nor would many readers be misled by his feigned naïveté in claiming not to know why Lady Adeline takes such extraordinary interest in Juan, or by his more blatant pretense of ignorance about what houris of the Moslem heaven want to do with the young Khan. Sometimes the narrator indulges in specious reasoning so irrational for a man of sense that the reader is actually expected to conclude the opposite. When lust is attributed to the sun and the greater degree of propriety found in "nations of the moral north" is therefore connected with their inhibiting cold, the reader is supposed to understand that this facetious logician cannot possibly hold the premises on which he grounds his arguments. He fully intends his readers to see through such mendacity and tacitly acknowledge that small talk is often nothing more than polite lying.

Had the narrator not already established his character, according to the rules of social etiquette, as an essentially reliable critic of all he surveys, his occasional deceptions might ruin his credibility. One of Byron's supreme achievements as a satirist—one that points beyond the eighteenth-century mode to that flourishing today—is his creation of a complex narrator whose relationship to both reader and subject matter cannot be taken wholly at face value since it is ironic and frequently shifting. Though his complicated, intriguing personality is stained with the social corruption he derides, nevertheless his compassion for the fallen world compels the reader to identify with both the satirist and the satiric targets. Never does the narrator assume, except in jest, an impeccably moral attitude that might erect psychological barriers between reader and satiric object. Far from alienating his readers, his implicit awareness that to be human is to be flawed compels the reader to reexamine the degree to which each individual, through hypocrisy, contributes to the world's corruption. Never as a solemn preacher or a cynical scoffer but rather as a sophisticated observer, he lives among us, implying the ideals he intends but seldom stating them, instead leaving them for the reader to infer. Though his effusions rarely produce the "honest simple verse" to which he modestly pretends in the Dedication, it is hard not to admire him, even when he resorts to duplicity to express his involvement with erring humanity. Despite occasional self-pity and laments for the meaninglessness of life, the narrator does not appear to me to be a predominantly alienated or tragic figure.[13] In my opinion he has come to terms with the progressive disillusionment he calls life and with an inconsistent, ever-changing world that he understands only in part. Though scarred, he has not been overwhelmed, and he obligingly invites us to profit from his experience. However chaotic and unfathomable he finds the universe to be, Byron's narrator continues to expand his consciousness of life's abundance.

NOTES

1. Byron told George Bancroft in 1822 that Johnson's Preface "contained the most correct judgment of Shakespeare"; both Leigh Hunt and Lady Blessington

claimed that Byron at times affected a Johnsonian manner. See *His Very Self and Voice: Collected Conversations of Lord Byron*, ed. Ernest J. Lovell, Jr. (New York: Macmillan, 1954), pp. 293, 328; and Blessington, *Conversations*, p. 20.

2. Jerome J. McGann, *"Don Juan" in Context* (Chicago: Univ. of Chicago Press, 1976), pp. 161–65.

3. George M. Ridenour, *The Style of "Don Juan,"* pp. 1–18; McGann, *"Don Juan" in Context*, pp. 68–69.

4. England, *Byron's "Don Juan" and Eighteenth-Century Literature*, pp. 15–22.

5. Anne K. Mellor, *English Romantic Irony* (Cambridge, Mass.: Harvard Univ. Press, 1980), pp. 49–50.

6. William Hazlitt, "Lord Byron," in *The Spirit of the Age, Works*, XI, 75.

7. Hazlitt, "Lord Byron," *Works*, XI, 75n.

8. Marshall, *The Structure of Byron's Major Poems*, p. 176. For the contrary view that the narrator is "a self-consistent speaker" whose many voices are the "manifestations of one voice," see George M. Ridenour, "The Mode of Byron's *Don Juan*," *PMLA*, 79 (1964), 442–46.

9. Marshall, *Structure*, p. 177.

10. Blessington, *Conversations*, p. 26. On 25 Dec. 1822 Byron wrote Murray: "No Girl will ever be seduced by reading D[on] J[uan]—no—no—she will go to Little's poems—& Rousseau's romans—for that—or even to the immaculate De Staël— —they will encourage her—& not the Don—who laughs at that—and—and—most other things" (*BLJ*, X, 68).

11. Blessington, *Conversations*, p. 155.

12. James R. Sutherland, *English Satire* (Cambridge: Cambridge Univ. Press, 1958), p. 76.

13. See Alvin B. Kernan, *The Plot of Satire* (New Haven, Conn.: Yale Univ. Press, 1965), pp. 212–22, for a description that characterizes the narrator as estranged, rejected, and tragic. By emphasizing the comic, the tragic, or the satiric elements in *Don Juan*, critics have inevitably arrived at widely disparate views on what they consider the dominant tone of the poem.

STUART CURRAN

Form and Freedom
in European Romantic Poetry

Natur und Kunst, sie scheinen sich zu fliehen
Und haben sich, eh man es denkt, gefunden;
Der Widerwille ist auch mir verschwunden,
Und beide scheinen gleich mich anzuziehen.
Es gilt wohl nur ein redliches Bemühen!
Und wenn wir erst in abgemessnen Stunden
Mit Geist und Fleiss uns an die Kunst gebunden,
Mag frei Natur im Herzen wieder glühen.

So ists mit aller Bildung auch beschaffen.
Vergebens werden ungebundne Geister
Nach der Vollendung reiner Höhe streben.
Wer Grosses will, muss sich zusammenraffen.
In der Beschränkung zeigt sich erst der Meister,
Und das Gesetz nur kann uns Freiheit geben.

           Johann Wolfgang von Goethe,
                "Natur und Kunst"[1]

I

The composite orders of Wordsworth, Byron, and Shelley are the most daring and sophisticated formal experiments in British Romantic poetry. The poets' knowledge of their literary heritage is brilliantly tempered to a

From *Poetic Form and British Romanticism*. © 1986 by Oxford University Press, Inc.

determined conceptual purpose, and yet their individual ideologies, if clearly associated in a shared concern with the values of process and progress that dominate their culture, are as distinctive in constitution as they are in purpose. The generic inclusiveness of *The Prelude, Don Juan*, and *Prometheus Unbound* is of such complexity that each poem becomes the locus for an encompassing world view, and thus it is natural for us as readers, generally speaking, to refer the entire canon of the authors to these supreme embodiments of their genius. So enveloping a synoptic form, we are wont to say, must constitute the poet's largest and ultimate vision of life. The critical instincts by which we enforce an ideological centering of such intensity are not only natural, but they also accord with our own experience, moral no less than aesthetic.

Nevertheless, they are implicitly reductive. We have only to look at the wanderers elsewhere in Wordsworth who cannot discover meaning or solace—his Female Vagrant, his burned-out old soldiers, the intellectually dessicated Solitary of *The Excursion*—to temper any simple sense of Wordsworth's faith in his progressive imaginative liberation. Providing the obverse of or necessary balance to Byron's fluid comic vision are the four historical tragedies he wrote contemporaneously with *Don Juan*, all centering on heroes ground down by cultural fixities each vainly tries to escape. And there can be observed in Shelley's writing another way of construing a universal democratic paradigm that inhibits any urge to read the final act of his lyrical drama sentimentally, the republic of despair enacted in *The Triumph of Life*. What is most to be celebrated in these poets, and their fellow artists of the Romantic movement as well, is not an encompassing ideological vision, but that they never remained still, even when formulating structures encompassing ceaseless mental movement. And the preceding chapters as a whole suggest an even more cautionary injunction against too facile an equation of art and life among these poets. If poetic forms embody a logic that constrains the intellect to its dictates and if genres necessarily presuppose that certain values will be honored over others, even with composite orders—perhaps most especially with composite orders—such interwoven generic constraints, though they may well enable creativity, exert a continual ideological pressure on imaginative vision. That is not to say that a genre constitutes an ideological absolute. The history of literary genres within the Romantic period suggests that, whatever the metal from which an artistic superstructure is formed, even an alloy of intricate molecular complexity, it is always malleable. Bend it as the poet wills, however, the metal does not change.

And yet, the continuing implication of this discussion, whether involving sonnets or epics, is that the ideological pressure of a genre can, at least in the hands of a major artist, be liberating. Classical pastoral offered Wordsworth a model for a democratic sufficiency of such balanced clarity that it took him a decade to plumb its implications. An entire generation in Blake's life as a poet issued from his endeavor to grapple with the logical possibilities inherent in the epic as it was left by Milton to his successors. The shift in cultural values that transpired during the Enlightenment allowed the entire period to reconceive, from a necessary distance, the ethos of the English Renaissance. In these instances, and many more suggested by the foregoing pages, recovery stimulated a process of reformation, of reimagining the past; and that in turn, at least from the midpoint of the eighteenth century to the political realignment that took place between 1827 and 1832, equally prompted the reimagining of the present, which, by the perverse logic of history, had in the Enlightenment lost much of its past and all of its mythology. The received traditions of literature, particularly as channeled through the centuries by their generic momentum, could compensate where other cultural embodiments had been emptied of palpable meaning. Against the failure of myth, the factionalism and proliferation of religious sects, the dissolution of iconographical knowledge, their resilient conceptual syntax kept its integrity and was thus able to counter and assimilate the demythologizing rationalism whose stream forged a new and dangerously rapid tributary in the eighteenth century.

The result was not so much a universally understood program—though there are assuredly contentious manifestoes among Romantic poets—as the necessary adjustment of European culture to fundamentally altered circumstances. The peculiar isolation of Britain from the continent coincided, fortuitously it would appear in retrospect, with the pressure of Enlightenment rationalism to create the charged arena of Romanticism in which a skeptical epistemology closed with, and transformed, its literary heritage within a single generation. The Renaissance hierarchy of genres was tested, inverted, then reconstituted through those inverted values. To place that transformation within a sharper ideological and cultural framework, where the literary inheritance had been conceived upon an aristocratic model, resolutely tempered to sacramental purposes, and generally secured against open-ended philosophical speculations, the shift of underlying cultural values necessarily subjected it to a democratic ethos, a progressive secularization, and the skeptical assumptions of Berkeley and Hume. Byron may disagree profoundly with Wordsworth's sense of the decorum appropriate to such an inversion, asserting the worldly voice of Pope and Gay against a reincarnation of "namby-pampy" Phillips, but he participates in the same process; and, indeed, his entire poetic career, viewed in a glance, is one extended inversion of the traditional genres in order to reconstitute them according to an aristocratic notion of the democratic, secular, and skeptical. As Byron's example suggests, the inherent logic of such a thorough transformation tends to ford a genre to pivot on its axis. In such a process of turning inside out, it is no wonder that paradox invests the entire process. Not the least of its results is that the more resistant to altered circumstances are the conventions of a genre, the more likely they are not to be discarded but rather forced into new alliances flaunting their shifted values. Of all the major Romantic poets Byron might be counted the least likely to write a religious quest romance, which, without our overstraining the logic, is probably why he did so. Yet also, as even such a reverse of expectations as this attests, the transformation of generic convention resolves itself in a continual process of testing. The consequences are major and, as the previous pages continually exemplify, they are twofold. Because the constituents of a genre cannot be simply appropriated without question, they become self-conscious in their application, which is to say self-reflexive in their very conception. Moreover, this process of testing also necessarily forces them into organic relationship with the overall artistic purpose, as Coleridge so perceptively argued from his own experience.

We have ourselves inherited a common metaphor for representing at least one element of this studied inversion, which is the mode by which light, enlightenment, is seen to be transmitted by the means of art. There are, on the one hand, mirrors and, on the other hand, lamps; and these two means of representation, which are not in fact means at all but simply metaphorical tropes, imply a rude dichotomy between simple mimesis and a self-conscious creativity. In the rough, this metaphorical extrapolation from the tangled maze of the history of consciousness helps to separate its strands. The accepted function of literature did perceptively shift ground in the eighteenth century, partly because the potential readership and the number of publications both vastly expanded, contributing to and being reinforced by the attendant alteration in cultural values we have been remarking. But to conceive that shift as also involving the spurning of tradition or a disregard for the generic underpinnings of that tradition is to be seduced by the apparent logic implicit in simplistic metaphor. In our own time that logic has become something of a historical assumption, and, unquestionably, there were some few souls in the nineteenth century who also pursued it. It is, however, significant that at least in England those who grasped for such an understanding did so while standing in the perplexing trough of genius that separated a definable Romantic period from what would come to be discerned as the early manifestations of Victorian art. John Stuart Mill's "What is Poetry?" of 1833 and John Keble's lectures from the Oxford Chair of Poetry from 1832 to 1841, published in 1844 as *De poeticae vi medica*, redefine poetry as the mere expression of lyrical emotion, an art of spontaneous overflow empowered by an aesthetic clearly derived from what were mistakenly conceived by the writers to be Wordsworth's notions of his art. That the chief beneficiary of this aesthetic in Great Britain, the short-lived Spasmodic School, bowed in and then out with less effect than the inhabitant of the previous generational trough sixty years earlier, the Della-Cruscan school (of which, it might be said, its lamp was the Spasmodics' mirror), should give us both pause and historical perspective. But, at least with Mill, the cultural ramification has been wrongly construed from the first, for the driving question of his essay is actually the nature of fiction; and it had far more importance for conceiving the ground rules of the Victorian novel as a repository of cultural stresses than for influencing in any lasting way its poetry. As an assessment of Romanticism, it participates in the fantasy by which Browning was to clear ground for his genius, defining the previous two generations as centers of lyric verse and ignoring their notable achievements in narrative poetry. The arguments by which Mill and Keble safely encompassed, and distorted, the poetry of the previous half-century are as transparently indicative of the insecurity of their decade as Shelley's celebration of his culture in the *Defence of Poetry*, separated by a mere dozen years from Mill's essay, is also inimitably of its time. Since, however, Mill and Keble provide the most substantial evidence adduced to promulgate the myth of a generic breakdown in British poetry, they have assumed an importance beyond their intellectual means and a centrality that masks their fearful belatedness.[2]

Yet, to give due credit to the sources of a distorting misapprehension, it is surely possible that the generation that followed the Younger Romantics mistook the remarkable freedom with which they learned to manipulate traditional genres, not the least from the example of Wordsworth and Coleridge themselves, for a total liberation from them. Though attempts to distinguish the two generations of British Romanticism generally founder because of the signal contributions of the older poets to the poetic ferment of the Regency, the patterns discernible from the evidence of the preceding chapters suggest that what may have been tentative generic experiments in the first generation quickly established firm principles for the artistry of the second. Yet against what in retrospective logic might be anticipated—and, perhaps because the logic seems so obvious, it has now been fairly embalmed in customary literary history—the enlarging skepticism of the Younger Romantics paradoxically coincides with an increasing preoccupation with generic possibility. A moment's contemplation should explode the seeming paradox and comprehend why inherited traditions would prove so imperative to a school of poetry that is self-professedly engaged in social and psychological liberation.

Where the Younger Romantics inherit the democratic, secular, and skeptical ethos of their predecessors, an ethos invested in a revitalization of generic traditions, they implicitly assume a notion of genre as both a mode of apprehension and a repository of conflicting values, exemplified in Wordsworth's resurrecting the paradigms of classical pastoral against Renaissance Christian allegory or eighteenth-century aristocratic mannerism. Through all these cultural manifestations, they recognize, the conventions remain and the metal bends to necessity. So from Ephesus to Haija Sophia to St. Peter's, Byron pursues his religious quest. So Keats, in *Hyperion*, juxtaposes the Miltonic fall into knowledge with its equivalent in classical myth. So Shelley, in *Prometheus Unbound*, intrudes a vision of the crucified Christ before the eyes of his hero martyred by Jupiter. As certainly as a conceptual syntax embodies an ideological syntax, it resists any single system of belief; and especially where such systems are brought into confrontation, the syntax allows the contemplation of essential mysteries of human experience through multivalent contexts and a liberating artistic perspective. What we learn from the ubiquity of deconstructive strategies in British Romantic poetry is that the generic perspective, if the poet is clever enough, can be profoundly exploratory. The art that results is therefore likely to have no purpose beyond that of exploration.

Needless to say, it is a defensible political posture. In an age of reaction, and with a European conflict that seemingly disallowed every alternative to a British compromise that had in those stresses barely held together—that had indeed through those stresses proved that the compromise was more a matter of conventional rhetoric than of law—not to serve, but to stand and wait openly, is perhaps the only comprehensible stance for those who can neither revert to the past nor do more than hope for the future. From our comfortable distance it is easy either to accord faith in a remythologized prospect as though it were a program uniting the culture, or to puncture those seemingly inflated hopes as if unaware that they were, as Shelley said of *Prometheus Unbound*, only saving "idealisms of moral excellence." One extreme of critical perspective inevitably produces its alternative, yet neither ultimately is true to the conditions of the culture.[3] What is profoundly true is that literary traditions, particularly those associated with generic tradition, allowed a neutral, yet critical and self-integrating, stance for poets who stood ineffectually outside it.

What we learn from the concentrated generic transformations of British Romanticism is a simple truth that can be expressed without resort to theoretical jargon or reductive abstractions, which is that art continually recreates life as well as further extensions of art. In one sense or another every poem of substance in the Romantic period reveals the pattern. Form is a refuge from the systems of belief forced, and understandably so, by a culture in siege and at war. It is a link with the past as a conceptual repository, its contents not construed as involving (though it was, of course, the case) even more constricting belief systems, but rather liberating imaginative structures that reaffirm the commitments all of us have to what transcends the necessary limitations of any cultural epoch. Shelley's remark in *A Defence of Poetry* that the poetry of Dante and Milton is essentially distinct from their religious beliefs is characteristic of how we may imagine they were read as well by a great many less candid admirers: "The distorted notions of invisible things which Dante and his rival Milton have idealized, are merely the mask and mantle in which these great poets walk through eternity enveloped and disguised.... The Divina Commedia and Paradise Lost have conferred upon modern mythology a systematic form" (pp. 498–499). A different time—indeed, a later time trying to contain the fearful energy released by Humean skepticism— might revert to the repository of traditional Christian paradigms for moral comfort or philosophical distance, as Arnold does in his claims for literary touchstones. But the British Romantics look to genre for a much more radical purpose, to supply a geometry for art that is, or can be made to be, itself both morally neutral and a driving force.

II

But does that then mean that an isolated Britain, however distinguished the literary productions of its Romanticism, is to occupy a no-man's-land, sharing an identifying term with continental literatures from which it would be better to differentiate it? By no means. And yet the very question suggests that the relationship between British and continental

Romanticisms is complex and requires a continual adjustment of cultural perspective if it is to be viewed without distortion. First of all, we have to recognize that Romanticism, conceived as a European phenomenon, lasted well over a century, yet at the same time occurred in national phases. Thus Goethe was already being enthusiastically celebrated as a genius before any of the Italian or French Romantics were born and stood as sage and septuagenarian when the great commotion of French Romanticism began with the *Méditations Poetiques* of Lamartine in 1820. Just four years after that milestone, with the death of Byron, the flowering of British Romanticism had abruptly ceased; but the central figure of the French movement, Victor Hugo, did not die until 1885, leaving, true to his nature as a cultural monument, two epic poems to be published after his death. The anomalies interwoven within such dates could be multiplied considerably but would only underscore the extent to which, even when we identify Romanticism as pan-European, it is keyed to the discrete exigencies of national cultures.[4] And yet the effort to discuss it in a transnational setting inevitably encourages a discourse about what is shared in, rather than what separates, these national Romanticisms, with the result that vital distinctions easily become blurred.

If we attempt to define the movement by contrast, we are bound to renew the polemical debate over classicism and Romanticism, but even that debate is culturally determined, surfacing in Germany in the 1790s, where it occupied something less than a decade of spirited polemics, reerupting in Italy in the 1810s, slightly tinging the British cultural scene at the same time, and then being suddenly resuscitated in France during the 1820s and 30s. The latter, almost comic, gesture of belatedness should alert us to the fact that the dispute between classic and romantic, so vague though noisy in its polemics and so incongruously reconceived within every stirring of national literatures, is a component of Romanticism itself, the surest mark of the self-consciousness by which the movement, in country after country, came to understand its power and to galvanize its momentum. Moreover, on close inspection it is almost impossible to mark a dividing line and identify anticlassical Romantics, at least among the intellectual and artistic giants of the period. In Italy one must rule out Foscolo, who so celebrated his birth on a Greek island that, even without his translation of *The Iliad*, claim might be made for him as Greece's Romantic poet, as well as Leopardi, who prided himself on his ability to read classical Greek poetry with the stylistic discernment of a native-speaker. In Germany we must exclude Hölderlin, who not only reinvented the Greek pantheon but earnestly tried to believe in it, and the arch neo-

Hellenists Goethe and Schiller, who defended classicism in the preliminary debate; but also, if we regard Friedrich Schlegel as their chief antagonist, we are faced with the irreducible fact that he was a learned antiquarian, wrote a history of classical poetry, and was by appointment a professor of Sanskrit. The Younger British Romantics all resuscitate classical myth, and it might even be said that Byron gave his life for the sake of a myth he had assiduously deconstructed. It is true that the study of Greek rather gave way to Roman martial arts under Napoleon's empire, but if the posthumous publication of Chenier's bucolics in 1819 offered the French Romantics their point of departure, Hugo's odes a central voice, and Sainte-Beuve's celebration of classical models in the 1840s and 50s a new impetus, the French debate appears to have continued at least into the 1870s when Rimbaud introduced modernism at the age of seventeen. And yet it is entirely symptomatic of this century of debate that the first indication of Rimbaud's prodigious genius was a Latin prize poem written at the age of fourteen.

Even when we locate the classic–romantic debate within Romanticism itself, however, it does not escape the inevitable cultural determinism. Broadly speaking, we might wish to see it in T. S. Eliot's terms, as a confrontation of a tradition and the individual talent, and often that was how the argument ran. But whose tradition and in relation to what talent? Foscolo's conception of himself as neo-Hellenist empowers his writing and, indeed, even mythologizes it in a poetry of endless exile: his Greece is irrecoverable, but incarnate in him. In a sense, that frees Foscolo from other components of literary tradition that any Italian poet must inherit, the quattrocento, and behind it, the heritage of Latin literature. And yet, for Foscolo's countrymen it would appear a specious freedom for a dispirited, partitioned, and repeatedly occupied country—if that term is even applicable—to throw off what gave it identity, continuity, and dignity.

If we cross the Alps, the entire argument shifts. Classical order becomes profoundly antinationalistic, at least as the Schlegels or Madame de Staël represent it. The romantic signifies the northern, the rugged poetry of the heroic past: the pine tree, not the palm, as Heine would succinctly mark the distinction. In generic terms Romanticism is the romance, Germany's indigenous mode, competing with the Homeric and Virgilian epic for literary primacy. Toward the west the issues are more academic and perhaps subtler. The neo-Hellenism of the British Romantics is, as we have continually remarked, an easy inheritance, one already assimilated in the Renaissance, but revived, along with the formidable classical scholarship spearheaded by Richard Porson, as a respectable cloak for skeptical, non-Christian thought. The very late classical revival of France had first to contend with the legacy of the Empire's Roman trappings and then with the academic canon of French literature. Sainte-Beuve's new classicism coincided exactly with the recovery of the French Renaissance, particularly Ronsard.[5] Yet, as the debate raged, it is apparent that both elements became crucial to the liberation the Romantic faction wanted. If classicism is seen as a lapidary, unchanging, and aristocratic order, then it is an aspect of rationalism, or benevolent despotism, or Aquinean Catholicism. But if it resides in the mythmaking of Hesiod, the dynamic energy of Homer, or the erotic spontaneity of Theocritus on the one hand, and on the other the plain honesty of Horace, the brooding double vision of Virgil, or the lyric virtuosity of Catullus, it represents an ancient freedom from the constraints of modern culture. The other side of the European defense of classicism, in other words, is Romanticism.

As British Romanticism constitutes a renaissance of the Renaissance, both a recovery of its earlier literature and of that earlier literary recovery itself, we can reliably transfer the applicability of this entire complex, with due allowance for what the past meant in each national literature and the extent to which it had been obscured, to the whole of western European Romanticism. And if we add to that recognition a balanced awareness that what writers do and what they propound are often distinct, we are also able to extend the significance of traditional forms that we have observed in British Romanticism to the poetic ferment on the continent. There is clearly a link binding British experimentation with genre to Hölderlin's attempts to forge a new free verse form in German from Greek iambs and hexameters and Schiller's recovery of the grand style, to Foscolo's *Odes and Sonnets* of 1803 and his driving Pindaric ode, *I Sepolchri*, of 1806, and to the splendid incongruity by which French Romanticism trumpeted its originality in Lamartine's elegies, Hugo's odes, and Musset's epyllions.[6] Yet if we concentrate attention just on the reappropriation and central positioning of the ode in all three cultures, we must acknowledge that what binds these revivals are radically different notions of the form. It is not the same kind in any of them, and even where there are certain correspondences, they are apt to strike us as anomalous rather than as generically constitutive. For instance, the early odes of Coleridge—"Ode to the Departing Year," "France: An Ode"—do share the public themes and hortatory inflations of Hugo's odes of a generation later. Yet, their poetical models are as different as their politics. Coleridge's poems derive their impetus from the political odes—particularly the Whig progress piece—of the British eighteenth century, whereas Hugo's are conditioned by the alexandrine encomium and by seventeenth-century French stage conventions. A new form of the ode will arise among the second group of French Romantics to compete with the grand rhetoric and dramatic postures of Hugo, but it will derive from reclaiming Ronsard, whose odes have nothing in common with Pindar's, to the French literary canon. The Pindaric odes of Hölderlin, Schiller, and Foscolo do stem from a single source but are similarly filtered through very different national understandings of classical form, the former two reconceiving Winkelmann's marble, the latter a Mediterranean passion. The characteristic odes of the later British Romantics, on the other hand, derive their power, as we have noted, from the choral odes of Greek tragedy, converting the oppositional structure of strophe and antistrophe into dialectical rhythms demanding a synthesis that usually the poet is unable or unwilling to effect. In each case Romanticism is dependent not simply on classicism but on versions of classicism that themselves betray the biases of the nation's scholarship and probably its program of education. Even more is this the case with the hymn. We can compare, but it is probably more fruitful to contrast, Novalis's *Hymnen an die Nacht*, Manzoni's *Inni Sacri*, Shelley's "Hymn to Intellectual Beauty," and the hymnic meditations of Lamartine. The religious climate of each culture is so distinct, so enveloped by centuries of national development, and so infused with contemporary European politics that only the fact of the kind itself allows common ground.

The complexity of these formal problems seems far removed from what might appear normative a century before, and therein lies an expansion of the singular paradox observed earlier in the relationship of British Romanticism and the Enlightenment. To survey European literature around 1750 is to discover common ground, something approaching an observed and universal canon over which reigns the flexible Voltaire. It was that because—at least in Britain, France, and Germany—it was so small a cultivated tract. Though neither Italy nor Spain ever lost its principal heritage, in the other three countries Romanticism coincides as a movement with reclaiming the wilderness beyond—which is to say, particularly medieval literature, and in England and France the sixteenth century as centered in Spenser and the Pléiade. The explosion of lyrical forms in Romanticism is exactly the reverse of poetic anarchy; rather, it testifies to the revelation of literary possibility from the past against which the dull sameness of heroic couplets and of bifurcated alexandrines suggested undeserved, long-endured, and wholly unnecessary poverty. Yet at least in the initial stages of this recovery, it is for obvious reasons intensely nationalistic, though connected to a further common ground in the resurgence of classical scholarship. Everywhere in European literature the observed canons were revealed as inadequate to encompass the burden not just, as a strictly historical overview might have it, of startling new material and creative conditions, but of a revived heritage. And after the first wave, national recovery, came its sharing through translation.

Another feature of that early Enlightenment landscape was the codification of generic rules by French arbiters of taste: Boileau, Rapin, Le Bossu, et al. But again, the British experience is written large when one crosses to the recovery of continental literatures. There were no rules to encompass the verse of the Troubadors and Minnesingern, or the *Niebelungenlied*, or the succession of Italian Orlando poems, or the ballad. Not only had neoclassical categories constricted literature to a small number of approved texts and an implicit hierarchy of genres, but it had through its exclusivity reduced generic possibility itself. The gradual critical enlargement of the number of stipulated genres we observe in England during the eighteenth century occurs throughout Europe as the history of literature was at last understood and for the very first time written. The hegemony of rules could not survive such a test. For a history of national literature is perforce diachronic and evolutionary, even when, as was the case with Bishop Percy and Thomas Warton, it is obsessed with prehistoric sources. To such a history critical arbiters of another culture and an opposite ideology—representing, as it were, a synchronic poetics— were irrelevant. It is not, then, to choose a single case, that the numerous attempts to write a new epic in England and France threw the prescriptions of Le Bossu to the wind. History had done so in the revival of romance throughout Europe. The dialectical relationship between the two perspectives on narrative offered intellectual and artistic challenge, and it was accepted on all sides, first in England and then, with a life force that is truly astonishing, throughout nineteenth-century France, culminating in the posthumous publication of Victor Hugo's unfinished theosophical epics, *La Fin de Satan* and *Dieu*.[7]

To underscore the extent to which European Romanticism grounded itself in an Enlightenment program whose dynamics reached far into the nineteenth century, however, is not to deny major shifts in sensibility and concomitant generic developments in literature. The pastoral, for instance, does not disappear but becomes so transfigured and, so to speak, naturalized that it takes a second glance to recognize how deeply it embues the exotic landscapes of Hugo's *Orientales*. On the continent, indeed, Wordsworthian naturalism is less discernible than Churchill's or Crabbe's austere antipastoral, which only accords with a generation of warfare on Europe's pastoral plains. French Romanticism truly finds its first voice, echoing across the gulf of history, in Chenier's *Bucoliques*, written in prison before his execution under the Terror and first published in 1819. His representation of the lambs of eighteenth-century aristocracy being led to their slaughter is, arguably, the farthest-reaching of modern antipastorals, inasmuch as its inversions mark the doom of an entire culture as well as its unfortunate author. Yet something of its like also emerges in the terrifying calm of Leopardi's "Canto notturno di una pastore errante dell'Asia"—"Night Song of a Wandering Shepherd of Asia." Leopardi's youth was spent in studying the classics, and his career began with translation of the bucolic poetry of Moschus. In the "Canto notturno" he systematically inverts the pastoral conventions he knew by heart: alienation intrudes where we expect fellowship; the nomad's illimitable desert blurs into an infinite sky instead of the *hortus conclusus* of the pastoral bower; the menace of midnight replaces the otium of noon; and even Virgil's melancholy shadows—his reiterated "umbrae"—are exaggerated into an "Abisso orrida, immenso"—the horrid, immense abyss into which all of value disappears. This haunting song of despair, however, issues in a compassion that is exactly commensurate with the assurance of its metrics and the refinement of its style, reproducing the balance between the beauty that sustains and the entropy that threatens in the First *Idyll* of Theocritus and the First *Eclogue* of Virgil. As great pastoral subsumes the antipastoral, insisting on the vulnerability of its enclosed circle, in the "Canto notturno" the circle is expanded to cosmic dimensions and the vulnerability is proportionately infinite.

One notable feature of the European Romantic landscape, self-evident in even the most cursory of surveys, is its remarkable exfoliation of verse forms, both in new patterns of rhyme and meter and revivals of older models. Despite the occasional experiments in prose poetry (such as Aloysius Bertrand's exercises in hortatory medieval exoticism, *Gaspard de la Nuit*) or gestures toward *vers libres* (Hölderlin's neo-Hellenist odes), it is almost impossible to think of unrhymed French and German verse during this period. Indeed, rather than concentrate on Bertrand's self-conscious experimentation, we should recognize its actual context, which is the tyranny—and astonishing resilience—of the alexandrine couplet or quatrain in nineteenth-century French verse. As late as the dazzling surrealism of Rimbaud's "Bateau Ivre" of 1873, its preeminence is taken for granted, so much so that Hugo created an uproar, and eventually his reputation as the national arbiter of poetic taste, by daring to shift the position of its caesura. Rhyme is scarcely the only constituent of poetic form, but especially in reference to German poetry, the mere examples of Eichendorff and Heine, who polished an already glistening marble, should keep the theoretical pronouncements of the Jena school about liberating poetry from its constraints in necessary perspective.[8] So, in fact, might the actual achievements of Friedrich Novalis, all too briefly its major poetic genius. For, though his *Hymns to the Night*, with their combination of breathless, rhapsodic prose and chiselled hymnody, vaunt their freedom from classical restraint, they do so from within the framework of Gothic lyricism provided Novalis by medieval German mystical poetry and the Christian meditative tradition. In Italy, significantly, the formal terms are wholly different. To unrhyme Italian verse seems to have been a cultural effort going back at least to Dante; so the relative delicacy of a Leopardi in this respect, and his concern for refined syllabic symmetries, have their indigenous cultural underpinnings that mirror these other constants.

It is true that rhyme and meter can be freely reconstituted for the circumstances of the moment and therefore have no necessary connection with the long tradition of European poetry, with generic expectation, or with the example of precursors. Yet, if we look specifically at the kinds of continuities in form examined in the early chapters, we discover not only their presence but even more importantly their revival and dissemination across national boundaries. The sonnet in England, as we have traced its path, has a truly resilient formal continuity. It had a potent prehistory for Italian poets as well, much less so for the French (who recovered the form before resuscitating its French history), and virtually none for the Germans. Yet, given that disparity, what we can immediately observe as a constant of comparative Romanticism, without quibble or cultural adjustment, is the ubiquity of sonnets on the sonnet, a self-reflexive subgenre containing multitudes. The epigraph to this chapter, Goethe's sonnet "Natur und Kunst," is a studied import, proclaiming Goethe's adherence to a pan-European literary tradition and, in effect, Germany's union with it: "Und das Gesetz nur kann uns Freiheit geben": only that law will give German poetry its freedom. Wordsworth's independent view in "Nuns fret not at their Convent's narrow room," the prefatory sonnet to his 1807 collection, is exactly congruent, even to the adoption of the same imagery of confinement: "In truth, the prison, unto which we doom / Ourselves, no prison is." In the perspective of Goethe's sonnet,

Wordsworth's resolute return to the nature of the Petrarchan and Miltonic sonnet forms in his 1807 volumes, to ground their dynamics in the psychology of perception, takes on added resonance. Wordsworth's use of the form as a metaphor for the self's reaching out to center space and time, to effect a unity between the mundane and supernal, is not only uncannily what it enacts, but, as with Goethe's sonnet, a statement about the nature of art itself. His comparison of the sonnet to an orbicular construction, the cosmos of a drop of dew, nicely invokes the geometric shape that, in Marshall Brown's view, haunts German Romanticism, particularly among the Jena school.[9] Though not so systematically self-reflexive as Wordsworth, Foscolo appears to have something of the same ends in mind in the sonnets he published in 1803, where the form becomes a bridge that reunites the isolated voice with human and mythic continuities from which it has been exiled. In England during the Regency, as we have seen, Leigh Hunt took up the quiet intensities with which Wordsworth had invested the form and domesticated it to his suburban circle, and Keats and Shelley in turn stretched its newly discovered elasticity to see just how much of the sublime could be held and intensified within its constraints. But Wordsworth's most striking influence is unexpected, for Sainte-Beuve also seems to have drawn from his sonnets possibilities for the domestication of the poetic voice. His introduction of the sonnet into French Romanticism had far-reaching consequences.[10] Nerval converted its polarities into an enclosed tabernacle enshrining symbolic mystery. Baudelaire similarly found in the sonnet what he called a "Pythagorean beauty" and through his long career continually elaborated its "constraining form" to reach a "more intense idea" of inherent correspondences.[11] And, deliberately following in their wake, finally Mallarmé compacted the sonnet into the oxymoronic *tombeau* of an art sustaining its vitality within an impenetrable labyrinth. Indeed, with French symbolism the sonnet is converted from the Miltonic reaching out toward cultural ideals into the embodiment of an art without relationship to anything else but its own dynamics. In an art that exists for its own sake, form is essential.

Yet that very fact should underscore why form was so inescapable a necessity for Romantic subjectivity, a ground for either commitment or disengagement, but always a ground for self-mirroring and self-creation. And simple logic would suggest the necessity within such a dialectical field of a complementary mirroring and recreation of the predicated other as well. Hence the crucial importance of Coleridge's definition of "organic form" as art's "self-witnessing and self-effected sphere of agency." What

Coleridge's term presents, and what Romanticism as a whole wanted to embrace, was the challenge of definition from the inside out, in life as in art. Sonnets are not written according to Petrarchan rules but according to the inherent dynamics and geometry of the form (to which Petrarch's own understanding is of course a guide), and that in essence is the most universal urge of generic development throughout Western literature. The sonnet's prominence throughout Romanticism and its remarkable candor in artistic self-reflexiveness make it a simple index to the nature of poetic form in culture after culture. Its history in the nineteenth century, with the necessary adjustments made for formal continuities and experiments, is replicated in the ode, the elegy, the ballad, the romance, the epic, and in every shade between.

Yet, its history also traces a growing disengagement, an involution into formal self-witnessing as a refuge from bourgeois culture, that could not have been intended by the Enlightenment renaissance, even if it was, by the strange quirks of history, its principal inheritance for modernism. The customary division of nineteenth-century French poetry between Romanticism and Symbolism, though notoriously hard to place, testifies to a general awareness that Romanticism, though forced to wait out the Napoleonic Wars, did not embrace its disengagement with pleasure or with pride. Indeed, generally speaking, it turned to art as a resource of forms of intellectual power, as a means to reconceive and expand a European conceptual syntax too restrictive to accommodate the new historical forces represented by the French Revolution. For Romanticism form became a guarantor of intellectual freedom, at once a framework for psychological exploration and a means, through reimagining the past, to enlarge future possibilities. Although the past chapters have indicated numerous ways in which this was accomplished, here at the end we might contemplate two opposite strategies—the one deconstructive and the other modelled on the total organization of scientific system—which, in their sum, demonstrate how imperative formal means were to the Romantic enterprise and how intellectually liberating was the result.

The Fall of Hyperion, composed at the end of Keats's tragically foreshortened career and resonant with the knowledge of what impends, bears witness through its strategies of ideological displacement to an intellectual bravery that will neither succumb to convention nor pretend to its irrelevance. The poem represents Keats's reassimilation and testing of the values tentatively asserted in the fragmentary trial of *Hyperion* a year and a half before. Yet this second fragment, even if it is far more intense in its multiple confrontations, never even approaches the point of forcing the cosmological impasse upon which the original poem faltered. The shift of generic models is the key. For the supposedly objective truths of epic tradition Keats substitutes the mode insinuated upon the genre by Dante, the dream vision, which forestalls distance and accentuates the ways in which truths are perceived and ordered within the mind.

But the genre is adopted only to be insistently questioned even as it organizes the poem. The first episode within its fiction is the poet's dream of a deserted Eden, our most primordial of cultural myths and memories, which, simply because it is so unavailing of satisfaction, gives way to a second and antithetical dream. There the poet comes upon dispossessed collosi, who, with their strange mythic distance, embody our exclusion from the paradise at the infancy of our cultural and psychological development—or our primal alienation. After a struggle to attain an equilibrium, figured as a matter of life or death (and perhaps, after all, that is exactly what it is), the poet looks deeply within the inarticulate eyes of Moneta and is afforded his third vision, which appears to be the culminating one. For a month, immobile, he contemplates the similarly immobile and inarticulate Titans, lost like them in an extended daydream in the twilight of the gods. Yet, whatever internal recognitions might have been elicited by that reverie are never articulated: they constitute a marked resemblance to the deep eyes of Moneta into which the poet stares and upon which he is reflected. As an oracle Moneta has nothing whatsoever to tell; she only parts the curtains on a scene, where, though we assume it to be a *tableau vivante*, nothing occurs through the month-long vigilance. Yet she does speak before unveiling this enigmatic vision, and then it is to question the understanding and pronouncements of "dreamers weak," which, if we have managed to keep our bearings in this conceptual labyrinth, is to question the very dream in which she appears. As it starts to assimilate the cosmic myth of the earlier poem, *The Fall of Hyperion* breaks off, having intimated a majesty and a portent of meaning that it will not allow us to delimit. Relatively short as it is, it offers an accumulation of visions, not just those described but also those far interwoven in the vortex of their succession, all displacing meaning into a further interior, transferring symbolic import to that distance which is never reached. The effect is exactly, yet symmetrically, opposite to the breaking-point of the original experiment, *Hyperion*, where Apollo is left forever in the process of coming convulsively to a knowledge neither he nor we will ever comprehend.

The state in which *The Fall of Hyperion* suspends its discourse, if such a term applies where there is no reality principle in evidence, is either a plenum of too many visions compacted or a vacuum in which all are mutually canceling, a visionary intensity or a visionless emptiness. In either case it is a state that questions the value of its own enterprise as sharply as Moneta—or as formatively as does its own preliminary premise: "Fanatics have dreams." The proem frames the dream vision by questioning its value, and the dreams accumulate without answer. They all begin from the inception of Cartesian mental process: "Methought I stood where trees of every clime...." The enclosed and self-referential mind contemplates the paradise of its own elaboration—its desperate, never-satisfied need—and can assert but one sole assurance, that it thinks, or that in doing so, it once forced a poem to be conceived: "Methought." The term, removed from the present moment by its tense no less than its archaism, by its nature implies self-questioning, and in its purity introduces us to visions that elaborate that self-questioning beyond the point where any answer is ascertainable. Is there then no truth in these embedded enigmas, no assurance that impels us forward? The very recognition of the reader's momentum ironically enforces what is the one solemn certainty that we can ever know from *The Fall of Hyperion*, which is at least a more comforting truth than is to be gleaned from the similarly involuted fragment of a dream vision with which Shelley ended his career. In "The Triumph of Life" Shelley looks metaphor directly in its face and recognizes that there may be nothing else. Keats's vision pursues the larger conflation of values, the conceptual syntax that is genre, affirming that there is in human history a legacy of dream visions, all of which testify to a genuine desire for universal truth, and which are, by the nature of art, composed of and recognized by conventions that are utterly arbitrary. That they have no intrinsic meaning Keats is at pains to demonstrate, but that they allow him to structure a poem that represents the deeper and deeper search for ultimate certainties is a value to be exemplified, even self-reflexively celebrated. "There is a budding morrow in midnight" he claimed on behalf of the blind bardic visionary who impelled Western literature on its course through endless traces of imaginative conception. Having characteristically represented an oxymoron at the very inception of generic traditions, Keats pursues his fascination with the Phoenix that forever survives its own consuming in this complicated visionary experience in which he juxtaposes multiple planes of reality, all of which are traditionally sanctioned and all of which, even as they deny what they affirm, leave untouched the shrine of affirmation they can never reach. That shrine is the embodiment of human desire that systems of belief may ultimately codify but that visions empower and genres organize. The seemingly arbitrary structures that compose the genres of literature are the means by which a poet realizes what in another context Keats called the negative capability of art. Genres allow an imaginative creation to be compounded of "uncertainties, Mysteries, doubts" (*Letters*, I, 193) and even, in the extreme case of *The Fall of Hyperion*, to embody a charged fullness empty of defined meaning, only and profoundly capable.

At the opposite pole from this fragment of dissipating visions lies the most extensive composite order of European Romanticism, Goethe's *Faust*, almost a lifelong undertaking, only finished within the year of the poet's death. Whether or not its multitude of scenes, composed over so many years, all quite fit together, it is the supreme example of *genera mixta* in all of literature, the consummate *Gesammtkunstwerk*. As the defense of the mixed genre invariably rested, Tasso states it clearly, on the poet's duty to create a heterocosm of God's universe in all its varied majesty and contradiction, so Goethe, though he hedged somewhat on the vexed question of God, pursues a like aim. He does so, first, through deliberately embodying and reconciling the debate between Romantic and classical ideals in the elaborate parallels he draws between Christian and Hellenistic structures of thought and art in the two parts of *Faust* and, second, through the most ambitious reclamation of genres that exists in literature. It is sufficiently ambitious that *Faust* should attempt to revitalize every mode of drama practiced on Western stages, from its double prologue to the opera libretto conceived for one scene of Part II. (Goethe went so far as to inquire of Meyerbeer whether he had time to volunteer his services and furnish the required music.) Even more striking, however, is the panoply of verse forms and of their attendant decorums with which he invests the work: though, as it were, the figured bass of *Faust* is provided by the heroic couplet conventional to the German stage, one scene is written in the stately alexandrine of French neoclassical tragedy, and an entire act recreates Greek tragic decorum. These form a backdrop to interpolated verse forms of almost every variety imaginable: from the antique balladry of "The King of Thule" to the homely *Knittelvers* of folk tradition to the breathless lyrical effusion in dimeter of "Gretchen am Spinnenrade"—and even, with startling appropriateness, to one scene being composed in prose to render the moment of Faust's total demoralization in Part I. It is not simply a multitude of genres and forms that are thus assimilated, but with them the concerns of every major religion of the West from primitive cult worship to ethical culture, the range of human sciences, and the vision of Europe's greatest poets as well: Euripides in Act Three of Part II, Dante in the final scene, even in the Euphorion episode the touching tribute to Byron.

The result goes beyond anything contemplated in Wordsworth's term composite order. Rather, Goethe aspires, in Angus Fletcher's phrase, to a "transcendental form," reaching for the infinity of human potentiality that was the subject of his art for sixty years. For Goethe the human lot is a continual striving to become—"immer streben"—against all odds and through every conceivable form. Goethe's attempt to rear a Gothic cathedral from the page, *Faust* in the multiple perfections of its parts incarnates the "Alles Vergängliche" of its final chorus, that "something ever more about to be" that Wordsworth characterized as human destiny and that a later time would come to see as a credo of Romanticism. Goethe poured his life, his art, and an encyclopedic learning into that capacious mold in the faith that it might contain even what he might only imagine and everything he could hope to know. And every block in its construction is a form retrieved, rethought, transformed. In this, as it is the grandest, it is also the exemplary conception of European Romanticism.

NOTES

1. Goethe's sonnet translates literally as follows: "Nature and Art—they appear to diverge, but before one even considers it turn out to be the same. For me their contention has disappeared; both seem to attract me equally. Only honest exertion has real value! And if, first having set time aside, we have bound ourselves in spirit and purpose to our art, then Nature will once again be able to stir the heart. So all things under formation are constituted. In vain will liberated spirits strive for a fulfillment of pure heights. Who desires great things must make great effort. Through restriction one proves oneself a master, and only law can give us freedom."

2. With all respect for the value of M. H. Abrams's *The Mirror and the Lamp: Romantic Theory and the Critical Tradition* (New York: Oxford University Press, 1953), its argument that Romanticism participated in a proto-Crocean expressionism, so strongly based on this evidence, has had a widespread and deleterious influence, especially as the putative evidence was gathered into a college handbook under the title of *Romantic Criticism: 1800–1850*, edited by R. A. Foakes (London: Edwin Arnold, 1968). Needless to assert, the evidence supporting the present argument is pointedly to the contrary and implies the need to rewire (or refuse) this as yet blazing Romantic lamp.

3. I refer to the scholarly controversy over "the Romantic ideology," a term that furnishes the title for Jerome McGann's refreshing critique of an earlier generation's willingness to raise to ideological certainties what are culturally determined and tentative celebrations of the imaginative propensities of an embattled humanity (*The Romantic Ideology* [Chicago: University of Chicago Press, 1983]). Such an antithetical statement, however, tends to reinforce a dialectic

founded on erroneous assumptions, for, as McGann argues, there never existed an independent entity to be construed by this term.

4. Aside from numerous indigenous historical determinants, the way each culture defined its literary canon profoundly influenced its Romanticism. On this aspect one should consult Ernst Robert Curtius' magisterial and cautionary account, "Modern Canon Formation," in *European Literature and the Latin Middle Ages* (1948), tr. Willard B. Trask (New York: Harper and Row, 1953), pp. 264–272.

5. See Margaret Gilman, *The Idea of Poetry in France from Houdar de la Motte to Baudelaire* (Cambridge: Harvard University Press, 1958), pp. 178–189, and Ruth E. Mulhauser, *Sainte-Beuve and Greco-Roman Antiquity* (Cleveland: Press of Case Western Reserve University, 1969).

6. Though Gilman (*The Idea of Poetry in France*, p. 162) argues that "Hugo with the ode, Lamartine with the elegy, Vigny with the 'poëme,' had created great poetry, because they had applied their talents to genres of which the French language offered either no examples or inadequate ones," at least with Hugo generic choices are also profoundly ideological. Laurence M. Porter rightly remarks that "Hugo's theoretical statements in his prefaces to the *Odes* clearly show that he associated the Ode form with the Ancien Regime. Progressively as he evolves from monarchical views towards liberalism, he experiences the ode as inadequate for his poetic vision"—*The Renaissance of the Lyric in French Romanticism: Elegy, "Poëme" and Ode* (Lexington, Kentucky: French Forum, 1978), p. 86.

7. For this history, with a chronological bibliography appended, consult Herbert J. Hunt, *The Epic in Nineteenth-Century France; a study in heroic and humanitarian poetry from* Les martyrs to Les siècles morts (Oxford: Blackwell, 1941).

8. The Jena circle of the 1790s, including Novalis, Wackenroder, and preeminently Friedrich Schlegel, from which we derive an Idealist Romantic poetics, represented their aesthetic of liberated poetry in the short-lived periodicals, *Atheneum* and *Lyceum*. Since contemporaneously Goethe and Schiller were developing their notions of a new classicism, it is perhaps natural for later historians to see in the *Atheneumsfragmente* the foundations of a Romantic aesthetics. But a meticulous historicism must paint a more complicated picture. Insofar as these figures were known outside Germany, they were represented by Madame de Staël's *De l'Allemagne* of 1810 in a suggestive but necessarily superficial fashion. Though her account spurred the classic–romantic debate, the ideas of the Jena circle were virtually ignored by Italian culture, generally disavowed by British empiricism and skepticism, and rather splendidly distorted the minute they crossed the borders into the France of the Bourbon Restoration. We might even infer that Schlegel's circle had a comparatively minor influence on the actual achievements of German Romanticism, since for all its energetic spirit of creative innovation, its pronouncements came a quarter of a century after Goethe's own fame was established, and he and Schiller dominated the European view of German Romanticism. Against those titanic presences the effusion of brilliant but gnomic ideas either in short-lived periodicals, through an extensive

but unpublished correspondence, or in untranslated philosophical lectures could not compete on a European stage—nor, for that matter, among the general reading public of the German-speaking states. In order to avoid a serious distortion of the record in the interest of theoretical paradigms, the experimentation of the Schlegel circle needs to be grounded in this large pan-European perspective, rather than Romanticism be cut to the proportions of the circle—an enthusiastic avant-garde of a kind that the ensuing century would see recreated repeatedly in Paris. Even so, even at its most radically innovative, this circle was obsessed with the nature and uses of artistic form, and Schlegel himself, in his prescription for criticism, firmly acknowledged that "The determination of the genre and structure, of the general proportions and the limitations of a work of art is ... one of the preparatory labors of actual critical evaluation." See Hans Eichner, "Friedrich Schlegel's Theory of Literary Criticism," in *Romanticism Today*, a collection of diverse essays without stipulated editor (Bonn-Bad Godesburg: Inter Nationes, 1973), p. 24.

9. *The Shape of German Romanticism* (Ithaca: Cornell University Press, 1979).

10. John Porter Houston, *The Demonic Imagination: Style and Theme in French Romantic Poetry* (Baton Rouge: Louisiana State University Press, 1969), pp. 51–53.

11. See Baudelaire, *Correspondance generale*, ed. Jacques Crepet (Paris: L. Conard, 1947–1953), III, 39.

JOHN L. MAHONEY

"We Must Away": Tragedy and the Imagination in Coleridge's Later Poems

And thus he sang: "Adieu! Adieu!
Love's dreams prove seldom true.
The blossoms, they make no delay:
The sparkling dew-drops will not stay
Sweet month of May,
We must away;
Far, far away!
Today, to-day!"

Song from Zapolya (2.1.74–81)

It has been almost a commonplace of Coleridge criticism to think of his greatest poetry as largely the work of the years before 1800, the years of the Conversation poems and of the great imaginative trio—*Christabel, The Rime of the Ancient Mariner, Kubla Khan*—poems of the wondrous worlds of preternatural and supernatural. These are poems not always unqualifiedly joyous—witness the disturbing presence of "pensive Sara" in *The Eolian Harp*, the eerie and distressing violation of the lovely and innocent Christabel by the tormented serpent-woman Geraldine—yet ultimately and with few exceptions they celebrate the power of mind, of imagination to shape diversity into harmony, to achieve a sympathetic oneness with the beauty of nature. So also do they capture the nuances and shadings as well as the divinity-bearing power of "the one Life within us

From *Coleridge, Keats, and the Imagination: Romanticism and Adam's Dream*, edited by J. Robert Barth, S.J., and John L. Mahoney. © 1990 by The Curators of the University of Missouri.

and abroad"; of "the whole World ... imag'd in" the "vast circumference" of "the stony Mount"; of "This little lime-tree bower," its "broad and sunny leaf," "that walnut-tree," "the ancient ivy ... fronting elms" that an accident has prevented him from sharing with his friends, but that imagination has enabled him to see and to "lift the soul, and contemplate / With lively joy the joys we cannot share."[1] These poems generally move toward triumphal conclusions of blessing and redemption, of acclaim for the poet who "on honey-dew hath fed, / And drunk the milk of Paradise," even conclusions that hint at the possibility of rescue for the magical Christabel from the savage spell of the serpentine Geraldine.

In discussing *Dejection: An Ode* with its terrifying descriptions of "A grief without a pang" and "the smothering weight" on "my breast," there has been a notable tendency in critical writing about Coleridge to see the early stages of a tragic valedictory to the great creative period. The poem *To William Wordsworth* is seen as a further example as the mournful and respectful speaker, having heard Wordsworth recite *The Prelude*, views his predicament "as Life returns upon the drowned, / Life's joy rekindling roused a throng of pains" (63–64), and views genius and knowledge as "but flowers / Strewed on my curse, and borne upon my bier / In the same coffin, for the self-same grave!" (73–75). Such a tendency, while providing certain superficial advantages of chronology and ordering, seems to undermine the artistic achievement of these early nineteenth-century poems, and the extension of the view that decline characterizes the large body of poetry after 1810 simply worsens the problem.

What is intriguing about this valedictory approach to the later or even latest Coleridge poems is that it fails to make key connections between these and the pre-1800 poems and—a crucial point—to see them in the larger context of Coleridge's ideas about literature as the work of imagination. This is not to say that these late poems have not received full and perceptive treatment. Anyone familiar with the work of Patricia Adair, W. J. Bate, James Boulger, Kathleen Coburn, Angela Dorenkamp, Beverly Fields, Edward Kessler, Paul Magnuson, Marshall Suther, George Watson, and others knows from what a number of fruitful angles they have been examined.[2] Especially interesting is J. Robert Barth's observation in his recent study concerning Coleridge's ideal of love. Speaking of *Constancy to an Ideal Object* and other late poems, he sees no affirmation, no positive resolution, yet there are for him "times of hope and even moments of joy, for even in the darkest times there was always love in Coleridge's life." Eschewing the easy dismissal of the late poems as a dramatic falling-off after the turn-of-the-century triumphs, he argues, "Both in substance and style they have a life of their own."[3]

Many of these considerations of this body of poetry have been necessarily brief, treating the works quite understandably as a relatively minor part of the larger Coleridge repertoire. Others—and Barth's new book is a good example—have been more concerned with relating the poetry to matters biographical, philosophical, or theological. Molly Lefebure, in her fine study of the fullness of Coleridge's opium addiction, sees the poet practically admitting in 1811–1812 that he could only transcribe, not create.[4] George Watson sees a great deal that is right in the later poetry, arguing that it would be redundant to debate all the things that went wrong. Praising Coleridge, the post-1802 "occasional poet," especially for poems like *The Delinquent Travellers*, *Work without Hope*, and *The Garden of Boccaccio*, he nevertheless chooses the single-theme approach, the theme for him being "unrequited love."[5]

Patricia Adair, finding that Coleridge's "unusual proneness to reverie and daydream, in which the conscious and unconscious powers of the mind are merged, is the secret of his greatest poetry," argues that as the dream faded, the poetry declined, and she concludes quite remarkably with a thesis very different from our own: "No one understood better than Coleridge himself that the loss of joy meant also the death of his imagination."[6] Specifically, she contends that "*Dejection* ... lacks the power of Coleridge's greatest poetry" and that at Highgate, cared for but hopeless, wandering from place to place, a slave to increasing doses of opium, "It is no wonder that the little poetry he wrote is an expression of despair."[7] Her analysis of individual later poems is perceptive if, I think, somewhat beside the mark, as in her contention that the images are "all too obviously fixed," their meaning "so confined and definite as almost to approach the method of allegory," "another sign of the death of the imagination."[8]

James Boulger, in his *Coleridge as Religious Thinker*, sees the poet of the later years as "the poet in prose of the post-Christian Kantian ontology." Regarding the early poetry as the work of the imagination, he notes that "the later may with some justice appear as that of the higher or religious reason." And because of the emotional failure of the late poetry, Coleridge is "not remembered as a great Christian poet."[9]

W. J. Bate, using 1817 as a beginning point for the late poems, sees poems like *Limbo*, *Ne Plus Ultra*, and *Fancy in Nubibus* as "intensely personal," as "what a poet may write when he no longer conceives of himself as a poet at all." Yet Bate finds in the best post-1817 poems "a denseness of thought often embodied in an odd original imagery, frequently homely, occasionally even grotesque," abstractions "thick with emotion and meaning." Coleridge, he says, "creates a mode of poetry entirely his own."[10] Norman Fruman, who sees the poems generally as "almost all short, personal statements, often revealing a fitful energy quickly exhausted," regards the decade following *Dejection: An Ode* as "the blackest of his unhappy life, ten years of almost complete failure and personal demoralization" and the period following as offering the image "of a great artist adrift on a wide, wide sea, without sextant or compass or rudder, but still capable of moments of brilliant seamanship."[11]

All of the above is not to say that the late poems have not had their admirers and advocates, although at times the admiration and advocacy seem to stem from considerations of subject matter—philosophy and theology especially—rather than from those of poetic achievement. I. A. Richards finds poems like *Youth and Age, Phantom and Fact, Self-Knowledge,* and *Epitaph* "more taut and self-sustaining" than the later prose and finds the poetry of *Phantom and Fact* and *Constancy to an Ideal Object* "highly distinctive."[12] Kathleen Coburn sees some of the later works as "too much neglected now" and argues that "Coleridge continued to the end to think and feel like a poet."[13] She is especially interesting in her remarks on Coleridge's use of the mirror as "the image of the inward self" as well as something that "distances the self from itself," inspiring "with whatever of fear or awe it is capable, the need to bridge the gap, whether by philosophy or by poetry, between the percipient and the perceived." The bridge is built occasionally, she argues, "not by any consistent system of thought, but by brilliant aperçus touching both the knower and the world to be known."[14]

George Whalley, who has done so much with the ordering of the composition of Coleridge's poems, bemoans the lack of a "full-scale discussion of these [late] poems and of their place in the development of Coleridge's poetic art." He takes to task those who hold a view of Coleridge "as a poet who squandered and neglected his poetic faculties and took to philosophy and theology *faute de mieux*."[15] While not denying Coleridge's intense and lifelong interest in philosophy and theology, he sees these disciplines as "correlate to, and not hostile to, poetry."[16] Interestingly, in what he calls the late "metaphysical" poems of Coleridge—*Human Life, Limbo, Ne Plus Ultra, Constancy to an Ideal Object,* and others—he takes as criteria "ingenuity of metaphor, violence of conceit, and the tendency to conduct argument through a train of images rather than by logical sequence."[17]

In *Coleridge's Nightmare Poetry,* Paul Magnuson argues that while *Dejection: An Ode* has the tone of a "last poetic utterance," there is rich evidence that Coleridge "is not totally devoid of feeling and imagination," that his "still active imagination may project an image of its own destruction," that "his imagination is not totally unresponsive."[18] And in his perceptive *Coleridge's Metaphors of Being*, Edward Kessler has a special concern with the late poems. He is particularly illuminating in his discussion of the philosophical reverberations of the poems, although he underplays the workings of the poetic imagination and the success of the late poetry as poetry. For him the late poetry is not so much the record of Coleridge's poetic quest as the fulfillment of a long struggle through the metaphors of poetry to realize the potential of Being; "physical imagery must be cast aside before Being can emerge as itself, substantial and not illusory. His own poetic evolution moves away from the 'concrete', the particular, the individual—elements that most modern readers expect to find in poems."[19]

Summarizing a body of scholarship on any group of poems is dangerous, of course, but what seems clear from the above perhaps general survey is a pronounced tendency to treat the late poems of Coleridge as inferior poems after the great years, as minor works of a major poet, as good examples of the poet as philosopher, or—more sharply negative—as signs of poetic or imaginative decline or even demise after the poet, plagued by physical and psychological suffering, found less inspiration for his art and turned increasingly to the firm foundations of philosophy and theology. Yet for some readers—and I am one of them—many of these poems dramatize imaginatively a yearning for the world of people and the power of nature, and simultaneously a feeling of alienation and isolation. While an essay of this length cannot explore fully the range of possibilities in these poems, it can perhaps suggest some new directions in reading them, some fresh ways of seeing the Coleridgean imagination at work within them.

The major argument of this essay is that Coleridge remained a poet almost to the end of his life, even though he produced an enormous amount of literary theory and philosophical and theological speculation during his last twenty-five years. The all-important corollary of this argument is that the poet's central ideas on imagination and its workings did not radically change even though the materials of his experience and the rhythms and patterns of his inner life did, and even though—ironically—he protested that he had lost his capacity to feel and to imagine. The frequent and, it seems, easy argument that he turned from art to the higher disciplines needs to be examined in the light of several factors. First, from his earliest days, as his letters and notebooks reveal,

Coleridge had been interested in all kinds of philosophy. The most confident and successful efforts of the great years reveal the creative artist articulating a vision nourished by his reading in Hartley, Kant, Schelling, the Schlegels, and many others. In this connection George Whalley's contention is telling. Coleridge, he contends, "had been fascinated by philosophy and theology almost from childhood. As his precocity settled into mature interest and concern, the philosophy and theology were still important to him though changed. His poetic imagination, specialized at times in the production of verse, commanded and unified the whole ambience of his mind."[20]

A word about chronological strategies. Beginning points for the so-called late poems are at best arbitrary and in the eye and ear of the beholder. Some would find convenient the period beginning with *Dejection: An Ode*; others would start with the so-called Highgate period. I have found Whalley's delineation of Coleridge's poetic career sensible and convenient for my purposes. "The poems," Whalley suggests, "fall into three clearly defined periods: from *Lyrical Ballads* to 'Dejection' (1797–1802); from 'Dejection' to 'To William Wordsworth' (April, 1802, to January, 1807), and from January, 1807 to 1834."[21] In the rest of this essay, I will use the poems of the second period, so fully and richly treated by a number of critics, as springboards for a fuller discussion of the post-1807 poems. The major concern will be close attention to certain key poems (and less close attention to others), with a view to providing new insight into the dominant themes and techniques of the poetry of the third period and offering a foundation for a later and more extensive study.

Returning to our central argument, there was rapid development in the poetry during the 1790s, development in poetic technique and in the unfolding of certain dominant concerns that would continue throughout Coleridge's life and work—the need for unity, for the full and active expression of that vital power of synthesizing, sympathizing, and creating called imagination. The Conversation poems evince that blend of description and rumination emerging from a solitary speaker. A silent listener—present or absent—serves as a vital force. The landscape plays a prominent part in the drama. The meter is a free-flowing blank verse; the manner relaxed and idiomatic; the language concise, rich, sensuous; the subject matter the probing of complex psychological states.[22] In "The Eolian Harp," the speaker, in the presence of a seemingly orthodox and cautious listener, moves from a description of a quiet, warm, comforting cottage setting—"How exquisite the scents / Snatch'd from yon bean-field! and the world *so* hush'd!" (9–10)—to a daring speculation on the lute in the casement—"its strings / Boldlier swept, the long sequacious notes / Over delicious surges sink and rise" (17–19)—to a powerful question rooted in an imaginative vision of the lute—"And what if all of animated nature / Be but organic Harps diversely fram'd, / That tremble into thought, as o'er them sweeps / Plastic and vast, one intellectual breeze, / At once the Soul of each and God of all?" (44—48)-to an awareness of the listener's dissatisfaction with such pantheistic talk, to a final statement about his "unregenerate mind" (55) and a prayer for God's gift of faith to "A sinful and most miserable man, / Wilder'd and dark" (62–63).

There is, on the one hand, the matter-of-factness of the opening of *This Lime-Tree Bower My Prison* as the speaker records the bad fortune that has kept him at home as his friends, especially Charles Lamb, to whom he addresses the poem, walk through dazzling natural settings. There is, on the other hand, that moving statement of confidence that, even though absent, he can share imaginatively, sympathetically with his sauntering friends the joys of "walnut tree," "ancient ivy," "late twilight." The underpinnings are clearly Coleridge's developing ideas of the power of mind, the linking of man and nature, yet philosophy seems always to be in the service of poetry:

> Henceforth I shall know
> That Nature ne'er deserts the wise and pure;
> No plot so narrow, be but Nature there,
> No waste so vacant, but may well employ
> Each faculty of sense, and keep the heart
> Awake to Love and Beauty! and sometimes
> 'Tis well to be bereft of promis'd good,
> That we may lift the soul, and contemplate
> With lively joy the joys we cannot share. (59–67)

The poems of the so-called great trio also reveal their share of poetic preoccupation with philosophical and religious motifs. There is the great moment of imaginative vision when the Mariner, having shot the albatross and brought death and sterility to his world, sees and blesses intuitively, imaginatively the water snakes:

> Within the shadow of the ship
> I watched their rich attire:
> Blue, glossy green, and velvet black,
> They coiled and swam; and every track
> Was a flash of golden fire.

> O happy living things! no tongue
> Their beauty might declare:
> A spring of love gushed from my heart,
> And I blessed them unaware:
> Sure my kind saint took pity on me,
> And I blessed them unaware. (277–87)

And there are, of course, the almost Dionysiac lines of *Kubla Khan*, lines that celebrate the visionary poet whose imaginative creations can outrival the greatest human creations:

> Could I revive within me
> Her symphony and song,
>   To such a deep delight 'twould win me,
> That with music loud and long,
> I would build that dome in air,
> That sunny dome! those caves of ice!
> And all who heard should see them there,
> And all should cry, Beware! Beware!
> His flashing eyes, his floating hair!
> Weave a circle round him thrice,
> And close your eyes with holy dread,
> For he on honey-dew hath fed,
> And drunk the milk of Paradise. (42–54)

Undoubtedly the growing physical and psychological pain—especially unhappy marriage, unrequited love, the prison of opium—that characterized Coleridge's life after 1800, the search for meaning as joy seemed to vanish, triggered a more intense quest for the method and consolation of philosophy and theology in an effort to understand and to articulate, as Richard Haven has argued, the patterns of his consciousness. Haven observes, "When philosophy replaced poetry as Coleridge's primary activity, the language and symbols of philosophy came to serve some of the same functions that had earlier been served by the language and symbols of poetry."[23] One can, of course, question Haven's distinction between "symbols" of philosophy and poetry—and I do—but that seems like another matter here. Coleridge, it is true, wrote less poetry after 1800; indeed he wrote a good deal less poetry throughout his career than Wordsworth or Byron or Shelley, for example. In no sense did he abandon poetry. He continued to write a variety of poems in a variety of manners, not only those of tragic disillusionment that are relatively well known and occasionally anthologized, but also those less well known expressions of joy, however transitory, and those more overtly religious poems of prayer and resignation. As in his earlier work, some of these poems are little more than pious, abstract moralizing. In others, however, and these are the chief interest in this essay, the creative impulse seems alive and free in the midst of sadness and loss, and the imagination brings the whole soul into unified action, capturing the moods of the spirit—bright and dark—with vividness and intensity.

Expressions of joy, of communion with nature, are never completely absent, indeed are cherished deeply and expressed lovingly in later poems like *To Nature* that must be kept in mind when examining the later Coleridge repertoire. There is, of course, in *To Nature* the note of self-deprecation, the turning to nature for evidences of love and unity:

> It may indeed be phantasy, when I
>   Essay to draw from all created things
>   Deep, heartfelt, inward joy that closely clings;
> And trace in leaves and flowers that round me lie
> Lessons of love and earnest piety.   (1–5)

Yet one senses here a hesitancy (Wordsworth's "If this / Be but a vain belief" comes to mind) to attribute complete authenticity to the imagination, to the emotion that transcends abstract dogma. However, the poet continues (again with echoes of Wordsworth), let the world mock. He will conquer "fear," "grief," "vain perplexity"; he will offer not the formulaic prayer, but a different kind of present to God, one alive with the fresh and vibrant natural phenomena that pervade an early poem like *Frost at Midnight*, one that links natural and supernatural—"fields," "blue sky," "wild flower," "God," "even me":

> So will I build my altar in the fields,
>   And the blue sky my fretted dome shall be,
> And the sweet fragrance that the wild flower yields
>   Shall be the incense I will yield to Thee,
> Thee only God! And thou shalt not despise
>   Even me, the priest of this poor sacrifice. (9–14)

What interesting if muted echoes of a deeply religious commitment are expressed in a letter to Thomas Meuthen from 2 August 1815. Desirous of the esteem of good men, Coleridge fears that many may say that he seems interested in the Gospel, that he has talents revealed in political essays, in plays, "'but what has he sacrificed on the altar?' To this, before God, I dare not answer; for I ought to have chosen the better part, and have *trusted*." If he were more gifted, he claims, he "most gladly and willingly would, with divine grace, have devoted all my faculties to one object, both in verse and prose." And he does plan such art. "Till the whole mind is given to God, no man can be happy; and who gives a part, and only a part, cannot even have quiet—that sad boon of lethargy—which the utterly unawakened enjoy."[24]

There is some of the same hopeful quality in the sonnet *Fancy in Nubibus*, significantly subtitled "The Poet in the Clouds." Written, according to Charles Lamb, on the seacoast, it isolates moments of joy close to nature, but, more interesting, these are moments of creativity when the imagination can shape natural beauties according to one's hopes and desires. The speaker echoes Keats's urbanite's exclamation, "'Tis very sweet to look into the fair / And open face of heaven," and revels in the joys of the mind when it can make images from beauty and happiness as they quickly pass. "O! it is pleasant, with a heart at ease, / Just after sunset, or by moonlight skies, / To make the shifting clouds be what you please" (1–3), he begins, skillfully painting an evening sky in which ever-moving clouds can be shaped to suit the energy and inventiveness of his imagination. Or in the same mood, he can be stirred by the creations of a fellow poet; he can "let the easily persuaded eyes / Own each quaint likeness issuing from the mould / Of a friend's fancy" (4–6). Or, even more venturesome, he can exercise that sympathetic aspect of the imagination, can become part of the scene he creates. In pictures of rich color and swift movement, he imagines himself "with head bent low / And cheek aslant see rivers flow of gold / 'Twixt crimson banks; and then, a traveller, go / From mount to mount through Cloudland, gorgeous land!" (6–9).

The joyous moment or condition can also be one of love for a person or a state of the spirit that renders it open and receptive to all creation. In the dramatic piece called *The Improvisatore*, Coleridge assumes the title role and deals with the question of what is true love posed by two young ladies, Katherine and Eliza. The core of his response moves beyond personal anecdote to the more philosophical dimension of sympathy in love, of the outward manifestations betokening a deeper power within the soul. Love, he tells the young ladies in his discursive response, is "a constitutional communicativeness and *utterancy* of heart and soul; a delight in the detail of sympathy, in the outward and visible signs of the sacrament within—to count, as it were, the pulses of the life of love" (I.464). Fascinated by the Improvisatore's response, the girls teasingly wonder whether one who speaks so beautifully of love in the abstract can have truly experienced it. His answer is a song of affirmation qualified: he loved in his imagination, which for a time created an ideal embodiment, but "She missed her wonted food" (15). "Fancy must be fed" (12); hope, the cardinal Coleridgean virtue, must be kept alive, but was not. Images of stormy sea, castaway, and bewilderment, images that recur in the later poetry, dominate Coleridge's self-portrait. In a mood reminiscent of Wordsworthian remembrance, he traces the decline of love's intensity, of hope, but speaks of new gifts that surpass all others. In richly figurative language that ironically anticipates the tragic later poem *Work without Hope*, he pictures a new calm, "Late Autumn's Amaranth, that more fragrant blows / When Passion's flowers all fall or fade" (56–57).

There are few more powerful evocations of joy revived in the midst of dejection, imagination reactivated in the midst of the dull ache of spiritual and physical pain, than *The Garden of Boccaccio*. A dream vision, the situation, rhythm, diction, and imagery of the opening lines recall *Dejection*. The mood is "dreary"; life seems "emptied of all genial powers"; the poet sits "alone" (1–4). All prayers for help seem to fail; the past cannot be revived. The "dull continuous ache" (8) seems the only vital sign as he hovers at the brink. Then the "Friend" of the poem, Anne Gilman, leaves at his side a striking illustration of Boccaccio's "First Day" from an edition of the *Decamerone* by Thomas Stothard, a contemporary painter and engraver. Again, as elsewhere in the poems being discussed, the theme is not rebirth or return to youthful sensuous awareness. The joy is vivid but not lasting; it is remembrance in its highest form, the product of the artist's ability to evoke and stir imaginative response. Wordsworth's "The picture of the mind revives again" is echoed. The idle eye becomes busy; the inward power is recharged; language and image are freshly recovered:

> Like flocks adown a newly-bathéd steep
>   Emerging from a mist: or like a stream
> Of music soft that not dispels the sleep,
>   But casts in happier moulds the slumberer's dream. (19–22)

The process is progressive. "The picture stole upon my inward sight" (24), and "one by one (I know not whence) were brought / All spirits of power that most had stirr'd my thought / In selfless boyhood" or "charm'd my youth" or "lent a lustre to the earnest scan / Of manhood" (24–34). The delights of Boccaccio move him to sing again, to hope until that "sober" matron reappears "Whom as a faery child my childhood woo'd / Even in my dawn of thought-Philosophy; / Though then unconscious of herself, pardie, / She bore no other name than Poesy" (46–51). There is here the intriguing implication that poetry and philosophy have, in spite of their obvious differences, a special kinship, that poetry, active in the creation of a youthful, realizable ideal, later becomes philosophy for some artists, but that philosophy can never completely divorce itself from the need to concretize, to vivify abstractions and make them real to the heart. The poem's conclusion is dramatic and stirring. Thanks to Boccaccio the poet is, at least for a time, "all awake!" There is a new immediacy to his life: "I see no longer! I myself am there, / Sit on the groundsward, and the banquet share" (59–65).

Such poems are, of course, not fully representative of the work of the last twenty-five years. The basic argument of the essay to this point has been that Coleridge's career cannot be neatly divided into a phase during which he produced his most memorable poetry and another in which, imagination and poetry failing, he turned to the solace of philosophy and theology. The key corollary of the argument is that Coleridge remained a poet to the end, that the controlling image of the later poetry, a poetry of uneven quality, is the ideal unity, a state in which the imagination discovers in nature analogues of an interior joy. If the analogues become fewer and fewer, if some seem abstract and lifeless, if disillusionment dominates at times, the triumphs still remain. The ideal for Coleridge may seem evanescent, but it still remains a goal to be pursued and cherished, and the imagination provides an extraordinary access route.

Yet the pain and sadness of so much of the later poetry are inescapable. The poems of this period and after catch a strongly tragic spirit. At times—and invariably the poetry suffers—he openly doubts the creative power and seeks the more solid foundations of philosophy or theology, or, like the fideist, throws himself totally on God's mercy. The result, as in earlier poems when intensity of religious zeal and strength of philosophical argument dominate, is an abundance of heavy-handed moralizing, a strong reliance on conventional poetic diction, and a rigidly regular, almost singsong, rhythm. Lines like the following from *A Hymn*, with their commonplace plea of the guilty man to an all-powerful God, illustrate the fideistic posture and the poetic effects described above:

Great God! thy works how wondrous fair!
Yet sinful man dids't thou declare
   The whole Earth's voice and mind!
Lord, ev'n as Thou all-present art,
O may we still with heedful heart
   Thy presence know and find!   (11–16)

Similar characteristics are seen in his translation *Faith, Hope, and Charity: From the Italian of Guarini.* They can be seen all too strikingly in the lackluster didacticism of *Love, Hope, and Patience in Education* with its distrust of the joys of spontaneity and its presentation of a new and stiffly personified heroine of comfort:

   When overtask'd at length
Both Love and Hope beneath the load give way.
Then with a statue's smile, a statue's strength,
Stands the mute sister, Patience, nothing loth,
And both supporting does the work of both. (22–26)

But the failure of such poems should not be allowed to hide a considerable number of triumphs, poetry still responsive to the predicament of the artist who creates from the exploration of human alienation and loss complex, abruptly expressed, and vividly realized images in free-flowing rhythms that seem modern. Coleridge's imagination is still at work, albeit its range is widened to include the tragic as well as the joyous, to catch the multifaceted nuances of human emotion. Coleridge was, of course, theorizing more about the imagination during these years—in *Biographia Literaria*, the notebooks, *The Statesman's Manual*, and other prose works touching on aesthetic questions. He was describing his vision of nature in greater detail, not as the "one, clear, unchanged, and universal light" of Pope, but as a process, a living force in which universal forms and concrete particulars are constantly interacting. He was offering his idea of imagination as the root of genius in the arts, the great completing power mediating between and reconciling opposites to create unity and, in words from his celebrated definition in *The Statesman's Manual*, giving "birth to a system of symbols, harmonious in themselves, and consubstantial with the truths, of which they are the *conductors*."[25] Symbol, far from a simple image, is a translation of a complex reality, capturing what is essential within the creative activity of nature.

Imagination, then, is not simply the faculty of triumph, of joyous unity with nature. It is also at home capturing the tragic notes of human experience, the sense of human suffering, loss, alienation. Nothing that is human can be foreign to imagination. Just as the great tragedians capture the predicaments of men and women who suffer and yet endure, who cry out against injustice, who achieve a kind of grandeur in spite of battles lost but fought nevertheless, so to a lesser extent Coleridge captures imaginatively sadness and struggle. Yet, as in great tragedy, he catches it in such a way that we feel, sympathize with, pity, but do not despair; "all disagreeables evaporate," as Keats says of the stark intensity of King Lear's loss of everything and his discovery of himself. There is, in Aristotle's words, a catharsis, not an avoidance of pain or an easy solution, but a genuine purging of the tragic emotions, a putting into perspective of the individual predicament so that those who read or watch feel their experience widened, their sense of the range of human possibility enlarged.

Michael Friedman offers an illuminating way of thinking about the tragic imagination. Writing about Wordsworth's pamphlet *The Convention of Cintra*, he argues, "Wordsworth suggests that the true sorrow of life is that reality offers so few experiences that are correlative 'to the dignity and intensity of human desires.'" Wordsworth, according to Friedman, saw the Convention as evoking only shame and sorrow and yet as offering "an opportunity for the release of emotions that would not be beneath the dignity and intensity of human desires. The sorrow of human life would be overcome in the experience of true shame and sorrow. A catharsis would have been achieved." Friedman concludes his analysis with the contention that the "discharge of emotion may well lessen the emotional tension in the sorrowing individual's psychic economy. The diminution of psychic tension is felt as a form of pleasure."[26]

Coleridge himself had been interested in the tragic and the purgation of tragic emotion. "The communicativeness of our nature leads us," he wrote, "to describe our own sorrows; in the endeavour to describe them, intellectual activity is exerted; and from intellectual activity, there results a pleasure, which is gradually associated, and mingles as a corrective, with the painful subject of the description."[27] He alerts his readers to the dark side of his spirit: "If any man expect from my poems the same easiness of style which he admires in a drinking song, for him I have not written." And carrying aesthetic theory into the realm of theology, he explains, "Poetry has been to me its own 'exceeding great reward:' it has soothed my afflictions; it has multiplied and refined my enjoyments; it has endeared solitude; and it has given me the habit of wishing to discover the Good and the Beautiful in all that meets and surrounds me."[28]

Coleridge's later works include many poems of the tragic imagination, poems basically of the inner life where truth seems most real, poems that struggle in gnarled, nightmarish, seemingly disconnected images to evoke a twilight state just short of absolute negation. The King Lear of act 4, scene 6, half-mad in his imaginings, comes to mind ("There's hell, there's darkness, there's the sulphurous pit, burning, scalding, stench, corruption"), but the "ounce of civet" is rarely found to "sweeten" his imagination, and we are left with the frightening picture of a man terrified, seemingly cut off from his inner sources of strength.

As suggested earlier, the poems of Whalley's second period, notably *Dejection: An Ode* and to a lesser extent *To William Wordsworth*, when matched with the imaginative power of the post-1807 poetry, provide a basis for the argument concerning the irony of Coleridge's cry for a lost imagination. With the seeming affirmation of Wordsworth's *Ode: Intimations of Immortality* still ringing in his ears, Coleridge wrote his *Dejection: An Ode* on 4 April 1802.[29] How different its tone, its language, its imagery, but especially its facing of similar questions from both the Wordsworth poem and his own earlier work. Using the familiar lines of the *Ballad of Sir Patrick Spence* as his point of departure and the omen of "the new Moon / With the old Moon in her arms" as an anticipation of stormy weather, the speaker pleads for "The coming-on of rain and squally blast" not simply for its physical power, but that it might minister to his deadened spirit, "Might startle this dull pain, and make it move and live" (14–20). Coleridge would have the reader see and feel his physical condition as complete. Indeed stanzas 2–3 dramatize a psychological predicament, a sense of deadness within, a sadness that transcends physical pain and that cannot be adequately conveyed in the language of common speech. It is

> A grief without a pang, void, dark, and drear,
> A stifled, drowsy, unimpassioned grief,
> Which finds no outlet, no relief,
> In word, or sigh, or tear— (21–24)

Yet—and how ironic—we see vivid images of "the western sky, / And its peculiar tint of yellow green," of "thin clouds above, in flakes and bars, / That give away their motion to the stars"; of "Yon crescent Moon, as fixed as if it grew / In its own cloudless, starless lake of blue." These are quickly followed, however, by the finality of "I see, not feel, how beautiful they are!" We find no Wordsworthian sense of the possibility of growth, of compensation, only the speaker's definitive assurance that "I may not hope from outward forms to win / The passion and the life, whose fountains are within" (25–46).

It is this deep conviction of the absolute need for an active, creative, psychological power—the imagination—that the speaker develops in the touching lines of stanzas 4–5. Only the mind's dynamic encounter with experience creates meaning. Sight and memory are inadequate; "we receive but what we give, / And in our life alone does Nature live." Meaning, felt truth, comes only from the self. The familiar Romantic image of effluence—the lamp, the fountain—comes to mind: "from the soul itself must there be sent / A sweet and potent voice of its own birth, / Of all sweet sounds the life and element!" The speaker calls the power "Joy," an inner force possessed by and given only to the "pure," a force "Which wedding Nature to us gives in dower / A new Earth and new Heaven." It creates a new reality "that charms or ear or sight" (59–75).

So much for the speaker's description of the woebegone state of his spirit, the depth of his loss, the impossibility of rebirth. Stanza 6 sharply echoes Wordsworth's opening stanza as the speaker plays on the words of the Immortality ode to dramatize the very different state of his own soul. He can, he says, recall a time when his mind could cope with misfortune, when he could hope in the midst of sadness:

> There was a time when, though my path was rough,
> This joy within me dallied with distress,
> And all misfortunes were but as the stuff
> Whence Fancy made me dreams of happiness. (76–79)

He had the gift of "hope" and could appreciate the Wordsworthian sense of the possibility of some gain in spite of eroding youthful blessings. Yet there is a finality, a firmness of tone, in his convictions about the present. "But now afflictions bow me down to earth," he says. "But oh! each visitation / Suspends what nature gave me at my birth, / My shaping spirit of Imagination." Such finality and firmness make him turn to "Abstruse research," only to have that turning result in the loss of the "natural man" and in a psychological infection that becomes "the habit of my soul" (80–93).

In the long, irregular stanza that follows, there is a flow of grotesque, terrifying imagery that graphically reveals the depth of difference in the answers of the speakers to the problems of both odes. The speaker of

Dejection finds no "joy" in the "embers," no gathering with the children, no union with nature. His are cries of anguish as he personifies the fantasies that torment him: "Hence, viper thoughts, that coil around my mind, / Reality's dark dream!" The "joyous song" of the "young lambs," the "gladness of the May" in the Wordsworth ode give way to "the wind, / Which long has raved unnoticed." The lute, so unlike the melodious Eolian harp of Coleridge's earlier poems, sends forth "a scream / Of agony by torture lengthened out." Here is no benevolent nature; instead appropriately frightening images dominate, the product of a tormented mind no longer possessed of that great prize "Joy." The setting is "Bare crag, or mountain-tairn, or blasted tree, / Or pine-grove whither woodman never clomb, / Or lonely house, long held the witches' home." The wind is not a Wordsworthian breeze but "Mad lutanist! who in this month of showers, / Of dark-brown gardens, and of peeping flowers, / Mak'st Devils' yule, with worse than wintry song" (94–120). The story is not one of triumph over loss, but, again ironically, an imaginative adaptation of the drama of Wordsworth's Lucy Gray:

> 'Tis of a little child,
> Upon a lonesome wild,
> Not far from home, but she hath lost her way:
> And now moans low in bitter grief and fear,
> And now screams loud, and hopes to make her mother hear.
> (121–25)

The concluding stanza has a special beauty in itself and a special significance in the way it illuminates the contrast between the two odes. Wordsworth's poem ends with a seeming confidence, firmly focused on the speaker and on his faith that age brought gifts greater than the losses, that memory had made it possible to feel thoughts "too deep for tears." Coleridge's concluding stanza begins on a similar self-centered note; he dwells on his sadness. Yet very quickly the self-centeredness gives way to an imaginative concern for the other, to a gentle good wish, a blessing for the "Lady." The lines are a prayer for an experience the speaker can no longer know—except imaginatively—but would nonetheless bestow. Fresh, vividly realized images convey his wish and prayer: "Visit her, gentle Sleep! with wings of healing"; "May all the stars hang bright above her dwelling" (126–33). His strongest prayer, however, is for inner strength, for the capacity to feel, to imagine, to know joy, to internalize the vitality of the process of nature:

Joy lift her spirit, joy attune her voice;
To her may all things live, from pole to pole,
Their life the eddying of her living soul! (134–36)

Dejection: An Ode provides a firm foundation for exploring the post-1807 poems with their pattern of physical and psychological pain, their rendering of this pain not through mere self-indulgent spurts of tormented rhetoric or maudlin religious sentiment, but through powerful images of the dark side of experience and the catharsis of hope, even when the hope is for another human being. So does the poem *To William Wordsworth*, a poem Coleridge composed, as the subtitle tells us, on the night after he had heard Wordsworth recite *The Prelude*. Again irony is striking as he addresses his "Friend" and "Teacher" and praises his poem with its recounting "Of the foundations and the building up / Of a Human Spirit" (5–6), of how:

Scarce conscious, and yet conscious of its close
I sate, my being blended in one thought
(Thought was it? or aspiration? or resolve?)
Absorbed, yet hanging still upon the sound—
And when I rose, I found myself in prayer. (108–12)

In the post-1807 poems, moments of relief are fewer; the pain is obviously deeper; the loss more decisive. Yet the poet, it seems, remains the dominant figure, ranging through the domain of his imagination for word and image to catch the state of the spirit. One notes, on the most obvious level, the simple cry of physical pain. "Sad lot, to have no Hope!" (1), he moans in a prayer for relief in *The Visionary Hope*, moving from routine abstractions to concrete feelings, sights, and sounds that dramatize his plight: "He strove in vain! the dull sighs from his chest / Against his will the stifling road revealing, / Though Nature forced" (5–7), "Sickness within and miserable feeling" (11). After a time the physical and psychological merge to create a phantasmagorical state: "Though obscure pangs made curses of his dreams, / And dreaded sleep, each night repelled in vain, / Each night was scattered by his own loud screams" (12–14). Yet pain is at least a sign of life, a basis for hope, so much so that he is tempted to "let it stay! / yet this one Hope should give / Such strength that he would bless his pains and live" (26–28). *Youth and Age*, a once-upon-a-time poem, contrasts his youthful exuberance with "This breathing house not built with hands, / This body that does me grievous wrong" (8–9), with "locks in silvery slips," with "This drooping gait, this altered size" (33–34). *The Garden of Boccaccio* records the "numbing spell" (5), "the dull continuous ache" (9). The poet in "To a Lady: With Falconer's *Shipwreck*" identifies with the hero, William Falconer, of the poem he sends to his lady. Like Falconer, and Cowper's castaway, he is a "shipwrecked man!" (16) whose verse is inspired by "The elevating thought of suffered pains, / Which gentle hearts shall mourn" (19–20).

As pathetic and debilitating as physical pain is, it is but prelude to the state of his spirit, to isolation from the nourishment of nature, from the ever-elusive ideal that one would grasp but cannot. The best poems of these years, like all successful poems, dramatize the condition rather than narrate it, fashioning a language and an imagery that match the deeply rooted malaise of the writer, creating metaphor and symbol that participate in the reality of which they are a part.

The state of the spirit, so much a part of the great *Dejection* ode just considered, stands out most sharply in the later poems as a kind of microcosm of Coleridge's larger vision of human nature. Conventional images of darkness, shipwreck, and physical pain have already been noted. What, however, distinguishes the best of these poems is what has already been briefly suggested—the workings of the imagination on the tragic side of life, the darker nuances of the psyche, with a resulting knotted, highly complex, and frequently disconnected language and imagery. These have been associated, not quite appropriately, by some critics with the Metaphysical poetry of the seventeenth century, but perhaps more rightly they should be seen as anticipating what we might call the modern tradition, perhaps the "terrible" sonnets of Hopkins, the bleak and jarring world of Eliot's Prufrock or *The Wasteland*, the troubled fantasies of Robert Lowell. The often fragmentary quality of the poems, the lack of logical connectives between clusters of images, the condensed and often free-flowing quality of the writing—all these suggest something new and different. If symbols are, in Coleridge's aesthetic, "consubstantial with the truths of which they are conductors," they seem a fair way of describing what we are dealing with here.

What is man? What is the nature of his condition? Does he have a basis for hope given his condition? These are the recurring questions. Man is consistently imaged as inexplicable in his essence, as uncertain of his destiny at best, indeed all too often unable to decipher the code of nature provided by a once-loving God as a way of achieving the "blessed mood" of happiness. *Human Life* sketches him in richly paradoxical and frightening images; at times—interesting phenomenon—even Coleridge's abstractions and personifications seem to possess a remarkable vitality and suggestiveness. Man is a "vessel purposeless, unmeant, / Yet drone-hive strange of phantom purposes" (8–9), the drone image suggesting the male of the honeybee, stingless and making no honey, living on the labor of others, lethargic, idle. He is a "Blank accident! nothing's anomaly!" (14) whose very essence is "contradiction" (9). *Self-Knowledge*, written just two years before Coleridge's death, describes him not proudly as "What a piece of work" but grimly as "Dark fluxion, all unfixable by thought" (7), as "Vain sister of the worm" (9), images of dehumanization. *Limbo* sees men caught in a strange arena between life and nonlife, shrinking from the light like "Moles / (Nature's mute monks, live mandrakes of the ground)" (6–7), frightened animals scurrying for some kind of safety.

Most terrifying is the dramatization of his spiritual life, a more compressed and powerful development of the nostalgic lines of *Dejection* like "I may not hope from outward forms to win / The passion and the life whose fountains are within" or "O Lady! we receive but what we give, / And in our life alone does Nature live." The power, so often seen in the figure of the fountain—"Joy's bosom-spring" (18) in *A Hymn*, the Fount of Cheer in *The Two Founts*—still remains, but it is choked, and the nature with which it must be reconciled and reunited to create life has become an Eliot-like wasteland, "A heap of broken images, where the sun beats, / And the dead tree gives no shelter, the cricket no relief, / And the dry stone no sound of water." Man is caught, indeed trapped, not in the bliss of heaven or the damnation of hell, but in "Limbo's Den," a macabre state of mental terror, "not a Place" but a realm "where Time and weary Space / Fettered from flight, with nightmare sense of fleeing, / Strive for their last crepuscular half-being" (11–14). Time and space have become meaningless scholastic categories, no longer susceptible to neat definition; poetry, however, with its image-making power, must do what philosophy cannot, must translate the untranslatable. Now one confronts

> Lank Space, and scytheless Time with branny hands
> Barren and soundless as the measuring sands,
> Not mark'd by flit of Shades,—unmeaning they
> As moonlight on the dial of the day! (*Limbo*, 15–18)

The den of Limbo is a hopeless one, a Kafkaesque existence lacking even the mild comfort of the old Christian description of Limbo. It is a condition not a place, "Wall'd round, and made a spirit-jail secure, / By the mere horror of blank Naught-at-all" (32–33). Angus Fletcher in his essay "Positive Negation" sees Coleridge as like Hamlet, fearful "lest events simply may not follow. His work can be conceived as an intensely interested struggle against this fear."[30] Rejecting the abstractions of philosophy and theology, he imagines Limbo as at the very boundary line of existence where Space and Time—one "lank," the other "scytheless"— seem to have lost all their power and prerogatives, indeed "unmeaning they / As moonlight on the dial of the day!" (17–18). How different from human time, human life, although it too offers little consolation. Human time is a blind old man—Gloucester-like—with a face all eye, with a new silent sight gratefully accepting a special kind of illumination. Coleridge's image is powerful, sharply drawn:

> With scant white hairs, with foretop bald and high,
> He gazes still,—his eyeless face all eye;—
> As 'twere an organ full of silent sight,
> His whole face seemeth to rejoice in light!
> Lip touching lip, all moveless, bust and limb—
> He seems to gaze at that which seems to gaze on him! (25–30)

As W. J. Bate says, "But even this blind hope is denied the soul in limbo. For there, if the redemption of man is not believed, hope turns to fear."[31] After seventeen relentlessly rhyming couplets, the poem is climaxed by a quatrain whose sense of finality and strategically positioned rhymes speak for themselves:

> A lurid thought is growthless, dull Privation,
> Yet that is but a Purgatory curse;
> Hell knows a fear far worse,
> A fear—a future state;—'tis Positive Negation! (35–38)

Fletcher's observation is again helpful as he surveys the poet's whole inner state. Coleridge, he argues, "whose heart is so full, if sometimes only of its own emptiness, its desire to be filled, seems fully aware that the betweenness of time-as-moment, pure thresholdness, barren liminality, at least in what Einstein would call a 'space-like' way, must be a nothingness."[32]

Few poems capture so well and so imaginatively the mood of Coleridge in the later years as *Time Real and Imaginary: An Allegory*. The quick rhythms and idiomatic manner of the opening lines suggest the joy and liveliness of youth when time seems an "endless race" run by "Two lovely children," "A sister and a brother!" (4–5). The sister gleefully runs onward, unaware of real time and age; in looking back, however, she spies the brother, no longer young and swift, but a blind, haggard, Bergman-like wraith who has felt the ravages of real time. The mood of the opening is abruptly reversed with the regular, almost stolid rhythm of the final couplet intensifying the pathos: "O'er rough and smooth with even step he passed, / And knows not whether he be first or last" (10–11). Coleridge in a January–March 1811 notebook entry tried to capture the sense of time that pervades the poem:

> Contrast of troubled manhood, and joyously-active youth, in the sense of Time. To the former ~~it~~ Time, like the Sun in a ~~cloud~~ empty Sky is never seen to move, but only to *have moved*—there, there it was—& now 'tis here—now distant—now distant—yet all a blank between / To the latter it is as the full moon in a fine breezy October night—driving in amid Clouds of all shapes & hues & kindling shifting colors, like an Ostrich in its speed—& yet seems not to have moved at all—This I feel to be a just image of time real & time as felt, in two different states of Being—The Title of the Poem therefore (for Poem it ought to be) should be Time real, and Time felt (in the sense of Time) in Active Youth / or Activity and Hope & fullness of aim in any period / and in despondent objectless Manhood—Time *objective* & subjective—[33]

Ne Plus Ultra captures more powerfully in sharp, staccato lines the haunted imagination. As suggested earlier, Coleridge's allegorical figures can at times take on an unusual strength and range of suggestion, and the picture of the Demon in these lines, with its play of opposites—especially the familiar "Night" and "Light"—and of striking adjectives—"primal," "Condens'd," "abysmal"—takes the poem beyond the conventional into an entirely new realm of poetic effect. Note the barrage of what might be called powerfully vague images of a demonic creature aimed at creating the effect of terror:

> Sole Positive of Night!
>   Antipathist of Light!
> Fate's only essence! primal scorpion rod—
> The one permitted opposite of God!—
> Condens'd blackness and abysmal storm

Compacted to one sceptre
Arms the grasp enorm— (1–7)

What is being dramatized, then, is a condition of imaginative and emotional paralysis, an entrapment by the Demon that, isolating man from the vital beauties of nature, triggers the creation of the nightmare world, a place of silent, fetid, lethargy-inducing darkness that envelops its victims and leaves them without that central Coleridgean virtue of hope. *Work without Hope*, one of the most interesting and crucial of the later poems, graphically captures the gap between the torpor of the poet and the active processes of nature:

All nature seems at work. Slugs leave their lair—
The bees are stirring-birds are on the wing—
And Winter slumbering in the open air,
Wears on his smiling face a dream of Spring!
And I the while, the sole unbusy thing,
Nor honey make, nor pair, nor build, nor sing. (1–6)

Every phase of nature is "at work," every creature directed toward its final cause, its proper activity; there is a wonderfully imaginative sense of an orchestrated process with self-fulfillment the goal and result. "Slugs leave their lair" to begin their annual activity; "bees are stirring," weary of their long sleep and plotting the long-range activities of later spring and summer; once again, after their annual vacation, "Birds are on the wing." These vivid, concrete images culminate in the lovely personification of Winter, still asleep, but with a magic sense of anticipation, wearing "on his smiling face a dream of Spring!" The poet seems almost categorical in describing himself as "the sole unbusy thing." He is useless. He can no longer create, find an outlet for his capacities, cannot "honey make, nor pair, nor build, nor sing." Like the antihero of *Dejection*, he can "see, not feel, how beautiful they are!" The full extent of his condition is captured in the last four lines. The first couplet juxtaposes a pathetic self-portrait, "With lips unbrightened, wreathless brow, I stroll," with a rhetorical question, "And would you learn the spells that drowse my soul?" The second, constructed around a brilliant and favorite Coleridge metaphor, answers that question: "Work without Hope draws nectar in a sieve / And Hope without an Object cannot live" (11–14). The precious nectar garnered from Work is lost in the sieve of Despair. Hope, without the vehicle of fulfillment, the power of making dreams concrete and realizable, the imagination, is a cruel hoax. The creative, life-giving fount has given way to the wasting sieve. Surely this sonnet anticipates the anguish of Hopkins's *Thou Art Indeed Just, Lord*.

> See, banks and brakes
> Now, leavèd how thick! lacèd they are again
> With fretty chervil, look, and fresh wind shakes
> Them; birds build—but not I build; no, but strain,
> Time's eunuch, and not one work that wakes
> Mine, O thou lord of life, send my roots rain. (9–14)

A number of later poems, with varying degrees of success, focus specifically on loss of love or on the parody of love as pity or kindness. Since love is a central concern for Coleridge, the inability to love or to find reciprocation for love distresses him greatly. In a seldom-discussed *Song*, he cleverly juxtaposes two stanzas, using the second to undercut the power of the first and concluding with one of his most grotesque and painful metaphors. The opening of the *Song* celebrates love as a flashing and sharp sword, "veiled in spires of myrtle-wreath," so sharp that it "cuts its sheath" (1–2). Once the unfolding takes place, once we see "through the clefts itself has made," the sword of love is "By rust consumed, or snapt in twain; / And only hilt and stump remain" (5–8). *The Pang More Sharp Than All: An Allegory*, after describing in rather uninspired fashion the departure of the boy Love ("Hope's last and dearest child without a name!— / Has flitted from me, like the warmthless flame," 2–3), turns inward to record how love has not so much departed from him as he has become "exiled" from love. Then in one of those extraordinary psychological images of creative interaction, one that draws on Spenser's *Faerie Queene*, Coleridge develops the motif of exile:

> For still there lives within my secret heart
> The magic image of the magic Child
> Which there he made up-grow by his strong art,
> As in that crystal orb-wise Merlin's feat,—
> The wondrous 'World of Glass,' wherein inisled
> All long'd for things their beings did repeat;—
> And there he left it, like a Sylph beguiled,
> To live and yearn and languish incomplete! (36–43)

In still another allegorical poem, *Love's Apparition and Evanishment: An Allegoric Romance*, a poem filled with echoes of *Dejection*, the tragic death of love is strangely portrayed. Using another favorite image, the "eyeless face," the poet compares himself to "a long Arab, old and blind" (1), who "listens for a human sound—in vain" (6). He describes his own "vacant mood" (8), "the sickly calm with aimless scope, / in my own heart" (15–16). The poem turns abruptly as he spies "thee, O genial Hope, / Love's elder sister" (17–18). What he sees now, however, is not the bright girl of his youth, but a Gothic horror, "Drest as a bridesmaid, but all pale and cold, / With roseless cheek, all pale and cold and dim, / Lie lifeless at my feet!" (19–21). Now Love, "a sylph in bridal trim" (22), stands beside him, but, unlike the memorable figure in George Herbert's *Love III* who finally brings warmth and hope, she has no power here. Indeed she brings despair as she "fades away / In the chill'd heart by gradual self-decay" (31–32).

In spite of pain, psychological trauma, and the onset of despair, hope flickers from time to time, hope in natural process, in human love, in poetry, in the ideal created by the power of mind/imagination. These poems, however, ultimately remove the flickers of that ideal, tracing its possibilities, its decline and fall and death, and preparing the way for a final resignation to God. Clearly one of the most beautifully realized poems in this vein is *Constancy to an Ideal Object*. It opens on a Renaissance note with a vision of the mutability of earthly things: "Since all that beat about in Nature's range, / Or veer or vanish" (1–2). The poet, inclined to hope in his ideal, quickly questions it, asking "why should'st thou remain / The only constant in a world of change, / O yearning Thought! that liv'st but in the brain?" (2–4). It is folly to "Call to the Hours, that in the distance play" (5); they will bring no "life-enkindling breath" (8). Outcasts, battered by the storms of existence, "Hope and Despair meet in the porch of Death!" (10). There can be no meeting of the "I am" and the "It is." As Boulger writes, "The ideal, fixed mode of thought, the spiritual image, must remain detached from the vibrant, mutable reality of Nature, through a paradox which is emotionally enervating for the poet."[34] Still the poet is haunted by the possibility of dreams realized, images rendered concrete, the ideal in the real. He envisions in his mind's eye "some dear embodied Good, / Some living Love" (13–14), "a home, an English home, and thee!" (18). Yet all seems vain; the ideal—of love, of hope, of peace—will vanish as two of Coleridge's recurring metaphors illustrate. The first is the familiar shipwreck image freshly conceived. The early plight of the Mariner comes to mind. Without the ideal, even the perfect home is "but a becalmed bark, / Whose Helmsman on an ocean waste and wide / Sits mute and pale his mouldering helm beside" (22–24). The second, rooted in a much-discussed contemporary phenomenon that Coleridge had himself observed and mentioned, is that of a person following his own projected shadow and attributing mysterious powers to the effect created. The image fashioned is a ghostly embodiment of his growing despair of finding the ideal. "And art thou nothing?" he questions, confronting the image, and the answer follows quickly and disturbingly:

> Such thou art, as when
> The woodman winding westward up the glen
> At wintry dawn, where o'er the sheep-track's maze
> The viewless snow-mist weaves a glist'ning haze,
> Sees full before him, gliding without tread,
> An image with a glory round its head;
> The enamoured rustic worships its fair hues,
> Nor knows he makes the shadow, he pursues! (25–31)

As I. A. Richards says, "There is something more terrible than loneliness here. It is the Ideal itself—not the actual or the fancied embodiment—he is questioning."[35]

Some of the later poems, especially those written at the very end, develop a kind of tranquillity, a sense of a new hope, or perhaps resignation, that comes not from human resources or poetic power but from a turning to God. In *Self-Knowledge* Coleridge is angered by the familiar adage "Know thyself" and proceeds to challenge it: "Say, cans't thou make thyself?—Learn first that trade" (3). With increasing rhetorical intensity he continues, "What is there in thee, Man, that can be known?" (6). The new answer is fideistic, more a counsel of religious perfection than a line of poetry: "Ignore thyself, and strive to know thy God!" (10). The poem *Reason* seems to challenge poetic vision and the mysteriousness of life as it elevates a new power to probe and to achieve the higher knowledge:

> Whene'er the mist, that stands 'twixt God and thee
> Defecates to a pure transparency
> That intercepts no light and adds no stain—
> There Reason is, and then begins her reign! (1–4)

Coleridge's Highgate years, as Angela Dorenkamp has demonstrated, were years of great unhappiness, but years in which he came increasingly to recognize the vanity of human endeavor and the absolute need for supernatural strength, for a power beyond mind, beyond imagination. This essay has followed the poetic rendering of unhappiness in a series of remarkably powerful poems. They are poems of hope and despair but ultimately of resignation, and several of the final works are more versified prayer than inspired poetry. Most readers know the famous epitaph. Fewer know the touching *My Baptismal Birth-Day* of the same year. No longer the quester, no longer the Unitarian preacher, no longer the poet of the holiness of the "One Life," he is finally "God's child in Christ adopted,—Christ my all" (1). He now preaches confidently a new orthodoxy: "Father! in Christ we live, and Christ in thee" (5). With Donne-like militancy, with a ringing challenge to the lure of the world, he rests his case:

> Let then earth, sea, and sky
> Make war against me! On my heart I show
> Their mighty master's seal. In vain they try
> To end my life, that can but end its woe—
> Is that a death-bed where a Christian lies!—
> Yes! but not his—'tis Death itself there dies. (9–14)

It is as if the orthodox religious thinker and man of faith and the artist meet, and poetry finally gives way. The restless Coleridge finds his rest in resignation to God.

NOTES

This essay is an outgrowth of my short article "The Reptile's Lot: Theme and Image in Coleridge's Later Poetry" in *Wordsworth Circle* 8 (Autumn 1977): 349–60. I am grateful to the editor for permission to use parts of that article.

1. All references to Coleridge's poetry are to *The Complete Poetical Works of Samuel Taylor Coleridge, Including Poems and Versions of Poems Now Published for the First Time*, 2 vols., ed. with Textual and Bibliographical Notes by Ernest Hartley Coleridge (Oxford: Clarendon Press, 1912).

2. See Adair, *The Waking Dream: A Study of Coleridge's Poetry* (New York: Barnes and Noble, 1967); Bate, *Coleridge* (New York: Macmillan, 1968); Boulger, *Coleridge as Religious Thinker* (New Haven: Yale University Press, 1961); Coburn, "Reflections in a Coleridge Mirror: Some Images in His Poems," in *From Sensibility to Romanticism*, ed. Frederick W. Hilles and Harold Bloom (New York: Oxford University Press, 1965); Dorenkamp, "Hope at Highgate: The Late Poetry of S. T. Coleridge," *Barat Review* 6 (1971): 59–67; Fields, *Reality's Dark Dream: Dejection in Coleridge* (Kent, Ohio: Kent State University Press, 1967); Kessler, *Coleridge's Metaphors of Being* (Princeton: Princeton University Press, 1979);

Magnuson, *Coleridge's Nightmare Poetry* (Charlottesville: University Press of Virginia, 1974); Suther, *The Dark Night of Samuel Taylor Coleridge* (New York: Columbia University Press, 1960); Watson, *Coleridge the Poet* (London: Routledge and Kegan Paul, 1966).

3. J. Robert Barth, S.J., *Coleridge and the Power of Love* (Columbia: University of Missouri Press, 1988), 105.

4. Molly Lefebure, *Samuel Taylor Coleridge: A Bondage of Opium* (London: Gollancz, 1974), 470–71.

5. Watson, *Coleridge the Poet*, 131–32.

6. Adair, *The Waking Dream*, 6.

7. Ibid., 220.

8. Ibid., 224.

9. James Boulger, *Coleridge as Religious Thinker* (New Haven: Yale University Press), 196, 198, 199.

10. Bate, *Coleridge*, 176–77.

11. Norman Fruman, *Coleridge: The Damaged Archangel* (New York: George Braziller, 1971), 332, 261.

12. I.A. Richards, "Coleridge: His Life and Work," in *Coleridge: A Collection of Critical Essays*, ed. Kathleen Coburn (Englewood Cliffs, N.J.: Prentice Hall, 1967), 23–24, 27.

13. Coburn, "Reflections in a Coleridge Mirror," 415.

14. Ibid., 433.

15. George Whalley, "'Late Autumn's Amaranth': Coleridge's Late Poems," *Transactions of the Royal Society of Canada* 2:4 (June 1964): 159.

16. Ibid., 162.

17. Ibid., 175.

18. Magnuson, *Coleridge's Nightmare Poetry*, 110.

19. Kessler, *Coleridge's Metaphors of Being*, 47.

20. Whalley, "'Late Autumn's Amaranth,'" 162.

21. Ibid., 164. Students of the dating of *Dejection: An Ode* are indebted to George Dekker's *Coleridge and the Literature of Sensibility* (New York: Barnes and Noble, 1978). Dekker argues persuasively for the poem as a later version of drafts from as early as the late 1790s. He contends that the verse letter "is, in effect, an intermediate and in many ways deviant draft of *Dejection: An Ode*." He further argues, "Of all Coleridge's poems *Dejection* was probably the least of an *ex tempore* performance. Of all his great poems, it was at once the most dearly earned and richly inherited." See also *Coleridge's "Dejection": The Earliest Manuscripts and the Earliest Printings*, ed. Stephen Maxfield Parrish (Ithaca: Cornell University Press, 1988). Dekker connects the ode with the eighteenth-century tradition of sensibility and the genre of the nocturnal lament. See especially pp. 7–57. See also Paul Magnuson, *Coleridge and Wordsworth: A Lyrical Dialogue* (Princeton: Princeton University Press, 1988), 273–317.

22. See M.H. Abrams, "Structure and Style in the Greater Romantic Lyric," in *Romanticism and Consciousness: Essays in Criticism*, ed. Harold Bloom (New York: W. W Norton, 1970), 201–29.

23. Richard Haven, *Patterns of Consciousness: An Essay on Coleridge* (Amherst: University of Massachusetts Press, 1969), 17.

24. *Collected Letters of Samuel Taylor Coleridge*, ed. Earl Leslie Griggs (Oxford: Clarendon Press, 1956–1971), 4:583 (2 August 1815).

25. *Lay Sermons*, ed. R. J. White (Princeton and London: Princeton University Press and Routledge and Kegan Paul, 1972), 29. This is vol. 6 in *The Collected Works of Samuel Taylor Coleridge*, ed. Kathleen Coburn.

26. Michael Friedman, *The Making of a Tory Humanist: William Wordsworth and the Idea of Community* (New York: Columbia University Press, 1979), 248–49.

27. *The Complete Works of Samuel Taylor Coleridge, with an Introductory Essay Upon His Philosophical and Theological Opinions*, ed. W. G. T. Shedd (New York: Harper and Brothers, 1856), 7:v.

28. Ibid., 7:viii.

29. The following section on the Immortality and Dejection odes is adapted from my "Teaching the Immortality Ode with Coleridge's 'Dejection: An Ode,'" in *Approaches to Teaching Wordsworth's Poetry*, ed. Spencer Hall with Jonathan Ramsey (New York: Modern Language Association of America, 1986), 92–95. Permission to adapt has been graciously granted by the Modern Language Association of America. Quotations from the Immortality ode are from *The Poetical Works of William Wordsworth*, ed. E. de Selincourt and Helen Darbishire (Oxford: Clarendon Press, 1947), 4:279–85.

30. Angus Fletcher, "Positive Negation," in *New Perspectives on Wordsworth and Coleridge: Selected Papers from the English Institute*, ed. with a foreword by Geoffrey H. Hartman (New York and London: Columbia University Press, 1972), 147.

31. Bate, *Coleridge*, 177.

32. Fletcher, "Positive Negation," 140.

33. *The Notebooks of Samuel Taylor Coleridge*, ed. Kathleen Coburn (Princeton and London: Princeton University Press and Routledge and Kegan Paul, 1957–1973), 3:4048 (January 1811).

34. Boulger, *Coleridge as Religious Thinker*, 209.

35. Richards, "Coleridge's Minor Poems." A lecture delivered in honor of the Fortieth Anniversary of Professor Edmund L. Freeman at Montana State University, 8 April 1960, p. 23.

THOMAS McFARLAND

Involute and Symbol
in the Romantic Imagination

Among the criteria that define Romanticism, or rather that the retrospective vision of later scholarship has hopefully put forward as defining that sensibility, organicism, imagination, symbol, and nature occupy significant places. The matter is too familiar to require extensive documentation, but perhaps a brief summoning of citations will refresh memories or provide introduction for newcomers to the topic. "The concept of organism is the key to the Romantic view of the world," said Oskar Walzel in 1923. On the other hand, James Engell in 1981 defined "the concept of the imagination" as "the quintessence of Romanticism." Rene Wellek, in a classic article, gave pride of place to a threefold requirement: "imagination for the view of poetry, nature for the view of the world, and symbol and myth for poetic style."[1]

There are other criteria as well.[2] Without attempting to enumerate them here, however, we may note a peculiar feature of any listing of characteristics. All criteria are themselves formations of the imagination. Imagination as one of those criteria seems to reside on a common plane with others, neither above nor below any of a dozen or more Romantic hallmarks. But all Romantic characteristics, either as emphasized by Romantic literature and attitudes as such or as isolated by commentary, are simply dispositions of imagination from the first. In that apprehension,

From *Coleridge, Keats, and the Imagination: Romanticism and Adam's Dream,* edited by J. Robert Barth, S.J., and John L. Mahoney. © 1990 by The Curators of the University of Missouri.

one might use a lowercase type for the imagination in which all Romantic structures exist, and capitalize the Imagination that loomed so large in the aesthetic theorizing of Coleridge and Wordsworth, of Blake and Baudelaire, of Hazlitt and Keats. Yet the two imaginations are at the same time, wherever the paradox may lead, one and the same human faculty.

Though doubtless we all are willing to concede out of hand the distinction between the two uses of imagination, it does not follow that it might not be useful to raise their paradoxical relationship more deliberately to our attention. In his influential work of 1964, *Wordsworth's Poetry, 1787–1814*, Geoffrey Hartman argued for a conflict between nature and imagination as underlying important aspects of Wordsworth's poetic production. But such a conflict can exist only as a construct of the imagination, and any validity it might have is precisely conditioned by the fact that it is imagination that is valorizing both terms of the opposition in every instance. As I have argued elsewhere:

> The primacy of nature must be stressed, because ... in certain emphases of Geoffrey Hartman and Harold Bloom, the role of nature in the Romantic sensibility is misconceived or diminished. Bloom, for instance, sees the 'context of nature as a trap for the mature imagination'. 'The internalization of quest-romance,' he says again, 'made of the poet-hero a seeker not after nature but after his own mature powers, and so the Romantic poet turned away, not from society to nature, but from nature to what was more integral than nature, within himself.' Hartman, for his part, speaks of 'the deeply, paradoxical character of Wordsworth's dealings with nature' and suggests that what Wordsworth calls imagination 'may be *intrinsically* opposed to Nature'. Hartman goes on to make extended play with an 'unresolved opposition between Imagination and Nature' that he posits for Wordsworth.
>
> These views, which are versions of Blake's idiosyncratic position that 'Natural objects always did & now do Weaken deaden & obliterate Imagination in Me', cannot it seems to me be maintained either for Wordsworth or for Romanticism as such except by disregarding overwhelming evidence to the contrary. Nature was not in opposition to Wordsworth's imagination; the vision of nature was itself the richest fulfillment of that imagination.[3]

To be sure, Hartman's is a subtle study, and one of unusual complexity and sensitivity as well. I do not suggest that as a practicing critic Hartman shows himself unaware of the centrality and depth of Wordsworth's response to nature, but rather that he has—and one wishes to reiterate the subliminal influence of Blake in the formation of his contentions—adopted an antithetical mode of conceiving imagination and nature that is invalid at the outset. Despite his subtleties of perception, Hartman is committed to an antithesis of nature and imagination that obscures the central fact that for Wordsworth nature is itself the chief and defining glory of imagination:

> Wordsworth's rhapsodic opening, muted too soon, does not express faith in nature but rather in the quickening relation of imagination to nature. Nature, however, is real and important enough.[4]

> At the beginning of *The Prelude* a poet returns to nature, yet the poem he writes is about the difficulties of that return. He cannot always sustain his quest to link what makes a poet, the energy of imagination, to the energy of nature.[5]

> ... two rival highpoints of *The Prelude*. In one, imagination breaks through to obscure the light of nature; in the other, the poet sees imagination directly via the light of nature.[6]

> the poet [Wordsworth] falls mute and corroborates Blake's strongest objection: "Natural Objects always did and now do weaken, deaden, and obliterate Imagination in me."[7]

> We see that the mind must pass through a stage where it experiences Imagination as a power separate from Nature, that the poet must come to think and feel as if by his own choice, or from the structure of his mind.[8]

Of particular interest for what follows in this essay is that Hartman considers himself joined not only to Bloom but also to the critic Paul de Man in his fundamental view of the antithesis of nature and imagination and the consequent devaluing of nature as a Wordsworthian centrality: "Harold Bloom in *The Visionary Company* (New York, 1961), our first systematic and eloquent questioning of the idea that the Romantics are fundamentally nature poets, and Paul de Man in his essay on the Romantic image, *Revue internationale de philosophie*, 14 (1960), 68–84, have also helped to destroy the 'large and lazy assumption' of which [John] Jones complained."[9] The importance of the bonding to De Man is augmented if we consider an article of 1962 that was the first version of Hartman's chapter of 1964 called "Synopsis: Via Naturaliter Negativa." For in the earlier statement Hartman says, "A very small group, finally—represented by occasional insights rather than by a sustained position—has pointed to the deeply paradoxical or problematic character of Wordsworth's dealings with Nature and suggested that what he calls Imagination may be *intrinsically* opposed to images culled or developed from Nature." And the footnote appended to the word *Nature* specifically says: "Only Paul de Man so far as I know, brought this out strongly in 'Structure intentionnelle de l'Image romantique,' *Revue Internationale de Philosophie*, No. 51 (1960), pp. 1–17 [*sic*] . As this study goes to press, I receive Harold Bloom's relevant and important study of the problem, *The Visionary Company* (New York, 1961)."[10]

The alliance of Hartman and De Man constitutes a formidable cultural alignment, and to take effective issue with it argument must proceed carefully. To begin such argument, I wish to reinvoke my contention asserted above: "Nature was not in opposition to Wordsworth's imagination; the vision of nature was itself the richest fulfillment of that imagination." It is true that Blake said that "Wordsworth must know that what he Writes Valuable is Not to be found in Nature." Yet it was Blake who also said, "The tree which moves some to tears of joy is in the Eyes of others only a Green thing that stands in the way."[11] The Romantic emphasis on nature was not the cognizance of external objects as such, which indeed is necessary to any experience in any era. The Romantic emphasis on nature was rather the imaginative intensification of the cognizance of external objects, a standing illustration for Blake's "All Things Exist in the Human Imagination."[12] Hazlitt said that Wordsworth "described the love of nature better than any other poet," and the way he did this, it was clear to Hazlitt, was by an imaginative intensification of perception. "Mr. Wordsworth's characteristic is one, and may be expressed by one word," wrote Hazlitt, "a power of raising the smallest things in nature into sublimity by the force of sentiment. He attaches the deepest and loftiest feeling to the meanest and most superficial objects." Elsewhere Hazlitt provides a specific example: "Wordsworth, looking out of the low, latticed window, said, 'How beautifully the sun sets on that yellow bank!' I thought within myself, 'With what eyes these poets sees nature!' and ever after, when I saw the sun-set stream upon the objects facing it, conceived I had made a discovery, or thanked Mr. Wordsworth for having made one for me!"[13]

The sun streaming on the yellow bank seems almost banal to us now, for we are the legatees of the Romantic revolution. That it seemed so wonderful to Hazlitt shows that Wordsworth's imaginative intensification of the perception of nature, as that of his fellow Romantics throughout Europe, did indeed constitute a fundamental change in awareness. The Neoclassic neglect of nature has been pointed to by many and diverse commentators; traditional commentary is equally correct when it insists that Romanticism is characterized by a new awareness of and response to the natural world. Rejecting the Neoclassic tradition of Boileau, which "sway'd about on a rocking horse, / And thought it Pegasus," Keats gave eloquent voice to the shift of sensibility by which the poet now must immerse himself in nature:

> Ah dismal soul'd!
> The winds of heaven blew, the ocean roll'd
> Its gathering waves—ye felt it not.
> The blue Bared its eternal bosom, and the dew
> Of summer nights collected still to make
> The morning precious: beauty was awake!
> Why were ye not awake? But ye were dead
> To things ye knew not of ...[14]

Certainly, Defoe, writing in the early eighteenth century, was dead to what we now regard as the sublime beauty of the Lake District. In his journal of a tour through England, published in 1726, he saw not beauty and wonder but simply obstacle. He said when barely north of Lancaster, "There, among the mountains, our curiosity was frequently moved to enquire what high hill this was, or that.... Indeed, they were in my thoughts, monstrous high.... Nor were these hills high and formidable only, but they had a kind of an inhospitable terror in them."[15] Upon entering the Lake District itself, Defoe confirmed the total disconnection between imaginative response and natural scene:

> Here we entered Westmoreland, a country eminent only for being the wildest, most barren and frightful of any that I have passed over in England ... the west side, which borders on Cumberland, is indeed bounded by a chain of almost

impassable mountains, which, in the language of the country,
are called Fells.... But 'tis of no advantage to represent horror,
as the character of a country ... yet here are some very pleasant,
populous and manufacturing towns.[16]

By 1769, however, with the trickling creek of Romanticism beginning to
broaden preparatory to its torrential deluge of European cultural
attitudes, Gray visited the Lake District and saw with new eyes: "pass'd by
the side of Skiddaw & Its cub called *Latter-rig*, & saw from an eminence
at two miles distance the Vale of Elysium in all its verdure, the sun then
playing on the bosom of the lake, & lighting up all the mountains with its
lustre."[17] Further penetration of "the Vale of Elysium" confirmed the
Romantic wonder of its natural spectacle:

our path here tends to the left, & the ground gently rising, &
cover'd with a glade of scattering trees & bushes on the very
margin of the water, opens both ways the most delicious view,
that my eyes ever beheld. behind you are the magnificent
heights of *Walla*-crag; opposite are the thick hanging woods of
L[ord] Egremont & *Newland*-valley with green & smiling fields
embosom'd in the dark cliffs; to the left the jaws of *Borodale*,
with that turbulent chaos of mountain behind mountain roll'd
in confusion; beneath you, & stretching far away to the right,
the shining purity of the *Lake*, just ruffled by the breeze
enough to shew it is alive, reflecting rocks, woods, fields, &
inverted tops of mountains, with the white buildings of *Keswick*,
Crosthwait-church, & Skiddaw for a background at distance. oh
Doctor! I never wish'd more for you.[18]

The new awareness here heralded by Gray's imaginative response
was enormously augmented by Wordsworth, who spoke of the Lake
District as

> tract more exquisitely fair
> Than is that paradise of ten thousand trees,
> Or Gehol's famous gardens[19]

And after detailing the beauties of those gardens (in rivalry with
Coleridge's description of Xanadu), Wordsworth says,

> But lovelier far than this, the paradise
> Where I was reared; in Nature's primitive gifts
> Favoured no less, and more to every sense
> Delicious, seeing that the sun and sky,
> The elements, and seasons in their change,
> Do find their dearest fellow-labourer there— (8.144–49)

Wordsworth's valuation of nature, indeed, so hugely occupied his imagination that one is at a loss to understand how a claim of opposition between nature and imagination can be maintained on any level:

> But he had felt the power
> Of Nature, and already was prepared,
> By his intense conceptions, to receive
> Deeply the lesson of love which he,
> Whom Nature, by whatever means, has taught
> To feel intensely, cannot but receive[20]

When Wordsworth surveyed his own course of life under the persona of the Wanderer, he testified that

> before his eighteenth year was told,
> Accumulated feelings pressed his heart
> With still increasing weight; he was o'erpowered
> By Nature[21]

The pedagogic role imaginatively prescribed for nature led in turn to a pedagogic role for Wordsworth's poetry. Those moving lines at the end of *The Prelude* in which Wordsworth calls himself and Coleridge "Prophets of Nature" focus the entire agenda of his poetic imagination:

> Prophets of Nature, we to them will speak
> A lasting inspiration, sanctified
> By reason and by truth; what we have loved,
> Others may love, and we will teach them how (13.442–45)

To be sure, Wordsworth then immediately specifies that the teaching will

> Instruct them how the mind of man becomes
> A thousand times more beautiful than the earth
> On which he dwells, above this frame of things (13.446–48)

But this recognition of a higher role for mind than for nature does not cast the division as an opposition but rather as an ascent. Indeed, the "great consummation" hailed in the Prospectus to *The Recluse* was precisely the marriage of mind and nature: "the discerning intellect of Man" was to be "wedded to this goodly universe / In love and holy passion." Wordsworth's great poem was designed to "chant, in lonely peace, the spousal verse / Of this great consummation."[22]

Let us follow this matter a bit further, because it is the purpose of this essay to suggest that there is a growing tendency in modern Romantic commentary to gain freshness by rejecting traditional understandings. One must to some extent agree with Jerome McGann's recent observation that "the critical literature on Romanticism has begun to lose its grip on the historical and structural peculiarities of Romantic works."[23] Indeed, in a number of instances that shall remain nameless here, it is, to utilize the *mot* of Dr. Johnson, as if modern commentators, finding the cow of truth already at the dairy, have set out to milk the bull. And some of the most sophisticated and influential modern studies seem to find their subtlety only by losing sight of established truths.

In any event, any attempt to displace nature from its centrality in Romanticism, and its centrality in Wordsworth, must collide with the most intense and powerful statements by the Romantics and by Wordsworth himself. If Wordsworth ever believed anything, he believed that he recognized

> In nature and the language of the sense,
> The anchor of my purest thoughts, the nurse,
> The guide, the guardian of my heart, and soul
> Of all my moral being[24]

If Wordsworth retained a faith

> That fails not, in all sorrow my support,
> The blessing of my life, the gift is yours,
> Ye mountains! Thine, O Nature! Thou has fed
> My lofty speculations; and in thee,
> For this uneasy heart of ours, I find
> A never-failing principle of joy
> And purest passion.   (*Prelude*, 2.4.59–66)

He testifies with passionate intensity that "the earth / And common face of Nature spake to me / Rememberable things" (1.586–88) and that

From Nature and her overflowing soul,
I had received so much, that all my thoughts
Were steeped in feeling   (2.416–18)

He recalls "That spirit of religious love in which / I walked with Nature" (2.376–77) and to his beloved sister he bequeaths the memory

That on the banks of this delightful stream
We stood together; and that I, so long
A worshipper of Nature, hither came
Unwearied in that service[25]

Though Wordsworth later repudiated the phrase "worshipper of Nature," the repudiation came when he was no longer a true and significant poet. His poetic genius and his poetic achievement were inseparable from an enormous imaginative intensity about nature and natural objects:

To every natural form, rock, fruit or flower,
Even the loose stones that cover the highway,
I gave a moral life: I saw them feel.
Or linked them to some feeling: the great mass
Lay bedded in a quickening soul, and all
That I beheld respired with inward meaning (*Prelude*, 3.124–29)

In other words, Wordsworth was irreducibly, in Shelley's apostrophe, "Poet of Nature."[26] For Shelley himself, as Mary Shelley reports, "The love and knowledge of Nature developed by Wordsworth" was part of his "favourite reading."[27] Shelley "loved to shelter himself" in "such imaginations as borrowed their hues from sunrise or sunset, from the yellow moonshine or paly twilight, from the aspect of the far ocean or the shadows of the woods,—which celebrated the singing of the winds among the pines, the flow of a murmuring stream, and the thousand harmonious sounds which Nature creates in her solitudes."[28]

In short, one must in the main agree with Paul de Man that "an abundant imagery coinciding with an equally abundant quantity of natural objects, the theme of imagination linked closely to the theme of nature, such is the fundamental ambiguity that characterizes the poetics of Romanticism."[29] Yet even in agreeing with De Man's statement, one must note a reservation. He says that the linkage of "the theme of imagination" to "the theme of nature" is part of a "fundamental ambiguity." But the ambiguity exists only in this hypothesis that he shares with Hartman and that Hartman hails him for asserting; otherwise the matter is straightforward enough. The gratuitous ascription of "ambiguity" seems a choice if small example of that reaching for subtlety referred to above, and also of the distortion that such reaching tends to entail.[30]

De Man, indeed, in one of his most subtle and influential essays deepens argument in a way that challenges traditional understandings of Romantic symbol. As I shall suggest in the remainder of this discussion, the deepening may also offer a distortion of what symbol means in its historical and cognitive context.

Symbol, like imagination, preoccupied the Romantic sensibility on both practical and theoretical levels. As Schiller wrote to Goethe in August 1798, with reference to dramatic characterization, there is a "higher poetic law" that justifies "deviations from reality":

> Sobald man sich erinnert, dass alle poetische Personen symbolische Wesen sind, dass sie, als poetische Gestalten, immer das Allgemeine der Menschheit darzustellen und auszusprechen haben, und sobald man ferner daran denkt, dass der Dichter sowie der Künstler überhaupt auf eine öffentliche und ehrliche Art von der Wirklichkeit sich entfernen und daran erinnern soll, dass ers tut, so ist gegen diesen Gebrauch nichts zu sagen.[31]

Likewise, Coleridge, in setting forth a symbolic interpretation of the harmony passage in Milton's *Comus*, used as background the claim that Milton "wrote nothing without an interior meaning."[32]

But along with a widespread awareness of symbolic and allegorical possibilities in art, the Romantics frequently on a theoretical level attempted to define the nature of symbol. In such attempts, they often juxtaposed symbol against allegory. As counterpart to his distinction between Imagination and Fancy, Coleridge produced an almost equally well known distinction between Symbol and Allegory:

> Now an Allegory is but a translation of abstract notions into a picture-language which is itself nothing but an abstraction from objects of the senses; the principal being more worthless even than its phantom proxy, both alike unsubstantial, and the former shapeless to boot. On the other hand a Symbol ... is

characterized by a translucence of the Special in the Individual or of the General in the Especial or of the Universal in the General. Above all by the translucence of the Eternal through and in the Temporal. It always partakes of the Reality which it renders intelligible; and while it enunciates the whole, abides itself as a living part in that Unity, of which it is the representative.[33]

In Germany a similar differentiation prevailed, and there too symbol was valorized above allegory. Though Schelling and Creuzer subscribed to such a dichotomy, it was Goethe who was most influential in its enunciation:

Symbol transfers the appearance into the idea, the idea into an image, in such a way that the idea remains always infinitely active and unattainable, and, even if expressed in all languages, remains in fact inexpressible.

Allegory transforms the appearance into the concept, the concept into an image, in such a way that the concept is forever delimited in the image and completely fixed and expressed there.[34]

Now De Man, in an article that has had wide currency in contemporary theory, argues that "the symbol, in the post-romantic sense of the terms, appears more and more as a special case of figural language in general, a special case that can lay no claim to historical or philosophical priority over other figures." Rather than being superior to allegory, argues De Man, symbol is lower than allegory and in fact a conception of little value at all: "After such otherwise divergent studies as those of E. R. Curtius, of Erich Auerbach, of Walter Benjamin, and of H.-G. Gadamer, we can no longer consider the supremacy of the symbol as a 'solution' to the problem of metaphorical diction."[35] But "the problem" exists only in De Man's postulates, as does the necessity of its "solution," and indeed both problem and solution are characteristic of De Man's way throughout his work, where nodes and crises elsewhere not troublesome are repeatedly addressed.

To be sure, De Man's is a sophisticated intelligence, and his views warrant serious attention. Yet a large part of his position on the relative status of allegory and symbol seems to rest on three twentieth-century sources, one the historical discussion of symbol and allegory in Gadamer's

Wahrheit und Methode, another the book on German tragic drama by Walter Benjamin, and the third Angus Fletcher's work on allegory. Gadamer is in part summarized:

> The subjectivity of experience is preserved when it is translated into language; the world is then no longer seen as a configuration of entities that designate a plurality of distinct and isolated meanings, but as a configuration of symbols ultimately leading to a total, single, and universal meaning. This appeal to the infinity of a totality constitutes the main attraction of the symbol as opposed to allegory, a sign that refers to one specific meaning and thus exhausts its suggestive potentialities once it has been deciphered.[36]

Fletcher is not summarized, but if one looks into his book, the following passage presents itself early:

> The word "symbol" in particular has become a banner for confusion, since it lends itself to a falsely evaluative function whenever it is used to mean "good" ("symbolic") poetry as opposed to "bad" ("allegorical") poetry.... A critic may say of *The Castle* or *The Trial* ... that they are "mythic", and then proceed to read them ... as the purest sort of allegory.[37]

Though that passage is not cited by De Man, one may perhaps be justified in assuming that it underlies his position. Not only did Fletcher's *Allegory: The Theory of a Symbolic Mode*, which was published five years before De Man's article, substantially broaden the reference of the term *allegory*, and enhance its prestige as well, but also De Man quotes Coleridge on symbol not from a Coleridgean context but from Fletcher's book.[38]

In any event, in the interests of "temporality" De Man decisively raises allegory over symbol: "The prevalence of allegory always corresponds to the unveiling of an authentically temporal destiny." Again:

> In the world of the symbol it would be possible for the image to coincide with the substance, since the substance and its representation do not differ in their being but only in their extension; they are part and whole of the same set of categories. Their relationship is one of simultaneity, which, in truth, is spatial in kind, and in which the intervention of time is merely

a matter of contingency, whereas, in the world of allegory, time is the ordinary constitutive category.[39]

But where allegory is brought forward in conjunction with the up-market term *authentic*, symbol is invoked in conjunction with the denigrative Sartrean formula of "bad faith": "we tried to show that the term 'symbol' had in fact been substituted for that of 'allegory' in an act of ontological bad faith."[40]

De Man may here specifically be speaking of Friedrich Schlegel, whom he has summoned to buttress his historical contention (he concedes the need to deal "in a historical manner before actual theorization can start"):[41]

> When the term "allegory" continues to appear in the writers of the period, such as Friedrich Schlegel, or later in Solger or E.T.H. Hoffmann, one should not assume that its use is merely a matter of habit, devoid of deeper meaning. Between 1800 and 1832, under the influence of Creuzer and Schelling, Friedrich Schlegel substitutes the word "symbolic" for "allegorical" in the oft-quoted passage of the "Gespräch über die Poesie": "... alle Schönheit ist Allegorie. Das Höchste kann man eben well es unaussprechlich ist, nur allegorisch sagen." But can we deduce from this, with Schlegel's editor Hans Eichner, that Schlegel "simply uses allegory where we would nowadays say symbol"? I could be shown that, precisely because it suggests a disjunction between the way in which the world appears in reality and the way it appears in language, the word "allegory" fits the general problematic of the "Gespräch", whereas the word "symbol" becomes an alien presence in the later version.[42]

But against this contention of De Man, one can point to a consideration grounded more deeply in comparative texts. Schlegel explicitly says that "the highest thing can be said only allegorically, precisely because it is inexpressible (*unaussprechlich*)." Clearly the word *inexpressible* is a key term; it is also the very word that Goethe, in the passage quoted above, uses to describe the necessary fate of the idea conveyed by a symbol: the symbolic idea must remain "inexpressible" (*unaussprechlich*). That being so, how then can Schlegel's substitution of *symbol* for *allegory* in his own central passage be seen as anything other than a bringing of his own insistence into alignment with the distinction established by Goethe? That distinction was vigorously proselytized by Goethe, as we can see by his introducing a man named Martin Wagner to Schelling in 1803 with the statement that "if you can make clear to him the difference between allegorical and symbolical treatment, you will be his benefactor, because so much turns on that axis."[43]

The ontological bad faith, indeed, seems rather to inhere in De Man's identification of symbol with "metaphorical diction." On the contrary, symbol has historically been a conception in the service of theological concerns, and only secondarily in the service of literary concerns. Coleridge, for instance, in the famous distinction between symbol and allegory quoted above, is referring not to literary theory, as a noncontextual reading might suggest, but to religious faith: "Faith is either to be buried in the dead letter, or its name and honors usurped by a counterfeit product of the mechanical understanding, which in the blindness of self-complacency confounds SYMBOLS with ALLEGORIES."[44] To understand how entirely Coleridge knew what he was doing, let us simply cite some titles from the bibliography of a modern work on early Christianity:

B. Capelle, *Le symbole romain au second siècle* ...
B. Capelle, *Les origines du symbole romain* ...
F. T. Dölger, *Die Eigliederung des Taufsymbols in den Taufvollzug* ...
G. L. Dossetti, *Il simbolo di Nicea e di Constantinopoli* ...
A. Harnack, *Apostolisches Symbolum* ...
A. Harnack, *Konstantinopolitanisches Symbol* ...
J. Lebon, *Les anciens symboles à Chalcédoine* ...
H. Lietzmann, *Symbolstudien* ...
A. M. Ritter, *Das Konzil von Konstantinopel und sein Symbol* ...
I. Ortiz de Urbina, *El simbolo Niceno* ...[45]

In view of Coleridge's overriding interest in theological matters,[46] it may be hardly surprising that for him the theological use of symbol always took higher place than the literary use; but for us, as literary critics, frequent reminders of this fact may be necessary:

There is, believe me, a wide difference between symbolical and allegorical. If I say that the flesh and blood (*corpus noumenon*) of the Incarnate Word are power and life, I say likewise that this mysterious power and life are verily and actually the flesh and blood of Christ. They are the allegorizers who turn the sixth chapter of the Gospel according to St. John ... they, I repeat, are the allegorizers who moralize these hard sayings, these high words of mystery, into a hyperbolical metaphor *per catachresin*.[47]

Such defining attachment of symbol to theology dictates two effects for its use in literary matters. First, it ensures that symbol has an ontological, not a critical, function. Symbol cannot be pressed into service as a tool of criticism: allegory is unraveled by criticism; symbol is not.[48] Judging by the number and variety of critical efforts to interpret their meaning, there may be no more palpably symbolic poems in all of English literature than *Kubla Khan* and *The Ancient Mariner*. Yet none of the multitudinous readings supplants the pregnant statement of either poem, or is even necessary to it; both poems generate their urgency from hidden sources, despite all the critical ingenuity lavished on them; both glow gorgeously and mysteriously, and their light does not fade (and it is intriguing that for both poems the most nearly persuasive interpretive readings tend to be theological and unspecific, rather than literary and tightly verbal).

Accordingly, when Angus Fletcher, in the passage quoted above, points out that in the act of critical analysis only allegory comes into play, he does not impeach the validity of symbol. The critic who reads "*The Castle* or *The Trial* ... as the purest sort of allegory" is doing just that; he is not, however, dismissing the possible symbolic meaning of his texts, which is presented to the mind through a combination of intuition and abstract logic, not through criticism.

Secondly, the theological primacy of symbol dictates, against De Man, that symbol does not reside in the realm of "metaphorical diction." The "symbolical," as Coleridge on the contrary insists, is "distinguished *toto genere* from the allegoric and the metaphorical." Again, Coleridge speaks against apprehensions by which "in the mysterious appurtenances and symbols of Redemption (regeneration, grace, the Eucharist, and spiritual communion) the realities will be evaporated into metaphors."[49]

The key word there is *realities*. The "purpose of a metaphor is to illustrate a something less known by a partial identification of it with some other thing better understood,"[50] but a symbol "partakes of the Reality which it renders intelligible; and while it enunciates the whole, abides itself as a living part in that Unity, of which it is the representative."[51] In no event is symbol coincident with metaphor; it is rather "a medium between *Literal* and *Metaphorical*." Furthermore, it, as well as allegory, participates in the temporal, despite De Man's efforts to relegate it to the spatial alone. Symbol is characterized "above all by the translucence of the Eternal through and in the Temporal."[52]

In general, it might be said that the unsatisfactoriness of De Man's analysis arises from a confusion of symbol with "rhetoric" and "figural language." Though in its literary appearances symbol is compatible with the rhetorical figure of synecdoche, it stems from different roots and is an entity of a different kind. The symbol was in its origins a physical thing, a *symbolon*, not a rhetorical trope. It was a fragment or part broken off from a larger physical whole in order to accredit the bearer when the part was recognized as belonging to that whole.[53] That physicality has never left the developed conception of symbol, and indeed the symbol has never been restricted merely to structures of language. To take a single example from the quotidian, the advertising line "a diamond is forever" is a symbolic statement. The "translucence of the Eternal" shines in the word *forever*, as does the idea of unchanging fidelity in a spiritual relationship that the diamond itself—a physical object, not a figure of rhetoric— symbolizes by its own permanence and purity. Furthermore, the symbolizing function made explicit by the slogan occurs without the slogan: when the diamond is presented as ring, the whole meaning of permanence and purity is indicated by the part, that is, by the diamond itself, without the mediation of language.

In thus bridging the cleft between material things and spiritual idea, and between part and whole, the symbol from its inception has been a unit of meaning (not a figure of language) with an integrative charge directed toward the whole of reality. As Goethe put it: "Everything that happens is symbol, and, while it perfectly represents itself, points to other matters [*das übrige*]."[54] Or as a modern commentator says, "It is clear that symbol potentially encompasses the depth of man himself and the height and breadth of all the world, in and out of time. Symbolic knowledge reaches out to all that man can know."[55] Or as Gadamer says:

> A symbol is the coincidence of sensible appearance and supra-sensible meaning, and this coincidence is, like the original significance of the Greek symbolon and its continuance in terminological use of the various religious denominations, not a subsequent coordination, as in the use of signs, but the union of two things that belong to each other.... The possibility of the

instantaneous and total coincidence of the appearance with the infinite in a religious ceremony on the basis of this tension assumes that it is an inner harmony between the finite and the infinite that fills the symbol with meaning. Thus the religious form of the symbol corresponds exactly to its original nature, the dividing of what is one and reuniting it again.[56]

De Man's apparent unawareness of or at least lack of emphasis on the secondary nature of literary symbol is not shared by an earlier praiser of allegory and denigrator of symbol. In 1928, in his *Ursprung des deutschen Trauerspiels*, Walter Benjamin in fact used as his ground of rejection the charge that literary symbol was an illegitimate substitute for theological symbol:

> For over a hundred years the philosophy of art has been subjected to the tyranny of a usurper who came to power in the chaos which followed in the wake of romanticism. The striving on the part of the romantic aestheticians after a resplendent but ultimately noncommittal knowledge of an absolute has secured a place in the most elementary theoretical debates about art for a notion of the symbol which has nothing more than the name in common with the genuine notion. The latter, which is the one used in the field of theology, could never shed that sentimental twilight which has become mere and more impenetrable since the end of early romanticism.[57]

Benjamin goes on to censure "this illegitimate talk of the symbolic" and notes that though its concept "insists on the indivisible unity of form and content," actually it "fails to do justice to content in formal analysis and to form in the aesthetics of content":

> For this always occurs whenever in the work of art the 'manifestation' of an 'idea' is declared a symbol. The unity of the material and the transcendental object, which constitutes the paradox of the theological symbol, is distorted into a relationship between appearance and essence. The introduction of this distorted conception of the symbol into aesthetics was a romantic and destructive extravagance which preceded the desolation of modern art criticism. As a symbolic construct the beautiful is supposed with the divine in an unbroken wholes.[58]

Benjamin urges that allegory in the context of a symbol/allegory distinction serves merely as a foil for symbol and therefore cannot reveal its own structure:

> Simultaneously with its profane concept of the symbol, classicism develops its speculative counterpart, that of the allegorical. A genuine theory of the allegory did not, it is true, arise at that time, nor had there been one previously. It is nevertheless legitimate to describe the new concept of the allegorical as speculative because it was in fact adapted so as to provide the dark background against which the bright world of the symbol might stand out.... The symbolizing mode of thought around 1800 was so foreign to allegorical expression in its original form that the extremely isolated attempts at theoretical discussion are of no value as far as the investigation of allegory is concerned—although they are all the more symptomatic of the depth of the antagonism.[59]

Where Coleridge had said that "allegory is but a translation of abstract notions into a picture-language which is itself nothing but an abstraction from objects of the senses," and where Goethe had said that "allegory transforms the appearance into the concept, the concept into an image, in such a way that the concept is forever delimited in the image and completely fixed, and expressed there," Benjamin on the contrary says that "in the context of allegory, the image is only a signature, only the monogram of essence, not the essence itself in a mask."[60] According to Benjamin, the German tragic drama of the baroque is peculiarly suited to allegory:

> Whereas in the symbol destruction is idealized and the transfigured face of nature is fleetingly revealed in the light of redemption, in allegory the observer is confronted with the *facies bippocratica* of history as a petrified, primordial landscape. Everything about history that, from the very beginning, has been untimely, sorrowful, unsuccessful, is expressed in a face— or rather in a death's head. And although such a thing lacks all 'symbolic' freedom of expression, all classical proportion, all humanity—nevertheless, this is the form in which man's subjection to nature is most obvious and it significantly gives rise not only to the enigmatic question of the nature of human existence as such, but also of the biographical historicity of the

individual. This is the heart of the allegorical way of seeing, of the baroque, secular explanation of history as the Passion of the world; its importance resides solely in the stations of its decline. The greater the significance, the greater the subjection to death, because death digs most deeply the jagged line of demarcation between physical nature and significance. But if nature has always been subject to the power of death, it is also true that it has always been allegorical.[61]

There is much in that passage to connect matters. Benjamin's insistence that nature "has always been allegorical" is not structurally at odds with Coleridge's insistence that allegory is "an abstraction from objects of the senses," though the evaluation of the concession is entirely different in the two thinkers. De Man's formula, that "the prevalence of allegory always corresponds to an authentically temporal destiny,"[62] seems to find its strong precursor in Benjamin's argument that allegory "gives rise not only to the enigmatic question of the nature of human existence as such, but also of the biographical historicity of the individual."

Yet neither Benjamin nor his successor De Man seems really to grasp the cognitive structure of symbol. It is interesting to note that neither gives adequate recognition to its context in the defining cluster of Romantic criteria. Benjamin finds no place for symbol in German baroque tragedy, and therefore can for the most part simply abandon its Romantic connections. De Man explicitly tries to divorce it from its place in the Romantic complex, even going so far as to make the extraordinary and untenable claim that "we are led, in conclusion, to a historical scheme that differs entirely from the customary picture. The dialectical relationship between subject and object is no longer the central statement of romantic thought, but this dialectic is now located entirely in the temporal relationships that exist within a system of allegorical signs."[63] No better example could be summoned as text for the present essay, which is concerned with the historical distortions introduced even by the most subtle modern commentators. The dialectic of subject and object is intrinsic to human awareness and therefore cannot be restricted to Romantic thought; nevertheless, and unequivocally against De Man, it does figure in that thought powerfully and definitively. It figures in many forms. Robert Langbaum has seen it as defining the very nature of Romantic poetry: "The romantic lyric or poetry of experience ... is both subjective and objective. The poet talks about himself by talking about an object; and he talks about an object by talking about himself."[64]

Philosophically, an abstract dialectic of subject and object, arising from Kant's first *Critique*, totally dominated German systematic thought, and it is intensely presented in the writings of Schelling, Fichte, and Hegel. But the dialectic of subject and object was ubiquitous. For a single locus as hilarious as it is pregnant, consider Carlyle's description of Coleridge: "I still recollect his 'object' and 'subject', terms of continual recurrence in the Kantean province; and how he sang and snuffled them into 'omm-m-ject' and 'sum-m-ject,' with a kind of solemn shake or quaver, as he rolled along." Again!,

> His talk, alas, was distinguished, like himself, by irresolution: it disliked to be troubled with conditions, abstinences, definite fulfilments;—loved to wander at its own sweet will, and make its auditor and his claims and humble wishes a mere passive bucket for itself. He had knowledge about many things and topics, much curious reading; but generally all topics led him, after a pass or two, into the high seas of theosophic philosophy, the hazy infinitude of Kantean transcendentalism, with its 'sum-m-jects' and 'om-m-jects.'[65]

Divorced from such anecdotal humor, the dialectic of subject and object, in the form of the interplay of "I am" and "it is," occupied the largest portion of Coleridge's thought for almost forty years.[66] It was also to be the chief topic of Wordsworth's great philosophical poem, which was to chant "the spousal verse / Of this great consummation." Wordsworth's poetic voice was to proclaim

> How exquisitely the individual Mind
> (And the progressive powers perhaps no less
> Of the whole species) to the external World
> Is fitted:—and how exquisitely, too—
> Theme this but little heard of among men—
> The external World is fitted to the Mind[67]

There is no need to draw more examples from the ocean available, for the point is clear. In attempting to supply "a historical scheme that differs entirely from the customary picture," De Man does violence to the simple truth of the situation. Furthermore, not only is the dialectic of subject and object a cornerstone of the Romantic way of looking at the world, but it and the other Romantic emphases are all intertwined, a fact not satisfactorily noticed by either De Man or Benjamin. Coleridge speaks of "living educts of the Imagination; of that reconciling and mediatory power, which incorporating the Reason in Images of the Sense, and organizing (as it were) the flux of the Senses by the permanence and self-circling energies of the Reason, gives birth to a system of symbols, harmonious in themselves, and consubstantial with the truths of which they are the *conductors*."[68] The intertwinement of imagination and symbol is taken up into the title of J. Robert Barth's study of 1977, *The Symbolic Imagination: Coleridge and the Romantic Tradition*, where it is pointed out that the imagination "is always for Coleridge the symbol-making faculty"; "the imagination" is "the symbol-making and symbol-perceiving faculty."[69] Other intertwinements exist also. For a single instance, a continental commentator notes, "The organic is therefore for Schelling an essential characteristic of symbol, which thereby fundamentally distinguishes itself from allegory. The symbol remains, in contrast to allegory, intimately bound up with the realm of organic nature. Where this reference to nature is not present, the true 'symbolic' character of an art work, according to Schelling, is lost."[70]

Allied with De Man's and Benjamin's unsatisfactory grasp of the dynamics of symbol's intertwinement with the other criteria of the Romantic complex is their dismissive understanding of symbol's cognitive structure. It is no accident that De Man repeatedly uses the word *mystification* when his argument veers toward an assessment of the symbolic. "It becomes a conflict between a conception of the self seen in its authentically temporal predicament and a defensive strategy that tries to hide from this negative self-knowledge. On the level of language the asserted superiority of the symbol over allegory, so frequent during the nineteenth century, is one of the forms taken by this tenacious self-mystification." Again, De Man says that

> the lucidity of the pre-romantic writers does not persist. It does not take long for a symbolic conception of metaphorical language to establish itself everywhere, despite the ambiguities that persist in aesthetic theory and poetic practice. But this symbolical style will never be allowed to exist in serenity; since it is a veil thrown over a light one no longer wishes to perceive, it will never be able to gain an entirely good poetic conscience.[71]

Thus, in calling for "a historical de-mystification" of symbol,[72] De Man reverts to a preference for "the lucidity of the pre-romantic writers" that in rejecting symbol is also rejecting the deep structure of Romanticism itself. Romanticism was profoundly involved with dreams, reveries, twilight states of consciousness[73]—all those "petites perceptions" summoned by Leibniz against Locke.[74] Behind Locke there lay the criterion of the "clear and distinct" enunciated by Descartes,[75] even though Locke in accepting the criterion testily refused to accept the phrase itself.[76]

It is that criterion, we realize on reperusing the passage from Angus Fletcher quoted above, that underlies the preference for allegory over symbol of which De Man is a late formulator. But a true Romantic such as Coleridge could ask "whether or no the too great definiteness of Terms in any language may not consume too much of the vital & idea-creating force in distinct, clear, full made Images."[77] Indeed, the Romantic poets and theorists, conditioned by Leibniz's *Nouveaux essais* and Rousseau's *Rêveries d'un promeneur solitaire*, felt at home, to utilize another concatenation by Coleridge, in states of "shadowy half-being," of "nascent Existence in the Twilight of Imagination, and just on the vestibule of Consciousness."[78]

The obscurity and vagueness of symbol were therefore not seen by the Romantics as defects, even though, as Coleridge said, it might be "hard to express that sense of the analogy or likeness of a Thing which enables a Symbol to represent it, so that we think of the Thing itself—& yet knowing that the Thing is not present to us."[79] Far from trying to make lucid the indistinct aura of symbol, the Romantics cherished that indistinct aura.[80] As I have elsewhere observed:

> It has been frequently pointed out, especially in recent years, that an actual critical process recognizes only allegory in its analyses, and that accordingly in the distinction between symbol and allegory so much favored by Romantic writers, the higher status accorded symbol would appear to be something of a mystification. In terms of what we have been saying about the numinous transfer of the predicates of soul, however, the seeming contradiction disappears. The whole point of symbol is not to open itself to critical analysis but precisely to defy such analysis: symbol strives to maintain, not dissipate, the aura of soul. "True symbolism," as Goethe says, is a "living and momentary revelation of the impenetrable [*des Unerforschlichehen*]." Symbolism, says Kant again, transfers "our reflection upon an object of intuition to quite a new concept, and one with which perhaps no intuition can ever directly

correspond.... All our knowledge of God is purely symbolic."
As Friedrich Creuzer noted in 1810, in the third chapter of the
first book of the first part of his *Symbolik und Mythologie den
alten Völker, besonders den Griechen*: "If it is true, as the ancients
understood, that the nature of symbol is precisely the dark and
twilit, how can a symbol deny its nature and be clear?"
Allegory, he says, is like "the luxuriantly spreading branches of
a climbing plant," but "symbol is more like the half-closed bud,
which locks in its calyx, undeveloped, the highest beauty."[81]

In cherishing an aura of indistinctness, symbol protected a
teleological function that moved toward the apprehension of a great and
incomprehensible whole. This both De Man and Benjamin concede. De
Man, summarizing Gadamer, says that "the world is then no longer seen
as a configuration of entities that designate a plurality of distinct and
isolated meanings, but as a configuration of symbols ultimately leading to
a total, simple, and universal meaning. This appeal to the infinity of a
totality constitutes the main attraction of the symbol as opposed to
allegory."[82] Benjamin, for his part, says that "as a symbolic construct, the
beautiful is supposed with the divine in an unbroken whole."[83]

But for the Romantics, One way the symbol, despite its obscurity,
indicates the whole is ultimately a cognitive structure of reason, not a
rhetorical structure of mystification. Thus Coleridge, significantly,
identifies as reason itself the symbolic progression from part to whole:
"The Reason first manifests itself in man by the *tendency* to the
comprehension of all as one. We can neither rest in an infinite that is not
at the same time a whole, nor in a whole that is not infinite."[84] As the
movement toward the whole is the hallmark of reason, so is the
apprehension of that whole the final task of reason. Coleridge speaks of
"that ultimate end of human Thought, and human Feeling, Unity and
thereby the reduction of the Spirit to its Principle & Fountain, who alone
is truly *one*,"[85] and this end underlies all reason's efforts: "Reason is the
knowledge of the laws of the WHOLE considered as ONE."[86]

If concern with the whole is the very nature of reason, then symbol's
concern with the whole reveals itself as wholly participating in reason
itself. Symbol cannot be a mystification. Rather it partakes of the highest
cognitive efforts of the mind; its structure is one of cognitive synecdoche,
not rhetorical mystification: "It always partakes of the Reality which it
renders intelligible; and while it enunciates the whole, abides itself as a
living part in that Unity, of which it is the representative."[87] Coleridge

was undeviating in this insistence. In 1815, for instance, he applied a phrase from Phineas Fletcher's *Purple Island* to his concept of symbol: "Symbols = 'the whole, yet of the whole a part.'"[88] Again, in 1825, he wrote: "Must not of necessity the first man be a symbol of mankind in the fullest force of the word symbol, rightly defined;—a sign included in the idea which it represents;—that is, an actual part chosen to represent the whole."[89]

But neither Benjamin nor De Man, nor for that matter Gadamer, treats the involvement of symbol with wholeness as anything that might have cognitive validity. For De Man especially it remains simply "mystification." On the contrary, the fragmentary nature of our intuitions, as I have elsewhere undertaken to demonstrate in detailed argument, demands the idea of a whole that can only be approached by symbol. No other approach to this idea is possible. Of the German *Trauerspiel* Benjamin concludes that "in the spirit of allegory it is conceived from the outset as a ruin, a fragment."[90] Precisely. Hence, in the phenomenological analysis of ruin and fragment, the need for another conception than allegory. In *Romanticism and the Forms of Ruin: Wordsworth, Coleridge, and Modalities of Fragmentation*, I undertake to show that the phenomenology of fragmentation expressed in the formula "incompleteness, fragmentation, and ruin" is at the heart of Romanticism. I then further undertake to demonstrate, in a concluding chapter called "The Place Beyond the Heavens: True Being, Transcendence, and the Symbolic Indication of Wholeness," that incompletion, fragmentation, and ruin logically involve the symbolic indication of wholeness.

To rehearse the phenomenological arguments presented in that chapter, however, is not the task of the present essay. Rather the task here is to show that the structure of symbol, considered not as an indicator of wholeness but as a response to the experience of reality, has a rationally cognitive validity. Symbol, far from being a mystification, is a direct accounting of human perception.[91]

In order to elucidate that relation to reality, which neither De Man nor Benjamin wishes to see, a Romantic formulation of symbolic function divorced from the dialectic of symbol and allegory shall be summoned. Its author is De Quincey. Using got even the name symbol, but rather the unique term *involute*[92]—which serves to locate his conception outside an existing critical tradition and center it rather on personal experience—the Romantic essayist provides a framework of considerations that introduces this essay's final arguments against De Man. De Quincey says:

Let me pause for one instant in approaching a remembrance so affecting and revolutionary for my own mind, and one which (if any earthly remembrance) will survive for me in the hour of death, to remind some readers, and to inform others, that in the original *Opium Confessions* I endeavored to explain the reason why death, *caeteris paribus*, is more profoundly affecting in summer than in other parts of the year, so far, at least, as it is liable to any modification at all from accidents of scenery or season. The reason, as I there suggested, lies in the antagonism between the tropical redundancy of life in the summer and the dark sterilities of the grave. The summer we see, the grave we hunt with our thoughts; the glory is around us, the darkness is within us. And the two coming into collision, each exalts the other into stronger relief. But in my case there was even a subtler reason why the summer had the intense power of vivifying the spectacle or the thoughts of death. And recollecting it, often I have been struck with the important truth that far more of our deepest thoughts and feelings pass to us through perplexed combinations of *concrete* objects, pass to us as *involutes* (if I may coin that word) in compound experiences incapable of being disentangled, than ever reach us directly and in their own abstract shapes.[93]

In declaring the perceptual inadequacy of experiences that "reach us *directly* and in their own abstract shapes," De Quincey is also declaring the inadequacy of the "clear and distinct" as a criterion. Yet he is adhering strictly to the nature not only of his own experience but of the experience we all share. For "compound experiences," not "clear and distinct ideas," are the true stuff not only of life but of significant literature as well. Not the "lucidity of the pre-romantic writers" but the "perplexed combinations" of De Quincey's involutes are the materials of experience and the art that mirrors it. As Coleridge said, in rejecting the "lucidity" of his pre-Romantic predecessor Hume:

How opposite to nature & the fact to talk of the one *moment* of Hume; of our whole being an aggregate of successive single sensations. Who ever *felt* a *single* sensation? Is not every one at the same moment conscious that there co-exist a thousand others in a darker shade, or less light; even as when I fix my attention on a white House on a grey bare Hill or rather long

ridge that runs out of sight each way ... the pretended single
sensation is it any thing more than the *Light*-point in every
picture either of nature or of a good painter; & again
subordinately in every component part of the picture? And
what is a moment? Succession with *interspace*? Absurdity! It is
evidently on the Light-punct, the *Sparkle* in the indivisible
undivided Duration.[94]

In arguing that no one "ever *felt* a *single* sensation," but rather that
every sensation co-exists with "a thousand others in a darker shade,"
Coleridge precisely declares for the "compound experiences incapable of
being disentangled" and the "perplexed combinations of *concrete* objects"
that De Quincey later made the characteristic of his involutes. Both
insistences are based on an examination of the experience we actually
have, not on "rhetoric" or "figural language"; both reject De Man's
"lucidity of the pre-romantic writers," which indeed they reveal, to use
another phrasing of De Man, as being actually itself a form of "ontological
bad faith." The insistences of Coleridge and De Quincey, moreover,
supply a cognitive justification for the indistinct and vague reference of
symbol.

That reality is in fact perceived in the way that De Quincey and
Coleridge assert was demonstrated by William James in 1890, in his
monumental *Principles of Psychology*. Where Coleridge insists that no one
"ever felt a *single* sensation," James in total agreement extensively argues,

No one ever had a simple sensation by itself. Consciousness,
from our natal day, is of a teeming multiplicity of objects and
relations, and what we call simple sensations are results of
discriminative attention, pushed often to a very high degree. It
is astonishing what havoc is wrought in psychology by
admitting at the outset apparently innocent suppositions; that
nevertheless contain a flaw. The bad consequences develop
themselves later on, and are irremediable, being woven
through the whole texture of the work. The notion that
sensations, being the simplest things, are the first things to take
up in psychology is one of these suppositions. The only thing
which psychology has a right to postulate at the outset is the
fact of thinking itself, and that must first be taken up and
analyzed.[95]

After subtle argument, James concludes that consciousness is not formed of clear and distinct parts, but rasher that

> Consciousness, then, does not appear to itself chopped up in bits. Such words as 'chain' or 'train' do not describe it fitly as it presents itself in the first instance. It is nothing jointed; it flows. A 'river' or a 'stream' are the metaphors by which it is most naturally described. *In talking of it hereafter, let us call it the stream of thought, or consciousness, or of subjective life.*[96]

In thus broaching that conception of the "stream of consciousness" that has had such vast subsequent effect in twentieth-century literature and thought, James was developing ideas set in motion by his Romantic predecessors. James's "stream of thought" flows in the satire bed as Wordsworth's "river of my mind":

> But who shall parcel out
> His intellect by geometric rules,
> Split like a province into round and square?
> Who knows the individual hour in which
> His habits were first sown, even as a seed?
> Who that shall point as with a wand and say
> 'This portion. of the river of my mind
> Came from yon fountain?' (*Prelude* 2.208–15)

With such Romantic lineage, it is hardly surprising that the conception of consciousness as a stream wholly invalidates eighteenth-century psychological postulates based on the "clear and distinct." Where Coleridge finds Hume's theory of perception an "absurdity," James finds it "ridiculous." He rejects the criterion of the clear and distinct:

> Now what I contend for, and accumulate examples to show, is that 'tendencies' are not only descriptions from without, but that they are among the *objects* of the stream, which is thus aware of them from within, and must be described as in very large measure constituted of *feelings of tendency*, often so vague that we are unable to name them at all. It is, in short, the re-instatement of the vague to its proper place in our mental life which I am so anxious to press on our attention.[97]

Having declared for the psychological importance of "the vague" (the reference of symbols, we remember, is generically vague), James pressed home his attack on the "lucidity" of pre-Romantic forebears:

> Mr. Galton and Prof Huxley, as we shall see in Chapter XVIII, made one step in advance in exploding the ridiculous theory of Hume and Berkeley that we can have no images but of perfectly definite things. Another is made in the overthrow of the equally ridiculous notion that, whilst simple objective qualities are revealed to our knowledge in subjective feelings, relations are not. But these reforms are not half sweeping and radical enough. What must be admitted is that the definite images of traditional psychology form but the very smallest part of our minds as they actually live. The traditional psychology talks like one who should say a river consists of nothing but pailsful, spoonsful, quartpotsful, barrelsful, and other moulded forms of water. Even were the pails and pots all actually standing in the stream, still between them the free water, would continue to flow. It is just this free water of consciousness that psychologists resolutely overlook.[98]

But if pre-Romantic psychologists mired in the "clear and distinct"—mired in De Man's "lucidity"—resolutely overlooked it, Romantic proponents of symbol did not. Romantic symbol, to use the terms of James's metaphor, took the pails and pots standing in the stream and insisted on the inseparability of the water they contained with "the free water of consciousness" that flowed around them. Romantic symbol witnesses the ineluctable truth established by James's epoch-making treatise:

> Every definite image in the mind is steeped and dyed in the free water that flows round it. With it goes the sense of its relations, near and remote, the dying echo of whence it came to us, the dawning sense of whither it is to lead. The significance, the value, of the image is all in this halo or penumbra that surrounds and escorts it,—or rather that is fused into one with it and has become bone of its bone and flesh of its flesh; leaving it, it is true, an image of the same *thing* it was before, but making it an image of that thing newly taken and freshly understood.[99]

It would be difficult to formulate a more complete description of the imagistic structure of the Romantic symbol. In truth, leaving aside its reaching after unity, Romantic symbol is just that indication of the "halo or penumbra" that in cognitive experience, as demonstrated by James, actually accompanies every lucidly defined object of consciousness. When, as noted above, Goethe said that "everything that happens is symbol, and, while it perfectly represents itself, points to others matters [das übrige],"[100] the *das übrige* is exactly the "free water" surrounding a defined object of attention, the "sense of its relations, near and remote," the coincidence of "supra-sensible meaning" with "sensible appearance." Conversely, the defined object is only "the *Sparkle* in the indivisible undivided duration," or the result "of discriminative attention, pushed often to a very high degree."

All this other material—*das übrige*—justifies the key term used by Goethe and Schlegel: the "inexpressible." To them the symbol, along with its imagistic presentation, convey, that which is "inexpressible" (*unaussprechlich*). It evokes, in other words, the truth that "every definite image in the mind is steeped and dyed in the free water that flows round it." The symbol is an assertion of relationships more, not less, responsible to actual experience than is the allegory of De Man and Benjamin: "With it goes the sense of its relations, near and remote, the dying echo of whence it came to us, the dawning sense of whither it is to lead. The significance, the value, of the image is all in this halo or penumbra that surrounds and escorts it."

Just as every seemingly "definite image" has other relations "fused into it" so that it is "an image of the same *thing* it was before," yet after taking these fused relationships into account, there is "an image of that thing newly taken and freshly understood," so too, definingly, for symbol. The symbol is what it appears to be, but it is also more than it appears to be: "by a symbol," said Coleridge, "I mean, not a metaphor or allegory or any other figure of speech or form of fancy, but an actual and essential part of that, the whole of which it represents."[101] That is the true cognitive structure of symbol, and that is what De Man, limited to "rhetoric" and "figural language," does not see.

Indeed, Benjamin himself, despite the blinkered vision of his *Ursprung des deutschen Trauerspiels*, elsewhere arrives precisely at Coleridge's awareness of the coexistence of perceptions and De Quincey's insistence on "perplexed combinations" and "compound experiences" as the stuff of perception. In an essay called "On Language as Such and on the Language of Man," posthumously published twenty-seven years after the work on the German tragic drama, Benjamin shows himself finally aware that in any deep statement the expressible always involves the "inexpressible," which for Goethe and Schlegel had been the common and defining factor in the conception of symbol. Benjamin says, in words that take their place beside those of De Quincey and of Coleridge, that "within all linguistic formation a conflict is waged between what is expressed and expressible and what is inexpressible and unexpressed. On considering this conflict one sees, in the perspective of the inexpressible, at the same time the last mental entity."[102]

   For the Romantics, the symbol, which signified the coincidence and fusion of the expressed and the inexpressible,[103] was indeed the last mental entity. It was deeply intertwined with their imaginative emphasis on nature, with their imaginative emphasis on imagination, and with their imaginative emphasis on the infinite. It was not, as De Man would have it, a "mystification." Nor, as he also would have it, was it, either then or now, merely "a special case of figural language in general, a special case that can lay no claim to historical or philosophical priority over other figures." It was rather a token for the idea of unity that became increasingly fragmented in the cultural experience of the Romantics. It was ultimately an assertion of meaning summoned against the nihilism that Nietzsche was to forecast as the inevitable form of future thought, and that even then loomed menacingly on the horizon toward which the Romantics were drifting.

NOTES

1. Oskar Walzel, *Deutsche Romantik; I. Welt-und Kunstanschauung*, 5th ed. (Leipzig and Berlin: 1923), 15; James Engell, *The Creative Imagination: Enlightenment to Romanticism* (Cambridge: Harvard University Press, 1981), 4; René Wellek, "The Concept of Romanticism in Literary History," in *Concepts of Criticism* (New Oskar Walzel, *Deutsche Romantik; I. Welt-und Kunstanschauung*, 5th ed. (Leipzig and Berlin: 1923), 15; James Engell, *The Creative Imagination: Enlightenment to Romanticism* (Cambridge: Harvard University Press, 1981), 4; Rene Wellek, "The Concept of Romanticism in Literary History," in *Concepts of Criticism* (New Haven and London: Yale University Press, 1963), 161.

2. For a discussion of some fifteen or more of these criteria see Thomas McFarland, "The Spirit of the Age," in *Romantic Cruxes: The English Essayists and the Spirit of the Age* (Oxford: Clarendon Press, 1987), 1–24, 27–31. See further Thomas McFarland, "Fragmented Modalities and the Criteria of Romanticism," in *Romanticism and the Forms of Ruin: Wordsworth, Coleridge, and Modalities of Fragmentation* (Princeton: Princeton University Press, 1981), 3–55.

3. Thomas McFarland, "Romantic Imagination, Nature, and the Pastoral Ideal," in *Coleridge's Imagination*, ed. Richard Gravil, Lucy Newlyn, and Nicholas Roe (Cambridge: Cambridge University Press, 1985), 9–10.

4. Geoffrey H. Hartman, *Wordsworth's Poetry, 1787–1814* (New Haven and London: Yale University Press, 1964), 68.

5. Ibid., 67.

6. Ibid., 63.

7. Ibid., 41.

8. Ibid., 44.

9. Ibid., 350–51.

10. Geoffrey H. Hartman, "A Poet's Progress: Wordsworth and the *Via Naturaliter Negativa*," *Modern Philology* 59 (1962): 214–24.

11. *The Complete Poetry and Prose of William Blake*, ed. David Erdman, commentary by Harold Bloom, newly revised ed. (Berkeley and Los Angeles: University of California Press, 1982), 665, 702.

12. Ibid., 223.

13. *The Complete Works of William Hazlitt*, ed. P. P. Howe (London: J. M. Dent and Sons, 1930–1934), 4:121, 9:243, 17:118.

14. *The Poems of John Keats*, ed. Jack Stillinger (Cambridge: Harvard University Press, 1978), 73.

15. Daniel Defoe, *A Tour Through the Whole Island of Great Britain*, ed. G. D. H. Cole and D. C. Browning, Everyman's Library (London: Dent; New York: Dutton, 1962), 2:269.

16. Ibid., 2:269–70.

17. *Correspondence of Thomas Gray*, ed. Paget Toynbee and Leonard Whibley (Oxford: Clarendon Press, 1935), 3:1079.

18. Ibid., 3:1079–80.

19. William Wordsworth, *The Prelude: A Parallel Text*, ed. J. C. Maxwell (Harmondsworth: Penguin Books, 1971), 362 (1805 version, book 8, lines 121–23); hereafter, all quotations are taken from this edition of the 1805 *Prelude* and cited by line number in the text.

20. *The Poetical Works of William Wordsworth*, ed. E. de Selincourt and Helen Darbishire (Oxford: Clarendon Press, 1940–1949), 5:14.

21. Wordsworth, *Poetical Works*, 4:17.

22. Ibid., 5:4–5.

23. Jerome J. McGann, *The Romantic Ideology: A Critical Investigation* (Chicago and London: University of Chicago Press, 1983), 20.

24. Wordsworth, *Poetical Works*, 2:262.

25. Ibid., 2:263.

26. *The Complete Works of Percy Bysshe Shelley*, ed. Roger Ingpen and Walter E. Peck (New York: Gordian Press, 1965), 1:206.

27. Ibid., 1:167.

28. Ibid., 4:79.

29. Paul de Man, *The Rhetoric of Romanticism* (New York: Columbia University

Press, 1984), 2. The passage occurs in an essay that, as De Man says, "was first printed, in a slightly different French version, as 'Structure intentionnelle de l'image romantique' in *Revue internationale de philosophie* (1960), no. 51, pp. 68–84." Compare Hartman's references to De Man noted above.

30. De Man bases his claim for ambiguity so far as Wordsworth is concerned— and in view of the weight of the passages adduced above, it is not an adequate base—on the passage about imagination in the sixth book of *The Prelude*: "Wordsworth praises the faculty that gives him access to this new insight, and he calls this faculty 'Imagination'.... But this 'imagination' has little in common with the faculty that produces natural images born 'as flowers originate.' It marks instead a possibility for consciousness to exist entirely by and for itself, independently of all relationship with the outside world, without being moved by an intent aimed at a part of this world" (pp. 15–16). This passage, one surmises, was of crucial importance for the evolution of Hartman's book. For a single instance, compare Hartman's statement that "what Wordsworth calls Imagination is, in this perspective, hope recognizing itself as originally or ultimately independent of this world" (*Wordsworth's Poetry*, 313).

31. Goethe, *Gedenkausgabe der Werke, Briefe und Gespräche*, ed. Ernst Beutler (Zurich: Artemis Verlag, 1948–1971), 20:614.

32. *Collected Letters of Samuel Taylor Coleridge*, ed. Earl Leslie Griggs (Oxford: Clarendon Press, 1956–1971), 2:866.

33. *Lay Sermons*, ed. R. J. White (Princeton and London: Princeton University Press and Routledge & Kegan Paul, 1972), 30. This is vol. 6 in *The Collected Works of Samuel Taylor Coleridge*, ed. Kathleen Coburn.

34. Goethe, *Gedenkausgabe*, 9:532.

35. Paul de Man, "The Rhetoric of Temporality," in *Interpretation: Theory and Practice*, ed. Charles Singleton (Baltimore: Johns Hopkins University Press, 1969), 176.

36. Ibid., 174.

37. Angus Fletcher, *Allegory: The Theory of a Symbolic Mode* (Ithaca: Cornell University Press, 1964), 14.

38. De Man, "Rhetoric of Temporality," 177 nn 9–11.

39. Ibid., 190. Compare a commentator on Coleridge: "What is there in his view of reality that allows him to see one Life within us and abroad, to assert implicitly that a given reality, whether material or spiritual, is essentially linked with all other reality—that we live in a world of symbols, and therefore of symbolic knowledge? The answer lies in what we may call his principle of the 'consubstantiality' of all being" (J. Robert Barth, *The Symbolic Imagination: Coleridge and the Romantic Tradition* [Princeton: Princeton University Press, 1977], 5).

40. De Man, "Rhetoric of Temporality," 194.

41. Ibid.

42. Ibid., 175–76.

43. *F. W. J. Schelling Briefe and Dokumente: Band III. 1803-1809*, ed. Horst Fuhrmans (Bonn: Bouvier Verlag Herbert Grundmann, 1975), 32.

44. Coleridge, *Lay Sermons*, p. 30.

45. J.N.D. Kelly, *Early Christian Creeds*, 3d ed. (London: Longman, 1972), x.

46. "If there by any two subjects which have in the very depth of my Nature interested me, it has been the Hebrew & Christian Theology, & the Theology of Plato" (Coleridge, *Collected Letters*, 2:866; to Sotheby, 10 September 1802).

47. Coleridge, *Aids to Reflection*, ed. Henry Nelson Coleridge (London: William Dickering, 1848), 1:254–55n.

48. Compare Gadamer: "Allegory originally belonged to the sphere of talk, of the logos, and is therefore a rhetorical or hermeneutical figure. Instead of what is actually meant, something else, more tangible, is said, but in such a way as to suggest the other. Symbol, however is not limited to the sphere of the logos, for a symbol is not related by its meaning to another meaning but its own sensuous nature has meaning" (Hans-Georg Gadamer, *Truth and Method* [New York: Seabury Press, 1975], 65).

49. Coleridge, *Aids to Reflection*, 1:207n, 240.

59. Ibid., 1:258

51. Coleridge, *Lay Sermons*, 30.

52. Ibid.

53. See, e.g., Max Schlesinger, "Die Geschichte des Symbolbegriffs in der Philosophie," *Archiv für Geschichte der Philosophie* 22 (1909): 72.

54. Goethe, *Gedenkausgabe*, 21:286.

55. Barth, *Symbolic Imagination*, 7.

56. Gadamer, *Truth and Method*, 69–70.

57. Walter Benjamin, *The Origin of the German Tragic Drama*, trans. John Osborne (London: NLB, 1977), 159–60.

58. Ibid., 160.

59. Ibid., 161.

60. Ibid., 214.

61. Ibid., 166

62. De Man, "Rhetoric of Temporality," 190.

63. Ibid., 191. De Man does take note of "the tendency shared by all commentators to define the romantic image as a relationship between mind and nature, between subject and object" (p. 178). But he argues that "if the dialectic between subject and object does not designate the main romantic experience, but only one passing moment in a dialectic, and a negative moment at that, since it represents a temptation that has to be overcome, then the entire historical and philosophical pattern changes a great deal" (p. 188).

64. Robert Langbaum, *The Poetry of Experience: The Dramatic Monologue in Modern Literary Tradition* (New York: W. W. Norton & Co., 1963 [1957]), 53.

65. *The Works of Thomas Carlyle in Thirty Volumes*, centenary edition, ed. H. D. Traill (London: Chapman and Hall, [1896–1999]), II:55, 56.

66. See Thomas McFarland, *Coleridge and the Pantheist Tradition* (Oxford: Clarendon Press, 1969), chaps. 2 and 3.

67. Wordsworth, *Poetical Works*, 5:4–5.

68. Coleridge, *Lay Sermons*, 29.

69. Barth, *Symbolic Imagination*, 6, 12.

70. Bengt Sørensen, *Symbol und Symbolismus in den ästhetischen Theorien des 18. Jahrhunderts und der deutschen Romantik* (Copenhagen: Munksgaard, 1963), 252.

71. De Man, "Rhetoric of Temporality," 191.

72. Ibid., 194.

73. For a standard treatment, see Albert Béguin, *L'Ame romantique et le rive* (Paris: Librarie Jose Corti, 1939).

74. *Die philosophischen Schriften von Gottfried Wilhelm Leibniz*, ed. C. J. Gerhardt (Hildesheim: Georg Olms Verlagsbuchhandlung, 1960), 5:46–48.

75. It is specifically against "un art confus & obscur, qui embarrasse l'esprit, au lieu d'une science qui le cultive" that Descartes formulates his four precepts of method: "Le premier estoit de ne receuoir jamais aucune chose pour vraye, que ie ne la connusse evidemment estre telle: c'est a dire, ... de ne comprendre rien de plus en tries iugemens, que ce qui se presentcroit si clairement & sie distinctement a mon esprit, que ie n'eusse aucune occasion de la mettre en doute." The "clairement" and "distinctement" criterion also occurs in conjunction with the certainty of the cogito: "Et ayuant remarqué qu'l n'y a rien du tout en cecy: *ie pense, done ie suis*, qui m'assure que ie dis la verité, sinon que ie voy tres clairement que, pour penser, il faut estre: ie jugay que ie pouuois prendre pour reigle generale, que les choses que nos conceuons fort clairement & fort distinctement, sont toutes vrayes" (*Oeuvres de Descartes*, ed. Charles Adam and Paul Tannery [Paris: Leopold Cerf, 1902], 6:18, 33).

76. "*Clear and distinct Ideas* are terms, which though familiar and frequent in Men's Mouths, I have reason to think every one, who uses, does not perfectly understand.... I have therefore in most places chose to put *determinate* or *determined*, instead of *clear* and *distinct*, as more likely to direct Men's thoughts to my meaning in this matter" (John Locke, *An Essay Concerning Human Understanding*, ed. Peter H. Nidditch [Oxford: Clarendon Press, 1975], 12-13).

77. *The Notebooks of Samuel Taylor Coleridge*, ed. Kathleen Coburn (Princeton and London: Princeton University Press and Routledge & Kegan Paul, 1957–), 1:1016.

78. Coleridge, *Collected Letters*, 2:814; to Sotheby, 19 July 1802.

79. Coleridge, *Notebooks*, 2:2275.

80. Compare Goethe: "The more incommensurable and incomprehensible for the understanding a poetic product may be, the better" (*Gedenkausgabe*, 24:636).

81. Thomas McFarland, *Originality and Imagination* (Baltimore: Johns Hopkins University Press, 1985), 186–87.

82. De Man, "Rhetoric of Temporality," 174.

83. Benjamin, *Origin*, 160.

84. Coleridge, *Lay Sermons*, 60.

85. Coleridge, *Notebooks*, 3:3247.

86. Coleridge, *Lay Sermons*, 59.

87. Ibid., 30.

88. Coleridge, *Notebooks*, 3:4253.

89. Coleridge, *Aids to Reflection*, 1:206n.

90. Benjamin, *Origins*, 235.

91. The establishment of this truth seems especially germane in view of De Man's position, both express and implied, that allegory alone responsibly renders reality. "Whereas the symbol postulates the possibility of an identity or identification, allegory designates primarily a distance in relation to its own origin, and, renouncing the nostalgia and the desire to coincide, it establishes its language in the void of this temporal difference. In so doing, it prevents the self from an illusory identification with the non-self, which is now fully, though painfully, recognized as a non-self. It is this painful knowledge that we perceive at the moments when early romantic literature finds its true voice" ("Rhetoric of Temporality," 191). Again: "Allegory and irony are thus linked in their common discovery of a truly temporal predicament. They are also linked in their common demystification of an organized world postulated in a symbolic mode of analogical correspondences or in a mimetic mode of representation in which fiction and reality could coincide" (pp. 203–4).

92. The present essay germinated from a paper by Robert Morrison, "The Autobiographical Art of De Quincey," delivered at the Wordsworth Summer Conference at Dove Cottage, 13 August 1986. For further discussion of De Quincey's involute see Hugh Sykes Davies, "Involutes and the Process of Involution," in *Wordsworth and the Worth of Words*, ed. John Kerrigan and Jonathan Wordsworth (Cambridge: Cambridge University Press, 1986), 121–85, and Jonathan Wordsworth, *William Wordsworth: The Borders of Vision* (Oxford: Clarendon Press, 1982), 61.

93. Thomas De Quincey, *Confessions of an English Opium Eater and Other Writings*, ed. Aileen Ward (New York and Scarborough, Ontario: New American Library, Signet Classics, 1966), 129–30.

94. Coleridge, *Notebooks*, 2:2370; Christmas Day 1804.

95. William James, *The Principles of Psychology*; ed. George A. Miller (Cambridge: Harvard University Press, 1983), 219.

96. Ibid., 233.

97. Ibid., 246.

98. Ibid.

99. Ibid.

100. Goethe, *Gedenkausgabe*, 21:246.

101. Coleridge, *Lay Sermons*, 79.

102. Walter Benjamin, *Reflections: Essays, Aphorisms, Autobiographical Writings*, ed. Peter Demetz, trans. Edmund Jephcott (New York: Harcourt Brace Jovanovich, 1978), 320.

103. Compare Gadamer's succinct formulation: "The symbol is the coincidence of the sensible and the non-sensible, allegory the meaningful relation of the sensible to the non-sensible" (*Truth and Method*, 67).

DAVID PERKINS

The Imaginative Vision of *Kubla Khan*: On Coleridge's Introductory Note

Coleridge's introductory note to *Kubla Khan* weaves together two myths with potent imaginative appeal. The myth of the lost poem tells how an inspired work was mysteriously given to the poet and then dispelled irrecoverably. The nonexistent lines haunt the imagination more than any actual poem could. John Livingston Lowes used to tell his classes, W. Jackson Bate remembers, "If there is any man in the history of literature who should be hanged, drawn, and quartered, it is the man on business from Porlock." He has become, as Elizabeth Schneider remarks, a byword for Philistine intrusion upon genius. Coleridge's self-portrait in the introductory note is another source of fascination, one that anticipates, as Timothy Bahti observes, the image of the poet later propagated by the *symbolistes* and *L'art pour l'art*.[1] The note describes the poet as a solitary, a dreamer, and a reader of curious lore, such as *Purchas His Pilgrimage*. He is not portrayed as a habitual taker of drugs but rather the opposite: an "anodyne" had been prescribed for an illness and had the profound effect the note describes because, as the reader is supposed to infer, Coleridge was not used to the drug. But the motif of being drugged is also part of the *symboliste* myth of the poet. Only to a poet of this kind, withdrawn in dreams and uncertain in his inspiration, could the person from Porlock be a serious intrusion. That the man from Porlock comes "on business" is

From *Coleridge, Keats, and the Imagination: Romanticism and Adam's Dream*, edited by J. Robert Barth, S.J., and John L. Mahoney. © 1990 by The Curators of the University of Missouri.

also typical of the *symboliste* ethos, in which ordinary life and "business" were viewed as antithetical to poetry..

How the introductory note should be printed has not been much discussed, but editors have disagreed in practice. In popular anthologies it may be omitted altogether. If it is, the poem may not be read with the assumption that it is unfinished, particularly when, as is generally done, the editor also deletes Coleridge's 1834 subtitle, "Or, A Vision in a Dream. A Fragment."[2] Since in Romantic poetry "Vision," "Dream," and "Fragment" are practically genres, a reader's experience of the poem must be quite different when the expectations evoked by these terms are not activated.

In many anthologies Coleridge's introduction is printed as a footnote, usually without the first paragraph and the conclusion (the note usually stops at "without the after restoration of the latter," deleting the self-quotation from *The Picture* and the paragraphs that follow it). This editorial decision gives the introductory note less importance and suppresses several of its themes: that Coleridge is reluctant to publish the poem, that he offers it only as a "psychological curiosity" and that he is dependent on involuntary inspiration. After the poem was first "given" to him and then lost, he says in the penultimate paragraph, he could not restore or finish it "for himself," though he frequently tried. When Coleridge's lines from *The Picture* are not included, the theme of lost inspiration loses one of its counterpointing developments.

Or editors may place the note before the poem as an introduction, as Coleridge did. My purpose in this essay is to inquire what difference it makes. The introductory note guides our reading of the poem from start to finish. Without it, most readers would interpret the poem as asserting the power and potential sublimity of the poet, who can be compared to the great Khan. With the introductory note, this assertion is still present, but it is strongly undercut; the poem becomes richer and more complex, and the theme of lost inspiration is much more heavily weighted. Since many critics have stressed that the introductory note apologizes for the poem and minimizes its significance, there is no need to dwell further on these points. Instead, I shall emphasize that the introductory note gives the poem a plot it would not otherwise have, indicates genres to which the poem belongs, and presents images and themes that interrelate with those in the poem.

In previous articles and books, the only critics who have discussed the problems I take up are Irene H. Chayes, Kathleen M. Wheeler, and Jean-Pierre Mileur.[3] For Chayes, the introductory note is a "literary invention" that "serves as an improvised argument" of the poem; it informs the reader that "the unacknowledged point of view" in the first thirty-six lines of the poem "is that of a man asleep, probably dreaming"; and it offers a "general structural parallel" to the poem, since in both the introductory note and the poem "poetic composition of one kind occurs in the past but in some way is imperfect, and poetic composition of another kind is planned for the future but remains unachieved" (pp. 2–4). Wheeler agrees with Chayes that the introductory note is "a highly literary piece of composition" and that it has thematic similarities to the last eighteen lines of the poem. She thinks that the speaker of the introductory note is not to be taken as Coleridge but as a literal-minded and naive persona whom Coleridge creates "as a model to the reader of how not to respond to the poem" (p. 28). Once the reader recognizes himself in the persona, Wheeler argues, he feels a revulsion and becomes more imaginative and perceptive. Since Coleridge intended all this, his ironic representation of himself in the persona as a "laughing-stock" was "a gesture of incalculable generosity" (p. 38). She arrives at this theory because she wants to make the introductory note analogous to the glosses of the *Ancient Mariner*.[4] Mileur also believes that the introductory note is a "self-conscious fiction" with literary quality. It "constitutes an interpretation of the poem" and itself "cries out for interpretation" (p. 26). He makes specific suggestions to which I am indebted, but his interest is less in the relation of the introductory note to the poem than in general issues this relation poses or illustrates—"immanence" and "presence" versus "revision" and "belatedness."

Complex parallels and contrasts link the introductory note and the poem. There is a sharp difference in scene and tone. The introductory note is realistic, everyday, faintly humorous, and prose, while the poem is romantic, exotic, sublime, and verse. The action of the one is located in contemporary England, between Porlock and Linton, while the other is in ancient China. But they have a similar theme: the character and power (or weakness) of the poet. In the introductory note the poet is a drugged dreamer; his momentary inspiration is dismissed as a psychological anomaly. He takes "pen, ink, and paper" to record his lines, and his poem dissolves when the ordinary world intrudes. In the concluding lines of the poem, however, the poet is an awful figure of supernatural inspiration. His poetry is voiced, spoken rather than written, and imposes itself on the ordinary world, for in the conclusion of the poem the man from Porlock is represented by the poet's auditors ("all"), who are compelled to hear the poet and see his vision. Nevertheless, both the poet of the introductory note and the one of the concluding lines of the poem have lost their inspiration; the difference between them is that the modest, rueful writer of the introductory note scarcely hopes to recover it, while the speaker of the poem imagines himself as possibly doing so and creates a sublime image of himself as poet. We might be tempted to say that the introductory note and the concluding paragraph ironize one another, so that in neither can the representation of the poet's character and relation to the world be read with naive faith.[5] But when brought into contact with Romantic conventions, whatever is expressed in realistic conventions, as is the introductory note, always preempts our sense of truth. Everything about the introductory note—its tone, its description; of the poet, the world it portrays—emphasizes by contrast that the poem is Romantic in the sense of unreal.

In his "lonely farm-house" the author of the introductory note may also be compared with Kubla Khan behind his walls; since no other persons are mentioned in the first thirty-six lines of the poem, the reader imagines Kubla as alone. Though it is not unconscious and inspired,[6] Kubla's creativity is similarly effortless; he decrees and the palace is built. Coleridge's reference in the introductory note to "images on the surface of the stream" has reminded some readers of lines 31–32;[7] in these lines the image or "shadow" of the dome of pleasure would similarly be in fragments, since it would be broken by the waves,[8] as also is the image reflected on the stream in *The Picture*. The word *anodyne* sounds a little like "Xanadu," suggesting that Kubla's palace is located in opium-land.

This brings me to the very interesting quotation in the introductory note from Coleridge's *The Picture*. The introductory note implies that a stone has been thrown into a stream. A youth, who is gazing into the stream, can no longer see the images reflected in it, since they are dispersed by the waves from the stone. The youth is a version of the poet in the introductory note. If we read only the extract from *The Picture* that Coleridge quotes, we cannot know what "lovely forms" are reflected in the stream. In the context of the whole episode in *The Picture*, they are the forms of natural objects along the bank and of a "stately virgin," who has coyly obliterated the reflection of herself, at which the youth was gazing, by dropping not a stone but blossoms into the stream. Coleridge's theme in this part of *The Picture* is the familiar Romantic one of nympholepsy as expressing attraction to the transcendent and ideal. Like the persons in the concluding paragraph of the poem, who would close their eyes "with holy dread" at sight of the supernaturally inspired poet, the youth hardly dares to look at the maiden directly ("scarcely dar'st lift up thine eyes"). His vision of her is lost ("all that phantom-world so fair / Vanishes"), and just as Kubla hears "Ancestral voices prophesying war," the "fair" vision seen by the youth becomes one of strife, as each of the "thousand circlets" created by the blossoms falling into the water "mis-shape[s] the other." But the extract from *The Picture* has a happier trajectory than the introductory note. For in the extract there is a second person, the poet speaker, who is watching or imagining this scene. He comforts the disconsolate youth by reassuring him that the visions will be restored, and in the lines Coleridge quotes they "Come trembling back," and the pool is again "a mirror." Reading only the fragment quoted in the introductory note, we would not know that this episode in *The Picture* actually ends with the loss of the vision. In the lines not quoted, the "shadow" of the maiden can no longer be seen after the stream has again smoothed over. She has departed, and thereafter the youth seeks her through the woods in vain, or gazes into "the vacant brook."

Whether the story Coleridge tells in the introductory note is true has been much debated but makes no difference to my argument. Most critics now doubt that the poem was interrupted by the man from Porlock, that it is a fragment, and that its composition was as involuntary as the introductory note suggests.[9] (On the Crewe manuscript Coleridge noted that it was "composed, in a sort of Reverie.") However, the state of the argument leaves one free to credit or question Coleridge's story at any of these points, and the main reason for denying that *Kubla Khan* is a fragment is the possibility of interpreting it as a coherent whole. If Coleridge's story is not true—or even if it is—one naturally asks why he told it. The usual answer is that Coleridge was embarrassed by the poem. He had "little confidence" in it (McFarland), wished to defend himself against the charge of obscurity (Yarlott), and was ashamed to publish another fragment (Schneider).[10] He wrote the introductory note to deflect judgment, for we cannot form a critical opinion of a fragment, or if we can, we cannot hold Coleridge responsible for a poem composed in a dream. Beer, Bate, Brisman, Patterson, and others argue that the meaning of the poem made Coleridge uneasy; hence in the introductory note he both abdicated responsibility for the poem and tried to minimize its significance.[11] I shall come back to this point later, but for the moment I shall assume that Coleridge wrote the introductory note for reasons quite different from those that have been suggested. He wished to impose a "plot" upon the poem and to invoke appropriate formal expectations.

Without the introductory note *Kubla Khan* would not have a plot but would consist of two separate passages, the second referring in some lines to the first but not continuing from it. Bate has argued that this structure corresponds to a common one in the greater Romantic lyric, in which the first part, the "odal hymn," postulates a "challenge, ideal, or prototype that the poet hopes to reach or transcend," and the "second part, proceeding from that challenge, consists of" a concluding "credo," a "personal expression of hope or ambition."[12] Bate cites Keats's *Ode to Psyche* and Shelley's *Ode to the West Wind* as examples. In these examples, however, the two parts are much more closely interconnected than in *Kubla Khan*, and Coleridge was strongly committed to the principle that a good poem is organically unified. He could hardly have been pleased with the structure he had created. By writing the introductory note he both explained the structure and converted the poem into the dramatic enactment of a story.

The story told in the introductory note and enacted in the poem is that Coleridge, having taken an "anodyne," fell asleep while reading *Purchas His Pilgrimage*. In his sleep he composed "from two to three hundred lines." He remembered them when he awoke, and wrote them down as far as line 30. At this point a person called on business from Porlock and stayed above an hour. When, thereafter, Coleridge tried to continue the poem, he found that "with the exception of some eight or ten scattered lines and images," he could no longer remember it. He wrote down. the "scattered lines and images," which make up lines 31–36 of the poem, and at some later time composed lines 37–54 as a conclusion. Since the introductory note does not explicitly say that Coleridge appended the "scattered lines" to the ones already set down, a reader could assume that the interruption to the poem, caused by the man from Porlock, comes at line 36. I prefer to locate it at line 31 ("The shadow of the dome of pleasure") because at that point the continuity breaks and because the poem again seems somewhat discontinuous at line 35 ("It was a miracle of rare device"); thus, to repeat, lines 31–34 and 35–36 can plausibly be viewed as the separate fragments Coleridge could still remember after the visitor from Porlock had left. Wherever the reader locates the interruption, he sees it taking place, but would not see it without the introductory note, which tells him to look for it. *Kubla Khan* is a poem on the Romantic theme of lost inspiration that represents the to occurring.[13]

That the final lines (37–54) are not to be read as among those given in the dream is a necessary inference from their content.[14] For otherwise a reader would have to assume that in the very moment when Coleridge was envisioning the Abyssinian maid ("the images rose up before him as *things*, with a parallel production of the corresponding expressions") he spoke of this vision in the past tense. Such deliberate confusions are expected in John Ashbery but impossible to imagine in earlier poets. The poet would hardly say "In a vision once I saw" while the vision was present to him. Neither would he desire to revive the vision in the midst of it. Hence the reader must assume that lines 37–54 were written at some time subsequent to the dream composition. The longer we suppose they came after the original experience, the more moving their nostalgia and wish, as we imagine Coleridge still remembering the vision and longing to "rebuild" it. Yet, though the final lines are in the subjunctive mood, the grammatical markers of this ("could," "would," "should") disappear after line 49. The reader half forgets that the lines express only a wish and glories in the sublime poet they describe as though he were present. Thus, though in logic and grammar the poem does not conclude positively, for the imagination it ends triumphantly, as though the dome were rebuilt. In this respect the conclusion develops a possibility given in a different tone in the introductory note through Coleridge's self-quotation from *The Picture*, which had promised that the "visions will return" and the "fragments ... unite."

The Abyssinian maid has been the focus of intensive commentary; while nothing in the introductory note, so far as I can see, explains why Coleridge referred to her in particular, the plot to this point makes it plausible that at line 37 the speaker would appeal to some external source of inspiration. For his poem has been interrupted, the vision it reports is lost, and he is unable to revive the vision "for himself." From his store of memory or imagination, therefore he invokes the Abyssinian maid as a muse. When in line 38 he says that he once saw the Abyssinian maid in "a vision," he refers to a different vision from that reported in lines 1–36 and referred to in the introductory note ("he still retained some vague and dim recollection of the general purport of the vision") and in the subtitle, for though a reader might imagine that the vision of the Abyssinian maid was included in the dream, the different associations of Abyssinia and China, Kubla Khan and a singing maiden, suggest otherwise. The formulation of line 38 suggests this also, for if "a vision" referred to the vision just narrated of Kubla Khan's pleasure grounds and dome, it would more appropriately read "the vision," and the word *once* would not be present.[15] To sum up: the introductory note says that the poet lost a vision and the final lines express a wish to rebuild this vision, but in order to rebuild the vision of Kubla's pleasure dome, the poet must first revive a different vision, seen on another occasion, of an Abyssinian maid.

Because of the introductory note, we read *Kubla Khan* as a dream-poem, a genre that appealed strongly in the Romantic period. Among the well-known dream-poems are *The Prelude* 5.70–140, *The Pains of Sleep*, *Darkness*, *The Four Zoas*, and *The Fall of Hyperion*; if we conflate "dream" with "vision" we would add many more, including *The Triumph of Life* and virtually all of Blake.

To say just what readers expected in poems in this genre would be a subject for a book, and I can touch only on some main headings. A dream-poem might be "nonsense" (Lamb's and Hazlitt's term for *Kubla Khan*). But it might be veiled revelation, especially when it was also a "vision." Dreams and visions escaped from realism, predesigned form, orderly sequence, and rational and ethical responsibility and were thus invested with the mystery and wonder also found in primitive myths, folk and fairy tales, and medieval romances. Dreams might embody our secret emotions, and for some Romantic readers dreams might emerge from a reality deeper than ordinary reality, or express a mind within us that is more profound and aware than the conscious mind; dreams might rise from our inmost being where we are one with the all. If, as several commentators assume, Coleridge wished in the introductory note to minimize the import of *Kubla Khan*, to describe it as a dream was not an effective method.

Among the formal characteristics of dreams, and hence of dream-poems, was their concreteness. Except when a character in the dream spoke, a dream was made up of images, and a dream-poem lacked discursive language. The images might be peculiarly vivid. This was prized, and the more so when the images were glamorous or exotic. The poetic effusion of Perdita Robinson on *Kubla Khan* suggests that she found no meaning in the images but was thrilled by them and that they set off similar, supplementary images in her mind. The sequence of dream imagery might be explained by laws of association; moreover, in dreaming such functions of the mind as the external senses, the reason, or the will might be suspended, making dreams more purely associational than the activity of the mind when awake. Or, in another theory, the imagery of dreams was not produced by association but expressed and varied with the emotional state of the dreamer. According to G. H. von Schubert's *Symbolik des Traumes* (1814), the images of a dream are metaphorical and symbolic; they achieve a rapidity, economy, and wealth of meaning impossible to words. A few strangely ordered images in a dream can express what it would take hours to say in verbal language.[16] But the images of a dream are not experienced as figurative by the dreamer. For as Coleridge explained in connection with stage illusion, a dreamer does not compare the images presented in the dream with others. Each is literal reality during the instant in which it is present. Obviously the persistently concrete, exotic, immediate, unexplained imagery of *Kubla Khan* would seem dreamlike to a Romantic reader.

In other dream poems the speaker remembers a dream and reports it; since it took place in the past, the dream, we assume, has been worked over by the poet with the intention of creating a poem. In *Kubla Khan*, according to the introductory note, the words of the poem were part of the dream and were not changed subsequently. That composition was involuntary would have meant to Coleridge that *Kubla Khan* could not be considered a poem in the full sense and would have justified his description of it as a mere "psychological curiosity." But for many Romantic readers Coleridge's introductory note would have suggested that *Kubla Khan*, as the work of the "poet hidden" within us, in Schubert's phrase, was a greater work than if the conscious mind and will had helped to create it.

What Coleridge conveyed to the reader in calling the poem a "fragment" is more doubtful. It was not, in any case, merely that the poem was incomplete. Of course, Coleridge thus made, as I said, loss of inspiration more emphatically the subject of the poem than it would otherwise have been, and he altered the image of the poet, who became less sublime and more pathetic. But at least in German Romanticism, with which Coleridge was familiar, a "fragment" was a recognized literary form.[17] It was valued because it activated the imagination; in fact, a fragment was more suggestive than the same words would be within a larger work, where the context would necessarily limit their implication. According to the theories of the Schlegel brothers, a fragment preserves the free, ironic stance of its author as a systematic work would not. And for Romantic feeling in general, as McFarland has shown, any existing particular must seem a fragment in relation to the infinite whole. In McFarland's *Romanticism and the Forms of Ruin* attention is also directed to fragmentation within what we naively consider as wholes. For the Romantic sense of things, as McFarland interprets it, poems, personalities, and lives are inevitably "diasparactive" or torn apart.

The theme of fragmentation runs through *Kubla Khan*. There is the subtitle, and the term *fragment* occurs again in the introductory note; the two to three hundred lines of which the poem originally consisted may or may not have been a fragment; after the person from Porlock has gone, Coleridge can recall only "scattered lines or images"; he quotes (misquotes) a fragment from *Purchas His Pilgrimage* and another from his own poem *The Picture*; in the latter quotation the images in the water are said to shatter into "fragments" and then reunite; in the poem "huge fragments" of rocks are hurled up by a "fountain"; the "shadow of the dome of pleasure" would be broken into fragments by "the waves"; and structurally the poem falls into at least two separate fragments. A fragment, as these items suggest, is torn from something larger, and it brings the larger context to mind. Just as the whole of *Purchas His Pilgrimage* is vaguely invoked by the extract from it, and the entire *The Picture* by the quotation from it, the original "two to three hundred lines" of *Kubla Khan* are shadowed forth by the lines we have, not as something we can read or even guess at, but as something we are tempted to guess at. Moreover, a fragment, as the "huge rocks" remind us, can be sublime in itself. Many of these references are to actions and describe things becoming fragmented, fragments being hurled forth, and fragments reuniting. Things become fragmented by accident, as in the introductory note, or deliberately, as in *The Picture*, or by the action of irresistible forces and pressures, as with the huge rocks. The two latter suggestions, I suspect, are closer than the introductory note to the truth concerning Coleridge's fragment

Lowes, who gives a source for almost every image in the poem, did not seek one for the man from Porlock, for he did not consider this famous person as a part of the poem but as real. If, taking the opposite point of view, we ask why the man from Porlock came, answers may be: to reestablish everyday, rational consciousness, to end the solitude of the poet and associate him again with ordinary human beings, to turn the poem into a fragment, and to stop a transgression. When Coleridge's mind was "Voyaging through strange seas of Thought, alone" (to use Wordsworth's great metaphor for the mind of Sir Isaac Newton), his speculations, emotions, and mental imagery might become deeply disturbing to him. The person from Porlock serves the same function in the plot as the mildly reproving glance darted from the eye of Sara in line 4.9 of *The Eolian Harp*; her glance causes the poet to retract the "dim and unhallow'd" speculations he has just been pursuing—"shapings of the unregenerate mind"—and to reestablish solidarity with ordinary, good people, "the family of Christ." The person from Porlock is also somewhat analogous to the "goodly company" with which the Ancient Mariner, at the end of the poem, would wish to walk to church, and he has affinities with the friend, in chapter 13 of the *Biographia Literaria*, who has read Coleridge's chapter on the imagination and advises him not to publish it.[18] Many critics have suggested what transgression was imminent in the poem. It had to do with the vision of poetry and the poet as rivaling the creative power of God and/or of the demonic.

APPENDIX

The Introductory Note

The following fragment is here published at the request of a poet of great and deserved celebrity [Lord Byron], and, as far as the Author's own opinions are concerned, rather as a psychological curiosity, than on the ground of any supposed *poetic* merits.

In the summer of the year 1797, the Author, then in ill health, had retired to a lonely farm-house between Porlock and Linton, on the Exmoor confines of Somerset and Devonshire. In consequence of a slight indisposition, an anodyne had been prescribed, from the effects of which he fell asleep in his chair at the moment that he was reading the following sentence, or words of the same substance, in "Purchas's Pilgrimage": "Here the Khan Kubla commanded a palace to be built, and a stately garden thereunto. And thus ten miles of fertile ground were inclosed with a wall." The Author continued for about three hours in a profound sleep, at least of the external senses, during which time he has the most vivid confidence, that he could not have composed less than from two to three hundred lines; if that indeed can be called composition in which all the images rose up before him as *things*, with a parallel production of the correspondent expressions, without any sensation or consciousness of effort. On awaking he appeared to himself to have a distinct recollection of the whole, and taking his pen, ink, and paper, instantly and eagerly wrote down the lines that are here preserved. At this moment he was unfortunately called out by a person on business from Porlock, and detained by him above an hour, and on his return to his room, found, to his no small surprise and mortification, that though he still retained some vague and dim recollection of the general purport of the vision, yet, with the exception of some eight or ten scattered lines and images, all the rest had passed away like the images on the surface of a stream into which a stone has been cast, but, alas! without the after restoration of the latter!

Then all the charm
Is broken—all that phantom-world so fair
Vanishes, and a thousand circlets spread,
And each mis-shape[s] the other. Stay awhile,
Poor youth! who scarcely dar'st lift up thine eyes—
The stream will soon renew its smoothness, soon
The visions will return! And lo, he stays,

And soon the fragments dim of lovely forms
Come trembling back, unite, and now once more
The pool becomes a mirror.
[*The Picture; or, the Lover's Resolution*, lines 91–100]

Yet from the still surviving recollections in his mind, the Author has frequently purposed to finish for himself what had been originally, as it were, given to him. Σαμερον αδιον ασω: but the to-morrow is yet to come.

As a contrast to this vision, I have annexed a fragment of a very different character, describing with equal fidelity the dream of pain and disease ["The Pains of Sleep"].

NOTES

1. Timothy Bahti, "Coleridge's 'Kubla Khan' and the Fragment of Romanticism," *Modern Language Notes* 96:5 (December 1981): 1037.

2. In the earlier printings of 1816, 1828, and 1829 the subtitle was "Kubla Khan; or, a Vision in a Dream," and the introductory note was entitled "Of the Fragment of Kubla Khan."

3. Irene H. Chayes, "'Kubla Khan' and the Creative Process," *Studies in Romanticism* 6:1 (Autumn 1966): 1–4; Kathleen M. Wheeler, *The Creative Mind in Coleridge's Poetry* (Cambridge: Harvard University Press, 1981), 17–41; Jean-Pierre Mileur, *Vision and Revision: Coleridge's Art of Immanence* (Berkeley: University of California Press, 1982), 24–33, 80–88.

4. Mileur, *Vision and Revision*, 66, and Warren Stevenson, *Divine Analogy: A Study of the Creative Motif in Blake and Coleridge* (Salzburg: Institut für Englische Sprache und Literatur, 1972); also compare the introductory note with the gloss to *The Rime of the Ancient Mariner*.

5. Mileur, *Vision and Revision*, 24, also notes that the introductory note and the poem each challenge "the other's literality."

6. Though there was a legend, which Coleridge probably knew, that Kubla Khan had envisioned his summer palace in a dream before he built it. See John Livingston Lowes, *The Road to Xanadu*, 2d ed. (Boston: Houghton Mifflin Co., 1930), 358.

7. Bahti, "Coleridge's 'Kubla Khan,'" 1046; Mileur, *Vision and Revision*, 31; and other commentators.

8. This point was suggested to me in conversation by Judson Watson.

9. Some opinions may be cited without giving complete references: Lowes, Abrams, Hanson, Shaffer, and Piper accept that the poem was produced much as the introductory note says; Schneider, Ober, Watson, Mackenzie, and Stevenson doubt that its composition was involuntary. Schneider thinks it is a fragment;

House, Bate, Beer, Bloom, and McFarland deny this.

10. Thomas McFarland, *Romanticism and the Forms of Ruin: Wordsworth, Coleridge, and Modalities of Fragmentation* (Princeton: Princeton University Press, 1981), 225; Geoffrey Yarlott, *Coleridge and the Abyssinian Maid* (London: Methuen, 1967), 128; Elizabeth Schneider, *Coleridge, Opium and Kubla Khan* (Chicago: University of Chicago Press, 1953), 27.

11. John Beer, "Coleridge and Poetry: I. Poems of the Supernatural," in *S. T. Coleridge*, ed. R. L. Brett (London: G. Bell & Sons, 1971), 66–69; Walter Jackson Bate, *Coleridge* (New York: Macmillan, 1968), 82–84; Leslie Brisman, *Romantic Origins* (Ithaca: Cornell University Press, 1978), 26–28; Charles I. Patterson, "The Daemonic in *Kubla Khan*: Toward Interpretation," *PMLA* 89 (1974): 1039.

12. Bate, *Coleridge*, 78.

13. Donald Pierce, "'Kubla Khan' in Context," *Studies in English Literature, 1500–1900* 21:4 (Autumn 1981): 581, points out that *Kubla Khan* is "a poem *about* suspended powers. The unfinishedness of 'Kubla Khan' is integral to the theme."

14. Most persons who have written about the poem seem to assume this, but I have found in conversation that many Coleridgeans do not. Hence I make the point explicitly.

15. David Simpson, *Irony and Authority in Romantic Poetry* (London: Macmillan, 1979), 92, points out that the 'once I saw' (l. 38) seems to invoke a time outside of and prior to the vision of Xanadu."

16. G.H. von Schubert, *Symbolik des Traumes*, 3d ed. (Leipzig: F. A. Brockhaus, 1840), 6. Drawing his notions of the formal characteristics of dreams and dream poems from Freud, John Beer remarks that the poem "has the arbitrariness and reductive economy of much dream work" and "provides a many-faceted example of the 'over-determination' that Freud traced in much dream-work" ("The languages of *Kubla Khan*," in *Coleridge's Imagination*, ed. Richard Gravil, Lucy Newlyn, and Nicholas Roe [Cambridge: Cambridge University Press, 1985], 220, 252). Since I do not know whether or not the poem was actually a dream, but do know that Coleridge wanted it to be read as a dream, I do not compare it with Freudian descriptions of dream form but with the ideas of Coleridge and his contemporaries on this subject.

17. Chayes, "'Kubla Khan' and the Creative Process," 2, remarks, "Among the Romantics, 'fragment' sometimes has almost generic meaning."

18. Mileur, *Vision and Revision*, 14, connects the introductory note with chapter 13 of *Biographia Literaria*; see also Brisman, *Romantic Origins*, 34.

PAUL de MAN

Time and History
in Wordsworth

Up till now, the double-barreled topic of these lectures has rather prevented us from reading our romantic authors with the kind of receptivity, the self-forgetting concentration, that we have been describing (in the case of Rousseau) as the proper state of mind for critical insights. The need to keep one eye on the text and another eye on the critical commentator has forced us into the rather tiresome grimace well known to anyone who has ever played in an orchestra, where one has to keep track simultaneously of the score and of the conductor. The grimace becomes even more painful when the directives of the score and those of the interpreter are pulling in different directions, as we found to be the case, to some extent, in the three preceding examples. The result often is that because of the unavoidable simplifications involved in a polemical discussion, one fails to do justice to both the writer and the critic. I probably had to overstate the degree of my disagreement with Girard and Starobinski, critics for whom I have a great deal of sympathy and admiration, and I was clearly not being critical enough, to your taste, with Heidegger, when I suggested that there might be perhaps something of merit in an imaginary figure, one that never existed in the flesh, who would have approached literature with some of the insights that appear in *Sein und Zeit*. More distressing are the one-sided readings given to some of the texts, in order to use them as a rebuttal of methodological

From *Romanticism and Contemporary Criticism: The Gauss Seminar and Other Papers*, edited by E.S. Burt, Kevin Newmark, Andrzej Warminski. © 1992 by The Johns Hopkins University Press.

assertions. Such overanalytical approaches are certainly not attuned to catch the subtle nuances of temporality and intent that a valid commentary should bring out. Fortunately, my topic today will allow for a more relaxed kind of presentation in which the voice of the poet might come through in a less garbled manner. Geoffrey Hartman's study of Wordsworth awakens in me no trace of methodological disagreement.[1] I read whole parts of it with the profound satisfaction of full agreement, only marred by the slight feeling of jealousy that I did not write them myself. The much hoped-for synthesis between the best qualities of American and Continental criticism certainly begins to come true in a book like this. It is based on a wide knowledge of the tradition in which the poet is writing, in this case true familiarity with Wordsworth's antecedents in Milton and in eighteenth-century poetry, combined with an ear that is finely attuned to the slightest nuances of Wordsworth's language. Moreover, by interpreting Wordsworth from the inside, from the phenomenological point of view of his own consciousness, Hartman can trace a coherent itinerary of Wordsworth's poetic development. His achievement will make it possible for us to limit ourselves to some indications derived from the reading of a few very short but characteristic texts, thus tracing, in turn, an itinerary through Wordsworth by means of some of those larger themes that Hartman has pursued. These themes, in the case of Wordsworth and Wordsworth scholarship, are quite obvious, and Hartman does not depart from a well-established custom when he makes the relationship between nature and the imagination into Wordsworth's central problem. The Arnoldian tradition of reading Wordsworth as a moralist has, for quite a while now, been superseded by a concern for the implicit poetics that are present in his writing and that have to be understood prior to the interpretation of a moral statement that seems conventional. This leads inevitably to such abstractions as nature, the imagination, self-knowledge, and poetry as a means to self-knowledge, all of which figure prominently in recent Wordsworth studies, not only because Wordsworth himself talks at times openly about them, but because his poetry, even at its most trivial, always seems to be supported by and to relate back to them.

As will be clear to all of you, the path I'll try to trace by this direct commentary overlaps with that proposed by Hartman in more places than I will have time to mention. It diverges from it in at least one point of some importance, and I will comment on this disagreement later, as a way to summarize a tentative view of Wordsworth's poetry.[2]

Let me start out with a very well known poem to which Hartman devotes a chapter, the text that Wordsworth placed at the head of the section of his *Collected Poems* entitled "Poems of the Imagination." He later incorporated it into *The Prelude* and seems to have, in general, attached a special importance to it. It was written in Goslar, during his stay in Germany, together with several of the childhood memories that went into the two first books of *The Prelude*. "The Winander Boy" is divided into two sections separated by a blank space, and all readers of the poem have been struck by the abruptness of the transition that leads from the first to the second part. Problems of interpretation tend to focus on the relationship between the two parts. (I would add that that these problems were solved in a definitive but somewhat peremptory fashion in a fine recent anthology of English literature in which the second part has simply been suppressed.)

> There was a Boy, ye knew him well, ye Cliffs
> And Islands of Winander! many a time
> At evening, when the stars had just begun
> To move along the edges of the hills,
> 5 Rising or setting, would he stand alone
> Beneath the trees, or by the glimmering Lake,
> And there, with fingers interwoven, both hands
> Press'd closely, palm to palm, and to his mouth
> Uplifted, he, as through an instrument,
> 10 Blew mimic hootings to the silent owls
> That they might answer him.—And they would shout
> Across the watery Vale, and shout again,
> Responsive to his call, with quivering peals,
> And long halloos, and screams, and echoes loud
> 15 Redoubled and redoubled; concourse wild
> Of mirth and jocund din! And when it chanced
> That pauses of deep silence mock'd his skill,
> Then, sometimes, in that silence, while he hung
> Listening, a gentle shock of mild surprize
> 20 Has carried far into his heart the voice
> Of mountain torrents; or the visible scene
> Would enter unawares into his mind
> With all its solemn imagery, its rocks,
> Its woods, and that uncertain Heaven, receiv'd
> 25 Into the bosom of the steady Lake.
>   This Boy was taken from his Mates, and died
> In childhood, ere he was full ten years old.

—Fair are the woods, and beauteous is the spot,
The Vale where he was born; the Churchyard hangs
30 Upon a Slope above the Village School,
And, there, along the bank, when I have pass'd
At evening, I believe that oftentimes
A full half-hour together I have stood
Mute—looking at the Grave in which he lies.[3]

The first part of the poem introduces us into a world that is, in the words of the text, both "responsive" and, as in the gesture of the hands, "interwoven." Voice and nature echo each other in an exchange of which the exuberance expresses a stability, a firm hold on a universe that has the vastness of rising and setting stars, but nevertheless allows for an intimate and sympathetic contact between human and natural elements. Not the "vaste et profonde unité" of Baudelaire's *Correspondances* should come to mind, but a more innocent, more playful, pleasure at finding responses, satisfying possibilities of relationship even for someone who, like the boy, "stands alone." The "watery Vale" that might separate him from an alien natural presence is easily bridged by the cry of the owls; it is, by itself, an eerie enough noise on a dark night, but little of this eeriness is allowed to enter the poem. If we mimic it well enough to engage the response of its originators, the gulf between ourselves and nature need not be unbridgeable. "The poet ... considers man and nature as essentially adapted to each other, and the mind of man as naturally the mirror of the fairest and most interesting qualities of nature." This statement from the Preface to the *Lyrical Ballads* would be a good commentary on the opening scene of the poem.[4] Much Wordsworth criticism still today considers this frequently as the fundamental statement not just of Wordsworth but of romantic naturalism as a whole, and refuses to go beyond it. Yet, even in this first section of the poem, one finds some strain at keeping up a belief in such an "interwoven" world. "Mimic hootings" is not the highest characterization imaginable for the human voice, and we have somehow to be told explicitly that this is "concourse wild / Of mirth and jocund din" to convince us of the persistent cheer of the scene.

As soon as the silence of the owls allows for the noise to subside, what becomes audible is poetically much more suggestive than what went before. The deepening of the imaginative level is not announced with any fanfare or pointed dramatic gesture. The "surprises" that Wordsworth's language gives are indeed such "*gentle* shocks of *mild* surprize" that the transition from stability to suspense can be accomplished almost without our being aware of it. Yet certainly, by the time we come to "*uncertain* heaven," we must realize that we have entered a precarious world in which the relationship between noun and epithet can be quite surprising. Coleridge singled out the line for comment, as being most unmistakably Wordsworth's: "Had I met these lines running wild in the deserts of Arabia, I should instantly have screamed out, 'Wordsworth.'"[5] The line is indeed bound to engender wonder and meditation. The movements of the stars, in the opening lines, had seemed "certain" enough, and their reflection in the lake was hardly needed to steady the majesty of their imperceptible motion. But the precariousness that is here being introduced had been announced before, as when, a little earlier, in lines 18 and 19, it was said that when "pauses of deep silence mock'd his skill, / Then, sometimes, in that silence, while he (the boy) *hung* / Listening, a gentle shock of mild surprize...." We would have expected "stood listening" instead of the unusual "hung / listening." This word, "hung" plays an important part in the poem. It reappears in the second part, when it is said that the graveyard in which the boy is buried "*hangs* / Upon a Slope above the Village School." It establishes the thematic link between the two parts and names a central Wordsworthian experience. At the moment when the analogical correspondence with nature no longer asserts itself, we discover that the earth under our feet is not the stable base in which we can believe ourselves to be anchored. It is as if the solidity of earth were suddenly pulled away from under our feet and we were left "hanging" from the sky instead of standing on the ground. The fundamental spatial perspective is reversed; instead of being centered on the earth, we are suddenly related to a sky that has its own movements, alien to those of earth and its creatures. The experience hits as a sudden feeling of dizziness, a falling or a threat of falling, a *vertige* of which there are many examples in Wordsworth. The nest-robbing scene from book I of *The Prelude* comes to mind, where the experience is a literal moment of absolute dizziness which disjoins the familiar perspective of the spatial relationship between heaven and earth, in which the heavens are seen as a safe dome that confirms at all times the earth's and our own centrality, the steadfastness of our orientation toward the center which makes us creatures of earth. But here, suddenly, the sky no longer relates to the earth

> Oh! at that time,
> While on the perilous ridge I *hung* alone,
> With what strange utterance did the loud dry wind

Blow through my ears! the sky *seem'd not a sky*
Of earth, and with what motion moved the clouds!
                [*1805 Prelude* 1:335–39 (bk. I, ll. 335–39), 291]

Later, when in the Preface to the 1815 edition of his *Poems*,
Wordsworth gives examples of the workings of the highest poetic faculty,
the imagination, as it shapes poetic diction, he chooses three passages,
from Virgil, Shakespeare, and Milton, in which the italicized key word is
the same word, "hang," not used literally as in the last instance from *The
Prelude*, but used imaginatively. The Milton passage begins

As when far off at Sea a Fleet descried
Hangs in the clouds, by equinoxial winds
Close sailing from Bengala

. . . .
                                        so seem'd
Far off the flying Fiend.
                        [Preface to *Poems* (1815), 248]

Wordsworth comments: "Here is the full strength of the imagination
involved in the word *hangs*, and exerted upon the whole image: First, the
Fleet, an aggregate of many Ships, is represented as one mighty Person,
whose track, we know and feel, is upon the waters; but, taking advantage
of its appearance to the senses, the Poet dares to represent it as *hanging in
the clouds*, both for the gratification of the mind in contemplating the
image itself, and in reference to the motion and appearance of the sublime
object to which it is compared" [248]. This *daring* movement of the
language, an act of pure mind, corresponds to the *danger*, the anxiety of
the moment when the sudden silence leaves the boy *hanging*, listening. In
the second part of the poem, we are told, without any embellishment or
preparation, that the boy died, and we now understand that the moment
of silence, when the analogical stability of a world in which mind and
nature reflect each other was shattered, was in fact a prefiguration of his
death. The turning away of his mind from a responsive nature toward a
nature that is not quite "of earth" and that ultimately is called an
"uncertain heaven" is in fact an orientation of his consciousness toward a
preknowledge of his mortality. The spatial heaven of the first five lines
with its orderly moving stars has become the temporal heaven of line 24,
"uncertain" and precarious since it appears in the form of a
preconsciousness of death.

The uncertainty or anxiety is not allowed, however, to go unrelieved. In the prefigurative first section the uncertain heaven is, with a suggestion of appeasement, "receiv'd / Into the bosom of the steady Lake," and in the second part, at the moment when we would have expected an elegiac lament on the death of the boy, we hear instead a characteristically Wordsworthian song of praise to a particular place, the kind of ode to spirit of place of which Hartman has traced the antecedents in eighteenth century nature poetry:

> Fair are the woods, and beauteous is the spot,
> The Vale where he was born; the Churchyard *hangs*
> Upon a Slope above the Village School
> And, there, along that bank, when I have pass'd
> At evening, I believe that oftentimes
> A full half-hour together I have stood
> Mute—looking at the Grave in which he lies.

The dizziness revealed in the "hung / listening" has indeed resulted in a fall, has been the discovery of a state of falling which itself anticipated a fall into death. Now become part of earth in the graveyard, the boy is part of an earth that is itself falling into a sky that is not "of earth." But the movement is steadied, the fall cushioned, as it were, when the uncertain heaven is received into the lake, when sheer dizziness is changed into reflection. The corresponding moment in the second part is the meditative half-hour, which introduces a long, extended period of continuous duration that exists outside of the ordinary time of daily activity, at the moment of a privileged encounter with a scene that merges the youth of the village school with the death of the graveyard, as boyhood and death merged in the figure of the Winander boy.

We understand the particular temporal quality of this slow half-hour better when we remember that the earliest version of this poem was written throughout in the first person and was referred to Wordsworth himself as a boy.[6] The text went: "When it chanced / That pauses of deep silence mocked *my* skill ..." The poem is, in a curious sense, autobiographical, but it is the autobiography of someone who no longer lives written by someone who is speaking, in a sense, from beyond the grave. It would be banal and inadequate to say that Wordsworth is praising and mourning, in the poem, his own youth, the boy he used to be. The movement is more radical, more complex. The structure of the poem, although it seems retrospective, is in fact proleptic. In the second part,

Wordsworth is reflecting on his own death, which lies, of course, in the future and can only be anticipated. But to be able to imagine, to convey the experience, the consciousness of mortality, he can only represent death as something that happened to another person in the past. [Dead] men,[7] as we all know, tell no tales, but they have an assertive way of reminding us of mortality, of bringing us eventually face to face with our own finitude. Wordsworth is thus anticipating a future event as if it existed in the past. Seeming to be remembering, to be moving to a past, he is in fact anticipating a future. The objectification of the past self, as that of a consciousness that unwittingly experiences an anticipation of its own death, allows him to reflect on an event that is, in fact, unimaginable. For this is the real terror of death, that it lies truly beyond the reach of reflection. Yet the poem names the moment of death in a reflective mood, and it is this reflective mood that makes it possible to transform what would otherwise be an experience of terror into the relative appeasement of the lines, "... that uncertain Heaven, receiv'd / Into the bosom of the steady Lake."

Another way of putting it is that what Wordsworth strives to conquer, on the relentless fall into death, is the time, the surmise that would allow one to reflect upon the event that, of all events, is most worth reflecting upon but hardest to face. This time is conquered at the end of the poem, in the curiously exact full half-hour that becomes available to him, a purely meditative time proportionate to the time it takes us to understand meditatively Wordsworth's own poem. But the strategy that allows for this conquest is temporally complex: it demands the description of a future experience by means of the fiction of a past experience which is itself anticipatory or prefigurative. Since it is a fiction, it can only exist in the form of a language, since it is by means of language that the fiction can be objectified and made to act as a living person. The reflection is not separable from the language that describes it, and the half-hour of the end also clocks the time during which Wordsworth, or ourselves, are in real contact with the poem. Hartman is quite right in saying that the poem "becomes an ... extended epitaph" (20), though one might want to add that it is the epitaph written by the poet for himself, from a perspective that stems, so to speak, from beyond the grave. This temporal perspective is characteristic for all Wordsworth's poetry—even if it obliges us to imagine a tombstone large enough to hold the entire *Prelude*.[8]

Wordsworth himself gives us sufficient evidence to defend this kind of understanding. The first of the *Essays upon Epitaphs* describes, in prose, insights that are very close to what we have found in "The Winander Boy."

What seems to start out as a simply pious statement about the consolatory power of a belief in the immortality of the soul turns very swiftly into a meditation on the temporality that characterizes the consciousness of beings capable of reflecting on their own death. The first characteristic of such a consciousness is its power to anticipate: "The Dog or Horse perishes in the field, or in the stall, by the side of his Companions, and is incapable of *anticipating* the sorrow with which his surrounding Associates shall bemoan his death, or pine for his loss; he cannot *pre-conceive* this regret, he can form no thought of it; and therefore cannot possibly have a desire to leave such regret or remembrance behind him" [605]. And Wordsworth characterizes a human being that, not unlike the Winander boy at the beginning of the poem, would have chosen to remain in a state of nature by an "inability arising from the imperfect state of his faculties to come, in any point of his being, into contact with a notion of death; or to an *unreflecting* acquiescence in what had been instilled in him" [606]. Very soon in the same essay, however, it becomes clear that the power to anticipate is so closely connected with the power to remember that it is almost impossible to distinguish them from each other. They seem like opposites, and are indeed at opposite poles if we think of time as a continual movement from birth to death. In this perspective, the source is at a maximal remove from the final point of destination, and it would be impossible to reach the one by ways of the other. In a more reflective, more conscious concept of temporality, however, the two poles will, in Wordsworth's phrasing, "have another and finer connection than that of contrast" [608]. "Origin and tendency are notions inseparably co-relative," [606] he writes, and the essay develops this notion in an extended voyage image:

> As, in sailing upon the orb of this Planet, a voyage, towards the regions where the sun sets, conducts gradually to the quarter where we have been accustomed to behold it come forth at its rising; and, in like manner, a voyage towards the east, the birthplace in our imagination of the morning, leads finally to the quarter where the Sun is last seen when he departs from our eyes; so, the contemplative Soul, travelling in the direction of mortality, advances to the Country of everlasting Life; and, in like manner, may she continue to explore those cheerful tracts, till she is brought back, for her advantage and benefit, to the land of transitory things—of sorrow and of tears [608].

Stripped of whatever remnants of piety still cling to this language,[9] the passage summarizes the temporality of the "Winander Boy" poem. In this poem, the reflection on death takes on the form, at first sight contradictory, of a remembrance of childhood. Similarly, in Wordsworth, evocations of natural, childlike or apocalyptic states of unity with nature often acquire the curiously barren, dead-obsessed emptiness of nonbeing.[10] The poetic imagination, what is here called the contemplative soul, realizes this and thus encompasses source and death, origin and end within the space of its language, by means of complex temporal structurizations of which we found an example in "The Winander Boy."[11]

Another brief poem of Wordsworth's will allow us to take one further step in an understanding of his temporality; it may also make the concept less abstract by linking it to its more empirical mode of manifestation, namely history. The poem belongs to the later sonnet cycle entitled *The River Duddon*, which appeared in 1820.

> Not hurled precipitous from steep to steep;
> Lingering no more mid flower-enamelled lands
> And blooming thickets; nor by rocky bands
> Held;—but in radiant progress tow'rd the Deep
> 5 Where mightiest rivers into powerless sleep
> Sink, and forget their nature; *now* expands
> Majestic Duddon, over smooth flat sands,
> Gliding in silence with unfettered sweep!
> Beneath an ampler sky a region wide
> 10 Is opened round him;—hamlets, towers, and towns,
> And blue-topped hills, behold him from afar;
> In stately mien to sovereign Thames allied,
> Spreading his bosom under Kentish downs,
> With Commerce freighted or triumphant War.
>
>   (699)

The *Essay upon Epitaphs* had already suggested the image of a river as the proper emblem for a consciousness that is able to contain origin and end in a single awareness. "Origin and tendency are notions inseparably co-relative. Never did a Child stand by the side of a running Stream, pondering within himself what power was the feeder of the perpetual current, from what never-wearied sources the body of water was supplied, but he must have been inevitably propelled to follow this question by another: 'Towards what abyss is it in progress? what receptacle can contain the mighty influx?'" (606). In this poem, we have what seems at first sight like a progression, a continuous movement that flows "in radiant progress" toward the triumphant ending:

> In stately mien to sovereign Thames allied,
> Spreading his bosom under Kentish Downs,
> With Commerce freighted or triumphant War.

Equally convincing seems to be the movement that leads, in the poem, from the idyllic setting of "flower-enamelled lands / And blooming thickets" to the political, historically oriented language at the end. The progression from nature to history, from a rural to an urban world seems to be without conflict. We move from a relationship between the personified river Duddon and its pastoral banks to a relationship that involves human creations such as "hamlets, towers, and towns," or human historical enterprises such as "Commerce" and "War." And this gliding passage, similar to what is called in *The Prelude* "love of nature leading to love of man" [in the title to book 8 of the 1850 version of *The Prelude*],[12] appears as a liberation, an expansion that involves a gain in freedom. The river is no longer restricted "by rocky bands" and now flows "with unfettered sweep." The order of nature seems to open up naturally into the order of history, thus allowing the same natural symbol, the river, to evoke the connection between them. The poem seems to summarize the "growth of a mind" as espousing this movement, and to prove, by the success of its own satisfying completeness, that language can espouse poetically this very movement.

Some aspects of the language, however, prevent the full identification of the movement with natural process and put into question an interpretation of the river, which a subsequent poem in the same series addresses as "my partner and my guide" ["Conclusion," l. 1, 699], as a truly natural entity. The beginning of the poem, for instance, casts a curious spell over the subsequent progression. It describes what the river no longer is in such forceful and suggestive language that we are certainly not allowed to forget what the river *has been* by the time we encounter it in its expanded form. The opening line, for example, cannot cease to haunt us, and no matter how strongly the italicized *now* (in "*now* expands") takes us to the present, so much has been told us so effectively about what came before that we can only seize upon this present in the perspective of its past and its future. The past is described as successive motions of falling and lingering. The dizziness of the Winander Boy poem and of the childhood scenes of *The Prelude* is certainly present in the image of the river "hurled precipitous from steep to steep," which introduces, from the start, a powerful motion that dominates the entire poem and that the various counterforces, including the initial *not*, are unable to stem. For the idyllic stage that follows, among flowers and blooming thickets, is a mere lingering, a temporary respite in a process that is one of steady descent and dissolution. The implications of this movement become clearer still when the radiant progress is said to be "toward the Deep / Where mightiest rivers into powerless sleep / Sink, and forget their nature." This description of the sea is certainly far removed from the image of a pantheistic unity with nature that one might have expected. It is presented instead as a loss of self, the loss of the *name* that designates the river and allows it to take on the dignity of an autonomous subject. The diction of the passage, with the antithetical balance of "mightiest" and "powerless," is all the stronger since the apparent strategy of the poem does not seem to demand this kind of emphasis. It makes the forgetting of one's nature that is here mentioned into a movement that runs counter to the original progression; this progression, which first seemed to lead from nature to history while remaining under the dominant sway of nature, now becomes a movement away from nature toward pure nothingness. One is reminded of a similar loss of name in the Lucy Gray poems, where death makes her into an anonymous entity "Roll'd round in earth's diurnal course / With rocks and stones and trees!" ["A slumber did my spirit seal," ll. 7–8, 165]. Similarly, the river Duddon is first lost into a larger entity, the Thames, which in turn will lose itself in still larger anonymity. There is no cycle here by means of which we are brought back to the source and reunited with it by natural means. No prospect of natural rebirth is held out, and the historical achievement at the end seems caught in the same general movement of decay.

Nevertheless, the poem can overcome the feeling of dejection that this irrevocable fall might suggest; it ends on a statement of assertion that is not ironic. Not altogether unlike the uncertain heaven in "The Boy of Winander" that was steadied in reflection, the fall here is not prevented, but made tolerable this time by the assertion of historical achievement. There seems to be an assertion of permanence, of a duration in what seems to be an irrevocable waste, a falling away into sheer nothingness. It is based on a certain form of hope, on the affirmation of a possible future, all of which makes it possible for man to pursue an enterprise that seems doomed from the start, to have a history in spite of a death which Wordsworth never allows us to forget.

In this poem, the possibility of restoration is linked to the manner in which the two temporalities are structurally interrelated within the text. If taken by itself, the progression toward history would be pure delusion, a misleading myth based on the wrong kind of forgetting, an evasion of the knowledge of mortality. The countertheme of loss of self into death that appears in the first and second quatrain introduces a temporality that is more originary, more authentic than the other, in that it reaches further into the past and sees wider into the future. It envelops the other, but without reducing it to mere error. Rather, it creates a point of view which has gone beyond the historical world of which we catch a glimpse at the end of the poem, but which can look back upon this world and see it within its own, relative greatness, as a world that does not escape from mutability but asserts itself within the knowledge of its own transience. We have a temporal structure that is not too different from what we found in "The Winander Boy." Instead of looking back upon childhood, upon an earlier stage of consciousness that anticipates its future undoing, we here look back on a historical consciousness that existed prior to the truly temporal consciousness represented by the river. This historical stage is named at the end of the poem, but this end is superseded by the authentic endpoint named in line 5. We see it therefore, with the poet, as destined to this same end. Like the boy experiencing the foreknowledge of his death, history awakens in us a true sense of our temporality, by allowing for the interplay between achievement and dissolution, self-assertion and self-loss, on which the poem is built. History, like childhood, is what allows recollection to originate in a truly temporal perspective, not as a memory of a unity that never existed, but as the awareness, the remembrance of a precarious condition of falling that has never ceased to prevail.[13]

Hence, in the concluding sonnet of the same cycle, the emphasis on the italicized word *backward* in "For, *backward*, Duddon! as I cast my eyes, / I see what was, and is, and will abide" ["Conclusion," ll. 3–4, 699]. As a mere assertion of the permanence of nature, the poem would be simply pious and in bad faith, for we know that as soon as we think of the river as analogous to a self, as a consciousness worthy of engaging our own, that it only reveals a constant loss of self. Considered as a partner and a guide, it has indeed "past away" [l. 2] and never ceases to do so. This is the "Function" it fulfills in the line, "The Form remains, the Function never dies" [l. 6], in which the Form corresponding to this Function is the trajectory of a persistent fall. The entire poignancy of the two sonnets is founded on the common bond between the *I* of the poem and its emblematic counterpart in the Duddon, which makes the river into something more than mere nature. Instead of merely letting ourselves be carried by it, we are able to move backwards, against the current of the movement. This backward motion does not exist in nature but is the privilege of the faculty of mind that Wordsworth calls the imagination, asserting the possibility of reflection in the face of the most radical dissolution, personal or historical. The imagination engenders hope and future, not in the form of historical progress, nor in the form of an immortal life after death that would make human history unimportant, but as the persistent, future possibility of a retrospective reflection on its own decay. The 1850 version of *The Prelude* makes this clearest when it defines the imagination as being, at the same time, a sense of irreparable loss linked with the assertion of a persistent consciousness.

> I was lost
> Halted without an effort to break through;
> But to my *conscious soul* I now can say—
> "I recognise thy glory."
>
> [*1850 Prelude*, 6:596–99]

The restoring power, in Wordsworth, does not reside in nature, or in history, or in a continuous progression from one to the other, but in the persistent power of mind and language after nature and history have failed. One wonders what category of being can sustain the mind in this knowledge and give it the future that makes imagination dwell, in the later version of *The Prelude*, with "something evermore about to be" [6:608].

This may be the moment at which a return to Hartman's book is helpful. Like all attentive readers of Wordsworth, he reaches a point at which the nature of this restorative power has to be defined as the main assertive power in Wordsworth's poetry. And the understanding he has of Wordsworth's own mind allows him to give a very full and penetrating description of the complexities involved. He has noticed, more clearly than most other interpreters, that the imagination in Wordsworth is independent of nature and that it leads him to write a language, at his best moments, that is entirely unrelated to the exterior stimuli of the senses. He has also noticed that there is a kind of existential danger connected with this autonomy, and that when Wordsworth speaks about the *daring* of his imagery in the 1815 Preface, this risk involves more than mere experimentation with words. Hartman refers to this danger as an apocalyptic temptation, in his words, "a strong desire to cast out nature and to achieve an unmediated contact with the principle of things" [x]. Carried by the imagination, Wordsworth would at certain privileged moments come close to such visionary power, although he reaches it without supernatural intervention and always in a gradual and gentle way. Still, in the climactic passages of *The Prelude*, and in the main poems generally, the evidence of a moving beyond nature is unmistakable. What characterizes Wordsworth, according to Hartman, and sets him apart from Milton, for instance, and also from Blake, is that the apocalyptic moment is not sustained, that it is experienced as too damaging to the natural order of things to be tolerated. Out of reverence, not out of fear, Wordsworth feels the need to hide from sight the vision he has glimpsed for a moment; he has to do so, if his poetry is to continue its progression. And he finds the strength for this avoidance of apocalyptic abandon in nature itself—a nature that has been darkened and deepened by this very insight, and that has to some extent incorporated the power of imagination. But it has naturalized it, reunited it with a source that remains in the natural world. "The energy of imagination enters into a natural cycle though apart from it" [69], writes Hartman. The return to a natural image at the end of the famous passage on imagination in book 6 of *The Prelude* "renews the connection between the waters above and the waters below, between heaven and earth. Toward this marriage of heaven and earth the poet proceeds despite apocalypse. He is the matchmaker, his song the spousal verse" [69]. The road apparently beyond and away from nature in fact never ceased to be a natural road, albeit nature in a negative form, the *via naturaliter negativa*.

We cannot follow him in speaking of an apocalyptic temptation in Wordsworth. The passages that Hartman singles out as apocalyptic never suggest a movement toward an unmediated contact with a divine principle. The imagination [in book 6 of the 1805 version] is said to be "like an unfather'd vapour" [l. 527] and is, as such, entirely cut off from ultimate origins; it gives sight of "the invisible world" [l. 536], but the invisibility refers to the mental, inward nature of this world as opposed to the world of the senses; it reveals to us that our home is "with infinitude" [l. 539], but within the language of the passage this infinity is clearly to be understood in a temporal sense as the futurity of "something evermore about to be" [l. 542]. The heightening of pitch is not the result of "unmediated vision" but of another mediation, in which the consciousness does not relate itself any longer to nature but to a temporal entity. This entity could, with proper qualifications, be called history, and it is indeed in connection with historical events (the French Revolution) that the apostrophe to imagination comes to be written. But if we call this history, then we must be careful to understand that it is the kind of history that appeared at the end of the Duddon sonnet, the retrospective recording of man's failure to overcome the power of time. Morally, it is indeed a sentiment directed toward other men rather than toward nature, and, as such, imagination is at the root of Wordsworth's theme of human love. But the bond between men is not one of common enterprise, or of a common belonging to nature: it is much rather the recognition of a common temporal predicament that finds its expression in the individual and historical destinies that strike the poet as exemplary. Examples abound, from "The Ruined Cottage" to "Resolution and Independence," and in the various time-eroded figures that appear throughout *The Prelude*. The common denominator that they share is not nature but time, as it unfolds its power in these individual and collective histories.

Nor can we follow Hartman in his assertion of the ultimately regenerative power of nature. His argument returns to passages like the passage on imagination in book 6 of the [1850] *Prelude* in which, according to him, after having shown the "conscious soul" as independent, Wordsworth has to return to a natural image. The soul is said to be

> Strong in herself and in beatitude
> That hides her, like the mighty flood of Nile
> Poured from her fount of Abyssinian clouds
> To fertilize the whole Egyptian plain
> > [*1850 Prelude*, 6:613–16; Hartman 69]

Perhaps enough has been said about the river Duddon to suggest that Wordsworth's rivers are not to be equated with natural entities. We don't even have to point to the further distancing from nature suggested by the exotic reference to an entity richer in mythological and literary than in natural associations; the abyss in "abyssinian" maintains the source far beyond our reach, at a dizzying distance from ordinary perception and certainly not in "any mountain-valley where poetry is made" [69], as Hartman would have it. The fertile plain at the end occupies the same position that the historical world occupies in the last lines of the Duddon sonnet and is thus not a symbol of regeneration. Hartman reads the "hiding" as naturally beneficial, as the protective act of nature that makes possible a fertile continuation of the poem and of life, in contrast to the "unfathered vapour" that rejects the source in a supernatural realm. The hiding rather refers to the invisibility, the inwardness, the depth of a temporal consciousness that, when it reaches this level, can rejoice in the truth of its own insight and find thoughts "too deep for tears." If rivers are, for Wordsworth, privileged emblems for the awareness of our mortal nature, in contrast to the natural unity of echoes and correspondences, then the use of an allegorical river at this point can hardly be the sign of a renewed bond with nature.

Hartman speaks of the need for Wordsworth "to respect the natural (which includes the temporal) order" if his poetry is to continue "as narrative" (46). The equation of natural with temporal seems to us to go against Wordsworth's most essential affirmation. He could well be characterized as the romantic poet in which the separation of time from nature is expressed with the greatest thematic clarity. The narrative order, in the short as well as in the longer poems, is no longer[14] linear; the natural movement of his rivers has to be reversed as well as transcended if they are to remain usable as metaphors. A certain form of narrative nevertheless persists, but it will have to adopt a much more intricate temporal movement than that of the natural cycles. The power that maintains the imagination, which Hartman calls nature returning after it has been nearly annihilated by apocalyptic insight, is time. The key to an understanding of Wordsworth lies in the relationship between imagination and time, not in the relationship between imagination and nature.

A late poem of Wordsworth's that appears among the otherwise truly sterile sequence of the *Ecclesiastical Sonnets* can well be used as a concluding illustration. Like all other romantic poets, Wordsworth claims a privileged status for poetic language—a formula which was most legitimately put into question during our last session as standing in need of closer explanation. In Wordsworth, the privileged status of language is linked with the power of imagination, a faculty that rates higher than the fancy, or than rhetorical modes such as imitation, which, unlike the imagination, are dependent on correspondence with the natural world and thus limited by it. The language of imagination is privileged in terms of truth; it serves no empirical purposes or desires other than the truth of its own assertion:

> The mind beneath such banners militant
> Thinks not of spoils or trophies, nor of aught
> That may assert its prowess, blest in thoughts
> That are its own perfection and reward
> Strong in itself ...
>
> [*1805 Prelude*, 6:543–47, 372]

This truth is not a truth about objects in nature but a truth about the self; imagination arises "before the eyes and progress of my Song" [l. 526], in the process of self-discovery and as self-knowledge. A truth about a self is best described, not in terms of accuracy, but in terms of authenticity; true knowledge of a self is knowledge that understands the self as it really is. And since the self never exists in isolation, but always in relation to entities, since it is not a thing but the common center of a system of relationships or intents, an authentic understanding of a self means first of all a description of the entities toward which it relates, and of the order of priority that exists among these entities. For Wordsworth, the relationships toward time have a priority over relationships toward nature; one finds, in his work, a persistent deepening of self-insight represented as a movement that begins in a contact with nature, then grows beyond nature to become a contact with time. The contact, the relationship with time, is, however, always a negative one for us, for the relationship between the self and time is necessarily mediated by death; it is the experience of mortality that awakens within us a consciousness of time that is more than merely natural. This negativity is so powerful that no language could ever name time for what it is; time itself lies beyond language and beyond the reach of imagination. Wordsworth can only describe the outward movement of time's manifestation, and this outward movement is necessarily one of dissolution, the "deathward progressing" of which Keats speaks in *The Fall of Hyperion*. To describe this movement of dissolution, as it is perceived in the privileged language of the imagination, is to describe it, not as an actual experience that would necessarily be as brusk and dizzying as a fall, but as the generalized statement of the truth of this experience in its universality. Dissolution thus becomes mutability, asserted as an *unfailing* law that governs the natural, personal, and historical existence of man. Thus to name mutability as a principle of order is to come as close as possible to naming the authentic temporal consciousness of the self. The late poem entitled "Mutability" comes as close as possible to being a language that imagines what is, in essence, unimaginable:

Mutability

From low to high cloth dissolution climb,
And sinks from high to low, along a scale
Of awful notes, whose concord shall not fail;
A musical but melancholy chime,

Which they can hear who meddle not with crime,
Nor avarice, nor over-anxious care.
Truth fails not; but her outward forms that bear
The longest date do melt like frosty rime,
That in the morning whitened hill and plain
And is no more; drop like the tower sublime
Of yesterday, which royally did wear
Its crown of weeds, but could not even sustain
Some casual shout that broke the silent air,
Or the unimaginable touch of Time.

[780]

Notes

This is the fourth of the six Gauss lectures. It was announced under the title,
"Nature and History in Wordsworth," and delivered at Princeton on Thursday,
April 27, 1967. All notes supplied by the editors except where otherwise indicated.
When de Man gave this lecture again (in 1971 or 1972), he wrote several
additional passages and interpolated them in the lecture of 1967. These passages
appear in notes number 2, 8, 11, 13, and 14.

1. References to Hartman's text throughout this essay follow the pagination
of *Wordsworth's Poetry 1787–1814* (New Haven: Yale University Press, 1964).

2. The opening paragraphs seem to have been left out when de Man gave this
lecture again (around 1971 or 1972). The new lecture began with some more
informal remarks about what it means to *read* based on a version of the following
notes:

reading

> not declaim it—pure dramatic, vocal presence
> not analyze it structurally—as in Ruwet
> > semantic, thematic element remains
> > present in Jakobson/Riffaterre

but *read*, which means that the thematic element remains taken into
consideration

we look for the delicate area where the thematic, semantic field and
the rhetorical structures begin to interfere with each other, begin to
engage each other

they are not necessarily congruent, and it may be (it is, as a matter of
fact, it *is* the case) that the thematic and the rhetorical structures are
in conflict and that, in apparent complicity, they hide each other from
sight

in truth, there are no poems that are not, at the limit, about this
paradoxical and deceptive interplay between theme and figure; the

thematization is always the thematization of an act of rhetorical deceit by which what seems to be a theme, a statement, a truth-referent, has substituted itself for a figure

I can't begin to prove this, but want to hint at what I mean by reading two Wordsworth poems

Wordsworth, because he is the antirhetorical, *natural* poet (i.e. thematic) par excellence, not only because he explicitly attacked the use of figure as *ornatus*, but also because the thematic seduction is particularly powerful, in its transparency and clarity—one gets very far very quickly by meditative participation

no one has reached the point where this question of Wordsworth's rhetoricity can begin to be asked, except Hartman.

3. *Wordsworth: Poetry and Prose*, selected by W. M. Merchant (Cambridge, Mass.: Harvard University Press [The Reynard Library], 1955), 352–53. *1805 Prelude*, book 5, lines 389ff. Merchant prints only the 1805 version of *The Prelude*. All quotations from Wordsworth and page references, unless otherwise noted, are from this edition (which de Man used).

4. Preface [1800], in Wordsworth and Coleridge, *Lyrical Ballads 1798*, ed. W. J. B. Owen (London: Oxford University Press, 1967), 150–79 at 167. De Man quotes from a section Wordsworth added for the 1802 edition.

5. Quoted in M.H. Abrams, gen. ed., *The Norton Anthology of English Literature* (New York: W. W. Norton, 1962), 2:152, n. 5.

6. The earliest version of "The Boy of Winander" can be found in the Norton critical edition of *The Prelude* edited by Jonathan Wordsworth, M. H. Abrams, and Stephen Gill (New York: W.W. Norton, 1979), 492. A carefully edited critical version (along with a facsimile of the manuscript page) can be found in Stephen Parrish's edition of the 1798–99 *Prelude* (Ithaca: Cornell University Press, 1977), 86–87.

7. De Man's manuscript reads "Death men." If words crossed out in the manuscript are restored, the sentence fragment reads: "Death men, as we all know from Western movies, tell no tales, but the same is not true of Western romantic poetry, which knows that the only interesting tale is to be told by a man who."

8. In the second version of the lecture, the final sentences of this paragraph seem to have been replaced by the following passage:

It is always possible to anticipate one's own epitaph, even to give it the size of the entire *Prelude*, but never possible to be both the one who wrote it and the one who reads it in the proper setting, that is, confronting one's grave as an event of the past. The proleptic vision is based, as we saw in the poem, on a metaphorical substitution of a first-person subject by a third-person subject, "the boy" for "I." In fact, this substitution is, of all substitutions, the one that is, thematically speaking, a radical impossibility: between the living and the dead self, no analogical resemblance or memory allows for any substitution whatever. The movement is only made possible by a linguistic sleight-of-hand in which the order of time is reversed, rotated around a pole called self (the grammatical subject [first and third persons] of the poem). The posterior events that are to occur to the first person, I, (usually death) are made into anterior events that have occurred to a third person, the boy. A pseudometaphorical and thematically inconceivable substitution of persons leads to a temporal reversal in which anteriority and posterity are inverted. The structural mechanics of metaphor (for, I repeat, the substitution of the dead *he* for the living *I* is thematically, literally, "unimaginable" and the metaphor is not a metaphor since it has no proper meaning, no *sens propre*, but only a metaphorical structure within the sign and devoid of meaning)—the structural mechanics of metaphor lead to the metonymic reversal of past and present that rhetoricians call metalepsis. The prolepsis of the Winander boy, a thematic concept—for we all know that we can proleptically anticipate empirical events, but not our death, which is not for us an empirical event—is in fact metalepsis, a leap outside thematic reality into the rhetorical fiction of the sign. This leap cannot be represented, nor can it be reflected upon from within the inwardness of a subject. The reassurance expressed in the poem when the "uncertain" heaven is received in the lake or when the meditative surmise seems to promise the reflective time of the meditation is based on the rhetorical and not on thematic resources of language. It has no value as truth, only as figure. The poem does not reflect on death but on the rhetorical power of language that can make it seem as if we could anticipate the unimaginable.

This would also be the point at which we are beginning to "read" the poem, or to "read" Wordsworth according to the definition I gave at the start, namely to reach the point where the thematic turns rhetorical and the rhetorical turns thematic, while revealing that their apparent complicity is in fact hiding rather than revealing meaning.

9. A crossed-out clause here reads: "and with the understanding that what is here called immortality stands in fact for the anticipated experience of death."

10. A sentence crossed out here reads: "Being the father of man, the child stands closer to death than we do."

11. In reworking this passage for the second version of the lecture, de Man wrote the word *rhetorical* above the word *temporal* here (without crossing out *temporal*) and then rewrote the opening sentence of the following paragraph as: "Another brief poem of Wordsworth's will give us another version of his rhetorical movement" in place of "Another brief poem of Wordsworth's will allow us to take one further step in an understanding of his temporality." But ultimately de Man seems to have replaced this passage (from "Stripped of whatever remnants ...") by interpolating the following transitional passage:

The metaphor of the voyage, with its vast stellar and heliotropic movements of rising and setting suns and stars here makes the link between life and death, origin and end and carries the burden of the promise. But this is precisely the metaphor that was "deconstructed" in the Winander boy, in which this kind of analogism is lost from the start and never recovered; as is often, but not always, the case, a poetic text like the Boy of Winander takes us closer to an actual "reading" of the poet than discursive statements of philosophical convictions and opinions, especially when these statements are themselves heavily dependent on metaphor.

Another brief poem by Wordsworth may make the movement we are trying to describe less abstract

12. All quotations of the 1850 version of *The Prelude* are from the Norton critical edition.

13. In the second version, the final sentences of this paragraph (beginning with "We see it therefore ...") seem to have been replaced by the following passage:

> Middle and end have been reversed by means of another metonymic figure in which history, *contained* within a larger dimension of time, becomes, in the poem, the *container* of a temporal movement that it claims to envelop, since it is present at the end of the text. But, again, as in the boy of Winander, this metonymy of a content becoming a container, of an *enveloppé* becoming an *enveloppant*, is a rhetorical device that does not correspond to a thematic, literal reality. When Wordsworth chooses to name mutability for what it is, in one of his most suggestive poems, the "Mutability" sonnet from the Ecclesiastical Sonnets, no historical triumphs are mentioned but only decay. It would take us a great deal more time and effort than we have available tonight to reveal the deconstructive rhetoricity of the "Mutability" poem, though it could be done. It would take us closer to an actual reading of Wordsworth, for which these remarks are only introductory exercises.
>
> My entire exposition could be seen as a gloss on a sentence in Hartman's admirable book on Wordsworth in which he speaks of the need, for Wordsworth, to "respect the natural (which includes the temporal) order" if his poetry is to continue as narrative. The narrative (which is itself metonymic) depends indeed on making the natural, thematic order appear as the container, the *enveloppant*, of time rather than as its content; the narrative is metonymic not because it is narrative but because it depends on metonymic substitution from the start. I can therefore totally subscribe to Hartman's reading of Wordsworth's strategy. The only thing I might

Note that in this interpolated passage de Man seems to be rereading his own metaphor of "enveloping" above (the more authentic temporality "envelops the other" in the fourth sentence of the paragraph), that is, is reading his own text rhetorically.

14. In the second version, the following passage was inserted after the words "no longer" to replace the rest of the sentence:

a natural metaphor but a veiled metonymy. Wordsworth's most daring paradox, the claim to have named the most unnamable of experiences, "the unimaginable touch of time," is still based on a metonymic figure that, skillfully and effectively, appears in the disguise of a natural metaphor. In this least rhetorical of poets in which time itself comes so close to being a theme, the theme or meaning turns out to be more than ever dependent on rhetoric.

STEPHEN GURNEY

Byron and Shelley

Disinherited sons of the ruling class, rebels against the code of conventional values, fellow exiles driven from England by courtroom scandals and the sting of social obloquy, Byron and Shelley were the notorious exponents of the Romantic spirit in the generation after Wordsworth and Coleridge. Following their almost simultaneous estrangement from England in 1816, they mutually benefited from the friendship and stimulus that grew from their common dedication to poetry. And yet they are poets of entirely different stamps. Worldly, cynical, torn by the contradictory extremes of Promethean aspiration and rueful disenchantment, Byron is a poet of dichotomous extremes, capable, at once, of reckless idealism and corrosive satire, rhetorical grandeur and deflating deadpan. Shelley, too, could adapt his poetic gift to a variety of moods and genres, from the familiar and conversational ease of *Julian and Maddalo* and the stately pomp of *Prometheus Unbound* to the sprightly playfulness of *The Witch of Atlas* and the Dantesque gravity of *The Triumph of Life*. But in Shelley's case this facility of varied expression is a consequence of aesthetic tact and ordonnance—in a word, the cunning incarnation of his thematic material in a verbal form perfectly adapted to the spirit that it embodies. In point of sheer craftsmanship, Shelley, according to Wordsworth, was the most accomplished of the Romantic school. But Shelley's accomplishments, for all their variety, are the

From *British Poetry of the Nineteenth Century*. © 1993 by Twayne Publishers.

expressions of a spirit far more homogeneous than Byron's. This homogeneity derives from Shelley's consistent engagement with the issues of abstract metaphysics.

To Shelley these were not the intangible nothings that the worldly-wise dismiss with blank indifference. To the contrary, they were of ultimate and inescapable importance, the very crux of human aspiration, and perhaps the only goods worthy of contemplation and pursuit. While Shelley had his moments of Byronic skepticism regarding the efficacy of this pursuit and the existence of these intangibles, he could not forbear in poem after poem to trace the fugitive essence of that unseen power "whose taste," as the poet wrote, "Makes this cold common hell, our life, a doom / As glorious as a fiery martyrdom" (411).

Byron, more brutally conscious of the discrepancy between the loftiness of human desire and the vanity of mortal life, sought relief in sensual dissipation and self-protective wit. Shelley, on the other hand, was a steadfast exponent of ideals dedicated to the regeneration of the human spirit and the search for abiding verities. Doubtless, Byron found in Shelley's poetry an expression of his own latent though tattered idealism, while Shelley saw in the works of Byron a declaration of his own repressed misgivings and doubts. In any case, their alliance—for they remained friends despite personal disagreements and temperamental differences— was highly propitious for both. After Shelley's death, at the age of twenty-nine, Byron became even more cynical and, in an effort at self-distraction, conceived the quixotic scheme of aiding the Greeks in their war against Turkish oppression. The scheme ended at Missolonghi, where Byron died at the age of thirty-six.

Byron's life has generated more critical commentary perhaps than his poetry. More than any of his contemporaries, Byron succeeded in identifying himself in the popular imagination with the incarnate spirit of Romanticism. His "inheritance of storms,"[1] as he termed it in an epistle to his half-sister and lover, Augusta Leigh, refers to an aristocratic lineage peopled by characters as colorful as those in the poet's oriental tales. Byron's father, who earned the sobriquet "Mad Jack" by dint of his wild behavior, was the son of "Foulweather Jack" Byron—a one-time naval officer whose nautical adventures ended, so it was said, in mutiny or shipwreck. Byron waggishly refers to this legend in his masterpiece *Don Juan*, when following the shipwreck of his hero, he wryly observes, "... his hardships were comparative / To those related in my granddad's 'Narrative'" (676). Part of his granddad's narrative involved a dispute with Byron's uncle, "Wicked" Lord Byron of Newstead Abbey, childless himself and possessed of inveterate hatred for his seafaring brother. When the "Wicked Lord" died, the estate, or what was left of it, passed into the hands of "Foulweather Jack." From thence it finally devolved upon the poet—but not before he had suffered many indignities as a child who bore the full brunt of his mother's resentment at being betrayed and abandoned by the poet's father, who led a dissolute life and died a premature death in France.

Byron was the offspring of his father's second marriage to Catherine Gordon of Gight, a rich though overweight noblewoman who promised to compensate Mad Jack for having squandered much of his inheritance following the breakup of his first marriage. Byron was brought up by the irascible and volatile Catherine, assisted by a Calvinist nurse who solaced her young charge with the consoling reflection that the clubfoot with which he was born was a mark of Satan and an unmistakable sign of his predestined damnation. This strangely twisted woman also gave the boy a premature taste of the life of the senses. But with the death of his father and grandfather, Byron came into the inheritance of Newstead and eventually, after attending Eton and Cambridge, took his seat in the House of Lords. While Byron invariably stood on ceremony when it came to questions of rank and privilege, his speeches in Parliament were distinguished by a compassionate concern for the plight of the working classes—just one of the contradictions endemic to this most contradictory of characters.

To compensate for his clubfoot, Byron became an expert marksman, horseman, and swimmer, and like the Greek hero Leander of old, actually swam the Hellespont. He was also, by all accounts, a man of uncommon physical beauty. "That beautiful pale face will be my destiny," wrote Lady Caroline Lamb, the wife of the future adviser to Queen Victoria. Though only one among Byron's amorous train, she was not the least colorful— slitting her wrists in lovelorn pique at Byron's infidelities and then retiring to the country to write the story of her affair, which Byron himself later reviewed in concentrated rhyme, "I read 'Glenarvon' too by Caro Lamb: / God damn!"

The legend of Byron and Byronism outgrew the fame of his poetry, and he did everything he could to enhance it. He drank out of a skull from one of his ancestors whom he had dug up at Newstead in order to make his head into a cup. He toured the Middle East and came back with a bundle of swashbuckling tales of pirates, adventurers, and aristocratic rogues whose criminal doings smacked of the nobility of Robin Hood and were perpetrated in any case to assuage the inconsolable sorrows of their ravaged hearts. This combination of Byronic swagger and Byronic gloom became all the fashion (even the young Keats picked it up for a thankfully brief spell)—and to the women of his age it proved irresistible.

But the chef d'oeuvre of Byron's continental tour was the first two cantos of *Childe Harold's Pilgrimage* (1812). With the publication of these Byron became overnight a household word. No one had succeeded as skillfully as he at putting his finger on the pulse-beat of an age. The cynicism of post-Napoleonic Europe, the despair of human arrangements and sense of failed ideals—the loss, in short, of those Romantic dreams that fired the French revolutionists—had thrown the younger generation back upon itself in a brooding search for vanished certitudes. But there were none, only an aching void at heart and the search for amatory compensation in Romantic love. But this too proved to be illusory, and hence the unceasing alternation of satiate desire, self-disgust, and rekindled aspiration. These are the essential characteristics of Byron's *Childe Harold*, at least in his earlier incarnations. In expressing the complex truth about himself, Byron had seized upon the spirit of the age.

The truth of Byron, however, was even more complex than that, though it would be several years before he acquired the skill and versatility to express the whole range of his complex personality in verse. In the meantime, he had grown weary of indiscriminate desire and succumbed to the advances of Lady Annabella Milbank, a mathematician and moralist who regarded the poet as a prime specimen upon which to impose her stringent code of eugenics. The marriage lasted a year, produced one daughter, and brought to a head the rumors that had been circulating about Byron's liaison with his half-sister, Augusta Leigh. Henceforth Byron was excluded from polite circles. Ostracized by his own class, Byron shook off the dust of England and traveled first to Switzerland (where he met Shelley, Mary Wollstonecraft Godwin, and Shelley's future sister-in-law, Claire Clairmont, who promptly got herself pregnant with Byron's child). He finally settled in Italy, preferring Venice as the appropriate backdrop for a life of histrionic exploits. He became the sometime lover of an Italian countess, Teresa Guiccioli, whose husband seemed willing to put up with the affair—at least until he learned that Byron was smuggling weaponry to Greek revolutionaries out of his basement.

After Shelley's death by drowning in 1822, Byron, though engaged without a sign of flagging on that masterpiece of irrepressible wit and energy *Don Juan*, decided to take a more active role in Greek politics. With a piratical friend, Edward Trelawny, he sailed in company with mercenaries to the isles of Greece. But the glory of battle was not to be his. Dying of dysentery in Missolonghi, one of his last observations on the subject of divine judgment was unrepentantly Byronic: "Shall I sue for mercy? Come, come, no weakness! Let's be a man to the last."[2]

Byron's earliest volume, *The Hours of Idleness*, published in 1807, is largely juvenilia. There is a pleasing facility about the volume, but the jog-trot dactylic rhythms that predominate lack the distinction of Shelley's more subtly crafted music. One poem, however, which hymns the bleak beauty of Scotland's Loch Na Garr, has a genuine ring and impetuous roll that sweeps the reader along in its ecstatic celebration of the wild and desolate: "Round Loch Na Garr while the stormy mist gathers, / Winter presides in his cold icy car: / Clouds there encircle the forms of my fathers; / That dwell in the tempests of dark Loch Na Garr" (29). Exploiting the exotic color of his Scottish heritage, Byron already paints himself as outcast and exile, only at home among the mountains, which reflect the sublimity of his independent spirit. To be sure, the pose is crudely obvious, but it adumbrates an important dimension of the future Childe Harold. The critics, however, were unedified by the performance and responded with crushing scorn. In consequence, Byron retaliated with his own criticism in pentameter couplets, "English Bards and Scotch Reviewers" (1810)—a literary lampoon that first revealed Byron's penchant for Augustan satire and his affinity with the world of Dryden, Johnson, and Pope. While never achieving the compact craftsmanship of his neoclassic predecessors or rising to height of satirical brilliance that elevates *The Dunciad*, for example, onto the plane of prophecy, the poem shoots its darts with accuracy, poise, and comic wit. Many of Byron's victims have been forgotten, but we can still relish his jibes at Wordsworth, Coleridge, and especially Southey, whom Byron pursued with mischievous gusto throughout his career.

Two Byrons thus emerge as early as 1810: the disconsolate lyricist only at home among the wilds of nature or at the feet of beauty, and the disabused man-of-the-world sardonically deflating the pretensions of the self-important and the second-rate. The cynical cosmopolitan emerges for a moment in "English Bards," then pretty much withdraws into the privacy of Byron's racy and ribald correspondence. Not until *Don Juan* would Byron find a way to integrate the poetically divided halves of his double consciousness. In the meantime, there was much to be gained financially from exploiting the mythos of the morose lord haunted by nameless transgressions and inexpiable sorrows. Though Byron was the most read, talked about, and influential of nineteenth-century English poets on the European continent, his uncertain status among English critics is in part traceable to the slapdash exuberance of his verse (a quality that does not lend itself to close textual analysis). But more than this, the vexed question of the poet's sincerity led to charges of disingenuousness that made him less than satisfactory to the earnest Victorians of the next generation. Still, he was extolled by Matthew Arnold for the qualities of "sincerity and strength,"[3] and no less a critic than T. S. Eliot, closer to our day, has applauded the poet's honesty: "With his charlatanism, he has also unusual frankness ... with his humbug and self-deception he has also a reckless raffish honesty."[4]

The earlier incarnations of Byron's poetic personae are, however, too theatrical in the main for modern taste. The series of swashbuckling verse-tales from *The Giaour* (1813) to *The Island* (1823), whose heroes all wear the same mask of melancholy weltschmerz, are largely forgotten except by students of the genre. The same attitudinizing makes *Childe Harold*, with its stilted back-glances in the direction of eighteenth-century Spenserians, equally meretricious. But these efforts were not entirely negligible. From the tales Byron mastered the arts of anecdote and narrative that would serve their turn in that consummate masterpiece *Don Juan*, while the themes of alienation and exile, the quest for glory and the fall of empires would be tapped with greater felicity in the lyrical outpourings of 1816.

For by 1816 *Childe Harold* was not just a mask put on for the opera ball of poetic melodrama, but an alter ego whose lineaments bore an increasing likeness to the poet himself. Following the breakup of his marriage Byron was indeed the remorseful exile whom he had celebrated somewhat factitiously in his earlier poems. The remorse was less a consequence of having flouted conventional behavior than it was a result of yielding to those conventions that the poet heartily despised. For Byron this meant exile from his sister, Augusta Leigh. Retreating to the Swiss Alps, Byron, like Blake before him, enunciated an ethic that anticipates the amoralism of the Nietzschean superman. As Manfred, one of Childe Harold's aliases, puts it rather rudely to a Swiss shepherd who saves him from suicide: "Patience and patience! Hence—that word was made / For brutes of burthen, not for birds of prey; / Preach it to mortals of a dust like thine,— / I am not of thy order" (395). This Byronic bird of prey, an object of dread to ordinary mortals, is gifted with a surprisingly mellifluous voice, for the poems of Byron composed in Switzerland at this time—the third canto of *Childe Harold*, *Manfred*, the "Epistles" to Augusta—are among the most successful and moving of his lyrical utterances. Whatever personal reasons may have contributed to this, there is no doubt that Shelley—whose influence became seminal at this time—was especially auspicious to the Byronic muse.

The pseudogothic trappings that disfigure the first two cantos of *Childe Harold* are absent in *Childe Harold III* and *IV*, which we may discuss here as a unit even though the last canto was completed two years later in Italy. The split between pious narrator and naughty "childe" that is maintained in the first two books is here replaced by a straightforward lyricism that collapses the distinction between the poet and his personae. The Spenserian stanzas are executed with a new speed and grace that has little in common with either Spenser or his Augustan imitators. Especially effective is the concluding alexandrine, which unfolds like the roll of a drum or the last fading chord of a symphony.

The poem as a whole is dominated by one big theme: the disparity between human wishes and mortal limits. For Byron the most cherished ideals of love, beauty, nobility, and truth painfully highlight the sordid actualities of our fugitive lives. The entire production is steeped in the doldrums of disillusion. But the disillusion is frequently transformed by Byron into a dashing act of heroic defiance. A thunderstorm among the Alps can thus become a sounding board to the poet's Promethean passions:

> Sky, mountains, rivers, winds, lake, lightnings! ye!
> With night, and clouds, and thunder, and a soul
> To make these felt and feeling, well may be
> Things that have made me watchful; the far roll
> Of your departing voices, is the knoll
> Of what in me is sleepless,—if I rest.
> But where of ye, O tempests! is the goal?
> Are ye like those within the human breast?
> Or do ye find, at length, like eagles, some high nest?
>
> Could I embody and unbosom now
> That which is most within me,—could I wreak
> My thoughts upon expression, and thus throw
> Soul, heart, mind, passions, and feelings, strong or weak,
> All that I would have sought, and all I seek,
> Bear, know, feel, and yet breathe—into *one* word,
> And that one word were Lightning, I would speak;
> But as it is, I live and die unheard,
> With a most voiceless thought, sheathing it as a sword.

$$(223)$$

Such poetry is hard to resist. To be sure, when examined closely, the stanzas are full of generalized emotion and indistinct imagery, but the pacing of the verse is impeccable. We can feel those eagle wings expanding in the long alexandrine of the first stanza and partake of their gradual ascent as the long vowels rise to a higher pitch and the line lengthens out in soaring flight. And the second stanza, with its series of periodic clauses rising to a climax on the resounding plosive "speak," carries us along with irresistible force, until in the last two lines the cathartic outburst subsides into stoic resignation and deliberate constraint. The concluding swagger with which Byron flings the sword of articulate aspiration back into the scabbard of voiceless despair is irresistible. In the very act of sheathing his eloquence Byron's showmanship is at its most daring; we cannot but admire the brazen ploy with which he tricks his reader into believing that the poet's sullen silence masks thoughts too unutterably splendid and inexpressively profound to submit to the limits of language.

Apart, however, from the histrionics, the stanza also reveals the crux of Byron's dilemma. While he cannot forbear to aspire in the direction of some ideal realm adequate to the compass of his longings, he is no less convinced of the futility of such aspirations. Like Wordsworth, Byron would pass beyond the outward and visible universe into some realm of transcendent and limitless beatitude; unlike Wordsworth, Byron is convinced such impulses are self-deceiving and unrealistic. In consequence, he remains permanently polarized between two incommensurates: the supernal world of supposititious ideals and the sublunary world of sad realities. Between these dichotomous extremes Byron alternates frenetically, until he sinks—agonized but stoical, despondent but defiant—into a pessimism that is the obverse side of star-bound perfection. In Canto III, Byron endeavors to lose himself in the enchanting recesses of the Alpine wilderness, but unlike Wordsworth, who genuinely forgets himself among the majestic forms of nature, Byron never quite lets us forget how exquisitely refined his spirit must be to experience such elevating moments and traumatic letdowns. Moreover, Byron is not humbled by being brought into contact with nature—as Wordsworth invariably is—but it is nature that is humbled by being brought into contact with Byron. Nature does not offer the poet an antidote to the introspective turmoil of his passions as it does Wordsworth; rather it is the only setting cosmic enough in scope to accommodate and express the sublime energy of those passions.

The fourth canto of *Childe Harold* moves from the Swiss Alps to the ruins of classical antiquity. The scene is changed to Italy: "Italia! oh Italia! thou who hast / The fatal gift of beauty" (233). The "Bridge of Sighs," the dying gladiator, the Venetian twilight, the marbles of ancient Rome, the grotto of Egeria, the Mediterranean Sea-things, in short, of vast expanse and timeless grandeur—these and these alone are adequate emblems of the poet's indomitable spirit. This is the poetry of melodrama, larger than life and verging on parody. The Grotto of Egeria is an especially revelatory instance of the Byronic syndrome. This shrine, dedicated to an ideal vision of unearthly beauty, only serves to underscore "the nympholepsy of [that] fond despair" (242) which racks the poet's heart. The *OED* defines "nympholepsy" as "a state of rapture supposed to be inspired by nymphs, hence, an ecstasy or frenzy of emotion especially inspired by something unattainable." For this ailment, however, there is no nostrum:

> Oh, Love! no inhabitant of earth thou art—
> An unseen seraph, we believe in thee,—
> A faith whose martyrs are the broken heart,—
> But never yet hath seen, nor e'er shall see
> The naked eye, thy form, as it should be;
> The mind hath made thee, as it peopled heaven,
> Even with its own desiring phantasy,
> And to a thought such shape and image given,
> As haunts the unquench'd soul-parched, wearied, wrung, and riven.
>
> (243)

The verse constantly skirts the edge of satire in its unrestrained ardors and surcharged emotions—but it proved irresistible to Byron's contemporaries and can still hurl us into the stars today. This is the aspect of Byron that the poets, composers, and painters of nineteenth-century Europe saw fit to emulate and admire.

Byron composed *Manfred* at the same time as the third canto of *Childe Harold*. Not surprisingly, the heroes share the same characteristics. Like Mary Shelley's Dr. Frankenstein, who was modeled in part on both Byron and Shelley, Manfred is a Faustian seeker of forbidden and occult knowledge. He repudiates his mortal status and earthly dust and, like Dr. Frankenstein, aspires to a state of pure or at least ersatz divinity. In a fine piece of metaphysical paradox, the French theologian Simone Weil observes that "if we forgive God for the crime of having created us finite, God will forgive us for the crime of being finite."[5] But Byron's Manfred will not forgive the "crime," nor will he acquiesce in the indignity of being "Half dust, half deity, unlike unfit / To sink or soar" (393).

In *Manfred* Byron deliberately titillates his readers with autobiographical insinuations of incest between Manfred and his deceased sister Astarte, whom he summons at one point from the dead in a necromantic spell defiant of both man and God. In the end Manfred dies, asserting the autonomy of his matchless spirit—but his defiance, like much of Byron's defiance in this period, strikes us as empty and unconvincing. Its individualist isolation is sterile and self-regarding, and in the end it contrasts unfavorably with the metaphysical rebellion of a writer of our age like Camus, whose philosophic formula, "I rebel, therefore *we* exist," shows a sense of solidarity with human suffering largely absent in Byron. Like Camus's metaphysical rebel, Byron too arraigns the universe for developing the incongruous mix of that creature called man—whose suffering is more intense in proportion as his spirit is more developed. But in Byron this rebellion does not translate into sympathy for the ordinary and oppressed, as it does with Camus. Byron is chiefly concerned with his own emancipation and his own uniqueness. It is observable, too, that the principal characteristics of the Byronic hero—those by which he claims his superiority to his fellow men and his exemption from the rules of conventional behavior—would be regarded in another age, say the medieval Christian, as signs of distinction to be sure, but distinction of a diabolic rather than exemplary order. The incessant self-communings are a mark of acedia—that moody, morose melancholy contemptuous of earthly limits and divine laws. Byron, fully aware of this, played the satanic role to the hilt.

There are, however, two poems of this period pitched in a subtler and more intimate key. The first is the "Epistle to Augusta," which, along with a handful of lyrics from *Hebrew Melodies* (1815), such as the ubiquitous "She walks in beauty," must be credited as among the most successful of Byron's shorter poems. The address to Augusta deliberately evokes Wordsworth's address to Dorothy in "Tintern Abbey," and indeed much of the poem echoes the sentiments and situations in Wordsworth's lyric. But the differences are more telling. Byron, for instance, cannot find in the Swiss Alps that natural counterpoise to human suffering that Wordsworth peacefully imbibes in the Wye Valley. And, of course, his estrangement from Augusta contains undertones of incestuous longing that are never allowed to surface in Wordsworth:

> My Sister! my sweet Sister! if a name
> Dearer and purer were, it should be thine;
> Mountains and seas divide us, but I claim
> No tears, but tenderness to answer mine:
> Go where I will, to me thou art the same—

A loved regret which I would not resign.
There yet are two things in my destiny,—
A world to roam through, and a home with thee.

(90)

The poem is disarmingly disingenuous especially for Byron. And the fact that he honored Augusta's request by not publishing it in his lifetime shows that for once, at least, the poet was unwilling to convert his sentiments into stock on the literary marketplace.

One other poem from the summer of 1816 deserves consideration— *The Prisoner of Chillon*. Its ostensible subject is the heroic defiance and subsequent imprisonment of the patriot François Bonivard and his two brothers in the dungeons of Chillon on Lake Geneva. But Byron converts this apparent paean to the spirit of liberty into an elaborate parable of the human condition. For the incarceration of Bonivard epitomizes for Byron the desperation of the human plight. The seven pillars to which the prisoners are chained represent the seven ages of man, and the inability of the brothers to comfort one another underscores the essential isolation of the human heart. The "living grave" of the dungeon is a metaphor of that death-in-life which characterizes an existence toiling under the conscious weight of its predestined end.

Byron explicitly rejects the Wordsworthian belief in salvation through nature when a bird alights at the dungeon grate and cheers Bonivard with the delirious dream that it is the soul of his dead brother. Like Wordsworth's daffodils, the song of the bird seems to offer the prisoner an opportunity for self-transcendence. But it departs with cruel suddenness, and Bonivard is left "twice so doubly lone, / Lone as a corpse within its shroud, / Lone as a solitary cloud" (340). Bonivard's epiphany ends where Wordsworth's begins, "lonely as a cloud / That floats on high o'er vales and hills." Instead of mediating divine visions, Byron's nature cruelly mocks the desperate credulity of enchained humankind. This is Romantic existentialism, and Byron's parable has the same significance for his age that Camus's *Myth of Sisyphus* has for ours. But Byron saves the ultimate irony for last. When Bonivard is finally freed—the only of the brothers to survive—he regains his freedom with a sigh: "My very chains and I grew friends, / So much a long communion tends / To make us what we are" (340). Bonivard may have lost his physical chains, but the chains that bind us to age, death, and loss are inexorable. In *The Prisoner of Chillon* Byron gives an objective and impersonal authority to those themes that *Childe Harold* expresses with confessional passion.[6]

But the preceding analysis of Byron's poetic career is less than half of the picture. While Byron would certainly be remembered if he had ceased to write in 1818, he would not have been deemed, by Matthew Arnold, the greatest poet of the Romantic Age after Wordsworth; nor would he be ranked as second only to Shakespeare by one of the Bard's most able critics in our day, G. Wilson Knight. For when Byron took off in 1818 on the subject of Don Juan, he found both a poetic form and a colloquial idiom elastic enough to accommodate the complex and often contradictory levels of his many-sided genius. Although *Don Juan* is a terribly self-indulgent poem, the self it indulges is irresistibly fascinating and immensely entertaining. It is the work of a born raconteur whose vivid anecdotes and penetrating observations we would not miss for the world. "I rattle on exactly as I'd talk / With anybody in a ride or walk" (834), observes Byron of the numerous digressions that diversify his tale.

Byron's Don is neither the dissolute rake of Spanish legend nor the tragic amorist of Mozart's opera; to the contrary, he is a generous-hearted and vulnerable pretty boy, more often seduced than seducing. He is of little intrinsic interest in himself, but as a provoker of authorial commentary he is indispensable. For, as every student of Byron knows, the real hero of *Don Juan* is the narrator, whose capricious wit and satirical innuendos punctuate the misadventures of Juan with humorous though devastating asides on social hypocrisy and human self-deception. Indeed, apart from the asides, the narrative is relatively thin.

Don Juan (pronounced to rhyme with *ruin*) is a gracious youth sent packing by his master following an affair with Donna Inez—a family friend married to a man many years her senior. When their affair is discovered, Donna Inez is placed in a convent by her husband and Juan is sent on a voyage by his mother. The ensuing shipwreck is one of the great set pieces in the poem—revealing another, less edifying side of nature than that which Wordsworth contemplates in the sheltered recesses of the Cumberland range. Grotesquely, the survivors are obliged to draw lots—torn rudely from strips of Donna Inez's last love letter to Juan—to determine who shall be sacrificed to keep the others from starving. So much for the beneficence of nature and the enchantments of love. Juan is finally cast ashore on a pirate island where he is nursed by Haidee, the captain's daughter, in a romantic interlude that mixes the tender with the sardonic. When Papa returns, Juan is sold into slavery. He is exhibited on the Turkish slave mart, where he catches the eye of a sultana who smuggles him into her service in the disguise of a female attendant—an indignity at which Juan fumes. But not for long—the ribaldry is cut short by an invasion of Russian troops with whom Juan join forces. The invasion prompts Byron to one of the most scathing attacks on the wastefulness of war to be found in English poetry: "'Let there be light' said God, and there was light! / 'Let there be blood' says man, and there's a sea!" (748). When Juan rescues an orphaned Muslim girl and becomes her protector, his heroism brings him to the attention of Catherine the Great, and he is accordingly sent to Russia, where he becomes—inevitably—the Empress' lover. Eventually, after Catherine sends him to England on a diplomatic mission, Juan becomes the center of intrigue and rivalry among three English noblewomen who vie for his favors. Throughout the poem's installments, Byron promises hundreds of cantos more by way of response to censorious critics who regard his efforts as immoral. But the poem was cut short by Byron's death.

Don Juan is first and foremost a gigantic spoof. The narrator's quicksilver changes of mood and emotion are exhilaratingly irreverent. Stanza after stanza builds to what appears to be a grandiose flourish of Romantic sentiment, but each time the whole structure comes crashing to a fall in a verbal equivalent of the banana-peel joke. This tactic is reinforced by the ottava rima stanza—a perfect medium for Byron's iconoclastic wit. With its tumbling roll of periodic rhymes (ababab) cut suddenly short by the deflating deadpan of the closing couplet, Byron found the perfect medium for his disabused look at marriage, war, fashion, the boast of heraldry, and the pomp of power. As the poet remarks with an accepting shrug, "the sad truth which hovers o'er my desk / Turns what was once romantic to burlesque" (699).

Don Juan most often recalls the picaresque novels of the eighteenth-century—especially Fielding's Tom Jones. Indeed, the poem as a whole hearkens back to Augustan satire, but with one signal and essentially Romantic difference. The disrobing of human vanities by writers such as Pope, Swift, or Johnson was empowered by a perception of enduring standards against which moral deviations could be measured. But Byron's exposure of human follies calls upon no standard other than that of the poet's own uncompromising and comprehensive nature. Though his defiance is leavened with laughter, it is still the defiance of a Manfred or Childe Harold whose nature is so rich, complex, varied, and dynamic that it sees through and repudiates the staid conventions, secondhand sentiments, and narrow-minded prejudices that hold the majority of his fellows in thrall. Byron's satire proceeds from the perceived superiority of the poet's nature, not from an established code of conduct or values.

Still, the changes that have taken place in the Byronic personae may be gauged by placing the following stanza from Don Juan on the illusory nature of love next to the stanza formerly cited from Childe Harold, "O Love no inhabitant of earth thou art!" While *Childe Harold* wails over this circumstance in accents of inconsolable grief, the narrator of *Don Juan* is more wryly philosophical:

> Love bears within its breast the very germ
>   Of change; and how should this be otherwise?
> That violent things more quickly find a term
>   Is shown through nature's whole analogies;
> And how should the most fierce of all be firm?
>   Would you have endless lightning in the skies?
> Methinks Love's very title says enough:
>   How should "the *tender passion*" e'er be *tough*?
>
> (831)

Byron's italicized epithets make it somewhat unclear whether we are talking about the throes of love or sides of beef. In any case, humorous acceptance has replaced Promethean defiance—though the poem never ceases to surprise, and on occasion the rueful melancholy of the old Childe Harold will surface. *Don Juan* is fatalism with a smile—but behind the bracing facade, one can detect a nihilistic undercurrent that skirts the borders of despair.

It was against this fatalism and despair that Percy Bysshe Shelley dedicated his poetic career. No poet of the Romantic movement was more enamored of ideas or more grounded in classical learning. Shelley's scholarly endowments were immense. He was adept in seven languages; his erudition was as formidable as his gift of lyrical expression. His translations of Homer, Plato, Euripides, Goethe, Calderon, and Dante make us wish that had been granted another lifetime to render the bulk of the world's classics into English—his instinctive feel for Dante being especially arresting. But since he was granted less than half a lifetime, Shelley sometimes lacked what Samuel Johnson calls "judgment" (though this was coming, nay, already had come, in his last extended efforts, *Adonais* and *The Triumph of Life*). At the early stages of his career, however, Shelley did not always perceive the contradictions inherent in his peculiar poetic mix. This mix initially involved an inflammatory rhetoric based on the revolutionary principles of that proto-Marxist philosopher William Godwin, whose *Political Justice* preached the abolition of private property, the virtues of free love, the benefits of a vegetarian diet, the overthrow of state-sponsored religion, and the general emancipation of the working masses. The philosophic underpinnings of this creed are materialistic and necessitarian. Blame for the world's evil is largely ascribed to a superstitious notion of deity and an unequal distribution of the world's goods. Shelley picked up on the necessitarian doctrine in his first year at University College, Oxford, when he indited "The Necessity of Atheism" and had the temerity to distribute it among the heads of Oxford's various colleges. Expecting a rational response to his arguments, he was instead summarily expelled—much to the dismay of his father, who expected the boy to enter Parliament. Shelley had other ideas, such as preaching revolution to the Irish and sending incendiary missives aloft in hot-air balloons filled with gases manufactured from the chemical apparatus in his own amateur laboratory.

But Shelley's vision of social utopia was predicated on the politics of nonviolence, and his aspirations, for all their affinity to those of William Godwin, Thomas Paine, and other rational skeptics of the revolutionary age, have more in common with the visionary politics of Virgil's fourth eclogue or the prophecies of Isaiah regarding the millennium of peace and happiness when the lion shall lie down with the lamb. Shelley, in short, was a seer; and despite his faith in the inexhaustible goodness of human nature, his utopian visions were millenarian and apocalyptic. It is this mix of revolutionary politics and sidereal perfection that makes his early poems an often incongruous farrago of contradictions.

Thus *Queen Mab* (1813), which enjoyed a wide circulation among nineteenth-century socialist circles, purports to be a paradisical vision of postrevolutionary Europe disclosed to Ianthe, the poem's heroine, in a dream. But the vision is delivered by the fairy Mab—not the sort of company usually kept by disgruntled radicals. And the fairy's speculations on death as some sort of divine transfiguration seem strangely out of place in a poem whose premises are grounded in necessitarian and materialist doctrines of human felicity. Similarly, *The Revolt of Islam* (1818) concludes with Laon and Cythna, those long-suffering martyrs to the cause of freedom and justice, being conducted in a magical boat to some postmortal paradise where they shall preside as patron saints to social altruists crucified in the cause of civil liberty. As with *Queen Mab*, Shelley's social criticism and secular concerns seems incommensurate with the gossamer imagery and otherworldly scenarios that compete with the ostensible subject matter of these poems.

Between *Queen Mab* and *The Revolt of Islam* Shelley wrote another poem of some length. Though the atmosphere of *Alastor* (1816) is pantheistic rather than Christian, the quest to which the protagonist is committed has more in common with the medieval dream vision than the reductive philosophy to which Shelley nominally subscribed. *Alastor* is, in fact, the first of Shelley's attempts to follow to their wellsprings those overflowing fountains of beauty, hope, love, and joy whose effects are apparent in works of imaginative genius and acts of self-sacrificing virtue, but whose essence remains enigmatic and inaccessible to human comprehension. *Alastor* represents that side of Shelley that keenly responded to the philosophy of Plato and rapturously extolled the *Paradiso* of Dante as "a hymn of everlasting love." Despite his repudiation of institutional religion, Shelley, as George Santayana remarks, "was also removed from any ordinary atheism by his truly speculative sense for eternity."[7] It is the "speculative sense for eternity" that impels the visionary in *Alastor* to abandon all human comforts in the search for an absolute that is ultimately sacred.

Critics have noted Shelley's ambivalence toward his hero, whose quest takes the form of a metaphorical voyage in a frail vessel down a winding river to discover the secret wellsprings of life and thought. He is guided in his quest by the lovely apparition of a disembodied maiden whose "voice was like the voice of his own soul / Heard in the calm of thought" (18). She is at once an emblem of that intellectual beauty on whose trace the poet is driven and a personification of the imaginative faculty that awakens the poet's nostalgia for that nameless something which the "Preface" describes as "all of wonderful, wise, or beautiful, which the poet, the philosopher, or the lover could depicture" (14). She is, in short, the first of Shelley's female incarnations of eternal spirit—an image of the human soul freed from the burdens of mortality and a conduit through whom the principle of everlasting love issues into the regions of this world. We shall see her again as Asia in *Prometheus Unbound*, Emily in *Epipsychidion*, Urania in *Adonais*, the lady with the green thumb in *The Sensitive Plant*, and finally the goddess who kindles the dormant aspirations of the youthful Rousseau in *The Triumph of Life*.

But her pursuit in *Alastor* leads, paradoxically, to the protagonist's ruin. It has been frequently noted that the "Preface" to *Alastor* censures a quest that detaches its partisans from the solid body of average humanity, while the poem itself—or, at least, the poem's narrator—involuntarily succumbs to the allure of the youth's idealism. The conclusion is most revealing. Though the youth expires in a quest that is evidently vain and unproductive, the narrator applauds his efforts despite their indisputable futility. The quest, to be sure, is chimerical and the youth destroyed; but this very fusion of magnanimity and folly, lofty sentiment and self-defeating credulity ultimately transfigures the very world the youth has abandoned. The mere psychological fact that a few choice spirits in each generation are impelled to pursue such a quest irretrievably alters our sense of reality. Though the absolutes of beauty, grace, and truth remain a mere hypothesis, and the fate of those who dedicate their lives to these absolutes appears unencouraging, there is a residue of glory that radiates from their very defeat—and it is this that fundamentally alters our perception of ourselves and the universe we inhabit: "Nature's vast frame, the web of human things, / Birth and the grave, that are not as they were" (30).

A year after *Alastor*, Shelley composed two lyrics that continue the search for the hidden sources of human thought. For Shelley, this search is sometimes so intense that it passes at its highest reaches into a kind of mystic and unpremeditated orison. The "Hymn to Intellectual Beauty" (1816) is one of these. The poem posits the existence of a transcendental power that the poet vainly seeks to confirm on the plane of rational demonstration. And yet this "Spirit of Beauty, that dost consecrate / With thine own hues all thou dost shine upon / of human thought or form ..." (526) can no more be disproved than it can be validated. In a world of metaphysical incertitudes, it remains an unsubstantiated vagary, intuitively present though tantalizingly out of reach. The images Shelley evokes to characterize this Spirit are as fleeting, evanescent, and unpredictable as the Spirit itself: moonbeams, clouds in starlight, dying music, rainbows, the onset of spring. "Doubt, chance, and mutability" are the only indisputable constants, but despite this disheartening conclusion and the poem's rejection of a naive supernaturalism—"No voice from some sublimer world hath ever / To sage or poet these responses given" (526)— the lyricist concludes with a hope that these indeterminate glimpses of "an unseen power that floats though unseen among us" will crystallize, at length, into an assured conviction giving support and serenity to his future years:

> The day becomes more solemn and serene
>> When noon is past—there is a harmony
>> In autumn, and a lustre in its sky
> Which through the summer is not heard or seen,
> As if it could not be, as if it had not been!
>> Thus let thy power which like the truth
>> Of nature on my passive youth
> Descended, to my onward life supply

Its calm—to one who worships thee
And every form containing thee ...

(528)

It is no wonder that C. S. Lewis wrote of this poet, "there is
something holier about the atheism of a Shelley than about the theism of
a Paley."[8] Paley was the eighteenth-century deist whose natural theology
Shelley endeavored to refute in "The Necessity of Atheism." Clearly, for
Lewis, Shelley's troubled but irrepressible intuition of intellectual beauty
was more compatible with the spirit of genuine faith than Paley's
impersonal syllogisms and complacent theological formulaes.

"Mont Blanc" is a companion piece to "Intellectual Beauty,"
similarly positing the existence of a supreme power enthroned behind the
shifting flux of the Swiss valley of Arve. But as in the "Hymn," the source
of that teeming wilderness of life and death, glory and desolation,
predatory fauna and opulent flora remains "Remote, serene, and
inaccessible," like the silent peak of Mont Blanc, which majestically rises
from the Alpine valley below. No voice speaks to Shelley from this
mountain, like the fabled voice that thundered from the top of Sinai. The
poet endeavors to rise above the world of material phenomena, as later his
skylark will do: in "a legion of wild thoughts, whose wandering wings /
Now float above [the mountain's base]" (529). But his only discovery is the
myth-making faculty of the human mind—that faculty which seeks, as
Shelley wrote in a letter, "to see the manifestation of something beyond
the present and tangible object." Shelley's dilemma is that of the mystic
who cannot bring himself to believe in the truth of revealed religion. In
consequence, the existence of that power which rolls through the Arve and
kindles the poet's mind with conjectures of possible divinity remains
hypothetical—unconfirmed by human experience and unmeasured by
scientific means. Yet as "Mont Blanc" implies, humanity is most true to
itself when it embroiders the silent surface of the material universe with
the hieroglyphics of myth, poetry, and, yes, praise. Mont Blanc is an
inscrutable cipher, a tabula rasa upon which, in an inversion of Locke's
epistemology, the poet projects his own tentative theorems of divine
power. But the mountain remains silent, like the vast power behind the
shows of things that it suggests. Upon the "vacancy" of this perplexing
universe the poet disburdens his metaphysical postulates as a saving
alternative to despair.

A philosophic skeptic dedicated to the improvement of the human
lot and an uncompromising visionary seeking to confirm, in a world

beyond the senses, the nebulous visions that ravish his soul, Shelley, in *Prometheus Unbound* (1820), successfully integrated the two sides of his complex nature in a poem Yeats described as one of the sacred books of the world. Its sacredness may be arguable, but as a mythopoeic expression of the Romantic spirit it must be regarded as one of the few successful long poems of the nineteenth century. Its success may be measured in part by its having eclipsed or at least modified our perception of Aeschylus's *Prometheus Bound* to the point that we can no longer think of it without Shelley's belated sequel. With *Prometheus*, the unripe ethos of Shelley's revolutionary politics evolves into a complex anatomy of the human psyche. "What a difference," observes Kierkegaard, "between youthfully desiring to change the whole world and then discovering that it is oneself that is to be changed."[9] In *Prometheus* Shelley is still beset by "a passion for reforming the world," but this passion is now applied to interior psychology and a recognition that change must be from the inside out. Even the most liberal of governments and advanced of societies remain moribund unless the men and women who constitute its polis are themselves spiritually awake. *Prometheus Unbound* is the drama of that awakening. Virtually all of the characters, with the exception of the somewhat shadowy Demogorgon, are fragmented particles of a single divided mind seeking reintegration and rebirth. The key word of the drama is "unite."

Shelley's drama reverses, of course, the assumptions of Aeschylus. Prometheus, as the "Preface" proclaims, is "the type of the highest perfection of moral and intellectual nature, impelled by the purest and truest motives to the best and noblest ends" (201). Jupiter is a nonentity, which is to say that he is nothing more than a projection onto the cosmos of human fears, anxieties, and self-contempt writ large. His earthly incarnations include all oppressive governments and sectarian bigotries. Prometheus is thus enthralled by a being of his own creation. His earlier curse upon Jupiter simply perpetuates the despotic reign against which Prometheus struggles. But hatred, Shelley implies, is the worst tyranny of all. It is this curse that keeps the Titan enchained. By recalling the curse and responding to oppression with patience, forbearance, forgiveness, and love, Prometheus is finally triumphant.

But there is work to be done besides the dethronement of Jupiter. For this, Prometheus's banished spouse, Asia, is required. For it is Asia who endeavors to discover the moral and spiritual roots of Prometheus's defiance, to trace to its source that demand for justice and mercy which emancipates Prometheus from the disfiguring authority of Jupiter.

Prometheus's rebellion, in short, is predicated on the existence of a higher heaven against which Jupiter's reign is implicitly judged. The Titan's rejection of revenge is thus complemented in Act II by Asia's quest, in the realm of Demogorgon, for the authentic sources of that moral law by which the Jupiters of the world are ultimately measured.[10]

In the cave of Demogorgon—the personification of that shadowy power which Shelley formerly intuited at the peak of Mont Blanc—Asia learns of a spiritual principle enthroned beyond the world of appearances and the workings of natural law. Demogorgon's replies to Asia are elliptical and enigmatic, for the "deep truth is imageless" and, hence, can only be suggested by metaphor and symbol: "What to bid speak / Fate, Time, Occasion, Chance, and Change? To these / All things are subject but eternal love" (234). Reborn through contact with Demogorgon, Asia is the purified emblem of the human imagination in the same way that Prometheus, in his exchange of forgiveness for revenge, is the emblem of the purified human will. As in *Alastor*, Asia's purification involves a metaphorical voyage on a winding river that leads the regenerated soul back to its primal origins and pristine beginnings:

> My soul is an enchanted boat,
>   Which, like a sleeping swan, doth float
> Upon the silver waves of thy sweet singing;
>   And thine doth like an angel sit
>   Beside the helm conducting it
> Whilst all the winds with melody are ringing.
>   It seems to float ever, for ever,
>   Upon that many winding river,
>   Between mountains, woods, abysses,
>   A paradise of wildernesses!
> Till, like one in slumber bound,
> Borne to the ocean, I float down, around,
> Into a sea profound, of ever-spreading sound.
>
> (237–38)

Acts III and especially IV are given over to a description and celebration of the new dispensation in a series of lyrics that burst across the page like fireworks, a succession of dazzling pyrotechnics that, in C. S. Lewis's words, seem composed of "air and fire" and produce a sensation as of "Untrammelled, reckless speed through pellucid spaces which make us imagine while we are reading it that we have somehow left our bodies behind."[11] The celebration is brought to an end by the appearance of Demogorgon, who utters both a benediction and a warning. The rush of anapests, dactyls, and tumbling syncopated varieties of metrical rhythm comes to a standstill, while the deep organ tones of Demogorgon's stately iambics rise from the very depths of being:

> To suffer woes which hope thinks infinite;
>   To forgive wrongs darker than death or night;
> To defy Power, which seems omnipotent;
> To love, and bear; to hope till Hope creates
>   From its own wreck the think it contemplates;
> Neither to change, nor falter, nor repent;
> This, like thy glory, Titan, is to be
> Good, great and joyous, beautiful and free;
> This is alone Life, Joy, Empire and Victory.
>
>   (264)

After *Prometheus Unbound*, Shelley's poetry is increasingly dedicated to the pursuit of Demogorgon—in short, to the intuition and adoration of that ground of being which Demogorgon vaguely shadows forth. In *Epipsychidion* (1821), for example, Shelley attempts, on the plane of personal confession and idealized biography, to discover through the mediating love of Emilia Viviani that ultimate reality which is likewise mediated to Prometheus through the ministrations of Asia. The poem is full of Dantesque echoes and begins with a free translation from *La Vita Nuova* by way of warning to unenlightened readers who may misconceive the poet's intentions or regard them as morally suspect. The warning notwithstanding, it must be admitted that the poem—though rising to levels of lyrical beauty worthy of Dante—often muddles the boundaries between physical desire and spiritual illumination. This is a common Romantic fallacy, which we shall see repeated in the Victorian poet Dante Gabriel Rossetti—though perhaps Rossetti is finally a little more honest than Shelley about these matters. But with *Epipsychidion* Shelley does begin to explore, if not resolve, the contradictions implicit in his scheme of things. The contradictions were both philosophical and personal. On the personal level, it is fair to say that Shelley's love life was something of a mess—even by contemporary standards. In the poem Shelley dignifies this mess through a series of astronomical images that represent the various women in his life.

Following his expulsion from Oxford, Shelley had run off with Harriet Westbrook, a sixteen-year-old classmate of Shelley's sisters who had come into contact with the poet's works and wrote to him expressing her sympathy for his vision of redeemed humanity. But she also hinted of suicide as the only refuge for the persecutions she sustained in consequence of being radicalized by the poet. Shelley quixotically intervened and the two were married. From this union a pair of children were born, and Harriet became more insistent that her husband reconcile with his father so that they could live in the aristocratic comfort that Shelley's lineage warranted. But the poet was intransigent and began to repent his impulsive chivalries. He found sympathy in the home of William Godwin—the radical philosopher who had fired his youth—and, at length, met Godwin's daughter, Mary Wollstonecraft-Godwin. Mary's mother, the illustrious champion of women's rights, Mary Wollstonecraft, had died when Mary was a child. In the churchyard where she was buried, Shelley declared his love for this daughter of double genius. But despite his advocacy of free love in *Political Justice*, Godwin, on learning of the affair, expelled Shelley from his house. Nothing daunted, Shelley and Mary eloped to the continent. Harriet committed suicide, and Shelley returned to claim his children. But his father-in-law contested the poet's parental fitness in the British courts, and the children were placed in a foster home. Shelley departed from England with Mary in 1816, and after a brief stay in Switzerland with Byron, settled in Italy, "the paradise of exiles." Mary was every bit the poet's equal intellectually, but as her novel *Frankenstein* reveals, she had many misgivings about Shelley's idealized conceptions of human nature. The loss of several children to illness and disease plunged Mary into increasing gloom; and Shelley, in need of sympathy and estranged from Mary, began a platonic flirtation with a young girl imprisoned in an Italian convent.

Emilia Viviani is celebrated in *Epipsychidion* as a Dantesque mediary between the divine and the human. Drawing on literary imagery from *The Song of Songs* and the works of Dante, Shelley describes the stages of a pilgrimage that has brought him, through Emily, to a contemplation of beauty itself, single and indivisible, an eternal essence that abides beyond the world of spatio-temporal shadows and things that ripen and decay. In the end, the Dantesque springs of Shelley's lyric eventually triumph over the repressed sensualism of the poem's undercurrents. In the concluding section, the poet conceives of an island where he and Emily shall ascend to an awareness of that abiding One which overcomes mortal distinctions and individual differences:

Let us become the overhanging day,
The living soul of the Elysian isle,
Conscious, inseparable, one. Meanwhile
We two will rise, and sit, and walk together.
Under the roof of blue Ionian weather,
And wander in the meadows, or ascend
The mossy mountains, where the blue heavens bend
With lightest winds, to touch their paramour;
Or linger, where the pebble-paven shore,
Under the quick, faint kisses of the sea
Trembles and sparkles as with ecstasy,—
Possessing and possessed by all that is
Within that calm circumference of bliss ...

                                              (417–18)

In *Epipsychidion*, as George Santayana shrewdly remarks, Shelley "shatters the world to bits, but only to build it nearer to his heart's desire, only to make out of its colored fragments some more Elysian home for love, or some more dazzling symbol for that infinite beauty which is the need—the profound, aching, imperative need—of the human soul."[12]

This is the crux of Shelley's dilemma. Committed since his youth to a necessitarian philosophy that denies the reality of metaphysical axioms, Shelley at the same time feels the need, the "profound, aching, imperative need" to discover some objective and impersonal source for those moral visions and immortal longings to which this world's circumstances seem unequal. Shelley asks, "What were virtue, love, patriotism, friendship— what were the scenery of this beautiful universe which we inhabit; what were our consolations on this side of the grave—and what were our aspirations beyond it, if poetry did not ascend to bring light and fire from those eternal regions where the owl-winged faculty of calculation dare never soar?"[13]

Epipsychidion concludes with the tacit acknowledgement that the love of which Emily had been the conduit, remains, on this side of paradise, a fugitive, uncertain, and infrequent guest. Its loss is bitter, but as the postscript avers, "Love's very pain is sweet, / But its reward is in the world divine / Which, if not here, it builds beyond the grave" (418–19).

Within a few months of the composition of *Epipsychidion*, the death of the young English poet John Keats provided Shelley with the opportunity to again "bring light from those eternal regions" to which the poet instinctively aspired. *Adonais* (1821) is the most distinguished of

Shelley's extended poems. Its architectonics are nothing short of dazzling. The poet weaves together a complex series of images associated with fire and moisture, heat and cold, flowers and stars, light and darkness, time and eternity, as the salient facts of Keats's poetic career are assimilated to the Greek myth of the dying vegetation god. Drawing on the Greek bucolic poets Bion and Moschus for inspiration, Shelley departs from their assumptions in one important respect. The Adonis of Bion's lament is mourned by an earthly Venus representing the cyclical patterns of life and death in nature. In Shelley's poem Adonis becomes Adonais—the extra vowel giving the name a mournful plangency appropriate to an elegy, and suggesting, by the same stroke, the transcendental origins of earthly life. Remove the final consonant, and Adonais reveals his sonship to the principle of everlasting life that Hebrew scripture reverently forbears to utter except by indirection—the *Adonai* or Lord of ineffable name. By the poem's conclusion it becomes apparent why Shelley's deceased poet is mourned by Urania, the goddess of astronomy, rather than Venus. The principle that impelled Keats to remodel the world according to the lights of his poetic vision is immutable. Its extinction is only apparent, like that of the stars whose radiance is obscured by the atmospheric mists of early morning. At the poem's conclusion the mists of earthly life are swept away and the starlike radiance of Adonais is perceived in its changeless essence—a fixed star in the firmament of infinity:

> The splendours of the firmament of time
> May be eclipsed, but are extinguished not;
> Like stars to their appointed height they climb,
> And death is a low mist which cannot blot
> The brightness it may veil.
>
> (436)

In the poem's most famous stanza, Hebrew and Platonic elements intertwine as the atmosphere of mortal life is compared to a "dome of many-coloured glass" behind which abides that ultimate One "whose smile kindles the universe" (438).

But the conclusion leaves us with certain misgivings. At some point in the poem's unfolding metaphysics, the search for an ultimate reality devolves into something less salutary—a death wish that reveals an unripe petulance, an immaturity of vision that still clings to the works of this gifted but youthful poet and tempts him to spurn the created structures of being for glorious shipwreck on the shoals of eternity:

The breath whose might I have invoked in song
Descends on me; my spirit's bark is driven
Far from the shore, far from the trembling throng
Whose sails were never to the tempest given;
The massy earth and sphered skies are riven!
I am born darkly, fearfully, afar;
Whilst, burning through the inmost veil of Heaven,
The soul of Adonais, like a star,
Beacons from the abode where the Eternal are.

(438–39)

That last stanza explicitly alludes to Shelley's great lyric of 1818, "Ode to the West Wind," where in a series of breathless, rapid stanzas in the difficult Italian meter of terza rima, the poet assumed the identity of the ancient vegetation god with whom Keats is associated in *Adonais*. In the earlier ode, Shelley regards this myth of the dying and resurrecting corn god as a true emblem of human growth and change—life itself being a series of initiatory deaths and rebirths into deepening levels of consciousness and humanity. In the ode this process is cyclical and recurrent—"O, Wind, / If Winter comes, can Spring be far behind?" (574)—and operates simultaneously in the life and death of empires, the phases of individual life, and the revolution of the seasons. In *Adonais*, however, this naturalistic framework is supplanted by an ultimate and irrevocable apocalypse. Like the skylark whose song, in Shelley's celebrated lyric, is

Keen as are the arrows
    Of that silver sphere,
Whose intense lamp narrows
    In the white dawn clear
Until we hardly see—we feel that it is there,

(597)

so the morning star of Keats's immortal spirit, though apparently quenched by the spreading light of dawn, still persists—an "intense lamp" whose ever-living radiance is obscured but not destroyed by the prismatic mists of our mortal day.[14]

In *A Defence of Poetry*, Shelley proclaims that poetry "strips the veil of familiarity from the world, and lays bare the naked and sleeping beauty, which is the spirit of its forms." So Shelley in *Adonais* intuits beyond the veils of thought and sense that ultimate reality to which *Adonais* has returned. But can a mortal being survive the vision thus unveiled? At one point in *Adonais*, Shelley compares himself to Actaeon, the mythic huntsman who had gazed unwittingly on the naked beauty of Diana. For this sacrilege he was changed by the goddess into a stag, while her nymphs, metamorphosed into hounds, dragged him to his death. In the same way, Shelley's visionary propensities could not but exacerbate his sense of earthly ills and human limits. "The consequence," as Santayana observes, "was that Shelley, having a nature ... tender, passionate, and moral, was exposed to early and continual suffering.... If to the irrepressible gushing of life from within we add the suffering and horror that continually checked it, we shall have in hand, I think, the chief elements of his genius."[15]

Shelley's last poem, the unfinished *Triumph of Life* (1822), is devoted to an anatomy of that "suffering and horror" which he saw in the world around him. It is the most sober and disillusioned of Shelley's works and develops with a gravity and restraint that are a kind of literary breakthrough. Yeats observed that Shelley "lacked a vision of evil" and, in consequence, did not attain to that greatness which belongs to poets of more comprehensive vision. But *The Triumph of Life* brings Shelley to the threshold of such greatness. Its vision of human life is frank, uncompromising, disabused; and the tercets in which it is composed are, as T. S. Eliot remarked, as close an approximation as we have in English to the majestic gravity and economical speed of Dante. Dantesque, too, is the image of human suffering that Shelley beholds in a dream-vision like that of *The Divine Comedy*. And just as Dante is hosted through hell by the Latin poet Virgil, so Shelley is hosted through his modern nightmare of spiritual lostness by the representative man of the Romantic age: Jean Jacques Rousseau. Shelley's tragic awareness of the way in which the visionary gleam of youthful idealism is gradually destroyed by the compromises, betrayals, and disloyalties of so-called maturity is far removed from the Godwinian belief in human perfectibility that enchanted the poet in his adolescence. Despite Rousseau's youthful vision of a radiant goddess—the personification of that "visionary gleam" whose passing Wordsworth laments in the "Immortality Ode"—he cannot constrain himself from joining the mad procession of greedy, appetitive, and discontented worldlings driven to distraction by the promises and betrayals of earthly existence. This procession of broken spirits and disfigured forms follows in the wake of a triumphal chariot drawn by a nebulous being of uncertain shape. The chariot represents the counterfeit joys and parodistic pleasures life holds forth, and the shapes that trail behind are the dehumanized specters of those who have betrayed their deepest selves in the pursuit of vanities:

> Old men and women foully disarrayed,
> Shake their gray hairs in the insulting wind,
>
> And follow in the dance, with limbs decayed,
> Seeking to reach the light which leaves them still
> Farther behind and deeper in the shade.
>
> (507)

In the whole of human history only two privileged beings are exempt from this brutalizing procession: Socrates and Jesus Christ. Though it is hazardous to venture an interpretation of a poem left incomplete by the poet's death, it seems clear that Shelley was subjecting his earlier visions of regenerate humanity to mature revaluation. For Rousseau's vision of the disfiguring chariot follows almost instantaneously upon his drinking from the proffered cup of that goddess who is the last of Shelley's incarnations of intellectual beauty. The only explanation for this is so startling that it reverses the assumptions which Mary Shelley first articulated regarding her husband's works and which most critics have subsequently endorsed, namely, that "Shelley believed that mankind had only to will there would be no evil and there would be none" (267). But in *The Triumph of Life* not only the vision but the desire of evil is directly consequent upon Rousseau's draining the cup held forth by that "Shape all light" whose "half-extinguished beam / Through the sick day in which we wake to weep / Glimmers, forever sought, forever lost" (512–14). What does this episode suggest but that human nature is such that its loftiest visions of surpassing loveliness and moral good activate the perverse desire to deface, to destroy, to profane those visions?

In this way humanity is free, though haunted by its former longings, to pursue self-interest and self-gratification, even to its own undoing. Such a realization implies a reversal of those assumptions that had formerly determined Shelley's philosophic outlook—a reversal that reveals, perhaps, the extent to which Shelley's reading of Dante and the Gospels in their original languages was beginning to modify his worldview. But this is conjecture. And the question with which the poem abruptly ends, "'Then what is life?' I cried," remains unanswered.

Shelley died in 1822 when his sailboat, the *Ariel*, went down in a storm eerily prefigured in the concluding stanza of *Adonais*: "my spirit's bark is driven / Far from the shore, far from the trembling throng / Whose sails were never to the tempest given" (438–39). Mary lived to see her only surviving son, Sir Percy Florence, inherit the Shelley estate and settle into the life of an English landowner untroubled by the perturbations of genius. Sir Percy's wife, Lady Jane Shelley, was an indefatigable champion of the poet's memory. Mary never remarried; her principal work, after *Frankenstein*, is the complete edition of Shelley's poems, to which she added copious notes on the poet's life and thought. These notes carry on a kind of posthumous debate with the spirit of the dead poet and sound what for many readers is a valid criticism of his works—namely, their tendency toward the "wildly fanciful ... discarding human interest and passion, to revel in the fantastic ideas that his imagination suggested" (382). But the instinctive bias of Shelley's nature inclined precisely in the direction that Mary faulted as vague and insubstantial. If it is true that Shelley sometimes leaves the world and the common reader behind, it must also be allowed, as George Santayana observes, that "his abstraction from half of life, or from nine-tenths of it was perhaps necessary if silence and space were to be won in his mind for its own upwelling, ecstatic harmonies. The world we have always with us, but such spirits we have not always."[16]

NOTES

1. Byron, *Poetical Works* (London: Oxford University Press, 1967), 90 (hereafter cited in text).

2. Cited by Elizabeth Longsford in *The Life of Byron* (Boston: Little Brown, 1976), 210. Yet after this expression of defiance, Byron apparently muttered, "I fancy myself a Jew, a Mahomedan, and a Christian of every profession of faith. Eternity and space are before me; but on this subject, thank God, I am happy and at ease. The thought of living eternally, of again reviving, is a great pleasure."

3. Matthew Arnold, *Essays in Criticism: Second Series* (London: Macmillan, 1941), 136.

4. T.S. Eliot, *On Poetry and Poets* (New York: Farrar, Straus, and Giroux, 1970), 239.

5. George A. Panichas, ed., *The Simone Weil Reader* (New York: David McKay, 1977), 433.

6. Perhaps the most pertinacious of commentaries on this commanding poem may be found in Robert Gleckner's *Byron and the Ruins of Paradise* (Baltimore: Johns Hopkins Press, 1967). For Arnold reference, see P. J. Keating, ed., *Matthew Arnold: Selected Prose* (Harmondsworth: Penguin, 1987), 404. For Knight reference, see G. Wilson Knight, *Byron and Shakespeare* (New York: Barnes & Noble, 1966), 1.

7. George Santayana, *Winds of Doctrine and Platonism and The Spiritual Life* (Gloucester: Peter Smith, 1971), 180.

8. C.S. Lewis, *Christian Reflections* (Grand Rapids: William B. Eerdmans, 1967), 70.

9. Søren Kierkegaard, *Edifying Discourses: A Selection* (New York: Harper & Row, 1958), 186.

10. For a brilliant discussion of Asia's significance in *Prometheus Unbound*, see F. A. Pottle, "The Role of Asia in the Dramatic Action of Shelley's *Prometheus Unbound*," in *Shelley: A Collection of Critical Essays*, ed. by George M. Ridenour (Englewood Cliffs: Prentice-Hall, 1965), 133–43.

11. C.S. Lewis, *Literary Essays* (Cambridge: Cambridge University Press, 1969), 204.

12. Santayana, *Winds of Doctrine*, 163.

13. Carlos Baker, ed., *Selected Poetry and Prose of Shelley* (New York: Random House, 1951), 317.

14. My reading of this poem is profoundly indebted to Earl Wasserman's magisterial discussion in *Shelley: A Critical Reading* (Baltimore: Johns Hopkins University Press, 1971), 462–502.

15. Santayana, *Winds of Doctrine*.

16. Ibid., 172.

M.H. ABRAMS

Keats's Poems:
The Material Dimensions

The chief concern of modern critics of Keats has been with the semantic dimension of his poems—their component meanings; their thematic structures; and what, in a well-known essay, Douglas Vincent Bush called "Keats and His Ideas."[1] This was the primary issue for the New Critics of the midcentury, who read Keats's poems with the predisposition to find coherence, unity, and ironies; it is no less the issue for poststructural theorists, who read the poems with the predisposition to find incoherence, ruptures, and aporias. The concern with semantics is understandable, for Keats was a remarkably intelligent poet, almost without parallel in the rapidity with which he grasped, elaborated, and deployed philosophical and critical concepts. To deal with Keats's poems exclusively on the ideational level, however, is to disembody them and so to delete what is most characteristic about them. My aim in this essay is to put first things first: What is the immediate impact of reading a passage by Keats? And by what features do we identify the passage as distinctively Keatsian?

I

Consider the following lines from Keats's poems:

> My heart aches, and a drowsy numbness pains
> My sense, as though of hemlock I had drunk.

From *The Persistence of Poetry: Bicentennial Essays on Keats*, edited by Robert M. Ryan and Ronald A. Sharp. © 1998 by The University of Massachusetts Press.

From silken Samarcand to cedar'd Lebanon.
Singest of summer in full-throated ease.

                    whose strenuous tongue
Can burst joy's grape against his palate fine.

Thy hair soft-lifted by the winnowing wind.

'Mid hushed, cool-rooted flowers, fragrant-eyed.[2]

The passages differ in what they signify, but we can say about all of them, as about hundreds of other lines, that if we were to meet them running wild in the deserts of Arabia, we would instantly cry out, "Keats!" On what features does this recognition depend?

Robert Frost used the word "sound" to describe the perceived aspect of a poem that is distinctive for each poet: "And the sound rises from the page, you know, a Wordsworthian sound, or a Keatsian sound, or a Shelleyan sound.... The various sounds that they make rise to you from the page."[3] The term is helpful, but it needs to be unpacked. In the current era of semiotics and Derrida's warnings against "phonocentrism," we commonly refer to literary works as "*écriture*" and to poems as "texts." The material medium of poetry, however, is not the printed word. To think so is a fallacy—a post-Gutenberg fallacy of misplaced concreteness. Yet neither is the poetic medium a purely auditory sound as such. The material medium (in current parlance, "the material signifier") of a poem is speech, and speech consists of enunciated words, so that the sound of a poem is constituted by speech-sounds. And we don't—we can't—hear speech-sounds purely as sounds. Instead what we hear (to use Derrida's apt phrase) is "always already," and inseparably, invested with two nonauditory features. One of these is the significance of the words, phrases, and sentences into which the speech-sounds are conjoined. The other is the physical sensation of producing the speech-sounds that we hear or read. For when we read a poem slowly and with close attention, even if we read it silently to ourselves, the act involves—often below the level of distinct awareness—the feel of enunciating the words of the poem by remembered, imagined, or incipient movements and tactile sensations in the organs of speech, that is, in the lungs, throat, mouth, tongue, and lips. Because this feature, although essential to the full experience of a poem, has been neglected in literary criticism, I want to dwell for a while on the material, articulative aspect of Keats's language.

In taking pains, as Keats once said, to make a poem read "the more richly,"[4] he characteristically manages his language in such a way as to bring up to, or over, the verge of an attentive reader's consciousness what it is to form and enunciate the component speech-sounds. He makes us sense, for example, the changing size and shape of our mouth and the configuration of our lips as we articulate a vowel; the forceful expulsion of breath that we apprehend as syllabic stress; the vibration or stillness of our vocal chords in voiced or unvoiced consonants; the tactile difference between a continuant consonant and a stopped (or "plosive") consonant; and in the pronunciation of the various consonants, the movements of our lips and gestures of our tongue. Keats also makes us aware, as we pronounce consonants, of the touch of our tongue to the roof of the mouth or upper gum, and the touch of our lower lip to the teeth or (in labial consonants) of our lower lip on the upper lip. It is not possible to extricate with any precision the role of enunciation from those of sound and significance in the overall experience of a poem. It is evident, however, that Keats, by using long vowels, continuant consonants, and consecutive strong stresses to slow the pace at which we read, heightens our attention to the palpability of his material signifiers, and makes their articulation, juxtaposition, repetition, and variation into a richly sensuous oral activity. Consider the beginning of *Ode to a Nightingale*:

My heart aches, and a drowsy numbness pains
My sense, as though of hemlock I had drunk. (1–2)

In such passages, Keats enforces the realization that a poem, like other works of art, is a material as well as a significant thing; its significance is apprehended only by being bodied forth, and the poem's body is enunciated speech, which has a complex kinetic and tactile as well as auditory physicality. Of all the forms of art, furthermore, the material base of poetry, whether spoken or sung, is the most intimately human, because it is constituted solely by our bodily actions, and because its vehicle is the breath of our life.

When discussing poems, we tend to attribute to the sound—the purely auditory qualities—of the words what are in much greater part the effects of enunciating the words conjointly with understanding the reference of the words. For example, in the line from *The Eve of St. Agnes*,

From silken Samarcand to cedar'd Lebanon (270),

we say that the words are euphonious—that is, they sound good. But they sound good to the ear only because, meaning what they do, they feel good in the mouth; their pleasantness, as a result, is much more oral than auditory. It is a leisurely pleasure to negotiate the sequence of consonants in "cedar'd Lebanon": the oral move from *r* to *d* to *l*, concluding in the duplicated *ns*, feels like honey on the tongue. And it is only because we articulate the phrase while understanding its references that we seem to hear in this line the susurrus of the silks from Samarcand.

All poets more or less consciously make use of the enunciative dimension of language, but Keats exceeds his predecessors, including his masters Spenser, Shakespeare (the Shakespeare of the sonnets), and Milton, in the degree and constancy with which he foregrounds the materiality of his phonic medium. In this aspect he also exceeds his successors, except perhaps Gerard Manley Hopkins, who stylized features he had found in Keats to stress the artifice of his coined compounds, repetitions and gradations of speech-sounds, and sequential strong stresses:

Though worlds of wanwood leafmeal lie.[5]

Keats's awareness of the orality of his medium seems clearly connected to his sensitivity to the tactile and textural, as well as gustatory, qualities of what he ate or drank. For example, in a letter to his friend Charles Wentworth Dilke, he suddenly breaks off to say:

Talking of Pleasure, this moment I was writing with one hand, and with the other holding to my Mouth a Nectarine—good god how fine—It went down soft pulpy, slushy, oozy—all its delicious embonpoint melted down my throat like a large, beatified Strawberry. I shall certainly breed. (*L*2:179)[6]

In our cultural moment of trickle-down Freudianism, Keats's orality of course invites charges of regression to the infantile stage of psychosexual development. Such speculations, I think, in no way derogate from his poetic achievement. A thing is what it is, and not another thing to which it may be theoretically reduced. Keats's remarkable sensible organization generated distinctive qualities of a great and original poetry, for which we should be grateful, whatever our opinion of its psychological genesis.

Keats's exploitation of the component features of a speech-utterance (oral shape, gesture, directionality, pace, and tactile sensations) helps account for another prominent aspect of his poetic language: its iconic quality. By "iconic" I mean the impression we often get, when reading Keats's poems, that his verbal medium is intrinsically appropriate to its referents, as though the material signifier shared an attribute with what it signifies. Alexander Pope, in a noted passage in *Essay on Criticism*, said that in poetry "the sound must seem an echo to the sense."[7] As Pope's own examples show, this echoism is by no means limited to onomatopoeia. Keats's iconicity is sometimes such a seeming mimicry of sound by sound: "The murmurous haunt of flies on summer eves" (*Ode to a Nightingale* [50]) and "The silver, snarling trumpets 'gan to chide" (*The Eve of St. Agnes* [31]), for example. But sound mimicry is only one of many types of utterance mimicry in Keats. Take, for example, his notorious description, in his early poem *Endymion*, of what it feels like to kiss

Those lips, O slippery blisses. (II.758)

Even after Christopher Ricks's acute and often convincing casuistry with respect to the morality and psychology of embarrassment in Keats's poetry,[8] many of us continue to find this line off-putting. This is not, I think, because Keats's phrase, in what Ricks aptly calls his "unmisgiving" way, signifies the moist physicality of an erotic kiss, but because the act of enunciating the line is too blatantly a simulation of the act it signifies, in the lip-smacking repetitions, amid sustained sibilants, of its double-labial stops. The blatancy is magnified by the effect of morpheme symbolism, that is, frequently recurrent combinations of speech-sounds in words that overlap in what they signify. In this instance, the iconicity of the *sl* combinations, heightened by the internal rhyme in "those lips" and "O slippery," is accentuated to the point of caricature by the underpresence of related sound-and-sense units such as "slither" and "slide," even, one must admit, "slobber" and "slurp."

But Keats is always Keatsian, and the oral gesture and sensation mimicry in his early and less successful passages remains the condition, subdued and controlled, of his later writing at its best. In the line "Singest of summer in full-throated ease" (10) from *Ode to a Nightingale*, the unhurried ease of articulating the open back vowels and the voiced liquids *r* and *l* in the spondaic "full-throated" is sensed, fully and deeply, within the resonant cavity of the throat to which the words refer. In Keats's description (in *Ode on Melancholy*) of one

whose strenuous tongue
Can burst joy's grape against his palate fine,

the plosive onset and muscular thrust of the tongue in uttering the heavily stressed "burst" duplicates the action of the tongue in crushing a grape, while, in enunciating the phrase "his palate fine," the touch of the blade of the tongue, in forming the consonants *l* and *n*, is felt on the palate that the words designate. In the line "as though of hemlock I had drunk" from *Ode to a Nightingale*, to articulate the word "drunk" is to move with the vowel *u* from the frontal consonant *d* back and down through the mouth and throat, by way of the intermediate *r* and *n*, to close in the glottal stop *k*, in an act that simulates the act of swallowing that the word denotes. The effect is heightened by the anticipation of this oral gesture in the second syllable of "hemlock" and by its repetition in the following rhyme word, "sunk": "and Lethe-wards had sunk."

An instance that is subtler and more complex is Keats's description in *Ode to Autumn* of a personified Autumn sitting careless on a granary floor,

Thy hair soft-lifted by the winnowing wind. (15)

The exquisite aptness of this utterance to what it signifies is in part the effect of its changing pace and rhythm: the slow sequential stresses in "háir sóft-líftĕd" give way to fast-moving anapests—"sóft líftĕd bў thĕ wínnŏwiñg wínd"—in a way that accords with the desultory movement of the wind itself, as this is described in the next stanza of the poem. But the iconicity is to a greater degree the effect of the pressure and sensation of the inner airstream, the breath, that is sensed first in the throat in the aspirated (i.e., air produced) *h* in "hair," then between the tongue and hard palate in the aspirated *s*, and on to the upper teeth and lower lip in the aspirated *fs* of "soft-lifted," to become most tangible when the air is expelled through the tensed lips to form the *w* that occurs no fewer than three times—each time initiating the puff of air that forms the syllable *win*—in the two words that denote the outer airstream, "winnowing wind."

II

The conspicuous materiality of Keats's linguistic medium accords with the dense materiality of the world that his poems typically represent. In the line about bursting joy's grape, for example, Keats converts an abstract psychological observation—only someone capable of the most intense joy can experience the deepest melancholy—into the specifics of eating a grape. And in this line from *Ode to Psyche*,

'Mid hushed, cool-rooted flowers, fragrant-eyed. (113)

the references of the seven words, themselves so richly sensuous to utter, run the gamut of the senses of hearing, sight, odor, and touch (a touch involving both temperature and kinetic thrust in the spondaic compound "cool-rooted"). The materiality of Keats's representations, however, seems to run counter to his frequent practice, when referring to poetry in his letters, of applying to the imaginative process and its products such terms as "ethereal," "spirit," "spiritual," "empyreal," and "essence." In the traditional vocabulary of criticism, such terms have commonly been indicators of a Platonic philosophy of art, and this fact has led some commentators to claim that Keats—at least through the time when he wrote *Endymion*—was a Platonist in his theory about poetry, which he conceived as aspiring to transcend the material world of sense experience.

Platonic and Neoplatonic idealism is a philosophy of two worlds. One is the material world perceived by the human senses—a world of space, time, and contingency that is regarded as radically deficient because subject to change, loss, corruption, and mortality. To this the Platonist opposes a transcendent otherworld, accessible only to the spiritual vision. The otherworld is the locus of ultimate human desire because, since it consists of immaterial essences that are outside of time and space, it is unchanging, incorruptible, and eternal.

In an enlightening discovery, Stuart Sperry, followed by other scholars, showed that Keats imported "essence," "spirit," "spiritual," "ethereal," and related terms not from Platonizing literary theorists, but from a very different linguistic domain. In Keats's time, they were standard terms in a natural science, chemistry, in which Keats had taken two courses of lectures during his medical studies at Guy's Hospital in the years 1815 and 1816.[9] In the chemical experiments of the early nineteenth century, the terms were applied to various phenomena, and especially to the basic procedures of evaporation and distillation. When a substance was subjected to increasing degrees of heat (for which the technical term was "intensity"), it was "etherealized," or refined; in this process, it released volatile substances called "spirits" and was purified into its "essences," or chemical components. The crucial fact, however, is that the products at the end of this process remain, no less than the substance at its beginning, entirely material things, except that they have been refined into what Keats called the "material sublime" (*To J.H. Reynolds, Esq*: [69]). ("Sublime" and "sublimation," as Sperry points out, were the terms for "a dry distillation.")[10] The technical vocabulary of chemistry, that is, provided for Keats's quick intelligence unprecedented metaphors for poetry-metaphors that made it possible to represent what he called the "silent Working" (L1:185) of the poet's imagination as a process of refining, purifying, etherealizing, spiritualizing, and essentializing the actual into the ideal without transcending the limits and conditions of the material world.

In the opening lines of his early poem *Endymion*, Keats says that he intended the work to be "A flowery band to bind us to the earth" (I.7), that is, to this material world. When copying out the poem, Keats inserted the famed passage (I.777ff) that he described, in a letter to his publisher, as setting out "the gradations of Happiness even like a kind of Pleasure Thermometer"; the writing of these lines, he added, "will perhaps be of the greatest Service to me of any thing I ever did" (L1:218). In these crucial but obscure lines, the gradations of happiness that culminate in what Keats calls "A fellowship with essence" have often been interpreted as a Platonic ascent to a supraterrestrial realm. Despite some coincidence of terminology, however, Keats's gradations are entirely opposed to the dematerializing process of philosophical meditation that Plato describes in the *Symposium*. In that dialogue, one climbs "as by a stair" from the beauty of a single material body up "to all fair forms," and then to "the beauty of the mind," in order to reach the goal of ultimate desire, the idea of "beauty, absolute, separate, simple, and everlasting." Keats's "Pleasure Thermometer," on the other hand (as the word "thermometer" implies) measures what he calls the "intensity" (the degree of heat applied to a retort in a chemical experiment)[11] in an imaginative ascent that is metaphorically equated with the stages of refinement in a process of evaporation and distillation. The ascent begins with the pleasurable sensations of physical things; these pleasures are successively refined and purified from all self-concern, until one achieves the selfless stage of "love and friendship." At the application of a final ("chief") degree of "intensity," the grosser (the "more ponderous and bulky") element of friendship is in turn separated out, leaving only, "full alchemiz'd," the purified "essence" that is love. Thus, at the end of the psychochemical procedure,

> at the tip-top,
> There hangs by unseen film, an orbed drop
> Of light, and that is love. (I.805–7)

As Donald Goellnicht acutely noted, this "orbed drop" is "an exact description of a drop of pure distillate condensing on the lip of a retort to drip into a beaker."[12]

The point is important, because to Platonize Keats—just as to Intellectualize or to textualize him—is to disembody him and thereby eliminate what is most Keatsian in his poems. To read him rightly, we need to recognize that he is preeminently a poet of one world, however painful his awareness of the shortcomings of that world when measured against the reach of human desire. And Keats's one world is the material world of this earth, this life, and this body—this sexual body with all its avidities and its full complement of the senses, internal as well as external, and what traditionally are called the "lower" no less than the "higher" senses. (Remember Keats's relish of a nectarine and of "Joy's grape.") His term for the goal of profoundest desire is "happiness," which he envisions as a plenitude of the physical and intellectual satisfactions in this earthly life, except that they have been purified from what he calls their "disagreeables." And in a "favorite Speculation," he imagines the possibility of enjoyments in a life "here after" as simply a repetition of "what we called happiness on Earth," except (this time Keats resorts to a musical instead of a chemical analogue) that it is "repeated in a finer tone and so repeated" (*L*1:185).

III

Lest I give the impression that I share the nineteenth-century view that Keats is a poet of sensations rather than of thoughts, I want to comment on the way that, at his mature best, he deals with matters of profound human concern but assimilates the conceptual import of his poems with the material qualities of his spoken language and the material particulars that his language represents.

I concur with the readers for whom Keats's short ode *To Autumn* is his highest achievement. The poem is about a season of the year, but as in his other odes, the ostensible subject (a nightingale, a work of Grecian art, the goddess Melancholia) turns out to be the occasion for engaging with the multiple dilemmas of being human in the material world, in which nothing can stay. In *To Autumn*, however, more completely than in the other odes, Keats leaves the concepts implicit in the choice and rendering of the things, events, and actions that the verbal medium bodies forth. My onetime teacher Douglas Vincent Bush was an acute, as well as learned, reader of poetry, but I think he was mistaken when he described Keats's *To Autumn* as "less a resolution of the perplexities of life and poetic ambition than an escape into the luxury of pure—though now sober—sensation."[13] On the contrary, Keats's poem is a creative triumph because, instead of explicitly treating a perplexity of life, he identifies and resolves a perplexity by incorporating it in a work that presents itself as nothing more than a poem of pure sensation.

A knowledgeable contemporary of Keats no doubt recognized what a modern reader is apt to miss, that *To Autumn* was composed in strict accord with an odd lyric model whose origins go back to classical times but which enjoyed a special vogue from the 1740s through Keats's own lifetime. This is the short ode (sometimes it was labeled a hymn) on a general or abstract topic. The topic is named in the title and formally invoked in the opening lines, where it is personified, given a bodily form, and accorded the status of a quasi divinity, usually female. The poem proceeds to praise, describe, and expatiate on the chosen subject, but it does this, strangely, in the grammatical mode of a second-person address to the personified topic itself. In this genre the direct precursors of Keats's *To Autumn* were the odes addressed to a time of year or a time of day, described by reference to scenes in nature; this subclass includes William Blake's short poems on each of the four seasons, written in the 1770s, in which Blake gives the standard matter and manner of the ode a prominently biblical cast and compacts them into the compass of sixteen to nineteen lines. Within this latter type, it seems to me likely that Keats's particular antecedent was William Collins's *Ode to Evening*, published in 1746.[14] But whether or not Keats remembered Collins while composing *To Autumn*, it is useful to note the similarities between the two poems—in their use of the linguistic medium, their subject matter, and their poetic procedures—in order better to isolate what is distinctively Keatsian in this most formulaic of Keats's odes and to identify the innovations by which he brought what was by his time a stale convention to vibrant life.

Collins's *Ode to Evening* is unrhymed; in place of the standard recurrences of terminal speech-sounds, his invocation exploits the enunciative changes in the procession of the speech-sounds inside the verse line:

> If aught of oaten stop, or pastoral song,
> May hope, chaste Eve, to soothe thy modest ear. (1–2)

That is, Collins foregrounds the oral feel of producing the succession of vowels in the first line and of effecting the transition from the open back vowels (in "hope" and "soothe") to the closed front vowel (in "Eve" and "ear") in the second line.[15] He makes us all but aware, in enunciating these lines, that we produce the different vowels, even though the vibration of the larynx remains constant, by altering the configuration of our mouth and lips and by moving our tongue forward or back. He also brings to the edge of our awareness that the stopped consonants that punctuate these lines are effected by interrupting, with our tongue or lips, the sounding of the vowels: "If aught of oaten stop...."

Collins goes on, always in the mode of an address to the personified evening, to detail selected scenes and events in the declining day, including prominently (as in *To Autumn*) the sounds of insects. Later in the poem he holds constant the time of day and describes the change in a typical evening during each of the four seasons. By an inverse procedure, Keats holds the season constant and describes the changes during the course of a typical day, from the mists of the autumnal morning in the opening line to the setting of the sun in the closing stanza.

These and other parallels however only highlight the differences between the two poems. Collins's linguistic medium is only subduedly physical, and his descriptions are exclusively visual, intangible, and expressly represented as generic items in a conventional eighteenth-century landscape modeled on the paintings of Claude Lorraine. He asks to be led, for example,

> where some sheety lake
> Cheers the lone heath, or some time-hallow'd pile,
> Or up-land fallows grey
> Reflect its last cool gleam. (29–32)

Keats, on the other hand, makes us feel, in the act of enunciating his words, the very weight, pressure, and fullness that he ascribes not just to the physical processes by which autumn conspires (an interesting word!) with her "close bosom-friend," the virile sun, to "load," "bend," "fill," "swell," and "plump" the vines and trees, but also to their conspicuously edible products. Collins's Eve is young and virginal; she is "chaste," a "Maid composed," a "calm Vot'ress" from whom the male sun is segregated "in yon western tent." She is attended by an allegorical retinue of hours, elves, and "Pensive Pleasures sweet" but remains elusively diaphanous, emerging only to merge again into the visibilia of the landscape. "Be mine the hut" that

> marks o'er all
> Thy dewy fingers draw
> The gradual dusky veil. (34–40)

But when Keats's autumn makes a personal appearance in his second stanza, it is as a mature woman who, far from dissolving into the outer scene, remains a full-bodied person who supervises, and sometimes herself engages in, the physical labors of the seasonal harvest.

This leads me to the important observation that whereas the setting of Collins's ode is the natural landscape, the setting of Keats's ode is not nature but culture or, more precisely, the union of natural process and human labor that we call agriculture. Keats's poem was in fact inspired by the sight of a cultivated field just after it had been reaped. "Somehow a stubble plain looks warm," Keats wrote to his friend John Hamilton Reynolds. "This struck me so much in my sunday's walk that I composed upon it" (L2:167). In fact, in *Ode to Autumn*, what Keats's descriptions denote or suggest allows us to reconstruct the concrete particulars of a working farm. Before us there is a cottage with a thatched roof around which grapevines have been trained. In the vicinity are the other plantings that provide what Keats calls the "store" of farm products—a grove of apple trees, a garden producing gourds and other vegetables, hazelnut trees, and a partly reaped grainfield. There are also a granary with a threshing floor, beehives, and on a near hillside a flock of sheep with their full-grown lambs.[16] In this Keatsian version of a georgic poem, two plants are mentioned that are not products of human cultivation, but both are explicitly related to the activities of farming: the autumn flowers (9–11) that are harvested by the bees to fill the "clammy cells" of the farmer's beehive and the poppies (17–18) that are cut by the reaper in mowing the stalks of grain that they entwine. In the first stanza, even the natural process of ripening is converted, figuratively, into a product of the joint labors of autumn and the sun, and in the second stanza, the four functions attributed to the personified autumn all have to do with the workings of a cottage farm during the harvest: autumn sits on the granary floor where the grain is winnowed; watches the oozings from the cyder-press; sleeps on a furrow that, tired by her labor, she has left only half-reaped; and carries on her head the basket of grain that has been gleaned in the cornfield.

Most important, finally, is the difference in the overall purport of the two poems. Collins's *Ode to Evening* is a fine period poem of the Age of Sensibility that is content to praise, with established odic ceremonial, the time and natural scenes favored by the lyric speaker, represented in the first person, who wanders through the poem as a typical penseroso figure and connoisseur of picturesque and sublime landscapes. He seeks out not only the "sheety lake" and "time-hallowed pile," but also, in stormy weather, the hut

> That from the mountain's side,
> Views wilds, and swelling floods,
> And hamlets brown, and dim–discover'd spires. (35–37)

In Keats's *To Autumn*, the lyric speaker never intrudes as a first-person participant or even by specifying his responses to what he describes. The descriptions, however, are represented not simply for their sensuous selves, but in such a way as to communicate what is never expressly said. Keats, that is, concretizes the conceptual dimension of his poem, which declares itself only by the cumulative suggestions of the phenomena that he describes, the constructions of his syntax, the qualities and interrelations of the speech-sounds in which he couches his descriptions, and the increasingly insistent implications of the metaphors he applies to these phenomena in the course of the autumn day.

It is notable, for example, that *To Autumn* ends not in a decisive closure, but on a triple suspension—in syntax, meaning, and meter:

> And gathering swallows twitter in the skies.

The suspension is syntactic, in that the line (set off from what precedes it by a semicolon)[17] concludes a sentence that lists the varied contributors to the music of autumn, in which the only connective is a noncommittal *and*; Keats enumerates the sounds made by gnats *and* lambs, hedge-crickets *and* red-breast; *and* gathering swallows ... with which the series simply breaks off. The suspension is also semantic, in that "gathering," a present participle used adjectivally, signifies a continuing activity still to be completed.[18] Lastly, the suspension is metrical. The line can be read, according to the metric pattern established in the ode, with five iambic stresses:

> And gáthering swállows twítter ín the skíes.

An expressive reading, however, does not stress the inconsequential preposition "in," but renders the line with only four strong stresses:

> And gáthering swállows twítter in the skíes.

The result is that the poem closes with an empty fifth beat that we experience as portending something yet to come. The effect, although less conspicuous, is like that of the truncated last line in each stanza of Keats's *La Belle Dame sans Merci*:

> O what can ail thee, knight at arms,
>   Alone and palely loitering?
> The sedge has wither'd from the lake,
>   And no birds sing.

The multiple suspension, coming so unexpectedly as the conclusion to *Autumn*, is inherently suggestive, and also heightens our retrospective awareness of earlier features of the poem. For example, there is the repeated use of present participles that indicate an ongoing, unfinished process, from "conspiring" in the third line to "gathering" in the last. We become more sensitive to the illusoriness of the bees' belief that "warm days will never cease" (10); to the emblematic associations, in stanza 2, with the scythe of a reaper only momentarily suspended; and to the portent in "the last oozings" of the cyder-press. The ending also sharpens our realization that in the last stanza the sunlit day of the preceding stanzas has lapsed into evening, and that although autumn, as the lyric speaker reassures her,[19] has her music, its mode, unlike that of "the songs of spring," is elegiac, in a tonality established by the gnats (27) who "mourn" in a "wailful choir" (the suggestion is of a church choir singing a requiem) even as the swallows are gathering for their imminent flight south. We come to realize that the poem is from beginning to end steeped in the sense of process and temporality. Critics have often noted the static quality of Keats's descriptions, especially in the second stanza, but the seeming stasis, as the closing line both suggests and exemplifies, is in fact only a suspension on the reluctant verge of drastic change and loss. The precise moment of poise on the verge is denoted by the "now" in line 31. I must have read the poem a score of times before I realized the full poignancy of that word, coming at the end of a sequence of temporal adverbs beginning at line 25: "While," "Then," "and now" ... the swallows are gathering. *Sunt lacrimae rerum*. What Keats expresses without saying, even as he celebrates the season of fruition, is awareness that in this world such fulfillment is only a phase in a process that goes on "hours by hours"; he expresses also his quiet acceptance of the necessity that this rich day must turn into night and this bountiful season into winter.

To return to the material base with which we began: Throughout the poem the interplay of the enunciated speech-sounds helps to effect—in fact, greatly enlarges—this conceptual reach beyond assertion. The final word of the last line, "skies," is itself experienced as a suspension, in that we need to go no less than four lines back for the word whose speech-sound, in the elaborate odic rhyme scheme, it replicates.[20] That word is "dies"—

Or sinking as the light wind lives or dies.

Collins applies the same metaphor to the wind in his opening invocation
to evening,

> Like thy own solemn springs,
> Thy springs and dying gales,

but "dying gales" was a stock phrase in the poetic diction of Collins's time,
and its function in his poem is simply to comport with the pervasive mood
of "the Pensive Pleasures sweet." In Keats's *To Autumn*, on the other hand,
the wind that lives or dies resonates with a number of earlier elements in
the poem; most markedly, it reiterates the metaphor in the phrase "the
soft-dying day." These two allusions, reserved for the stanza that ends
with the premonitory flocking of the swallows, widens the reach of
reference from the processes of the natural world to the human speaker of
the poem, for whom living and dying are not, as for the wind, the day, and
the season, merely metaphors. The initial allusion to death, however, is
oblique and is mitigated by its embodiment in a sequence of speech-
sounds that are a delight to utter: "While barred clouds bloom the soft-
dying day." The procession is slowed for our closer apprehension by the
two sets of successive strong stresses; as we enunciate the line, our
awareness of the evolving changes in the seven long vowels (no vowel
occurs twice) is enhanced by the slight impediments to be overcome in
negotiating the junctures between adjacent consonants; while in the last
two words the first syllable of "dying," by a vowel shift forward and up,
modulates into "day," even as we realize that although the sunset can color
("bloom"), it cannot impede the death of the day.

Repetition cannot dull the sense of ever-renewing discovery in
attending to the interrelations of material medium, metrical pace, syntax,
tone of voice, and spoken and unspoken meanings in this marvelous
stanza:

> Where are the songs of spring? Ay, where are they?
>   Think not of them, thou hast thy music too,—
> While barred clouds bloom the soft-dying day,
>   And touch the stubble-plains with rosy hue;
> Then in a wailful choir the small gnats mourn
>   Among the river sallows, borne aloft
>   Or sinking as the light wind lives or dies;

And full-grown lambs loud bleat from hilly bourn;
Hedge-crickets sing; and now with treble soft
The red-breast whistles from a garden-croft;
And gathering swallows twitter in the skies.

Since we are celebrating the two-hundredth birthday of Keats, it seems appropriate to end this essay by situating his poem in the context of his life. *To Autumn* was the last work of artistic consequence that Keats completed. His letters and verses show that he achieved this celebratory poem, with its calm acquiescence to time, transience, and mortality, at a time when he was possessed by a premonition, little short of a conviction, that he had himself less than two years to live.[21] As it turned out, Keats died of tuberculosis only a year and five months after he composed his terminal ode. He was twenty-five years old. His career as a poet between his first successful poem, *On First Looking into Chapman's Homer*, October 1816, and *To Autumn*, September 1819, was limited to a span of thirty-five months.

NOTES

1. Douglas Vincent Bush, "Keats and His Ideas," *English Romantic Poets: Modern Essays in Criticism*, ed. M. H. Abrams (New York: Oxford University Press, 1960).

2. All quotations of Keats's poetry are from *The Poems of John Keats*, ed. Jack Stillinger (Cambridge, Mass.: Harvard University Press, Belknap Press, 1978).

3. Robert Frost, lecture on the bicentennial of Wordsworth's death (April 1950); transcribed from the tape recording in *The Cornell Library Journal* 11 (spring 1970): 97–98.

4. *The Letters of John Keats: 1814–1821*, ed. Hyder E. Rollins (Cambridge, Mass.: Harvard University Press, 1958), 2:106. Quotations of Keats's letters are from this edition, abbreviated *L* in text; volume and page numbers are given in parentheses in text.

5. Gerard Manley Hopkins, *Spring and Fall*, in *Poems of Gerard Manley Hopkins*, ed. Robert Bridges and W. H. Gardner, 3d ed. (Oxford: Oxford University Press, 1948), 8..

6. I take "I shall certainly breed" to signify Keats's awareness that this kind of sense experience was effective in the poetry he composed.

7. Pope, *An Essay on Criticism*, 2.365.

8. Christopher Ricks, *Keats and Embarrassment* (Oxford: Clarendon Press, 1974), 104–5.

9. Stuart M. Sperry, *Keats the Poet* (Princeton: Princeton University Press,

11973), chap. 2. For a detailed treatment of Keats's medical training and its role in his poetry, see Donald C. Goellnicht, *The Poet-Physician: Keats and Medical Science* (Pittsburgh: University of Pittsburgh Press, 1984).

10. Sperry, *Keats the Poet*, 45.

11. Keats's use of "intensity" as the measure of the degree of heat in a process of evaporation is especially clear in his oft-quoted statement that "the excellence of every Art is its intensity, capable of making all disagreeables evaporate" (*L*1:192).

12. Donald C. Goellnicht, "Keats's Chemical Composition," in *Critical Essays on John Keats*, ed. Hermione de Almeida (Boston: G. K. Hall, 1990), 155.

13. Bush, "Keats and His Ideas," 337.

14. *The Norton Anthology of English Literature*, ed. M. H. Abrams et al., 6th ed. (New York, 1993), 2:2465–66.

15. Collins's vowel play brings to mind Benjamin Bailey's testimony that one of Keats's "favorite topics of discourse was the principle of melody in Verse ... particularly in the management of open and close vowels.... Keats's theory was that the vowels ... should be interchanged, like differing notes of music to prevent monotony" (*The Keats Circle*, ed. Hyder E. Rollins [Cambridge, Mass.: Harvard University Press, 1948], 2:277). For an analysis of some of Keats's elaborate vowel patternings, see Walter Jackson Bate, *John Keats* (Cambridge, Mass.: Harvard University Press, 1963), 413–117.

16. In Keats's draft of *To Autumn*, a canceled line adds a barn to the cottage setting, after line 15: "While bright the Sun slants through the husky barn" (Stillinger, *The Poems of John Keats*, 477). The sacramental aura with which Keats invests the rich yields of the harvest season is suggestive of the rural scenes that Samuel Palmer was to paint some six years later, in the mid-1820s.

17. Although the punctuation varies in the various manuscripts of *To Autumn*, the preceding line ends with a semicolon in the printed text of 1820, which Keats oversaw and for which he may have written out a printer's copy manuscript. (For this matter, and for the variations between "gathered" and "gathering swallows" below, I am indebted to Jack Stillinger's annotations in *The Poems of John Keats* and to his analysis of the facts in a letter to me dated May 19, 1997).

18. In this passage Keats very probably recalled the lines in James Thomson's *Seasons*: "Warned of approaching Winter, gathered, play / The swallow-people.... / They twitter cheerful" (*Autumn* [836–38, 846], see *The Poems of John Keats*, ed. Miriam Allott [London: Longman, 1970], 654–55). Keats, after some vacillation between "gathered" and "gathering," fixed on the latter form in the printing of 1820. It is notable that Thomson makes explicit the "approaching Winter," whereas Keats, although he names the spring, summer, and autumn, only implies the coming of the fourth season.

19. The quick sympathy with which Keats consoles autumn for her lack of the songs of spring—"Think not of them, thou hast thy music too" (24)—parallels the poignant moment in *Ode on a Grecian Urn* when Keats interrupts himself to console the young lover, frozen in marble: "never, never canst thou kiss,"

—yet, do not grieve;

. . . .

Forever with thou love, and she be fair! (18–21)

20. In *Autumn* Keats added an eleventh line to the ten-line stanzas of four odes he had written in spring 1819 (*Nightingale, Grecian Urn, Melancholy*, and *Indolence*). In these poems, the rhyme in the concluding line is suspended over only three lines. In *Autumn*, the extra line suspends the recurrence of the final rhyme word over four lines.

21. Aileen Ward, *John Keats: The Making of a Poet*, rev. ed. (New York: Farrar, Straus, Giroux, 1986), 185 and 431 n. 4; 109–200 and 432 n. 13b.

G.A. ROSSO

The Religion of Empire: Blake's Rahab in Its Biblical Contexts

Blake created Rahab, a malevolent figure in his later poetry, at the end of his three-year sojourn at Felpham (1800–1803) when a vocational crisis of epic proportion moved him to transform *Vala* into *The Four Zoas* and to engrave the title-plates to *Milton* and *Jerusalem*. Emerging in marginal passages and added pages to Night 8 of *The Four Zoas*, Rahab functions as a biblical version of the secular Vala; she is the female aspect of a hermaphroditic creature Blake identifies with the harlot and dragon of Revelation.[1]

> Rahab triumphs over all she took Jerusalem
> Captive A Willing Captive by delusive arts impelld
> To worship Urizens Dragon form to offer her own Children
> Upon the bloody Altar. John Saw these things Reveald in Heaven
> On Patmos Isle & heard the Souls cry out to be deliverd
> He saw the Harlot of the Kings of Earth & saw her Cup.
> (*FZ* 111.1–6; E385–86)

In *The Four Zoas*, Rahab triumphs by crucifying Jesus the Lamb, her thematic opponent, and she gains dominion over his religion by practicing the "delusive arts" that impel or seduce his followers (Jerusalem) to worship at the altar of empire (the dragon form). Although Blake gives

From *Prophetic Character: Essays on William Blake in Honor of John E. Grant*, edited by Alexander S. Gourlay. © 2002 by Alexander Gourlay.

Rahab a distinct role and character in *The Four Zoas*, he reiterates these basic terms in *Milton* (1811–18) and *Jerusalem* (1820–27), combining dragon, harlot, and Rahab imagery in his composite figure.[2] In all three works, Rahab symbolizes the collusion of religion (the harlot) and empire (the dragon) that Blake encapsulates in the phrase "Religion hid in War" (*M* 37.43; *J* 75.20). Considering the intervals between her introduction into *The Four Zoas* and the publication of his engraved epics, Rahab's fundamental symbolic congruence across these years is striking.

This congruence depends on Rahab's connection to the book of Revelation, a connection that is both definitive and problematic. Revelation is undoubtedly the primary source of Blake's composite figure: in each epic he names her "Babylon," associates her with the harlot and dragon, and blames her for the destruction of Jerusalem. Equally important, Blake's identification of Rahab as the agent of Jesus' crucifixion is dependent on his reading of the Gospel narratives through the lens of Revelation.[3] And, in one of his more daring moves, Blake portrays Rahab as the element of corruption within John's seven churches, which he recreates as part of his own symbolic entity, the twenty-seven heavens and their churches.[4] This cosmic-historical construct includes what Blake characterizes as seven hermaphroditic "Dragon Forms," each of which contains a harlot (Rahab) within.[5] In *Milton* (37.35–43) and *Jerusalem* these seven churches are described in nearly identical terms:

> Abraham, Moses, Solomon, Paul, Constantine, Charlemaine,
> Luther. these Seven are the Male Females: the Dragon Forms
> The Female hid within a Male: thus Rahab is reveald
> Mystery Babylon the Great: the Abomination of Desolation
> Religion hid in War: a Dragon red, & hidden Harlot
>
> (J 75.16–20)

It seems clear that Blake draws directly on John's Revelation for the symbolic context of his Rahab.[6] However, the problem with Blake's symbolic identification is that, unlike John (who does not name either his dragon or harlot), Blake names the harlot-dragon "Rahab" and claims that John saw her in vision on Patmos isle. At the conclusion of *Milton*, following Ololon's speech, Blake writes:

> No sooner she had spoke but Rahab Babylon appeard
> Eastward upon the Paved work across Europe & Asia
> Glorious as the midday Sun in Satans bosom glowing:

> A Female hidden in a Male, Religion hidden in War
> Namd Moral Virtue; cruel two-fold Monster shining bright
> A Dragon red & hidden harlot which John in Patmos saw
> (*M* 40.17–22)

Why does Blake make the bizarre claim in two of his epics that John sees his Rahab? And how might it contribute to an understanding of Blake's composite figure? To answer these questions requires a fairly thorough inquiry into the biblical Rahab. In what follows, I will not provide a detailed reading of these Rahab passages, but present them here, up front, to show the conjunction of images that I am interested in.

In the Bible, Rahab appears as two distinct, and differently gendered, figures. First, he is the chaos dragon that Yahweh (Israel's God) quells in the waters of the deep at creation. Second, she is the Jericho harlot in Joshua (2–6) who hides the Israelite spies and earns lasting honor in both the Old and New Testaments as a type of the converted gentile. As Northrop Frye comments: "It is difficult to see what these two Rahabs can have to do with one another until we come to the Apocalypse" (139). Frye does not pursue the point except to state that Joshua's Rahab is a harlot like John's Babylon.[7] He thus leaves the question open whether John connected the two figures or if he had scriptural warrant for doing so. The answer is no on both counts: neither John nor any other scriptural writer identifies the two. We must, therefore, dig deeper into Blake's reading of two Old Testament traditions that both he and John inherit: the chaos dragon myth, in which empire is symbolized as a dragon, and anti-harlot polemic, in which collaboration with empire and its gods is figured as prostitution. These traditions remain separate throughout their long trajectories in the Hebrew Bible and merge only in Revelation chapter 17. Again, John does not name his dragon Rahab (or Leviathan, his cousin), but he clearly draws on the chaos dragon myth. Furthermore, since John creatively adapts both traditions using a form of biblical typology, Blake takes the next step and reads Joshua's Rahab as the principal type of the Babylon harlot's collusion with empire. Blake thus fuses John's harlot with Joshua's Rahab through an unorthodox but politically astute hermeneutic strategy: he applies the anti-empire, anti-harlot polemic of prophetic tradition to Joshua's Rahab in order to critique Israel's theology of conquest.

Blake conveys his critique of Israel's imperial ambitions through an original and careful reading of Rahab texts in both the Old and New Testaments. The Rahab chaos dragon passages in Psalm 89.10 and in

Isaiah 51.9, with the Rahab saga in Joshua 2 and 6, are the primary Rahab
texts, and they emerge at critical junctures in the history of Israelite
religion. In Joshua, Rahab is pivotal to the shift from exodus to conquest
traditions; her alliance with Joshua's spies enables occupation of the land
that eventually becomes the site of the Israelite Empire. Ps. 89 concerns
the difficult transition from the tribal to the royal cult, or from Moses and
Sinai to David and Zion traditions that introduce the Rahab dragon into
Old Testament symbolism. This symbolism, drawn from Canaanite myth,
serves to legitimate the transfer of power from the tribal confederacy to
the monarchy and, ultimately, to the empire under Solomon. However, in
response to the crisis induced by the fall of the Judean monarchy to
Babylon in 587 B.C.E., Second Isaiah reunites Mosaic and Davidic
traditions, using the Rahab dragon myth to announce the eschatological
future in a new Exodus and new creation.[8] This eschatology (handed
down through Daniel) is taken up in relation to the new Babylon, Rome,
in John's Revelation, which deploys the dragon myth and harlot at another
critical moment in biblical history. At this moment, when Christianity
emerges and the issue of its relation to both the Roman Empire and
Judaism arises, Joshua's Rahab reappears in several key New Testament
texts as an important figure of the new faith, especially in Paul's Letter to
the Hebrews (11.31).[9] But Blake reads black where others read white.
That is, against the grain of Hebrews' positive treatment of Rahab, Blake
reads Paul's Letter as evidence that the religion of Jesus is being turned
into an institutional church. He thus counters Hebrews with Revelation,
which he takes as his primary text because it retains the apocalyptic
emphasis of early Christianity and resists the transmutation of the Gospels
into the "Church Paul" (*J* 56.42).

No other writer or commentator that I know of puts the Rahab texts
together as Blake does. His reading is unique and, I hope to show, based
on a profound grasp of the turning points of biblical history. Blake is tuned
into these transitional moments through an apocalyptic sensibility rooted
in antinomian dissent and nourished in the revolutionary currents of his
age. He thus is able to perceive meaning and connection where others not
as interested in apocalypse and empire see only disparate strands. This
hypothesis I believe can account for why Blake saw what others did not
see, making Rahab of Jericho relevant to the Rahab dragon in more than
name.

RAHAB THE CHAOS DRAGON

There is no connected narrative of the chaos dragon myth in the Bible. It was not until 1895, when Hermann Gunkel pulled together various fragments of the myth from the prophets, Psalms, Job, and Revelation that serious study of the chaos dragon began.[10] In two of his pioneering works, *Schöpfung und Chaos in Urzeit und Endzeit* (1895)—"Creation and Chaos in Beginning-Time and End-Time"—and *Genesis* (1901), Gunkel drew parallels between ancient Near Eastern texts and biblical creation narratives in which he associated the dragons Leviathan and Rahab with the elements of chaos and the "deep" (Hebrew *tehom*), whose cognate Babylonian term "tiamat" was the name of the sea dragon in the creation epic *Enuma elish*.[11] In this text, Tiamat is defeated in battle by the divine warrior Marduk who, after creating the universe out of her carcass, is built a temple and is crowned king of cosmos and society.[12] Gunkel heard echoes of the dragon myth in Old Testament texts about the primordial sea and drew typological connections between Yahweh's victory over chaos at the creation and the new creation at the end of time. "This battle with the dragon, which parallels the drying up of the primordial sea, is clearly Yahweh's battle with the Chaos dragon," writes Gunkel: "This battle is also applied to the eschaton ... and then often interpreted in relation to the empire hostile to Israel" (124). This last notion is significant in that it points to the politics of the chaos dragon myth. Gunkel did not explore the issue, but political meaning inheres in the tension between the historical and mythical aspects of the dragon symbol. Indeed, at critical moments throughout Israelite history, all the Near Eastern empires that oppressed the Israelites—Egypt, Assyria, Babylon, Persia, Greece, and Rome—are denounced as the chaos dragon. This historicizing of the chaos myth is especially important in relation to the Exodus, for Rahab undergoes a transformation from a mythic dragon into a pejorative nickname for Egypt. (First) Isaiah, writing in the eighth century B.C.E., counsels his king not to join anti-Assyrian coalitions led by Egypt, for even though Assyria's domination is despised, Egypt is the Hebrew archetype of oppression: "Egypt's help is worthless and empty, therefore I have called her, 'Rahab who sits still'" (Isa. 30.7; NRSV).[13] The prophet says it is foolish to rely on Egypt against Assyria because Egypt is as impotent now as it was when Yahweh crushed the chaos monster at the Red Sea or at the creation.

The Rahab dragon, however, first appears in Hebrew tradition in relation to the difficult transformation of the tribal league into the

monarchy, sometime in the tenth century B.C.E. (Cross 135). Evidence
for this appearance comes from archeological findings in 1929 at Ras
Shamra, a sacred mound near the ancient city of Ugarit in Phoenicia,
which unearthed the Canaanite (Baal) version of the chaos myth.[14] In this
version, Yam (deified Sea) battles Baal for sovereignty over heaven and
earth; Baal defeats him and assumes kingship, receiving a temple as a sign
of his everlasting rule (Cross 93). Fundamentally similar to the Babylonian
version, the Canaanite chaos dragon myth emphasizes Baal's "everlasting
sovereignty"—a feature missing from the Babylonian version (Cross 25).
This feature is incorporated by the Israelites, whose earliest traditions are
primarily historical, based on Yahweh's unique revelations at the Red Sea,
Sinai, and the conquest. In their pre-monarchic cult, according to
Bernhard Anderson, the Israelites did not celebrate "the annual triumph of
cosmos over chaos" or the chaos dragon, but rather the epic "creation of the
people, that is, creation as a historical event" (Anderson, *Creation* 55). In the
period of the early monarchy, however, the Israelites adapted Canaanite
myth to legitimate the transfer of power from the tribal to the royal cult.
The tribal cult was associated with Moses, Joshua, and the northern tribes:
the royal cult was associated with David, Solomon, and the tribes of Judah
to the south. At this important juncture, the writer of Ps. 89 builds on the
dragon myth of the Canaanites in order to smooth the ideological transition
to monarchy. He grafts the royal cult myth onto Israelite history—Exodus,
Wilderness, Conquest—which is "now understood to culminate in the
election of David ... and Zion" (Anderson, *Creation* 68).[15] Yahweh's defeat of
Rahab strengthens the claim of this covenant transfer:

> Thou rulest the raging of the sea: when the waves thereof arise,
> thou stillest them. Thou hast broken Rahab in pieces, as one
> that is slain; thou hast scattered thine enemies with thy strong
> arm. The heavens are thine, the earth is also thine: for the
> world and the fulness thereof, thou has founded them. (Ps.
> 89.9–10)

By his victory over the primeval sea and chaos dragon, Yahweh creates the
universe and imposes order on the world; and this victory grants him the
power to establish forever David's throne and dynasty (89.29, 36).
Moreover, Yahweh's promise to "set his [David's] hand also in the sea, and
his right hand in the rivers" (v. 25) recalls Baal's victory over Yam the
chaos dragon. In both instances, the reenactment of the drama of creation
through the figure of the king ties history to the cult, and the political to the

cosmic (Ricoeur 191–94). Thus, even though the waters in Ps. 89 do not allude to the Exodus, the chaos myth contains an intrinsic political meaning. For the sea embodies the chaotic, insurgent elements that Yahweh must defeat before he begins creation and assumes eternal kingship. And these elements continually resurface throughout biblical history: at the flood, at the Red Sea, at the Jordan, and at several crisis moments when Near Eastern or Mediterranean empires take on dragonic form against the Israelites.

There are important differences between the two Rahab passages (Ps. 89.10 and Isa. 51.9) and they have to do with the relation of Israelite religion to empire. The transition from the Mosaic to the Davidic covenant was not smooth, as registered in the proverb "Is Saul also among the prophets" (1 Sam. 10.11) and in Nathan's oracle to David (2 Sam. 7). Saul retained the prophetic qualities of the charismatic judge even as he became the anointed king; however, Yahweh took away his kingdom and through the prophet Samuel gave it to David. In the "Samuel Compromise," as Paul Hanson coins it, the judgeship splits in two, with the charismatic office staying with the prophet and the holy warrior going to the prince or king. In this split Hanson locates the origins of the "tension-filled coexistence of the kings and prophets of Israel" (15). This tension is displayed in a key text that draws on the creation theology of Ps. 89. 2 Sam. 7.4–17, Nathan's oracle from Yahweh, both affirms and questions David's desire to build a temple: verses 4–7 direct David not to violate tribal cult tradition; verses 11–16 support building a royal "house," a pun yoking temple and dynasty. Although David does not get to build the temple—his son Solomon does—Yahweh promises David: "I will stablish the throne of his kingdom forever" (v. 13). The Rahab passage in Ps. 89 appears in a similar context. And Frank Cross observes a like strategy at work in the Yahwist or J documentary strand as a whole, which he calls "a propaganda work of the Israelite empire" (261). Ps. 89 and the Yahwist both replace the mutual, conditional covenant of Abraham and Moses with the unconditional oath sworn to David, reshaping the epic pattern by linking its promises "with ultimate fulfillment in the empire" (261). "Kingship in Israel," Cross writes, "became rooted in creation and fixed in eternity" (261). This development endangers the promise of Israel's blessing to "all the families of the earth" (Gen. 12.3), at least for the other nations of the Near East. For while Israel draws on its epic past and borrows from Canaanite myth to legitimate an important transition in its history, that history and mythic borrowing serve to emphasize the holiness and authority of the Israelite turn toward empire. For Blake, the holiness of empire is precisely what his Rahab symbolizes, albeit in negative fashion.

The fundamental difference between Ps. 89 and Isa. 51 lies in historical context: by the time of Second Isaiah, the monarchy has collapsed, throwing into question the divine promise of perpetuity to the house of David. Ps. 89 anticipates such a calamity in its final movement (verses 38–52), which laments an unnamed national disaster in which Yahweh voids David's covenant and casts his crown into the dust. But there is no more profound moment in Israelite history than the fall of Judah and sacking of Jerusalem by Babylon in 587 B.C.E. What is most intriguing for my purpose is that chaos dragon mythology appears in both transitional moments, in the foundation as well as in the downfall of the Davidic house. Yet this latest transformation is the polar opposite of the first. Monarchy has been destroyed and the Davidic promise negated by what was to become the ultimate oppressor, Babylon. With the apparent failure of Yahweh's covenant with David, royal cult theology is put into question. In fact, it disappears. Second Isaiah thus deploys Rahab dragon symbolism outside of an official cultic context. Where Ps. 89 focuses on Yahweh's defeat of the primordial dragon of creation and his establishment of a real king, Second Isaiah combines creation, exodus, and conquest traditions to announce the arrival of an eschatological kingdom in which the future messiah, not an actual king, reigns.[16]

Writing in the Babylonian captivity, Second Isaiah turns the chaos dragon myth in an eschatological direction and highlights its dual emphasis on creation and liberation, on cosmogony and history. Isa. 51.9–11 is a profoundly important source for Blake's Rahab, one whose symbolism, theology, and lyrical refrain "Awake, awake" are echoed throughout his epics. The passage appears just before the prophet announces the return of the exiled community to Jerusalem, which he figures in the dual terms of the Exodus and the chaos dragon myth. He opens with a desperate plea to Yahweh to "put on strength" and awaken "as in the ancient days," conjuring up a stark contrast between past redemptive acts and present non-intervention. He then asks rhetorically,

> Art thou not he that hath cut Rahab,
> and wounded the dragon
> Art thou not he which hath dried the sea [yam],
> the waters of the great deep,
> that hath made the depths of the sea
> a way for the ransomed to pass over?

> (Isa. 51.9–10)

This brilliant series of questions alludes not only to the creation, to Yahweh's primordial victory over the sea dragon, but to the beginning of the people's history when Yahweh defeated Egypt at the Exodus. By bringing the Canaanite dragon (Yam) into association with the Song of the Sea (Exod. 15), Second Isaiah identifies Egypt as Rahab (Cross 136–37). Perhaps more impressively, however, by applying the Exodus and the chaos dragon myth to the new oppressor, Babylon, the prophet moves from the cosmogonic and the historic planes to the eschaton, or end-time. "In three verses," Paul Hanson writes, the prophet "recapitulates the entire development of Yahwism from the cosmic vision of myth, to the translation of that vision into the categories of history, to the future orientation of prophetic eschatology" (311). Second Isaiah exhorts his people to move beyond the first creation and first Exodus, for their present historical crisis forms the core of a new myth, a new creation and Exodus from Babylon. This is no mere cyclical return to the ancient days, but a decisive break into the post-imperial future, as suggested by the prophet's transformation of conquest and monarchic traditions. In his account of the "way" that Yahweh's victory over Rahab opens up (51.10, 40.3, 43.19), Second Isaiah redirects the Exodus-Conquest route through the wilderness to Zion (52.1), as in Ps. 89. But in a move of tremendous import for the Gospels and Revelation, he eschatologizes holy war and kingdom ideology, turning Joshua's divine warrior and David's actual king into the coming messiah, the suffering servant (52.13–53.12). As a "lamb brought to the slaughter" (53.7), the servant is prophesied to redeem the people "not as a victorious king, but by his suffering and death" (Mowinckel 255). In this act of heroic martyrdom, to borrow a phrase from Milton, the servant becomes the prototype of the Lamb of Revelation, a figure that Blake always puts in opposition to Rahab.

Second Isaiah's prophetic contemporary Ezekiel also applies chaos dragon mythology to Egypt and Babylon, and he too eschatologizes the myth in terms that bear directly on the Babylon dragon of Revelation.[17] While less focused on Zion traditions than was his prophetic counterpart, Ezekiel's oracles against Tyre (26–28) and Egypt (29–32) rival Second Isaiah in their importance to Blake's conception of Rahab. The oracles against Tyre in particular are a primary source for Blake's association of Rahab with the Covering Cherub, a figure created in *Milton* and *Jerusalem* to contain the finale (Satan) and female (Rahab) aspects of the harlot-dragon. Blake connects his Covering Cherub with the imperial cities "Rome Babylon Tyre" (*M* 9.51): Tyre was the leading city of Phoenicia's vast maritime empire, and Egypt its ally. Focusing on Babylon's siege of

Tyre in 586–573, Ezekiel proclaims that Yahweh has brought the Babylon dragon from the north to destroy Tyre's wealth and pride. Alluding to Tyre's location on an island, Ezekiel likens Babylon's attack to the cosmogonic dragon of the deep who rises from the sea to desolate the city: "when I shall bring up the deep upon thee, and great waters shall cover thee" (26.19). This allusion to the sea-dragon cuts both ways: it praises the power of Babylon while it associates Babylon with Yahweh's primordial enemy. This double meaning is reiterated in chapters 28–31, which describe both Tyre and Egypt in terms that contribute to Blake's conception of Rahab as "covering" and "shadow." In chapter 28, Ezekiel taunts Tyre for its arrogance—"thine heart is lifted up because of thy riches"—and for the violence that its commercial traffic engenders: "By the multitude of thy merchandise they have filled the midst of thee with violence ... o covering cherub" (28.16). Ezekiel declares that Yahweh will thus bring justice to Tyre, causing it "to die the deaths of them that are slain in the midst of the seas" (28.7), or the death of those allied with the chaos dragon. In chapter 29 he calls the Egyptian Pharaoh "the great dragon" (29.3) and in chapter 31 he describes Egypt (or Assyria as an example to Egypt) as a cedar "with a shadowing shroud" whose branches are made great by the waters of the "the deep" (31.3–4). As with Tyre, whose cedar wood was a chief article in its commerce, Assyria is adversely judged by Yahweh for pride: "His branches are fallen ... and all the people of the earth are gone down from his shadow" (31.12). These symbols-dragon, empire tree, and shadow-attend Rahab's entrance into *The Four Zoas*.

Thus far Rahab has appeared only in "his" dragon form, where he surfaces in two fundamental transition moments in Israelite history: from tribal confederacy to monarchy and from monarchy to exile in Babylon. And with these changes in historical thinking come semiotic changes. In the first transition, Rahab is the chaos dragon of creation while in the second he becomes the end-time dragon of eschatology, which Second Isaiah and Ezekiel further identify with Egypt and the Exodus. But Rahab is primarily known as the harlot from Jericho who hides Joshua's spies from her own king and thus wins lasting praise, in both Judaism and Christianity, as a heroic example of the pagan convert. This Rahab also appears in a key moment of transition in Israelite history, namely in the pre-monarchic movement from exodus to conquest traditions narrated in the book of Joshua. Here, Rahab's collusion with the spies makes possible the invasion of Jericho, which is strategically important to the occupation of Canaan. Rahab's involvement with conquest lies at the core of Blake's conception of her, one that carries over into his view of her role in the New Testament, especially in Paul's Letter to the Hebrews, where she appears conspicuously in the transition from the old to the new covenant.[18]

RAHAB THE HARLOT

Because of her crafty partisanship on behalf of the Israelites, Joshua's Rahab is revered to this day in both Jewish and Christian traditions.[19] By the time that Christianity emerges in Palestine, Rahab already is an important enough figure for Matthew to include her in the genealogy of Jesus (1.5) and for Paul (Hebrews 11.31) and James (2.35) to compete in making her an exemplar of faith and works respectively. Early patristic commentary likewise treats Rahab in highly favorable terms, interpreting her scarlet cord (by which she helps the spies to escape) as a type of Christ's blood and her house as a type of the church.[20] Even Protestant accounts, while critical of her prostitution and deceit toward the king, justify Rahab's behavior on the grounds of her providential faith in God.[21] And the one group from whom we might expect something akin to Blakean unorthodoxy on the subject, the radical dissenters of the seventeenth century, largely follows the mainstream Protestant line. In his commentary on Hebrews, John Owen (Cromwell's chaplain) speaks of Rahab in very positive terms, identifying her as "a type and pledge of calling a church from among the Gentiles" (234). Bloom suggests that this identification of Rahab with the early Christian church is so common as to be practically universal, so that Blake probably knew of it (259). However, Blake's critical reading of Rahab is unique: unique in the sense that, unlike previous commentators, Blake actually places Rahab at the crucifixion scene, where she takes part in Jesus' trial and death.

In a highly unorthodox move, Blake construes Rahab's behavior—her sacrifice of the Jericho people to the Israelite conquerors—as a negative type of Jesus or the Lamb's sacrifice in the New Testament. Since Blake defines Joshua's Rahab by her complicity with the conquerors, and since he defines Jesus by his act of self-sacrifice, the two figures form a clear and dramatic opposition in his works. Indeed, Rahab is brought into Night 8 of *The Four Zoas* as the Lamb's mortal opponent.[22] She oversees his crucifixion "Rahab beholds the Lamb of God / She smites with her knife of flint" (113.32–33)—which exposes her as Urizen's "secret holiness" and leads to Urizen's transformation into the chaos dragon (105.5–106.45). And in *Milton*, the narrator invokes the muse to tell of the

"False Tongue," of "its sacrifices and / Its offerings; even till Jesus, the image of the Invisible God / Became its prey; a curse, an offering, and an atonement" (2.10–13). The narrator relates atonement to the "cruelties of Moral Law" (5.12), and he equates moral law with "the cruel Virgin Babylon" (5.27), whom he names Rahab (40.17). These passages show that Blake contaminates Rahab's figural purity in order to nullify her as an exemplary type of the crucifixion and church.

Blake builds on the typological connections that Paul sets up between the books of Joshua and Exodus in his Letter to the Hebrews, one of the primary texts in the history of Christian typology. In the Letter, Paul regards Joshua's Rahab as a model of faith and the crucifixion of Jesus as a fulfillment of atonement theology in Exodus. Chapter 11 is especially important in this regard as Paul includes Rahab in a long and illustrious line of Jewish heroes, among them Abraham and Moses, who with Joshua are associated with the priestly rites of blood sacrifice. Abraham offers up Isaac, "his only begotten son" who is interpreted as a "figure" of Jesus crucified and raised up from the dead (11.17–19). Moses is presented in the context of the Passover slaying of the Egyptian firstborn: "Through faith he kept the passover, and the sprinkling of blood, lest he that destroyed the firstborn should touch them" (11.28). "Them" refers to the Israelites, the people who "passed through the Red Sea as by dry land" (11.29), a miracle that evokes the ritual crossing of the Jordan in Joshua and the surrounding of the walls of Jericho seven days before they come crashing down (11.30). Rahab's verse follows: "By faith the harlot Rahab perished not with their that believed not, when she had received the spies with peace" (11.31). Although she is not directly related to atonement, Rahab's close connection with Joshua in Hebrews 11 may have inspired Blake to identify Paul's Rahab not only with the conquest but also with the high priest atonement ritual carried into Joshua from Exodus.

Rahab's affiliations with the conquest and ritual sacrifice are deepened by Paul's elaborate application of high priest atonement theology to the crucifixion of Jesus. Paul forges the Hebrews–Exodus link in the central section (chaps. 3–9) of the Letter that precedes the Rahab chapter. As in Romans 3.19–31, Paul equates crucifixion and faith by stating that redemption comes through the righteousness in Jesus Christ, "whom God hath set forth to be a propitiation through faith in his blood" (Rom. 3.21–25). The term "propitiation" ("sacrifice of atonement" in NRSV) translates the Greek *hilasterion*, which refers to the covering or lid of the holy of holies in the ark of the covenant, the place where the high priest sprinkled the blood of sacrifice on the day of atonement.[23] This theme and imagery is developed in the proclamation of Jesus as high priest whose blood sacrifice propitiates the sins of the people: "for without shedding of blood is no remission" (9.23). For Paul, Christ fulfills and surpasses the Jewish high priest, whose once-yearly entry into the holy of holies to make an atonement offering is now made once-for-all: "by his blood he entered in once into the holy place, having obtained eternal redemption for us" (9.12). This offering shows that Christ's death is sufficient for founding a new covenant (9.15) and that "by means of death" Christ redeems the faithful, based on an analogy with the blood sacrifices of the ancient high priest (9.18-22).

In a deft and complicated strategy, Blake incorporates into his version of Rahab both the Hebrews typology of crucifixion–atonement and the Exodus account of the high priest's separate holiness. For example, as part of his consecrated garments, Aaron is made a "breastplate of judgment" (Exod. 28.15), a robe with scarlet thread (28.33), and a headpiece with "HOLINESS TO THE LORD" engraved on it (28.36). In *Milton*, Blake names Rahab "the Holy" (19.54) and records her boast "And I will put on Holiness as a breastplate & as a helmet" (18.21). Indeed, in all three epics, Blake associates Rahab with both imperial conquest and high-priest atonement ritual, putting her in charge over what he calls "the cruelties of holiness" (*FZ* 105.12, *M* 19.34, *J* 68.14) that take ultimate form in the crucifixion of Jesus. Such a move enables Blake to turn Rahab from a type of the crucified redeemer to a persecutor of Christ, profaning Rahab's typological sanctity, her exemplary role as a "pledge of calling a church from among the Gentiles" (Owen 234).

While Blake follows Hebrews in subordinating Jewish Scripture to New Testament typology, he ultimately subjects the Letter to critique by reading it against the Gospel accounts of crucifixion or, more accurately, against his own apocalyptic approach to the Gospel narratives.[24] In the Gospels, Jesus' trial and crucifixion stem from his remarks concerning the kingdom and its connection to Daniel's messianic prophecy in 7.13–14. Jesus offers these remarks to Caiaphas the high priest and his council when asked if he is the Christ. He answers, "Hereafter shall the Son of man sit on the right hand of the power of God" (Luke 22.69); Matthew is more explicit, adding "and coming in the clouds of heaven" (26.64; see Mark 13.26).[25] In Matthew and Mark, once Jesus announces that he will fulfill Daniel's prophecy, Caiaphas "rent his clothes" and invokes the death penalty against him for blasphemy (Matt. 26.63). Blasphemy, however, is not a crime against the Roman State, and thus Caiaphas must collude in more obviously political terms with Pilate the imperial governor. In Luke, the Jewish priests declare "We found this fellow perverting the nation, and forbidding to give tribute to Caesar, saying that he himself is Christ a king" (23.2). This accusation is undercut by Jesus' disclaimer (Luke 23.3) and his "render unto Caesar" statement (Matt. 22.21), but the priests capture Pilate's attention by saying "He stirreth up the people, teaching throughout all Jewry" (Luke 23.5). When Jesus' pacifist reply—"My kingdom is not of this world" (John 18.36)—satisfies Pilate, the Jewish priests turn up the pressure on him: "If thou let this man go, thou art not Caesar's friend" (John 19.12). Pilate in response seeks to appeal to their nationalist sentiment, asking if he should kill the king of the Jews? But the Jewish priests retort, "We have no king but Caesar" (John 19.15). In political terms, the Jewish priests are right. Their compliance with the Roman authorities legitimates their power and the rule of the temple hierarchy.[26] But Jesus upsets this moral order, and its power relations, by offering a rival kingdom.

Taking his cue from Jesus' own eschatological perspective, Blake reads the Gospel crucifixion narratives against Paul's treatment of Christ in Hebrews, framing those narratives in the context of Daniel and Revelation. This reading enables Blake to identify both Joshua and Paul's Rahab with John's harlot, as all three exemplify collaboration with and sacrifice of others to empire. The duplicity of Joshua's Rahab is crucial here, for Blake's own Rahab participates in Jesus' crucifixion even as she venerates his death on the cross.

> Thus was the Lamb of God condemnd to Death
> They naild him upon the tree of Mystery weeping over him
> And then mocking & then worshipping calling him Lord & King
> Sometimes as twelve daughters lovely & sometimes as five
> They stood in beaming beauty & sometimes as one even Rahab
> Who is Mystery Babylon the Great the Mother of Harlots
>   (FZ 106.2–6, E379)

In *Jerusalem*, Blake opposes Rahab's duplicity and atonement theology with Jesus's concept of "self-sacrifice." Albion asks "Cannot Man exist without Mysterious / Offering of Self for Another," and Blake's Jesus replies:

> Wouldest thou love one who never died
> For thee or ever die for one who had not died for thee

And if God dieth not for Man & giveth not himself
Eternally for Man Man could not exist.

(96: 20–26, E256)

The "mystery" of sacrifice articulated in this passage does not stem from priestly ritual or from Jesus' one-time act of atonement, but from the daily ("Eternal") acts of self-sacrifice which undermine Rahab's selfishness. Similarly, at the end of *Jerusalem* chapter three, Blake stages a dramatic visual confrontation between "Rahab Babylon" and Jesus: Rahab's appearance with the seven-headed dragon from Revelation on plate 75 is countered by the full-page crucifixion scene on plate 76, in which Albion worships a risen Christ.[27]

Before turning to the issue of Rahab and Revelation, a final point may further explain why Blake connects Joshua and Paul's Rahab with John's harlot. This point concerns Rahab's role as a symbol of the Church in the New Testament and early Christian exegesis. As Jean Danielou shows in "Rahab as a Type of the Church," not Paul but Clement of Rome inaugurates the Christian typology of Rahab, interpreting the scarlet cord which "hung from her window as a sign and protection from extermination ... a type of the blood of Christ which saves" (246). Building on Clement, Origen adds the allegory of Rahab's house as a type of the Church (251), a crucial development for Blake's conception, and Gregory consummates the tradition in terms that anticipate Blake. Quoting Gregory, Danielou writes:

> Pay great attention to the purpose of this mystery (*sacramentum*). There is a prophetic reason in this reception of the spies in Joshua by a harlot.... Of whom, then, is this harlot the type? Though Rahab was a harlot, yet, as a prophetess, she enshrined the mysteries of a Virgin Church and the shadow of things to come until the end of time. (257)

I have not found evidence that Blake read the Church fathers. But he develops a similar apocalyptic interpretation of Rahab, although he applies it negatively to the Christian cult of the Virgin, which he conceives in terms of mystery and harlotry.[28] In *Jerusalem*, Blake refers to Rahab Babylon as "the Goddess Virgin-Mother" (18.29) and the "proud Virgin-Harlot! Mother of War!" (50.16). He develops these ideas explicitly in chapter 3, his most extended treatment of Rahab. On plate 56, he combines mother, harlot, and virgin in the image of the three Marys at the cross, cited in John 19.25. The women lament that their fear makes them hide the divine vision with curtain, veil, and (fleshly) tabernacle, which evokes Los the prophet's identification: "Look back into the Church Paul! Look! Three Women around / The Cross!" (56.42–43). On the next plate (57) Blake pictures two of the women weaving the veil of the tabernacle directly above St. Paul's Cathedral in the design.[29]

Blake's identification of Paul with *the* Christian church (understandable in his era) needs to be revised in light of modern scholarship, although Paul's presence in the transitional moment remains important because the letters authored in his name, Colossians and Ephesians, do speak of establishing a church. These texts appear in the crucial stage (circa 70–90 C.E.) when Christian writers were impelled to develop an institutional response to several major problems: the fall of Jerusalem and the Temple (70 C.E.), the delay of the Second Coming, and the challenge of Gnosticism.[30] The focus of Colossians and its sequel Ephesians is to prepare Hellenistic Christians to live in the Roman Empire at a time when the return of Christ was no longer imminent. In the interim, the burning of the Jerusalem Temple and the rise of Gnosticism had to be confronted, a need Colossians and Ephesians address by advocating a distinct and separate institutional church. In response to Gnostic claims about special divine "knowledge," Christian writers established a canon around Paul's letters, which they placed on a par with Hebrew Scripture (2 Pet. 3.16). With canon and creed in place, an episcopate could follow, based on Paul's claim that his own authority descended from the apostles (Gal. 2.8–9). We must acknowledge, however, that the authors of Colossians and Ephesians speak of Christ as the head of the "body" or church and employ the term "mystery" in ways that Paul avoided. While it was Paul's mission to the Gentiles that transformed Christianity from an apocalyptic sect within Judaism to a missionary cult in the Greco-Roman world, the language of "church" and "mystery" indicates a deeper commitment to organized religion than found in Paul.[31] Colossians speaks of the office of "minister" in a formal and developed manner and argues that "the blood on the cross" (1.20) not only makes church members "holy" (1.22) but manifests "the mystery which hath been hid from ages" (1.26). Ephesians develops these points, referring to the apostles as "holy" due to their special insight into "the mystery of Christ," in whom the "fellowship of mystery" has been hid until now (3.4–10). It is "when we come to Ephesians in the New Testament," write Duling and Perrin, "that we hear about the Christian Church, with a capital C" (282).

For Blake, a canon built on creed rather than vision can only contribute to the formation of a church that places Rahab—"the System of Moral Virtue" (*J* 5.10)—ahead of the Lamb. The Lamb's resurrection becomes the occasion for a new morality or religion based on mystery rather than an aesthetic based on revelation. Blake criticizes this didactic process as early as *The Marriage of Heaven and Hell* and as late as *Jerusalem*. In the *Marriage* he associates the process with priesthood in general and describes it as "Choosing forms of worship from poetic tales" (E38). In *Jerusalem* he locates the process more boldly in the Roman-Jewish alliance that converts the Gospel story into an apology for the crucifixion:

> When Satan first the black bow bent
> And the Moral Law from the Gospel rent
> He forgd the Law into a Sword
> And spilld the blood of mercys Lord
>
> (*J* 52.17–20)

Also in *Jerusalem*, Blake's ideal canon for the New Testament contains only "The Four-fold Gospel, and the Revelations" (48.12), although in the prose introduction to chapter 4, "To the Christians," he includes the apostles. Yet even there he is keen to separate didacticism from inspired utterance, claiming that the "Apostles knew of no other Gospel" but "the liberty both of body & mind to exercise the Divine Arts of Imagination" (*J* 77, E231). Without these arts, Christianity is reduced to the moral doctrines and political compromises that Blake epitomizes in the "Church Paul."

Again, Paul did not call for a single institutional church, as did the so-called "Deutero-Pauline" letters and "Pastoral" epistles (James; 1 and 2 Peter; Jude; and 1, 2, and 3 John) that appeared between 90–125 C.E. But while he did not participate in this movement, the "Pauline" compromise with the Roman imperial world, furthered in the pastoral epistles, is what John of Patmos vehemently opposes in his own letters to the Christian churches in Asia Minor (96 C.E.). Blake follows John in opposing this compromise, which is what Rahab means to him. As for the authors of Colossians and Ephesians, so for John, the crucial issues are the fall of Jerusalem and the delay of the Second Coming, which John answers by envisioning the messiah's return in language whose symbolic vividness surpasses anything in the writings of Paul or his disciples. Indeed, this symbolic power is what most captivates Blake and influences his aesthetic. Yet John casts his apocalypse in the form of a letter, beginning with a salutation in the Pauline style (1.4–6) and closing with a benediction (22.21), to situate his work in relation to the Pauline school (Duling and Perrin 460). As soon as he offers his salutation, he exclaims, "Behold, he cometh with clouds" (1.7), citing Daniel's prophecy of the Son of man (7.13) that Jesus quoted to the high-priest Caiaphas. John here returns to a classic text of early Christianity in order to inspire the churches to resist compromise with the dragon harlot of Roman imperialism.

DRAGON AND HARLOT IN REVELATION

The dragon and harlot traditions (which remain distinct in the Old Testament) finally, and for Blake, crucially, converge in the image of the harlot riding the dragon in Revelation 17. Although well known, the text is worth having before us:

> And there came one of the seven angels which had the seven vials, and talked with me, saying unto me, Come hither; I will show unto thee the judgment of the great whore that sitteth upon many waters; With whom the kings of the earth have committed fornication, and the inhabitants of the earth have been made drunk with the wine of her fornication. So he carried me away in the spirit into the wilderness: and I saw a woman sit upon a scarlet-colored beast, full of names of blasphemy, having seven heads and ten horns. And the woman was arrayed in purple and scarlet color, and decked with gold and precious stones and pearls, having a golden cup in her hand full of abominations and filthiness of her fornication. And upon her forehead was a name written, MYSTERY, BABYLON THE GREAT, THE MOTHER OF HARLOTS AND ABOMINATIONS OF THE EARTH (17.1–5)

It would be hard to overestimate the importance of this passage to Blake's conception of Rahab, whom he always associates with the harlot and dragon, the number seven, the color scarlet, the golden cup, and "Mystery Babylon." John of course does not name either the harlot or dragon Rahab. Frye's reading of Blake connects John's Babylon and Joshua's Rahab simply because they are harlots (299). In an effort to explain more fully why Blake names John's harlot "Rahab," I examine Revelation's merging of the chaos dragon and harlot traditions, building on but developing the sources that Frye cites. Of particular importance are the oracles against Babylon and Tyre in Isaiah 23 and 47. From these sources, John draws his symbols of the harlot and dragon: Tyre provides the image of the harlot and Babylon the symbolic name for Rome, as Richard Bauckham shows.[32] Moreover, in an oracle against Egypt, Ezekiel personifies Pharaoh as "the great dragon" (29.3), whom Second Isaiah (in his prophecy against Babylon) identifies as Rahab (51.9) and John transforms into "the great red dragon" (12.3). John's Babylon then symbolizes dual aspects of Roman imperial power: the military power of the dragon and the religious duplicity of the harlot. John portrays this duplicity first in his critique of the rival prophet "Jezebel," who "fornicates" with the Roman authorities in her teachings to the church at Thyatira. John's approach is reflected in *Milton*, where Blake identifies Rahab with "Rome Babylon & Tyre" (9.50–51) and, more significantly, places her on Mount Carmel (19.28), the site of Jezebel's holy war with Elijah (1 Kings 17–19). "Jezebel's" appearance in Revelation 2.20–23 anticipates the Babylon Harlot in 17–18: as both are defined by their acts of colluding with empire, Blake identifies them both with Rahab. Before turning to these texts, a sketch of the Old Testament harlot tradition may help clarify Jezebel's role in Revelation and connect her behavior with the chaos dragon of chapter 13 and the Babylon harlot of 17.

The roots of the anti-harlot tradition reach back to Solomon's empire, which adopted Phoenician Baalism into the royal cult in violation of the strict anti-idolatry code of Mosaic Yahwism. Building on an alliance established by David, Solomon put Hiram king of Tyre in charge of a labor force that Solomon conscripted by a tax on his own people (1 Kings 5.13–18) in order to build the Jerusalem Temple, which was modeled on the Baal temple at Tyre. Upon its completion, Solomon ordered his priests to bring the ark of the covenant into the sanctuary: "sacrificing sheep and oxen" unnumbered, the priests bore the ark "to the most holy place, even under the wings of the cherubim" (1 Kings 8.5–9). I mention these details not only to connect Solomon to Tyre and to the covering cherub of Ezekiel but also to uncover the roots of prophetic anti-harlotry. According to the book of Kings, the two primary causes that divide the United Monarchy are the people's revolt against Solomon for his exploitation of their labor and his "abomination" with Baalism.[33] Because Solomon "went after Ashtoreth" and built sacrificial altars to Chemosh and Molech—fire gods whose worship involved dedicating first-born children (1 Kings 11.5–7, 33–34)—Yahweh split the kingdom in two. However, in the wake of Solomon's "Canaanizing despotism" (Cross 264), Baal worship flourished under his successor Omri (876–869 B.C.E.), who arranged a marriage between his son Ahab and Jezebel, daughter of a Phoenician king. It is worth noting that Omri consolidated his reign at Tirzah before moving the Israelite capital to Samaria, for Blake identifies Tirzah and Rahab as kin, forming a twofold tabernacle (*J* 67.1–2, 33–34). Jezebel's zealous devotion to Asherah and Melkart (the Tyrian Baal) precipitated a violent struggle between Yahweh and Baal cults that culminated in the equally zealous Elijah's victory over the Baal prophets on Mount Carmel (1 Kings 18.17–40). While Elijah's program was adopted in earnest by King Jehu (843–815), whose bloody purge of Jezebel and the house of Ahab rallied the prophets behind him, the reform movement failed and Jehu's break with Phoenicia left Israel exposed to the imperial ambitions of Assyria.

Enter Hosea, creator of the anti-harlot metaphor in prophetic tradition. Hosea opposes Assyrian imperialism, but his focus is on Israel's continuing Baal worship, which he denounces in the figure of a prostitute (chapters 2, 4).[34] In his oracle against the fertility cult in chapter 2, Hosea prophesies that Yahweh will strip the harlot naked before the nations and expose her "lewdness," a theme developed by Isaiah, Jeremiah, Ezekiel, and John. And in chapters 4–5, in important passages for Revelation, and for Blake's critique of Paul, Hosea equates the sacrificial rites of Baal worship with harlotry (4.13–14) and announces Yahweh's judgment: "Therefore have I hewed them by the prophets; I have slain them by the words of my mouth.... For I desired mercy, and not sacrifice; and the knowledge of God more than burnt offerings" (6.5–6).[35] Hosea's thematic ties between sacrifice, harlotry, and empire attract both John and Blake to the fierce anti-harlot symbolism of the Old Testament prophets.

The issue of sacrifice forms the brunt of the problem with Jezebel in Revelation, and it broaches the wider issue of the Roman imperial cult, symbolized as the chaos dragon in chapter 13 and the harlot in chapter 17. "Jezebel" is John's derogatory name for a rival female prophet who preached the "doctrine of Balaam" (2.14) to the church at Thyatira, allowing members to eat food sacrificed to idols (Rev. 2.20–23). In the wealthy churches at Thyatira, Ephesus, and Pergamum, important trading centers in the eastern part of the empire, pressure was put on Christians employed in business and trade guilds to attend feasts that required such sacrifices (Hemer 120–23). John's uncompromising position would have caught Blake's attention because it ran counter to Paul's own preaching on the issue, which "Jezebel" adopts.[36] The antagonism is toward compromise with empire in general, not the specifics of food sacrificed to idols. Paul's epistles (Rom. 13.1–7; 1 Cor. 8.1–13; 10.14–31) offer a more benign view of empire than John's letters to the seven churches in that they "affirm responsible Christian citizenship *within* the power structures of the world" (Boring 258). John's letters reject Paul's more reasoned or less prophetic stance on the idolatry issue. John admonishes the churches to follow Christ's example, to resist empire by witnessing against the beast to the point of death. In effect, John takes literally the Gospel proclamation that the kingdom already has arrived and the powers of darkness no longer rule. Those who would suffer unto death bear witness to the priority of Christ over Caesar's kingdom: they "dispute that the world belongs to those who claim to rule over it" (Wengst 133). John thus prompts the moderate Christians to rethink their stance on empire as a matter of utmost urgency. His letter to Thyatira beseeches the church to refuse collaboration with "that woman Jezebel" because she attempts to "seduce my servants to commit fornication" (Rev. 2.20), language that he reiterates in chapter 17. In effect, John sees "Jezebel" as opening the door to the Roman dragon from within the Christian community, for which he denounces her in the anti-harlot idiom of Hebrew prophecy.[37] Blake imports this idiom directly into his Rahab symbolism but recasts it as hermaphrodism to emphasize its duplicity and perversity (not in the ordinary sexual sense but as spiritual deformity).[38]

John's judgment against Jezebel anticipates the larger judgment against the dragon and harlot in chapters 12–13 and 17–18. In both instances, "fornication" represents political and spiritual collaboration with the Roman Empire. In particular, John fuses the false prophet ("Jezebel"), the dragon, and the harlot into a monstrous symbol of Rome and the Roman imperial cult's coercive pressure on the Christian churches.[39]

In chapter 13, the great red dragon transfers his power and dominion to the chaos dragon, the beast from the sea, and a second beast from the land representing Domitian's emperor cult and his provincial agents. The emperor cult originated in the East, in the area of the seven churches, where such kings as Alexander the Great and Ptolemy I had been regarded as divine benefactors.[40] Augustus allowed his worship in the provinces but only when combined with that of the goddess Roma, the personified deity of Rome. The Augustan mission of "Eternal Rome," promoted as the *Pax Romana*, associates Augustus and Roma in terms that make both emperor and empire divine. As Richard Koebner puts it, Roman world government was visualized "as participating in the divine character of the *urbs Roma* itself" (7). More importantly, in tandem with the mission of eternal rule, in which "the whole imperial philosophy reached its climax" (Stauffer

157), the Augustan emperor cult provided a focus of common loyalty for the polyglot empire.[41] Emperor worship thus was enforced throughout the empire, particularly in the cities of Asia Minor that John addresses in Revelation. He connects the Roman dragon of military power with the Roman harlot of religious coercion, forging them into a twofold symbol. The sea beast, whose seven heads align him with the great red dragon, symbolizes Roman imperial power: "And I stood upon the sand of the sea, and saw a beast rise tip out of the sea, having seven heads and ten horns, and upon his horns ten crowns, and upon his heads the name of blasphemy.... And they worshipped the dragon which gave power unto the beast" (13.1). John's description comes straight out of Daniel 7, in which the beasts from the sea symbolize the four successive world empires, from Babylon to Greece, that oppose Yahweh's spiritual kingdom. But John further politicizes the beasts in Rome's brutality, in its superior military might: "and they worshipped the beast, saying, Who is like unto the beast? who is able to make war with him?" (13.4). In addition to the first beast's militarism, the second beast seduces the world to worship him by working miracles, making cultic images of the first beast, and branding workers with marks on their foreheads or hands (13.14–16). And he performs these feats in a sinister parody of the Lamb's power (his horns are "like a lamb" 13.11), recalling Jezebel's efforts on behalf of the dragon in the Lamb's name.[42]

The judgment against Babylon in Revelation 17–18 brings together the disparate traditions of dragon and harlot symbolism, the biblical contexts of Blake's Rahab. John's harlot sits upon the "many waters" of the Roman Empire and of the chaos dragon, trafficking with "peoples, and multitudes, and nations, and tongues" (17.15); her scarlet and purple match the imperial colors of the beast, associated with the Roman emperors and imperial cult; and her cup both intoxicates the people and deceives them with the sorceries of her commerce (18.23). Indeed, since war and conquest alone are insufficient to promote the *Pax Romana*, the harlot's cup—"whose golden exterior symbolizes the attraction of Rome's wealth" (Bauckham 348)—is needed to disguise Rome's dragonic power. Roman power needs the deception and seduction of the harlot to make empire seem desirable. Since Rome's wealth depends on Roman military dominance and as dominance, in turn, is sanctified by Rome's imperial religion, John declares that paying homage to Rome amounts to idolatry. It is fornication with a system that masks exploitation and brutality as the spread of Augustan prosperity and peace.[43] The beast and harlot thus symbolize the alliance of Rome's economic-military dominance and its state religion, which deifies worldly rule in the divine titles adopted by the Roman emperors.[44]

It is in this deification of state power, inscribed as "Mystery" on the harlot's forehead (17.5), that Blake's Rahab most closely derives from John's harlot. In *The Four Zoas*, during the crucifixion scene when Vala morphs into Rahab, Blake says that Vala is drawn down into the vegetative body where the synagogue of Satan "Clothed her with Scarlet robes & Gems / And on her forehead was her name written in blood Mystery" (105.14–15). This ceremony leads to Rahab's exposure as Urizen's "secret holiness" and Urizen's metamorphosis into dragon form (116.6–45). It is followed by Blake's most explosive and ferocious attack on Mystery in his entire work (119.1–120.51, 134.5–29), in which Mystery's violent end is announced in terms that draw directly from Revelation: "O Mystery.... Behold thy end is come / Art thou she that made the nations drunk with the cup of Religion" (134.5–6). Rahab carries this cup with her into the penultimate scene in *Milton* when "Milton" descends into Blake's garden at Felpham, appearing within the "Twenty-seven-fold mighty Demon" (37.11) lashing the sea like the chaos dragon. Blake enters the Demon's bosom, "In which dwells Mystery Babylon," and discovers the source of her power: "here is her secret place / From hence she comes forth on the Churches in delight / Here is her Cup filld with its poisons.... And here her scarlet Veil woven in pestilence & war" (38.23–26). And in Blake's most brilliant verbal–visual rendition of Rahab, plate 75 of *Jerusalem*, she again appears with her poisonous cup, pompous duplicity, and abominable "hermaphrodism," for which she is exposed as "Religion hid in War: a Dragon red, & hidden Harlot" (75.20). But if Revelation 17 remains the primary source of Blake's harlot symbolism, that is because the chapter consolidates the key prophetic traditions of the Old Testament, two of them stemming from Isaiah.

Isaiah 23 and 47 are of particular significance because they contain portraits of Tyre and Babylon as harlots whose commercial wealth is equated with pride and self-glorification. In Revelation, John's harlot nearly deifies herself in the proud boast "I sit a queen, and am no widow, and shall see no sorrow" (18.7) even as she inflicts sufferings on others, especially Yahweh's prophets (18.24). Bauckham relates this passage to Babylon's boast in Isaiah—"I am, and none else besides me; I shall not sit as a widow" (47.7–8)—and to Rome's self-promotion as the eternal city (344). The passage also relates closely to the representation of Tyre as a harlot in Isaiah 23, which joins the harlot symbol with a critique of

commerce in language that leads directly to Revelation 17. "And it shall
come to pass in that day, that Tyre shall ... sing as a harlot ... and she shall
turn to her hire, and shall commit fornication with all the kingdoms of the
world" (Isa. 23.15–17). Or perhaps *directly* is not the right word, for Isaiah
yokes Tyre with Sidon (23.3), homeport of Jezebel the Phoenician queen,
supplying John with a link to the Thyatiran "Jezebel" of Revelation 2.20.
Most importantly, both Isaiah and John depict Tyre-Babylon's pride in
wealth as self-deification that provokes Yahweh's wrath, his judgment
against empire and its harlots as a demonic force (Isa. 47.13–14).

This notion of empire brings us to John's unique merging of the
chaos dragon and Genesis serpent in the figure of Satan, an association
that helps clarify why he names the harlot "Mystery." John evokes "that
old serpent, called the Devil, and Satan" in the war in heaven episode (Rev.
12.9), which he connects with the imperial cult beast in chapter 13 by
citing the dragon's enmity against the woman's seed (Gen. 3.15; Rev.
12.17). He derives this association from the Leviathan figure in Isaiah
27.1, in which God's judgment against the dragon is paralleled with his
slaying of the crooked, twisting serpent (the seven-headed Lotan of
Canaanite myth). Bauckham suggests that by linking the chaos dragon and
Genesis serpent, John recalls the beast that "initiated humanity's
estrangement from God with the bait of becoming like Gods," which he
says resembles the pagan deities of Asia "who made the same promises to
their worshippers in the mysteries" (198). In a similar vein, Blake connects
the Genesis tree of temptation with his own tree of Mystery, drawing dual
associations from the first and last books of the Bible (*FZ* 101.24). John
may also refer to contemporary myths, particularly in the areas of the seven
churches, which associate serpents with divine power. In any case, the
unveiling of the harlot dragon's mystery in the serpent symbol contained a
fundamental ambiguity for John's audience because of its association with
God's adversary in the chaos dragon tradition (Bauckham 195–96). John
exploits these allusive possibilities in his treatment of the "*Nero redivivus*"
myth, the myth of Nero's return from the dead, a parody of the Lamb's
resurrection that contains the ultimate meaning of the harlot's mystery.

John lived through the persecution of Christians by Nero and the
destruction of Jerusalem by the Flavian emperors. But between Nero's
suicide in 68, which ended the Julio-Claudian line, and the beginning of
the Flavian dynasty in 69, he also experienced the first major breach in the
Pax Romana, the chaos of the so-called "year of the four emperors"
(Bauckham 443). This lapse of empire was as significant for John as
experiencing the temporary failure of the British Empire during the

American Revolution was for Blake.[45] When the empire recovered under Vespasian (69–79), Greek cities in Asia Minor began to circulate rumors about Nero's "faked" suicide and his return at the head of an eastern army to reclaim dominion over the western portion of the empire.[46] Nero's "philhellenism" had endeared him to the East, where he encouraged his own deification more eagerly than in Rome. Three false Neros appeared under the Flavians, the last one in the year 88, during Domitian's rule (Griffin 214). The return of Nero myth may partly explain why John identifies him with the second beast, who inherits his power from the chaos dragon, one of whose seven heads has a lethal wound that is healed (13.3,12). John refers here to the breakdown of empire and its recovery under the Flavians, whose dynasty culminated in Domitian's reign (81–96), which strongly promoted the imperial cult (Schüssler Fiorenza 193). But John exploits a contradiction, for the second beast also refers to Nero, whose symbolic number 666 was based on the sum of the letters of "Nero Caesar" written in Hebrew characters. Since the myth of Nero's return also embodies imperial survival, it posed a threat to the Flavians, especially to Domitian, who sought to solidify power in the East by deifying himself in a monumental statue erected at Ephesus. John thus blasts Nero and Domitian for seeking to delude the world into believing their idolatrous pretensions to divinity. That pretension is the most fundamental aspect of the harlot's mystery, as the angel of apocalypse reveals: "For I will tell thee the mystery of the woman, and of the beast that carrieth her" (17.7). The beast is none other than the revived Nero, "the beast that was, and is not, and yet is" (v. 8). John already told the seven churches that he writes in the name of the Lamb, "him which is, which was, which is to come" (1.4). He thus creates a Christian parody out of the Nero myth and sets up an eschatological contrast between Caesar and Christ (Yarbro Collins, *Combat* 186; Bauckham 384). The outcome of this battle reveals yet another aspect of the harlot's mystery, her unexpected defeat at the hands of the beast.[47] Or mouth, we should say, for he eats her and, as Nero did Rome, burns her. John thus focuses his symbolism on the mystery of the harlot's self-destruction and violence. Yahweh compels the imperialist heart to self-divide (17.16–17), so that the beast's ten horns turn on the harlot herself. The revealed mystery is that the parody resurrection is doomed to failure.

The Mystery theme helps to establish that Revelation is about resurrection, not crucifixion (which is Rahab's dominion), and to show that John offers an eschatological alternative to the Pauline Church. Paul's own eschatology or the idea of John consciously opposing him is not at issue.[48] Rather, the point is that Blake reads John against Paul in a very specific way. He sees that John's rhetoric urges his auditors to stand against the beast, sacrificing their lives, as Christ did, in the face of overwhelming imperial odds. Paul sacrificed his life in just this way under Nero. But specifically in "Paul's" letter to the Hebrews, sacrifice is geared toward atonement for sin, whereas in John's Revelation sacrifice is conceived primarily as an uncompromising witness to justice.

In the second chapter of *Jerusalem*, addressed "To the Jews," Blake expresses a similar view. He champions the "willing sacrifice of Self" against the "sacrifice of (miscall'd) Enemies / For Atonement" (28.20–21), and he contrasts the "spiritual deaths of mighty men / Who give themselves, in Golgotha, Victims to Justice" (34.53–54) with the death sentences required by the "System of Moral Virtue, named Rahab" (35.10). In the same way, the Lamb's sacrifice in Revelation is not to remove sin, but to inspire the active participation of the witnesses in the end-time struggle. John does not focus on the crucified Jesus as much as on Daniel's messianic Son of Man (Rev 1.13, 14.14), the figure that Jesus identifies as his resurrected form in the crucifixion narratives. Likewise in the Last Judgment (Night 9) of *The Four Zoas*, Blake equates Jesus ("him who was Crucified") with Daniel's "Son of Man," who returns to render justice against those who "piercd" him and oppressed the wretched of the earth (123.20–29). It is this anti-imperial, apocalyptic frame that Daniel and Revelation form around the New Testament writings that Blake uses against the institutional Church.

Blake thus incorporates Joshua's "good harlot" into Revelation's harlot-dragon symbolism in order to repudiate the whole ideology of Judeo-Christian conquest. He makes Rahab's duplicitous collaboration with Joshua's spies the primary type in a series of transitions in which the alliance of religion and empire is symbolized as a harlot dragon. Blake may be drawing on his antinomian roots, on writers such as the Ranter William Erbery, who traces the various churches ("beast-whores") from the apostolic age to the mid-seventeenth century, concluding that "the sinful Woman the great Whore ... is none else but the Apostate Church" (269).[49] Or it may be that Blake's apocalyptic intuition, shaped by the radical dissenting tradition, has attuned him to these revolutionary turning points and led him to the symbolic power of the mixed image. By merging two symbolic streams, the anti-empire Rahab dragon with the collusive Rahab harlot, Blake creates a composite figure of tremendous depth and range. This figure allows him to unify the violence of empire with the pragmatic complicity of people forced to live under it. Blake thus synthesizes the two traditions of Rahab for his own unique creative use.

RAHAB IN BLAKE'S EPICS

A concluding comment on the relation of these biblical contexts to Blake's Rahab is in order. The first point to make is that as both chaos dragon and Jericho harlot, Rahab functions in fundamentally political ways in the Bible. Blake retains this political valence. Rahab is his most potent symbol of the state religion of empire. As such, Rahab can help break down the widely held scholarly view that after the 1790s Blake's work becomes apolitical, or that it retreats from the overt social-political focus of his earlier work. This position has been held by scholars as diverse as Morton Paley and E.P. Thompson, G.E. Bentley and Leopold Damrosch.[50] However, a study of Rahab symbolism in the epics shows that Blake's politics deepened and broadened rather than faded away or became quiescent after 1800. Part of this evolution comes from Blake's immersion in the Bible, especially in the book of Revelation, during the first decade of the 1800s. From this immersion, Rahab emerges as the female half of the hermaphroditic form of Satan; she is the holiness or religious justification of empire in all three epics. Also, in each epic Blake creatively associates Joshua's Rahab with the chaos dragon and anti-harlot traditions that converge in Revelation 17. As Frye suggests, Rahab's profession associates her with the anti-harlotry polemic of the prophets. But harlotry is not mere prostitution; it is seduction in religious and political guise. The dragon cannot function by brute force alone but needs Rahab's "delusive arts" to impel people to accept brutality as the price of state power. Finally, in all three epics, Blake sets Rahab in dramatic structural and thematic opposition to the Lamb of God, whom she crucifies, although the crucifixion simultaneously reveals both her deceptive holiness and the Lamb's power to reclaim his kingdom from the empire dragon. Thus the revelation of Rahab, crucial to each epic's narrative resolution, shows that Blake portrays her from a consistently apocalyptic perspective.

While not as remarkable as the similarities, the differences in Blake's conception of Rahab are important to her meaning within each epic. Conceived in the deep personal ambiance of Felpham, Rahab exhibits an interior character in *The Four Zoas* that she lacks in *Milton* or *Jerusalem*. This interiority stems in part from her collusive nature: she is divided against herself (*FZ* 111.8–21) much as John's harlot-dragon self-divides or

Joshua's Rahab is pulled by the claims of self-survival and communal loyalty. This interiority may also account for her redemption in Night 9 of *The Four Zoas* (120.49–51), another feature lacking in the engraved epics. But besides being introduced into a work already in progress, the major difference between Rahab's role in *The Four Zoas* and the engraved epics is that in *Milton* and *Jerusalem* she functions as an eternal state or system. Blake names the system "Moral Virtue" (*M* 40.21; *J* 35.10) and constellates it with a host of other symbols, primarily the Covering Cherub, Vala's Veil, and Albion's Fatal Tree. In *Milton*, Rahab retains her biblical associations, but she represents the specific historical conjunction of British "natural religion" and empire that usurps Milton's legacy from 1650 to 1800. Picking up where *Milton* leaves off, Rahab in *Jerusalem* is absorbed into the Covering Cherub, Blake's Antichrist (89.52–63), but her symbolism expands in both scope and depth. Blake now calls the chaos dragon the Druid dragon, and he treats Druidism much as Bryant and other syncretists treated pagan religion, as a type of Christianity. Where *The Four Zoas* emphasizes Rahab's fundamental role in the institution of Christianity, and where *Milton* focuses on her role in the formation of Anglican state religion, *Jerusalem* expands her scope to encompass all dying-god or fertility religions, from Canaanite to Babylonian to Greco-Roman and Catholic-Protestant variants. In the last analysis, Rahab is the polar opposite of *Jerusalem*, who "is named Liberty / Among the sons of Albion" (*J* 26, in art) and who signifies liberation from the unholy alliance of morality and empire that Rahab personifies. Yet Rahab retains her power to the end. Blake is fascinated by, and not a little jealous of, her. Rahab is his most potent symbol of the religion of empire that people must resist if they are to achieve their full spiritual and political potential.

NOTES

1. For Rahab's appearance in *The Four Zoas* manuscript, see Bentley, *Vala* 162–66 and Pierce 127–39, 167. For reproductions, see Erdman and Magno 219–24, 229.

2. For dating of Blake's epics, see Viscomi 378–81.

3. While Rahab does not appear in the watercolors that he did for Thomas Butts between 1800 and 1809, Blake painted some 48 pictures on biblical subjects for Butts between 1803 and 1805 when Rahab made her appearance in *The Four Zoas*. Approximately 25 of these paintings deal with Gospel narratives about Jesus, with 7 of them focused on the crucifixion, entombment, or resurrection and another 7 devoted to themes from Revelation. One of the paintings, *The Entombment* (B 498), has a verse inscribed on the mount from Luke 23.53, referring

to Joseph of Arimathea's burial of Jesus. In deleted lines to *The Four Zoas* 110.29–31 (E843), Blake initially had Rahab, not Los, dig the sepulchre for Jesus, alluding to the Luke passage. For analysis, see Bentley, *Vala* 164–65 and Pierce 129–35.

4. On the twenty-seven heavens, see *M* 37.35–43 and *J* 175.1–27; for exposition, see Percival 114–22, Frye 130–34, 343–46, and Hobson 83–84.

5. In Blake, hermaphrodism does not refer simply to sexuality but to a kind of duplicitous monstrosity. For analyses of this complex idea, see Hobson, *Blake* 167–72 and Paglia 289–93.

6. Between 1803 and 1805, when he conceived of Rahab, Blake painted a subset of four Revelation watercolors on the Great Red Dragon (*B* 519:22). With the series of Last Judgments that he executed between 1806 and 1809, which include the harlot and dragon of Babylon, these works indicate the deep and pervasive influence that Revelation exerts on Blake's conception of Rahab, his own Babylon Harlot.

7. There is precious little commentary on the biblical contexts of Blake's Rahab. Frye of course is an exception, but he does not fully analyze the biblical texts; neither do Damon 385 or Percival 34–35, who links Vala, Mystery, and the Christian Church in an important connection that Bloom develops (E965; Bloom 259–60). In perhaps the best historical treatment of Rahab, Sandler builds on Frye's account of the chaos dragon, exploring Rahab's relation to Canaanite as well as Mesopotamian dragon traditions and to the Canaanite fertility cult (37–47). The only recent work on the biblical contexts of Rahab comes from Goldsmith, who develops a poststructural feminist critique of "Blake's Babylon" that includes a defense of Rahab against Blake, in the grain of recent feminist approaches to Revelation that exonerate the harlot (see Pippin and Keller). This interpretive approach, however, has not born fruit in the most current work on Rahab, which has returned to the form-critical methodology of Bentley's facsimile study of *The Four Zoas*. In an otherwise solid study, Lincoln unfortunately offers little on Rahab, treating her mainly as the "false" counterpart to Jesus (273), much as Ault does (320–25). And Pierce, who gives Rahab an entire chapter of her own (127–39), focuses on the formal process through which Vala turns into *The Four Zoas*. Pierce's labors in excavating the various layers of the manuscript, and Rahab's place within them, are praiseworthy, but they do not help determine her meaning in a substantial way.

8. "Second Isaiah" is a twentieth-century designation for chapters 40–55 of the book of Isaiah (Seitz 472–73). In Blake's time, the German biblical scholar J. G. Eichhorn found "secondary" oracles in Isaiah, and W. Gesenius spoke of a distinct writer whom he called "Pseudo-Isaiah," but they did not distinguish a "First" or "Second" Isaiah. In 1892, Bernhard Duhm attributed chapters 56–66 to a "Third Isaiah," thus inaugurating the modern study of Isaiah as a compilation of earlier and later prophets (Seitz 474–77).

9. While modern scholarship indicates that Paul did not write the letter (Doling and Perrin 282), Blake and his contemporaries accepted the traditional attribution. I will thus refer to the Letter as Paul's.

10. Before Gunkel's time, Blake had access to a version of the Babylonian creation myth in Bryant's *A New System of Ancient Mythology* (1774). In the chapter "Of the Original Chaldaic History" (3:95–126) Bryant cites Berosus of Babylonia, a third-century BCE "priest of Belus [Marduk]," as his source, claiming that Milton used him in *Paradise Lost*. Aside from name changes—Belus for Marduk and Thalath for Tiamat—Bryant's account matches Gunkel's in important details, including the god's cutting of Thalath ("the sea" in Greek) in half and forming the cosmos out of her body (3.103–04). Bryant also indicates the closeness of the Babylonian "chaotic history" to Genesis 1 and, possibly influencing Blake, refers to the monsters of the deep as hermaphroditic (3.102–03).

11. Scholars disagree about the cultural origins of Tiamat. Keller argues that "the noun *tehom* translates the Sumerian *tiamat*—the creator-mother-dragon of the *Enuma Elish*" (69). Day, to the contrary, claims that although *tehom* and Tiamat "are certainly etymologically related," the form "*thm*" comparable to Hebrew *tehom* is "attested in Ugaritic ... thus supporting the view that the Old Testament term is Canaanite" (7). Despite these differences, Rahab's connection to the sea and thus to the sea dragon is accepted by most scholars (Wakeman 56–82).

12. An English translation appears in Pritchard. For analysis, see Cross and Cohn.

13. All citations to the Bible are from the King James Version, unless otherwise indicated. I abbreviate citations to the New Revised Standard Version as NRSV.

14. For the Ras Shamra material, which revolutionized modern biblical study, see Gray and Forsyth.

15. Anderson believes that Israelite writers who developed royal covenant theology adopted the Canaanite dragon myth "to buttress the stability of Yahweh's sanctuary in Zion (Ps. 78.69) and the permanence of the Davidic dynasty (Ps. 89.36–37)" (*Understanding* 506).

16. Mowinckel states that the messianic kingdom derives from the royal cult: "The only essential difference is that the ideal of kingship belongs to the present ... whereas the Messiah is a purely future, eschatological figure.... 'Messiah' is the ideal king entirely transferred to the future, no longer identified with the specific historical king, but with one who, one day, will come" (123).

17. See also Jeremiah 51, a chapter that exerts a deep influence on Revelation's concept of Rome as harlot and chaos dragon. Jeremiah prophesies that Yahweh will restore what the chaos dragon destroys by violently overthrowing Babylon (51.44–45).

18. As mentioned in note 8, Paul did not write Hebrews. It was accepted as Paul's in the late fourth century by Augustine and was thus included by Jerome in the Vulgate (Duling and Perrin 283).

19. See the valuable commentary and bibliography in Nelson, who writes "The Rahab story has attracted a great deal of attention in recent decades" (40). Nelson, Ulanov, Frymer-Kensky and other modern scholars approach Rahab as a trickster figure of ancient folklore. Bird and Newman add a social dimension to the

trickster analysis. Bird argues that Rahab's marginal social role as harlot makes her emblematic of the Hebrews' outcast status in Canaan. Newman places Rahab—and "the anti-monarchical Rahab story" (173)—in the context of a peasant uprising against the Canaanite overlords.

20. In a significant contribution to the history of Rahab exegesis, Clement of Rome sought to reconcile the Rahab passages in Hebrews and James by arguing that the scarlet cord in Joshua is a prophecy of Christ's redemption on the cross (see A. T. Hanson 58).

21. Beginning with Luther and Calvin, Protestant commentators point to a negative tradition of rabbinical and patristic exegesis about Rahab's vocation and behavior. But they and the exegetes that Blake probably read—Thomas Coke, Matthew Henry, and Thomas Scott—defend Rahab against the ancient fathers and rabbis who condemn Rahab's lying and deceit by rationalizing it as part of God's providence (Coke 2:5). Scott admits, "Some object that her treachery to her king and country cannot be vindicated" (an objection that Blake shares), but he responds that "in her circumstances she could not have acted otherwise, if influenced by a true and living faith (Note, James ii.26)" (1:8). Henry comments similarly (2:13), but he adds an argument that praises Rahab's collusion with the Israelites that may have caught Blake's critical attention: "She foresaw the conquest of her country; and, in the belief of that, bespoke in time the favour of the conquerors" (2:16).

22. Rahab appears in *The Four Zoas* amidst a series of full-page drawings and proofs for Young's *Night Thoughts* featuring the crucifixion and resurrection of Jesus. See Erdman and Magno 220–22, 229.

23. Cousar says that the word "hilasterion" is the most contested image for atonement in the Pauline letters. He provides evidence that counters Blake's reading of Paul by arguing that Paul's atonement theology is "truncated without taking account of its apocalyptic depth," which emerges when the crucifixion is seen as a transpersonal, "earth-changing" event prophetic of the final resurrection (43).

24. Heppner believes that Hebrews is "clearly a text for which he [Blake] had a high regard," one that "played a key role in Blake's development of the notion of self-sacrifice" (198). In an illuminating analysis of Blake's watercolor *Christ in the Sepulcher, Guarded by Angels* (B 500), Heppner further contends that Blake basically adopts Paul's perspective on the crucifixion. He focuses on the inscription to Exodus 25.20 written just below the head of the entombed Jesus, which refers to the mercy seat above the ark of the covenant guarded by two cherubim. Heppner shows that this "surprising reference" appears also in Hebrews 9.5, which alludes to the earlier text in its allegory of the two covenants. By illustrating these two texts together, Blake reads the sacrifice of Jesus "in the light of ... Hebrews' interpretation of the relation between the two testaments" (199). This reading is both plausible and insightful. However, I believe Blake goes a step further and juxtaposes these texts in order to critique Hebrews' theology of atonement.

25. The King James Version of Daniel reads: "I saw in the night visions, and, behold, one like the Son of man came with the clouds of heaven.... And there was

given him dominion, and glory, and a kingdom, that all people, nations, and languages, should serve him" (7.13–14).

26. For a thoughtful discussion of the politics of crucifixion and of Jesus' self-conscious challenge to the Jewish leadership in Jerusalem, see Green 26–30.

27. Mitchell observes that Albion pays homage not to the "dead body of Jesus" but to what he calls the "prophetic crucifixion." That is, Albion perceives the crucifixion not "as an atonement for his sins" but "as an act which must be reenacted in the annihilation of his own Selfhood" (210).

28. *The Everlasting Gospel* states explicitly that the Roman Church makes the crucifixion its core element of worship: "He took on Sin in the Virgins Womb / And put it off on the Cross & Tomb / To be Worshipd by the Church of Rome" (E524).

29. Los's comment on the "three women" is arguably his mistake, as Mary Magdalen and Mary Jesus' mother appear in a positive light on pages 60–62 of *Jerusalem*.

30. I am indebted to Duling and Perrin on the phases of New Testament Christianity (114–30) and on the Deutero-Pauline movement (279–82).

31. In Ephesians, Duling and Perrin show, "there is a striking movement toward understanding the church as the "Great Church" characteristic of later centuries, but not typical of Paul" (275).

32. Bauckham reads John's portrayal of Babylon as the culmination of Old Testament prophecies about Babylon and Tyre (345): "If Babylon gave Rome its name," he writes, "it is probably Tyre that supplied the image of the harlot" (346).

33. For Solomon's abominations with Baalism, see 1 Kings 11.1–11. For his program of forced labor as the cause of the monarchy's division, see Hayes 148–49. Bright suggests that the prophets "regarded both Solomon's highhanded treatment of his subjects and his fostering of foreign cults ... as gross violations of Yahweh's covenant" (211).

34. In an autobiographical allegory, Hosea takes a harlot for his wife and with her raises children whose names symbolize the story of Israelite idolatry: his son "Jezreel," for example, recalls King Jehu's battle in the Jezreel Valley against the Baal cult (1.4).

35. The priestly cult of sacrifice was not universally accepted. In addition to Hosea and Amos (5.24–27), several psalms subordinate formal sacrifice to heartfelt devotion (40.6; 50.7–14; 51.15–17; 69.30–31). Psalm 106, for example, employs the harlot metaphor: "Yea, they sacrificed their sons and their daughters unto ... the idols of Canaan: and the land was polluted with blood. Thus were they defiled with their own works, and went a whoring with their own inventions" (106.37–39). See Snaith 88–120.

36. For positive readings of John's Jezebel, see Goldsmith 72–84 and Pippin 64.

37. Building on Derrida's influential essay "Of An Apocalyptic Tone Recently Adopted in Philosophy," recent scholars take John to task for his uncompromising,

or intolerant, stand (see Goldsmith, Pippin, and O'Leary). In addition to this perspective, it should be acknowledged that those who adopted John's stance faced ostracism, imprisonment, exile, and execution (Wengst 118).

38. Camille Paglia suggests that Blake's hermaphrodites are negative because of "their imperious self-containment," their "incapacity for emotional opening," and their spiritual blockage (289–93).

39. The definitive study of the imperial cult is by Price. The extent of coercion is an earnestly debated topic: contrast Leonard L. Thompson 171–97 and Yarbro Collins, *Crisis* 69–73, who argue against the claim, and Schüssler Fiorenza 6–9, who supports it.

40. Hayes states that Alexander saw himself as successor to both the Egyptian Pharaoh and Persian great king and that upon his death he was deified throughout the empire. "This amalgamation of royal ideologies," he writes, "marked the beginning of the Hellenistic ruler cult that was to culminate in the later worship of the Roman emperor" (276).

41. Hardt and Negri claim that Empire (in both its Roman and postmodern forms) not only covers "the entire space of what it considers civilization" but puts an end to history: "In other words, Empire presents its order as permanent, eternal, and necessary" (11).

42. G.K. Beale suggests that although the dragon is revealed as the mythic Satan, his seven crowned heads "represent blasphemous claims to earthly kingship by his beastly representatives," the two beasts of chapter 13 who rule "in feeble imitation of Christ's true kingship" (635).

43. As Gibbon puts it in his famous panegyric to imperial Rome: "The vast extent of the Roman empire was governed by absolute power, under the guidance of virtue and wisdom" (1:61). In more theoretical terms, Hardt and Negri argue that the Roman tradition of empire "is peculiar in that it pushes the coincidence of the ethical and juridical to the extreme," so that a "unitary power" both "maintains the social peace and produces its ethical truths" (10). They critique this version of empire and acknowledge that apocalyptic offers "an absolute alternative to the spirit of imperial right" (21).

44. Caligula demanded divine worship and provoked the Jews by planning to erect a statue of himself in the Jerusalem Temple, the "abomination of desolation" that Mark (13.14) and Matthew (24.15–21) adopt from Daniel (11.31). Nero appeared on coins wearing the crown of a deified emperor and Vespasian, while eschewing deification, issued coins with *aeternitati augusti* inscribed on them and the goddess Roma "enthroned on the seven hills" (Stauffer 154). Domitian was addressed as "lord and god" and erected a huge statue of himself at Ephesus, which from the time of Paul's mission was the center of Christian worship in Asia Minor (Yarbro Collins, *Crisis* 71–73; Stauffer 174; Gibbon 1:53–54).

45. For John, see Bauckham 444–46; for Blake, see Rosso 252, 268.

46. See Yarbro Collins, *Combat* 185–86 and Bauckham 412–14.

47. As Beale writes, "the kingdom will turn against itself and start to self-destruct even before Christ returns. The political side of the evil system will turn against the religious-economic side and destroy it" (858).

48. Discussing the ethical nature of Paul's apocalyptic perspective, Cousar pushes Paul closer to Revelation than Blake does: "the primary issue of ethics [in Paul] is not to determine what is good or how one chooses the good, but knowing who is the Lord and whose side one is on" (44).

49. Apostasy is a term the sectaries use to denounce corrupt fellow Christians, beginning with Roman Catholics, but extending to Anglicans and even to the dissenting sects themselves. Isaac Penington, who also places the Apostasy in the apostolic era, echoes Erbery and anticipates Blake by concluding "that the several ways of religion in the Christian world are but so many coverings; and that which is covered with them is the whorish spirit" (191). Compare *Milton* (plates 9, 38) and *Jerusalem* (plate 89).

50. See Paley 161–65, Thompson 175, Bentley, *Stranger* 196, and Damrosch 341. Clark and Worrall have dubbed this idea of Blake's retreat from the social-political focus of his earlier work the "thesis of fracture" (10). The idea recently has been challenged, perhaps most compellingly in Hobson 20–33 and 46–92.

WORKS CITED

Anderson, Bernhard W. *Creation versus Chaos: The Reinterpretation of Mythological Symbolism in the Bible*. Philadelphia: Fortress, 1987.

—. *Understanding the Old Testament*. Abridged 4th ed. Upper Saddle River, NJ: Prentice Hall, 1998.

Ault, Donald. *Narrative Unbound: Re-Visiting William Blake's "The Four Zoas."* Barrytown, NY: Station Hill, 1987.

Bauckham, Richard. *The Climax of Prophecy: Studies on the Book of Revelation*. Edinburgh: T & T Clark, 1993.

Beale, G. K. *The Book of Revelation: A Commentary on the Greek Text*. Grand Rapids: Eerdmans, 1999.

Bentley, G. E., Jr. *Stranger from Paradise: A Biography of William Blake*. New Haven: Yale UP, 2001.

—, ed. *William Blake*: Vala, or The Four Zoas: *A Facsimile of the Manuscript, A Transcript of the Poem, and A Study of Its Growth and Significance*. Oxford: Clarendon, 1963.

Bird, Phyllis. "'To Play the Harlot': An Inquiry into an Old Testament Metaphor." *Gender and Difference in Ancient Israel*. Ed. Peggy L. Day. Minneapolis: Fortress, 1989. 75–94.

Bloom, Harold. *Blake's Apocalypse: A Study in Poetic Argument*. Ithaca: Cornell UP, 1963.

Boring, Eugene M. "The Theology of Revelation: 'The Lord Our God the Almighty Reigns.'" *Interpretation* 40 (1986): 257–69.

Bright, John. *A History of Israel*. Philadelphia: Westminster, 1959.

Bryant, Jacob. *A New System, or, An Analysis of Ancient Mythology*. 3 vols. London: T. Payne, 1774.

Butlin, Martin. *The Paintings and Drawings of William Blake*. 2 vols. New Haven: Yale UP, 1981.

Clark, Steve, and David Worrall, eds. *Historicizing Blake*. New York: St. Martin's, 1994.

Cohn, Norman. *Chaos, Cosmos, and the World to Come: The Ancient Roots of Apocalyptic*. New Haven: Yale UP, 1993.

Coke, Thomas. *Commentary on the Holy Bible*. 4 vols. London: G. Whitfield, 1801–1803.

Cousar, Charles B. "Paul and the Death of Jesus." *Interpretation* 52:1 (1998): 38–52.

Cross, Frank Moore. *Canaanite Myth and Hebrew Epic: Essays in the History of the Religion of Israel*. Cambridge, MA: Harvard UP, 1973.

Damon, S. Foster. *William Blake: His Philosophy and Symbols*. Gloucester, MA: Peter Smith, 1958.

Damrosch, Leopold. *Symbol and Truth in Blake's Myth*. Princeton: Princeton UP, 1980.

Danielou, Jean. "Rahab as a Type of the Church." *From Shadows to Reality: Studies in the Biblical Typology of the Fathers*. Trans. Dom Wulstan Hibberd. London: Burnes & Oates, 1960. 244–60.

Day, John. *God's Conflict with the Dragon and Sea: Echoes of a Canaanite Myth in the Old Testament*. Cambridge: Cambridge UP, 1985.

Derrida, Jacques. "Of an Apocalyptic Tone Recently Adopted in Philosophy." *Semeia* 23 (1982): 63–99.

Duling, Dennis C., and Norman Perrin. *The New Testament: Proclamation and Perenesis, Myth and History*. 3rd ed. Fort Worth, TX: Harcourt, 1994.

Erbery, William. *The Testimony of William Erbery, Left Upon Record for the Saints of Succeeding Ages*. London: Giles Calvert, 1658.

Erdman, David V., ed. *The Complete Poetry and Prose of William Blake*. Commentary by Harold Bloom. Rev. ed. Berkeley: U of California P, 1982.

Erdman, David V., and Cettina Tramontano Magno, eds. The Four Zoas *by William Blake: A Photographic Facsimile of the Manuscript with Commentary on the Illuminations*. Lewisburg, PA: Bucknell UP, 1987.

Forsyth, Neil. *The Old Enemy: Satan and the Combat Myth*. Princeton: Princeton UP, 1987.

Frye, Northrop. *Fearful Symmetry: A Study of William Blake*. Princeton: Princeton UP, 1947.

Frymer-Kensky, Tikva. "Reading Rahab." *Tehillah le-Moshe: Biblical and Judaic Studies in Honor of Moshe Greenberg*. Ed. Mordechai Cogan, Barry L. Eichler, and Jeffrey H. Tigay. Winona Lake, WI: Eisenbrauns, 1997. 57–67.

Gibbon, Edward. *The Decline and Fall of the Roman Empire*. 3 vols. Ed. J. B. Bury. New York: Heritage, 1946.

Goldsmith, Stephen. *Unbuilding Jerusalem: Apocalypse and Romantic Representation*. Ithaca: Cornell UP, 1993.

Gray, John. *The Legacy of Canaan: The Ras Shamra Texts and Their Relevance to the Old Testament*. Leiden: E. J. Brill, 1965.

Green, Joel B. "The Death of Jesus and the Ways of God." *Interpretation* 52:1 (January 1998): 24–37.

Griffin, Miriam T. *Nero: The End of a Dynasty*. New Haven: Yale UP, 1984.

Gunkel, Hermann. *Genesis*. Trans. Mark E. Biddle. Macon, GA: Mercer UP, 1997.

Hanson, A. T. "Rahab the Harlot in Early Christian Tradition." *Journal for the Study of the New Testament* 1 (1978): 53–60.

Hanson, Paul D. *The Dawn of Apocalyptic: The Historical and Sociological Roots of Jewish Apocalyptic Eschatology*. Philadelphia: Fortress, 1975.

Hardt, Michael, and Antonio Negri. *Empire*. Cambridge, MA: Harvard UP, 2000.

Hayes, John. *Introduction to the Bible*. Philadelphia: Westminster, 1971.

Hemer, C. J. *The Letters to the Seven Churches of Asia in Their Local Setting*. Sheffield, Eng.: JSOT Press, 1986.

Henry, Matthew. *An Exposition of the Old and New Testament*. 6 vols. Edinburgh: Bell and Bradfute, 1790.

Hobson, Christopher Z. *Blake and Homosexuality*. New York: St. Martin's P, 2000.

—. *The Chained Boy: Orc and Blake's Idea of Revolution*. Lewisburg, PA: Bucknell UP, 1999.

Keller, Catherine. *Apocalypse Then and Now: A Feminist Guide to the End of the World*. Boston: Beacon, 1996.

Koebner, Richard. *Empire*. Cambridge: Cambridge UP, 1961.

Lincoln, Andrew. *Spiritual History: A Reading of William Blake's "Vala" or "The Four Zoas."* Oxford: Clarendon P, 1995.

Midrash Rabba: Ruth. Trans. L. Rabinowitz. London: Soncino, 1983.

Mitchell, W. J. T. *Blake's Composite Art: A Study of the Illuminated Poetry*. Princeton: Princeton UP, 1978.

Mowinckel, Sigmund. *He That Cometh*. Trans. G. W. Anderson. Oxford: Blackwell, 1959.

Nelson, Richard D. *Joshua: A Commentary*. Louisville: Westminster, 1997.

Newman, Murry L. "Rahab and the Conquest." *Understanding the Word: Essays in Honor of Bernhard W. Anderson*. Ed. James T. Butler, Edward W. Conrad, and Ben C. Ollenburger. Sheffield, UK: JSOT Press, 1985. 167–77.

O'Leary, Stephen D. *Arguing the Apocalypse: A Theory of Millennial Rhetoric*. New York: Oxford UP, 1994.

Owen, John. *Hebrews*. Wheaton, IL: Crossway Books, 1998.

Paglia, Camille. *Sexual Personae: Art and Decadence from Nefertiti to Emily Dickinson*. New York: Vintage, 1991.

Paley, Morton D. *Energy and the Imagination: A Study of the Development of Blake's Thought*. Oxford: Clarendon, 1970.

Penington, Isaac. *The Works of the Long-Mournful and Sorely-Distressed Isaac Penington*. 3rd ed. London: James Phillips, 1784.

Percival, Milton O. *William Blake's Circle of Destiny*. 1938. New York: Octagon, 1964.

Pierce, John B. *Flexible Design: Revisionary Poetics in Blake's* Vala or The Four Zoas. Montreal and Kingston, ON: McGill-Queens UP, 1998.

Pippin, Tina. *Death and Desire: The Rhetoric of Gender in the Apocalypse of John*. Louisville: Westminster, 1992.

Price, S. R. F. *Rituals and Power: The Roman Imperial Cult in Asia Mirror*. Cambridge: Cambridge UP, 1984.

Pritchard, J. B., ed. *Ancient Near Eastern Texts Relating to the Old Testament*. 3rd ed. Princeton: Princeton UP, 1969.

Ricoeur, Paul. *The Symbolism of Evil*. Trans. Emerson Buchanan. New York: Harper, 1967.

Rosso, G. A. "Empire of the Sea: Blake's 'King Edward the Third' and English Imperial Poetry." *Blake, Politics, and History*. Ed. Jackie DiSalvo, G. A. Rosso, and Christopher Z. Hobson. New York: Garland, 1998. 251–72.

Sandler, Florence. "The Iconoclastic Enterprise: Blake's Critique of 'Milton's Religion.'" *Blake Studies* 5 (1972): 13–57.

Schüssler Fiorenza, Elisabeth. *The Book of Revelation: Justice and Judgment*. Philadelphia: Fortress, 1985.

Scott, Thomas. *The Holy Bible Containing the Old and New Testaments with Original Notes, Practical Observations, and Copious Marginal References*. 3 vols. Philadelphia: William W. Woodward, 1804.

Seitz, C. R. "Isaiah, Book Of." *The Anchor Bible Dictionary*. Vol 3. Gen. Ed. David Noel Freedman. New York: Doubleday, 1992.

Snaith, Norman. *Mercy and Sacrifice: A Study of the Book of Hosea*. London: SCM, 1953.

Stauffer, Ethelbert. *Christ and the Caesars: Historical Sketches*. Trans. K. and R. Gregor Smith. London: SCM, 1955.

Thompson, G. P. *The Making of the English Working Class*. New York: Vintage, 1966.

Thompson, Leonard L. *The Book of Revelation: Apocalypse and Empire*. New York: Oxford UP, 1990.

Ulanov, Ann Belford. "Rahab." *The Female Ancestors of Christ*. 34–45. Boston: Shambhala, 1993.

Viscomi, Joseph. *Blake and the Idea of the Book*. Princeton: Princeton UP, 1993.

Wakeman, Mary K. *God's Battle with the Monster: A Study in Biblical Imagery*. Leiden: E. J. Brill, 1973.

Wengst, Karl. *Pax Romana and the Peace of Jesus Christ*. Trans. J. Bowden. London: SCM, 1987.

Yarbro Collins, Adela. *The Combat Myth and the Book of Revelation*. Missoula, MT: Scholars P, 1976.

—. *Crisis and Catharsis: The Power of the Apocalypse*. Philadelphia: Westminster, 1984.

Chronology

1755	Work begun on the building of the Pantheon in Paris.
1756	Wolfgang Amadeus Mozart born.
1757	William Blake born in London on November 28. Edmund Burke, *Philosophical Enquiry on the Origin of the Sublime and Beautiful*.
1762	Jean Jacques Rousseau, *The Social Contract*.
1764	Richard Arkwright invents the spinning jenny.
1770	William Wordsworth born at Cockermouth in Cumberland on April 7. Ludwig von Beethoven born.
1772	Samuel Taylor Coleridge born in the vicarage at Ottery, St. Mary, Devonshire, on October 21.
1774	Johann Wolfgang von Goethe, *The Sorrows of Young Werther*.
1775	American Revolution against England.
1776	American *Declaration of Independence* written. Thomas Paine, *Common Sense*; Adam Smith, *Wealth of Nations*. David Hume dies.
1778	Beethoven gives his first public concert.
1781	Immanuel Kant, *Critique of Pure Reason*.
1782	Britain negotiates peace with America.
1783	Blake, *Poetical Sketches*.

1784	Samuel Johnson dies. Wordsworth publishes first poetry in *The European Magazine*.
1787	United States *Constitution* written.
1788	George Gordon, Lord Byron born in London on January 22.
1789	Blake, *Book of Thel* and *Songs of Innocence*. French Revolution begins; fall of Bastille in Paris.
1790	Wordsworth takes walking tour of Europe. Blake, *The Marriage of Heaven and Hell*. Edmund Burke, *Reflections on the Revolution in France*.
1791	Mozart's *Requiem*. Death of Mozart. Thomas Paine, *The Rights of Man*.
1792	Shelley born in Horsham, Sussex on August 4. Mary Wollstonecraft, *A Vindication of the Rights of Women*. Louis XVI imprisoned with his family; September Massacres in Paris; monarchy abolished in France. War of the First Coalition begins when France declares war on Austria and Prussia.
1793	Reign of Terror; Louis XVI guillotined; France and England declare war; Marie Antoinette executed; Treaty of Versailles. Wordsworth, *An Evening Walk* and *Descriptive Sketches*. Eli Whitney patents the cotton gin.
1794	Blake, *Songs of Experience*, *Europe*, and *The Book of Urizen*. Thomas Paine, *Age of Reason*. Wordsworth and Coleridge meet.
1795	Keats born in London on October 31.
1796	Coleridge, *Poems on Various Subjects*.
1798	Wordsworth and Coleridge publish *Lyrical Ballads*, marking the beginning of high Romanticism. War of the Second Coalition begins and continues through 1801.
1802	Hostilities between France and England cease with signing of the *Treaty of Amiens*.
1803	Amiens peace fails. France and England declare war. Louisiana Purchase is made in the United States.
1804	Napolean crowned emperor. Britain at war with Spain.
1805	War of the Third Coalition against France, lasting until 1807.
1807	Wordsworth, *Poems in Two Volumes*. Hegel, *Phenemenology of Spirit*. Parliament passes general abolition act, enacted in 1808.
1809	Charles Darwin born. Alfred, Lord Tennyson, born.

1810	Sir Walter Scott, *Lady of the Lake*.
1811	Luddite riots. Jane Austen's first novel, *Sense and Sensibility*, published anonomously.
1812	Byron, first two cantos of *Childe Harold's Pilgrimage*. Charles Godwin and Shelley meet. United States and England at war. Charles Dickens born, Portsmouth, Hampshire. Robert Browning born, London.
1813	Robert Southey becomes Poet Laureate of England after Sir Walter Scott declines appointment.
1814	Byron, *The Corsair* and *Lara*. France invaded by allies of the Fourth Coalition; Paris falls; Napoleon abdicates and is exiled. Peace between United States and England with *Treaty of Ghent*. First steam locomotive. Steam-powered printing presses introduced at the *London Times*.
1815	Wordsworth publishes *Poems of 1815*. Blake's pictures produced in *Laocoön*. Napoleon returns to France, is defeated at Waterloo by allied armies, surrenders, and is exiled.
1816	Coleridge, *Christabel and Other Poems*. Byron, third canto of *Childe Harold*.
1817	Keats, *Poems*. Coleridge, *Biographia Literaria*. Death of Jane Austen.
1818	Byron, *Beppo* and the fourth canto of *Childe Harold*. Keats, *Endymion*. Mary Shelley's *Frankenstein* published anonomously. Karl Marx born.
1819	Wordsworth, *The Waggoner*. Byron, Cantos I and II of *Don Juan*. Birth of Queen Victoria in London.
1820	Shelley, *Prometheus Unbound*. Keats gravely ill with tuberculosis; publishes *Lamia, Isabella, The Eve of St. Agnes, and Other Poems*. George III dies. Friedrich Engels born. Sir Walter Scott, *Ivanhoe*. Charles Lamb publishes critical essays in *London Magazine*.
1821	Keats dies on February 23. Byron, *Cain* and Cantos III, IV, and V of *Don Juan*. Napolean dies.
1822	Shelley drowns on July 8. Matthew Arnold born.
1823	Byron, Cantos VI to XIV of *Don Juan*. Monroe Doctrine proclaimed.

1824	Byron, Cantos XV to XVI of *Don Juan*; dies on April 19. Shelley's *Posthumous Poems* published. Opening of National Gallery in London.
1825	William Hazlitt, *The Spirit of the Age, or Contemporary Portraits*. Erie Canal opens. First railway service in England.
1827	Blake dies on August 12. Beethoven dies March 26.
1828	Coleridge, *Poetical Works*.
1830	Alfred, Lord Tennyson, *Poems, Chiefly Lyrical*. Berlioz, *Le Symphonie Fantastique*.
1832	Édouard Manet born. Reform Bill.
1834	Coleridge dies on July 25.
1836	Samuel Morse invents the telegraph.
1838	Thomas Carlyle, *Critical and Miscellaneous Essays*. Wordsworth, *Sonnets*.
1840	Claude Monet born. Shelley, *A Defense of Poetry*. Queen Victoria marries Prince Albert.
1841	Auguste Renoir born.
1843	Wordsworth becomes Poet Laureate of England.
1844	Elizabeth Barrett Browning, *Poems*.
1847	Karl Marx and Frederick Engels, *The Communist Manifesto*. Emily Brontë, *Wuthering Heights*; Charlotte Bronte, *Jane Eyre*.
1850	Wordsworth dies on April 23. *The Prelude* is published posthumously in fourteen books.
1853	Vincent van Gogh born.
1861	Work begun on The Opéra in Paris, signaling the final phase of Romantic architecture.

Contributors

HAROLD BLOOM is Sterling Professor of the Humanities at Yale University and Henry W. and Albert A. Berg Professor of English at the New York University Graduate School. He is the author of over 20 books, including *Shelley's Mythmaking* (1959), *The Visionary Company* (1961), *Blake's Apocalypse* (1963), *Yeats* (1970), *A Map of Misreading* (1975), *Kabbalah and Criticism* (1975), *Agon: Toward a Theory of Revisionism* (1982), *The American Religion* (1992), *The Western Canon* (1994), and *Omens of Millennium: The Gnosis of Angels, Dreams, and Resurrection* (1996). *The Anxiety of Influence* (1973) sets forth Professor Bloom's provocative theory of the literary relationships between the great writers and their predecessors. His most recent books include *Shakespeare: The Invention of the Human* (1998), a 1998 National Book Award finalist, *How to Read and Why* (2000), *Genius: A Mosaic of One Hundred Exemplary Creative Minds* (2002), and *Hamlet: Poem Unlimited* (2003). In 1999, Professor Bloom received the prestigious American Academy of Arts and Letters Gold Medal for Criticism, and in 2002 he received the Catalonia International Prize.

SEAMUS HEANEY has taught at Harvard University and Oxford University. He has published more than 25 books of poetry, as well as works of criticism and a best-selling translation of *Beowulf*. He received the Nobel Prize for Literature in 1995.

GEOFFREY HARTMAN is Sterling Professor Emeritus of English and Comparative Literature at Yale University. He is the author of a book on Wordsworth's poetry and of several other books, such as *A Critic's Journey* and *Fateful Question of Culture*.

HELEN VENDLER is Professor of English at Harvard. She is the author of *The Bedford Book of Poetry* and the editor of *The Harvard Book of Contemporary American Poetry*.

JOHN CLUBBE is Professor Emeritus of English at the University of Kentucky. He is the author of a book on Byron and is the author, editor, or co-editor of numerous other titles, covering such authors or topics as Carlyle, Thomas Hood, and Victorian perspectives.

ERNEST J. LOVELL, JR. was Professor of English at the University of Texas at Austin and widely regarded as the most distinguished Byron scholar of his generation. He wrote books on Byron and edited editions of Byron's conversations.

JEROME J. McGANN teaches at the University of Virginia. He is editor of *The New Oxford Book of Romantic Period Verse* and the six-volume *Complete Poetical Works of Byron*. Also, he is the editor or author of numerous other titles, including *Byron and Romanticism, Fiery Dust: Byron's Poetic Development*, and *Towards a Literature of Knowledge*.

WILLIAM KEACH teaches at Brown University. He is the author of *Shelley's Style* and the editor of a work by Samuel Taylor Coleridge.

FREDERICK L. BEATY is the author of *Light in Heaven: Love in British Romantic Literature* and other titles.

STUART CURRAN is Professor of English at the University of Pennsylvania. He is the editor of *The Cambridge Companion to British Romanticism* and the editor or joint editor of other titles as well. Also, he has been the editor of the *Keats-Shelley Journal*.

JOHN L. MAHONEY is the Dean/Director of Admissions and former Chairman of the English Department at Boston College. He is the author or editor of a number of titles, among them *William Wordsworth: A Poetic Life* and *The English Romantics: Major Poetry and Critical Theory*.

THOMAS McFARLAND is Murray Professor of English Literature at Princeton University. He is the author of numerous books, many on Romanticism, including *The Mask of Keats: The Endeavour of a Poet*, *Paradoxes of Freedom: The Romantic Mystique of a Transcendence*, and *Shapes of Culture*.

DAVID PERKINS teaches at Harvard University. He is the author or editor of several titles, among them two volumes on the history of modern poetry, *Wordsworth and the Poetry of Sincerity*, and *Theoretical Issues in Literary History*.

PAUL DE MAN was Sterling Professor of Comparative Literature at Yale University and the author of several books, including *The Rhetoric of Romanticism, Blindness and Insight: Essays in the Rhetoric of Contemporary Criticism*, and *Allegories of Reading*.

STEPHEN GURNEY is Professor of English at Bemidji State University in Minnesota. He is a poet and also has published *British Poetry of the Nineteenth Century*, as well as a book on the author Alain-Fournier for Twayne's World Authors Series.

M.H. ABRAMS, widely regarded as the most distinguished living scholar of Romanticism, is the Class of 1916 Professor of English Emeritus at Cornell University. He is the author of *The Mirror and the Lamp: Romantic Theory and the Critical Tradition*, a definitive study of Romantic critical theory, as well as the author of *Natural Supernaturalism: Tradition and Revolution in Romantic Literature* and *The Correspondent Breeze: Essays on English Romanticism*. Also, he is the editor of a few editions of *The Norton Anthology of English Literature*.

G.A. ROSSO is Professor of English at Southern Connnecticut State University. He has published *Blake's Prophetic Workshop: A Study of The Four Zoas* and is the co-editor of *Blake, Politics, and History* and *Spirits of Fire: English Romantic Writers and Contemporary Historical Methods*.

Bibliography

Abrams, M. H. *English Romantic Poets: Modern Essays in Criticism*. London: Oxford University Press, 1975.

———. *The Mirror and the Lamp*. New York: W. W. Norton, 1958.

———. *Natural Supernaturalism*. New York: W. W. Norton, 1973.

Alexander, Meena. *Women in Romanticism: Mary Wollstonecraft, Dorothy Wordsworth, and Mary Shelley*. Totowa, NJ: Barnes and Noble, 1989.

Ault, Donald. *Narrative Unbound: Revisioning Blakes's "The Four Zoas."* Barrytown, NY: Station Hill Press, 1987.

Bate, Walter Jackson. *John Keats*. New York: Oxford University Press, 1966.

Beer, John. "Nature and Liberty: The Linking of Unstable Concepts." *Wordsworth Circle* 14, no. 4 (Autumn 1983).

Bewley, Marius. *The English Romantic Poets: An Anthology with Commentaries*. New York: Modern Library, 1970.

Bhattacharyya, Arunodo. *The Sonnet and the Major English Romantic Poets*. Calcutta: Firma KLM, 1976.

Bloom, Harold. *The Anxiety of Influence: A Theory of Poetry*. New York: Oxford University Press, 1973.

———. *Blake's Apocalypse: A Study in Poetic Argument*. New York: Doubleday, 1963.

———. *The Ringers in the Tower: Studies in Romantic Tradition*. Chicago: the University of Chicago Press, 1971.

———, ed. *Romanticism and Consciousness: Essays in Criticism*. New York: W.W. Norton, 1970.

———. *Shelley's Mythmaking*. New Haven: Yale University Press, 1959.

———. *The Visionary Company: A Reading of English Romantic Poetry* (rev. ed.). Ithica: Cornell University Press, 1971.

Brewer, William D. "Questions without Answers: The Conversational Style of 'Julian and Maddalo.'" *Keats-Shelley Journal* 38 (1989).

Brisman, Leslie. "Mysterious Tongue: Shelley and the Language of Christianity." *Texas Studies in Language and Literature* 23 (1981).

———. *Romantic Origins*. Ithaca: Cornell University Press, 1978.

Brisman, Susan Hawk. "'Unsaying His High Language': The Problem of Voice in *Prometheus Unbound*." *Studies in Romanticism* 16 (1977).

Bush, Douglas. *Mythology and the Romantic Tradition in English Poetry*. Cambridge: Harvard University Press, 1969.

Chandler, James. "Romantic Allusiveness." *Critical Inquiry* 8, no. 3 (Spring 1982).

———. *Wordsworth's Second Nature: A Study of the Poetry and Politics*. Chicago: University of Chicago Press, 1984.

Chatterjee, Visvanath, ed. *The Romantic Tradition*. Calcutta: Jadaupur University, 1984.

Claridge, Laura. *Romantic Potency: The Paradox of Desire*. Ithaca: Cornell University Press, 1992.

Cooke, Michael G. *Acts of Inclusion: Studies Bearing on an Elementary Theory of Romanticism*. New Haven: Yale University Press, 1979.

Cooke, Michael G., and Alan Bewell, eds. "*The Borderers*: A Forum." Special issue of *Studies in Romanticism* 27 (Fall 1988).

Cooper, Andrew M. *Doubt and Identity in Romantic Poetry*. New Haven: Yale University Press, 1988.

Crompton, Louis. *Byron and Greek Love: Homophobia in 19th-Century England*. Berkeley: University of California Press, 1985.

Cronin, Richard. *Shelley's Poetic Thoughts*. New York: St. Martin's, 1981.

Curran, Stuart. *Shelley's Annus Mirabilis: The Maturing of an Epic Vision*. San Marino, CA: Huntington Library, 1975.

Everest, Kelvin. *English Romantic Poetry: An Introduction to the Historical Context and the Literary Scene*. Philadelphia: Open University Press, 1990.

Ferguson, Frances. "Coleridge on Language and Delusion." *Genre* II (1978).

———. *Wordsworth: Language as Counter-Spirit*. New Haven: Yale University Press, 1977.

Fischer, Hermann. *Romantic Verse Narrative: The History of a Genre*. New York: Cambridge University Press, 1991.

Furst, Lilian R. *Fictions of Romantic Irony*. Cambridge: Harvard University Press, 1984.

Frye, Northrop. *Fearful Symmetry*. Boston: Beacon Press, 1967.

Gaull, Marilyn. *English Romanticism: The Human Context*. New York: W. W. Norton, 1988.

Gill, Stephen. *William Wordsworth: A Life*. Oxford: Oxford University Press, 1989.

Gingerich, Solomon F. *Essays in the Romantic Poets*. New York: Octagon, 1970.

James, D. G. *The Romantic Comedy*. London: Oxford University Press, 1963.

Jordan, Frank. *The English Romantic Poets: A Review of Research and Criticism*. New York: Modern Language Association of America, 1985.

Lau, Beth. *Keats's Reading of the Romantic Poets*. Ann Arbor: University of Michigan Press, 1991.

Lucas, John. *Romantic to Modern Literature: Essays and Ideas of Culture, 1750–1900*. Totowa, NJ: Barnes & Noble Books, 1982.

Nemoianu, Virgil. *The Taming of Romanticism*. Cambridge: Harvard University Press, 1984.

Newey, Vincent. "Shelley and the Poets: *Alastor*, 'Julian and Maddalo,' *Adonais*." *Durham University Journal* 85:54, no. 2 (July 1993).

Pater, Walter. *Appreciations*. London: Macmillan, 1900.

Piper, H. W. *The Active Universe: Pantheism and the Concept of Imagination in the English Romantic Poets*. London: Athlone Press, 1962.

Schapiro, Barbara A. *The Romantic Mother: Narcissistic Patterns in Romantic Poetry*. Baltimore: Johns Hopkins University Press, 1983.

Sperry, Stuart. *Keats the Poet*. Princeton: Princeton University Press, 1973.

Swanson, Donald R. "Carlyle on the English Romantic Poets." *Lock Haven Review* 11 (1969).

Thomas, Gordon K. "'The Thorn' in the Flesh of English Romanticism." *Wordsworth Circle* 14, no. 4 (Autumn 1983).

Vogler, Thomas A. "Rhetoric and Imagination." *Stanford Literature Review* 6, no. 1 (Spring 1989).

Wasserman, Earl. *The Finer Tone*. Baltimore: Johns Hopkins Press, 1967.

———. *Shelley: A Critical Reading*. Baltimore: Johns Hopkins University Press, 1971.

Webster, Sarah McKim. "Circumscription and the Female in the Early Romantics." *Philological Quarterly* 61, no. 1 (Winter 1982).

Acknowledgments

"The Internalization of Quest-Romance" by Harold Bloom. From *Romanticism and Consciousness: Essays in Criticism*, edited by Harold Bloom: 3–24. First appeared in *The Yale Review* 58, no. 4 (Summer 1969). Copyright 1969 by Harold Bloom.

"The Makings of a Music: Reflections on Wordsworth and Yeats" by Seamus Heaney. From *Preoccupations: Selected Prose, 1968–1978*: 61–78. © 1980 by Seamus Heaney. Reprinted by permission of Farrar, Straus, and Giroux, LLC..

"The Poetics of Prophecy" by Geoffrey Hartman. From *High Romantic Argument: Essays for M. H. Abrams*, edited by Lawrence Lipking: 15–40. © 1981 by Cornell University. Reprinted by permission.

"Truth the Best Music: The *Ode on a Grecian Urn*." Reprinted by permission of the publisher from *The Odes of John Keats* by Helen Vendler: pp. 114–52, Cambridge, Mass.: The Bell Press of Harvard University Press, copyright © 1983 by the President and Fellows of Harvard College.

"English Romanticism: the Grounds of Belief," by John Clubbe and Ernest J. Lovell, Jr. From *English Romanticism: the Grounds of Belief*: 146–60. © 1983 by John Clubbe and the Estate of Ernest J. Lovell, Jr. Reprinted by permission.

"Phases of English Romanticism," by Jerome J. McGann. From *The Romantic Ideology: A Critical Investigation*: 107–117. © 1983 by The University of Chicago. Reprinted by permission.

"Rhyme and the Arbitrariness of Language," by William Keach. From *Shelley's Style*: 184–200. © 1984 by William Keach. Reprinted by permission.

"The Narrator as Satiric Device in *Don Juan*" by Frederick L. Beaty. From *Byron the Satirist*: 123–37. © 1985 by Northern Illinois University Press. Reprinted by permission.

"Form and Freedom in European Romantic Poetry," by Stuart Curran. From *Poetic Form and British Romanticism*: 204–220. © 1986 by Oxford University Press, Inc. Used by permission of Oxford University Press, Inc..

"'We Must Away': Tragedy and the Imagination in Coleridge's Later Poems," by John L. Mahoney. From *Coleridge, Keats, and the Imagination: Romanticism and Adam's Dream*, edited by J. Robert Barth, S.J., and John L. Mahoney: 109–34. © 1990 by The Curators of the University of Missouri. Reprinted by permission.

"Involute and Symbol in the Romantic Imagination," by Thomas McFarland. From *Coleridge, Keats, and the Imagination: Romanticism and Adam's Dream*, edited by J. Robert Barth, S.J., and John L. Mahoney: 29–57. © 1990 by The Curators of the University of Missouri. Reprinted by permission.

"The Imaginative Vision of *Kubla Khan*: On Coleridge's Introductory Note," by David Perkins. From *Coleridge, Keats, and the Imagination: Romanticism and Adam's Dream*, edited by J. Robert Barth, S.J., and John L. Mahoney: 97–108. © 1990 by The Curators of the University of Missouri. Reprinted by permission.

"Time and History in Wordsworth," de Man, Paul. From *Romanticism and Contemporary Criticism: The Gauss Seminar and Other Papers*, edited by E. S. Burt, Kevin Newmark, Andrzej Warminski: 74–94. © 1992 by The Johns Hopkins University Press. Reprinted with permission of the Johns Hopkins University Press.

"Byron and Shelley," by Stephen Gurney. From *British Poetry of the Nineteenth Century*: 70–99. © 1993 by Twayne Publishers. Reprinted by permission of the Gale Group.

"Keats's Poems: The Material Dimensions," by M. H. Abrams. From *The Persistence of Poetry: Bicentennial Essays on Keats*, edited by Robert M. Ryan and Ronald A. Sharp: 36–53. © 1998 by The University of Massachusetts Press. Reprinted by permission.

"The Religion of Empire: Blake's Rahab in Its Biblical Contexts," by G.A. Rosso. From *Prophetic Character: Essays on William Blake in Honor of John E. Grant*, edited by Alexander S. Gourlay: 287–326. © 2002 by G.A. Rosso. Reprinted by permission.

Index